D0941354

Childhood, Marriage, and Reform

Childhood,

Lewis Perry

Marriage, and Reform

Henry Clarke Wright 1797–1870

The University of
Chicago Press
Chicago and London

The University of Chicago Press, Chicago 60637
The University of Chicago Press, Ltd., London

Printed in the United States of America
83 82 81 80 79 5 4 3 2 1

Library of Congress Cataloging in Publication Data

Perry, Lewis.
Childhood, marriage, and reform.

Includes bibliographical references and index.
1. Wright, Henry Clarke, 1797–1870. 2. Social reformers—United States—Biography. I. Title.
HN64.W95P47 301.24′2′0924 [B] 79-13649
ISBN 0-226-61849-8

Lewis Perry is editor of the *Journal of American History* and professor of history at Indiana University. Previously he taught for twelve years at the State University of New York at Buffalo. He is the author of *Radical Abolitionism: Anarchy and the Government of God in Antislavery Thought* (1973) and coeditor of *Patterns of Anarchy: A Collection of Writings on the Anarchist Tradition* (1966) and *Antislavery Reconsidered: New Perspectives on the Abolitionists* (1979).

For Elisabeth

Contents

Illustrations

Henry Clarke Wright. *Top:* in Ireland, about 1847. *Bottom:* probably in the late 1850s (courtesy of the New York State Historical Association, Cooperstown, New York).

Preface

"There is properly no history; only biography." Henry Clarke Wright borrowed these words from Emerson for the title page of his life story, *Human Life: Illustrated in My Individual Experience as a Child, a Youth, and a Man* (1849). Scorning the history of politics and war, he emphasized obscure events of farm and household, school and profession. By giving this shape to his own life he sought to encompass great changes in the experience of his countrymen. He believed that America was rushing into a modern era, in which the hidden, domestic side of life assumed new importance. Throughout his career he studied families and lectured on the proper sentiments of parents toward children, of husbands toward wives. His interest in the changing experiences of ordinary human beings has a counterpart in the endeavor of modern historians to create a non-elitist history. By analyzing his life and thought we may understand dimensions of the past that would otherwise be nearly inaccessible.

But no matter how intensively Wright studied family life, no matter how earnestly he aspired to merge his life in great movements of his times, it is also true that, examined closely, no life is exactly representative of others. Contemporaries frequently regarded Wright as radical and eccentric; historians have praised his originality or condemned his nonconformity. Try as he might to affiliate with the main currents of his age, he regularly felt so isolated and out of place that he cherished the motto, "Alone with God in the Wide Universe." In no respect was his divergence from other men more marked than in his habit of painstaking self-examination, a habit that led to a huge and astonishingly intimate collection of diaries. Here was the record, as he put it at the end of his life, of "my Interior, rather than Exterior life . . . a record of Isoteric [*sic*] & Exoteric life, but mostly of the former."

Wright affords us unique glimpses of the intimate history of a man who professed in public to be an authority on all of "Human Life." In calling this book *Childhood, Marriage, and Reform,* I have in mind both his private experience and public expertise. In this study of psychology and ideology I try to unravel Wright's tangled experiences as son and husband; at the same time, I trace his discovery of a large audience of parents and spouses who believed that the reform of domestic life held the key to social progress.

These counterpoints are carried out in five chapters, the first of which surveys Wright's public life as it might have appeared to contemporaries. It looks closely at his beginnings as an orthodox clergyman and at his highly controversial work in the antislavery cause. The main theme of the chapter is the difficulty of defining and justifying new careers in a fluid and increasingly specialized economy. The second chapter turns from the buzz of public life to persistent emotional meanings of childhood. In memories of death and conflict it locates some origins of Wright's style as a reformer and of doctrines that he advocated.

Wright liked to think of his life as embodying a great historical change from theological dogma to scientific concern for human needs. My third chapter analyzes the crises of faith in his early years and his subsequent labors, only partially successful, to break loose from his religious past. The fourth chapter treats human needs, particularly those that he emphasized as a reformer of marriage and sexuality. It discusses his marriage, his intimacies with women, and the ideals of domestic behavior that he shared with his audiences. The theme of the fifth chapter is Wright's ideological response to the vast political and economic changes of his lifetime. It traces his youthful romanticism, his exploration of Europe, and his vision of free labor and unbounded progress. It was this vision that condemned Southern slavery; it also made way for a future characterized by ceaseless change.

Acknowledgments

I am grateful for assistance by librarians at these institutions: the Boston Public Library, Harvard College Library, the Congregational Library (Boston), the Essex Institute (Salem), the William L. Clements Library (University of Michigan), the New York State Historical Association (Cooperstown), the George Arents Research Library (Syracuse University), Lockwood Library (State University of New York at Buffalo), Western Reserve Historical Society, Guernsey Memorial Library (Norwich, N.Y.), the Chenango County Historical Society, Yale University Library, the Historical Society of Pennsylvania, the Presbyterian Historical Society (Philadelphia), the Henry E. Huntington Library, the Institute of Historical Research (University of London), the John Rylands Library (Manchester), Dr. Williams's Library (London), the Historical Collections of the Society of Friends (Dublin), and the Bancroft Memorial Library (Hopedale, Mass.). Particular notes of gratitude go to Marshall Blake (Syracuse), Carolyn Jakeman (Harvard), Virginia Hawley (Western Reserve), and Louis C. Jones (Cooperstown), each of whom pointed me toward useful collections that I might otherwise have missed.

Many quotations from Henry Wright's diaries and other papers appear by permission of the Houghton Library (Harvard). Many other quotations appear by courtesy of the Trustees of the Boston Public Library. These courtesies are much appreciated.

Summer fellowships from the State University of New York Research Foundation and small grants from the Committee on Research and Creative Activity, State University at Buffalo, supported much of the research that led to this book. A fellowship from the American Council of Learned Societies permitted me to give most of one year to drafting the book (and gave me the chance to visit some of Henry Wright's haunts). During a year at the National Humanities Institute, New Haven, I enjoyed many opportunities to try out my ideas with scholars from other disciplines. Particularly helpful was a semester-long "cluster group" in family history. I also appreciated opportunities to test parts of this book among my former colleagues in the

American historians' discussion group and the Group for Applied Psychoanalysis, State University at Buffalo.

Several scholars generously shared their research or gave me useful advice. My thanks go to Paul Johnson, Douglas Riach, Duncan Rice, Nancy Cott, Henry Glassie, Robin Winks, David Davis, Peter Loewenberg, J. Earl Thompson, Jr., Robert M. Taylor, David Hollinger, Michael Pearson, Warren Bennis, and Dorothy Porter. I am greatly indebted to friends who took time from their own important work in order to read my long and often ragged chapters: Thomas Haskell, Ronald Walters, Murray Schwartz, Kathryn Kish Sklar, Donald Scott, David Bailey, Michael Fellman, and Georg Iggers. Elisabeth Israels Perry read every word and pressed me onward to greater clarity. Not always Pleasure, this was always Progress.

One

A Belligerent Nonresistant

> The whole country is in such a constant state of mutation, that I can only liken it to the game of children, in which, as one quits his corner another runs into it, and he that finds no corner to get into, is the laughing-stock of the others. . . . In short, everything is condensed into the present moment; and services, character, for evil as well as good unhappily, and all other things cease to have weight, except as they influence the interests of the day.
>
> James Fenimore Cooper, *Home as Found* (1838)

Upward Mobility

Henry Clarke Wright's decision to join the abolitionists in 1835 was the crossroads of his career, one of those vexed moments when a man forsakes the work of half a lifetime and sets forth in a new direction. Previously much of his life had gone to preparing for the ministry and finding his place as pastor in a small New England town. After turning from the ministry to abolitionism, he spent his remaining thirty-five years as a traveling expert on social evil and public improvement.

Antislavery was of such crucial importance in an era of profound and unsettling change that to call a man like Wright "an abolitionist" may appear to define him sufficiently. That, after all, is the identity he bravely chose in 1835 and never relinquished, an identity glorified in Northern memory by the Civil War.[1] As an abolitionist he won admiration for the steadfastness with which he endured the angry controversies that always swirled around him; as an abolitionist he also earned sharp criticism for lumping the cause of the slave together with irrelevant heresies. But "Christian reformer" may better define the way in which he thought of himself. It may capture more successfully his underlying vocational purpose as he attacked a shifting list of great evils, ranging from war to slavery to loveless marriage, and championed a list of panaceas that shifted from biblical education to nonresistance to male continence. He was always, in his favorite slogan, "alone with God in the universe"; he was secure and calm regardless of changes in personal circumstance or adjustments in opinions he held dear. In later years he adopted a second slogan to indicate that he welcomed change and adaptability: "Institutions for men, not men for institutions."

Wright's career revealed how difficult it was for individuals in a fluid society to cover new occupations with religious sanctions. Only as a Christian reformer could he escape from the unsatisfying life of a clergyman. Because he still served God he was free of the accusation of self-interestedness and could speak scathingly of the temporizing of others. In an article on the "Christian Reformer" in the *Union Herald* in 1840, he emphasized the possiblility of unselfish, guiltless aggression: "The gospel is a reformatory system. Its warfare is aggressive, not defensive. It has nothing to do with self-defence—but its business is attack—aggression upon the empire of sin. Christ is the Prince of moral reformers—the great Captain of agitators in aggressive warfare, as well as the Prince of Peace." Leaders of the church and nation were paralyzed by "subserviency to the will of man"; this was the vice of the day. But the reformer lived with the sole object of pleasing God. Rescued from care about earthly reputation, he could bravely "encounter the giant evils that block up the pathway of the kingdom of heaven."[2]

This self-effacing formulation appealed to Wright even though his labors at self-advancement had met considerable success. He almost exemplified the ideal of the self-made man: the poor boy who through education, morality, hard work, and fortunate marriage raised himself to a higher station—in his case the clergy of the eastern seaboard. But he entered the ministry at a time when its leadership in society was eroding and many were experiencing dissatisfaction with it as a vocation; it was a time when new callings were emerging and old ones had to redefine their authority. He became a self-made man in a new sense, inventing for himself the role of itinerant radical at war with all institutions that failed to respect his autonomy. In this role he expounded the vision of a new America, liberated from the institutions of the past, where all would live in peace with freedom to perfect their souls and bodies. He made his living by carrying this message.

His early career may justly be called orthodox. A talented but poor young apprentice, he was converted during a revival in Norwich, New York, in the winter of 1817. He was one of thousands reborn in the fires of religious excitement that crossed upstate New York so frequently that the area was known as the "burned-over district."[3] The term "burned-over" evoked old suspicions of the destructive and impermanent effects of religion not carefully confined within traditional procedures and teachings. But most of American Protestantism was obliged to make peace with the revival; such an accommodation was almost guaranteed by the disestablishment of churches and the flow of population westward. Largely because of the revivals, church membership increased geometrically in the first decades of the nineteenth century. "Evangelicalism" became synonymous with orthodoxy as revivalistic churches joined ranks on their eastern front against Unitarianism and free thought.[4] Young Wright stepped forward as an ardent champion of the rule of God in his hometown, gave up the trade to which he was apprenticed, made his way through Andover Seminary, and advanced to his place among the New England clergy.

After his conversion Wright urged the Presbyterians of his town not to shirk their part in the international battle against heathenism. In particular, the town might do good by setting up a scholarship fund to help would-be ministers secure the education they needed. The world needed ministers and missionaries; many young men stood ready to answer the call if they could only afford the tuition.[5] Perhaps with this kind of aid, Wright made his own way to Andover, a fortress of evangelical faith that boasted of the self-renunciatory lives and good works of missionary graduates all over the world. Andover was also a step upward in social rank. As Wright promptly observed, most of the other students were better educated and came from wealthier backgrounds.[6]

After two years at Andover Henry Wright took a year off to work as a teacher in Newburyport. A poetic epitaph poked fun at him as a kind of Ichabod Crane who was not averse to using the whip.

Here lies Master Wright,
When he bade us good night
The glory of Andover fainted;
He's read his last rule,
Whipped his last rogue in school,
And now he has gone up to be sainted.[7]

Teaching was simply a stop on the way up to better things. During his stint in Newburyport, he met a wealthy widow, Elizabeth Le Breton Stickney. After returning to Andover for his final year, he married her. He received his license to preach from the presbytery of Otsego, New York, in August 1823; this return to the land of his upbringing was especially triumphant because he was so much better educated than his ministerial examiners.[8] Even with a license, however, it took some time to find a parish appropriate to his training and his bride's social standing.

Wright served briefly in the small towns of Warner and Franklin in New Hampshire, while acting as supply minister to the First Church in West Newbury, Massachusetts. The Presbyterians and Congregationalists were at this time acting together as an evangelical coalition; despite his rural Presbyterian credentials Wright was admitted to the Essex County North Association of Congregational Ministers. At last, in 1826, he was examined by these brethren, voted upon by church and parish, and settled as the regular minister in West Newbury, not far from Andover, closer still to his wife's home in Newburyport. The new pastor lived in the style to which his wife was accustomed: there were servants, a beautiful dinner service, an expensive education for the stepchildren. He wore silk gloves. He loved to read in his study and to discourse on languages and history with other ministers of Essex County.[9]

He fully shared the hatred of Jacksonians and Unitarians that went with his role in society. He attacked those "busy Reformers—who break up our Parishes & interrupt the peace & harmony of our social intercourse for the sake of introducing your new fangled notions about Religion. . . . It may be a pretty thing to you *to be called* a Reformer—but be assured—it is misery & sorrow to us—you may feel it necessary to use every possible means *to support the appearance* of Zealous Reformers—but your conduct is proving our ruin."[10] In his new social station Wright was highly sensitive to masks and pretensions in public controversy, but he could not avoid them. Since it was improper for ministers to meddle in politics, he adopted a pseudonym—"Sincerity"—to write the *Essex Gazette* a letter of protest against the Jackson party and, more generally, the way in which men followed the roles they had assigned themselves, rather than reason, in deciding how to vote.[11]

In many ways Henry Wright was a successful minister. Membership in his church, which had seen hard times, expanded greatly. He had his own chance to preside over a revival and to witness the spreading of new light over neighboring parishes. He was loved by his flock.[12] The position in West Newbury, furthermore, offered the advantage of regular contact with distinguished and well-educated ministers from nearby churches as well as professors from Andover. Wright was respected for his proficiency in Greek and Hebrew, and he took an extremely active role in the pious and learned meetings of his colleagues.[13] He seemed completely comfortable in this world of mercantile fortunes and subsidiary agriculture, of an elegant lifestyle and affectionate parishioners. He expressed distaste for the factories he saw on a trip to Rhode Island. They were producing a generation with loose morals, unfit for civic responsibilities. They threatened to ruin farm families, put women to work, and debase the moral tone of New England.[14]

His role as a minister meant that he was preoccupied with education and social control. He helped form a lyceum, officiated at the county teachers association, and joined in the work of benevolent societies. For the most part he followed the lead of older and more prominent ministers, but there was no doubt of his eagerness for the work. In one meeting where there was hesitation over the best means of instituting a lyceum, Wright spoke against waiting for action from various parts of Essex County. By setting up one central lyceum, they might fan up "excitement in the different towns. Lecturers might be employed and sent round the County."[15]

Some of his opinions contrast ironically with his later reputation for radicalism. He advocated a three-pronged attack on crime: first, strict punishment; second, destroying such "sources of pollution" as gambling halls and grog shops; and third, improved schools for children and extensive opportunities for the intellectual and moral improvement of adults. A defective education failed to restrain loose passions, which he regarded as a principal cause of crime; an effective education stressed the claims of society, habits of industry, and traits of morality. The necessity of work was a recurrent theme in his educational writings: teaching children distinctions between savagery and civilization would impart reasons for vigilance against idleness. He feared "that our poor laws tend to produce the very evils which they are designed to alleviate": they increased the number of paupers and forced women who were willing to work to live instead off charity. He offered some criticism of the indolent rich, but much more of the intemperate poor, as he developed the theme: "*The idle & vicious must be supported by the industrious & frugal.*"[16]

From this perspective on advancing civilization and refractory idleness, nothing seemed more important than a good, efficient school system. Schools ought to be overseen by a few supervisors, according to Wright, rather than by voters at town meetings. There ought to be more supervision, more professionalism, more attention to the qualifications of teachers and progress of students. District schools were suffering from unwise competition with local arrangements. Parents and the community should give scarce resources to the common schools rather than to sabbath schools and other less important competitors. Pastors should support the common schools in their districts instead of the more prestigious colleges and academies. Teaching should become a respected occupation instead of part-time work for persons en route to other stations (as it had been for Wright). Mothers and fathers should support the authority of the schools during hours at home. Looking backward, Wright praised the New England tradition of public education; looking forward, he stressed the importance of moral and intellectual improvement of citizens in order to keep the republic under control and give meaning to political equality. The mood of his writings in these years was exhortatory. He was a busy conservative who feared the loss of an industrious, well-ordered society.[17]

Wright had not inherited his station in this society, and while he copied the bookish gentility habitual to its ministers, he felt the need for something more. It was up to the clergy to support an efficient school system that would strengthen feelings of responsibility, industriousness, and political obligation. There was no room in his world view for the perception that industriousness might subvert a tidy social system, no room for the old Federalist educational emphasis on hierarchy and subordination.[18] What was crucial was the good order of citizens and workers in a society countenancing mobility like his own.

While advocating anti-heathenism in his hometown and while preparing for the ministery, Wright had cherished the goal of missionary service and imagined himself in distant barbaric lands. His years as a pastor in West Newbury represented a suspension of that dream. There were some connections between his faith in domestic education and the work of God's emissaries overseas: he wrote that missionaries should begin by building schools because it was impossible to be progressive or Christian while uneducated.[19] God's cause was unequivocally linked to social progress. By fighting the evils of crime, illiteracy, drunkenness, and thoughtless voting, wherever he was, he took it for granted that he was advancing Christianity. Essex County was not Africa, however; and his settled pastorate and comfortable home separated him from the heroic, sacrificial life he had once imagined. In the early 1830s he began to express once more his yearning for a mission in the service of the Lord, preferably on far-off shores. The life he had made began to crumble, and vocation became a wracking problem.

His first experiment in a new kind of life occurred in 1832, when evangelical Amherst College faced a large debt and failed to get financial assistance from the legislature. The crisis evoked themes of both professionalism and piety. One complaint against the college was that it was superfluous; there were too many educated men already. In the words of one critic: "There were more lawyers than could get a living honestly. . . . There were doctors to be found in every street of every village, with their little saddlebags; and they must have a living out of the public. There were too many clergymen who, finding no places where they could be settled, went about the country begging for funds and getting up rag-bag and tag-rag societies." While opponents portrayed a mobile, predatory class of professional misfits, the college presented itself as an orthodox alternative to infidelity at Harvard. In one year it successfully raised $50,000, much of it in little donations from evangelical men and women.[20]

Henry Wright took time away from his ministry to work as a traveling agent of Amherst College during this crisis. He lectured in numerous Massachusetts towns, collecting small gifts and rallying audiences against the Harvard aristocracy. There was no redundancy of educated men; public morality depended on the willingness of the middle classes to encourage the aspirations of their talented children to rise to better positions. The opponents of the college, in his view, were "the growing aristocracy of the region" who hoped that Unitarianism would submerge the Bible and hold the lower classes in ignorance and vice. Therefore he stressed "the importance of raising up a sort of litterary [*sic*] men from among sons of midd[l]ing classes—of farmers & mechanics to fill the public offices & to give a tone to public opinion as the only means to save us from the oppression of Unitarianism & Cambridge. The community would soon learn to appreciate the active & enterprising sons of farmers & mechanics & prefer them to the proud sons of the rich."[21]

His agency for Amherst was a trial run in the vocation of a missionary; though far from Africa, he was on the move almost every day. He was now an itinerant rather than a settled pastor. Although the agency expired when the $50,000 was raised, Wright never settled down again. In July 1833, he took formal leave of his flock in West Newbury and looked around for a new life.

Between the ministry and the outer world lay the empire of benevolence, the network of societies that evangelical Christians had devised to control vice and promote piety in the cities, on the frontiers, wherever old-time faith stood in jeopardy from population movements or economic changes. These societies relied on funds from the churches. Wright noted eagerly how one Newburyport congregation "voted themselves to be a Benevolent Society to raise funds to spread the Gospel." Then they designated six national societies as financial beneficiaries, each receiving two months a year during which the minister gave appropriate sermons and a special committee solicited money. Here was work that linked dull towns to lofty purposes. Here, too, were new occupational opportunities, for each of these national movements ought to have a "permanent Agent" in each state to furnish persuasive facts and regularize the "taking up of collections for benevolent purposes."[22]

To supporters of these societies Christian reform went hand in hand with education. They supplied edifying things to read, instituted schools, subsidized the training of ministers and teachers, and equated the self-improvement of individuals with restoring the order of communities. Henry Wright knew many of the employees—sometimes they were called "agents," sometimes missionaries"—from his days at Andover Seminary. They were in many instances surplus clergymen or escapees from the old ideal of a settled ministry, but it was not "rag-bag and tag-rag societies" that they were trying to establish. Their purposes may be gleaned from the instructions given an agent sent by the American Home Missionary Society to Oregon in the 1840s. He was to establish "churches, schools, whatever would benefit humanity—temperance, virtue"; the outcome should be "the industrial, mental, moral and religious training of the young, and the establishment of society upon sound principles by means of institutions of religion and learning."[23] The benevolent societies envisioned a system of institutions that would ensure both virtue and progress in America.

In the summer of 1833 the American Home Missionary Society appointed Henry Wright a missionary and assigned him to Chicago. The trip west apparently involved deprivations that he was not yet steeled to endure: it was difficult to part from wife and family and leave them unprotected. He held this position only for a few months, and did not make it to Chicago. Instead he landed an agency with the American Sunday School Union; his territory was Essex County and New Hampshire and so, while wandering, he could still be close to home. By his own estimate he traveled over 3,500 miles in 1833, mostly in a gig. Sometimes he came to an "ignorant vicious place" like Marblehead where young men and women impeded his work by assembling on street corners, on Sunday evening, "to talk & laugh."[24] But usually traveling deepened his assurance that he was serving adequately in a holy scheme. He sent communications to evangelical papers, especially the great *Boston Recorder,* which brought together news and opinions of right-minded men (more often than not those of Andover) and reformatory enterprises. He visited Boston during the solemn week each June when all of the societies held their annual meetings. In 1834 he expressed his belief that they were "doing more for the world" than politicians and armies, "more even than civil government." There were a few discordant notes in his reflections. For one thing, speeches tended to be too studied and formal. There was "not enough sympathy & feeling & weeping over a lost world." He feared "that these annaverseries [*sic*] will degenerate into theatrical exhibitions." In addition, he made what he called *"discoveries of myself."* In assemblies with other ministers and agents he recognized his envy and ambition.[25] These were unsettling discoveries. Besides its work of ensuring social virtue and progress, Christian reform was supposed to be a vocation untainted by role playing and self-aggrandizement.

Henry Wright's task as agent of the American Sunday School Union was to promote schools that would supplement the common school system by stressing the gospel. In carrying out this task he rapidly discarded views that he had advocated fervently a few years before when he was a parish minister. Cooperation between churches and common schools was imperiled by the controversial "law of 1827" prohibiting schoolbooks that favored any religious denomination. Horace Mann's decision on behalf of the common-school system in Massachusetts was to search for nonsectarian textbooks portraying "the obligations arising from social relationships."[26] But to Henry Wright and other evangelicals, social obligation was meaningless if the student had no impression of man's future accountability before the throne of God. Some of the new textbooks, as Wright bitterly pointed out in the *Boston Recorder,* were the handiwork of a Unitarian heretic, John Pierpont. Either American children were going to be raised to know their savior and respect their ministers or they would receive a bland education that would pose no problems for a Mohametan: there was no neutral ground. Reversing his earlier emphasis on an efficient school system, Wright now urged parents to examine all schoolbooks and to refuse to delegate important decisions to committees and professionals. District schools now seemed too costly. The failure to teach sectarian truth, the association of pious children with infidels, the secularized moralistic textbooks—all subverted education in its truest sense, "the formation of character."[27] He also recoiled, at least temporarily, from his this-worldly emphasis on the upward aspirations of farmers and mechanics. The entire world from the moment of birth was a "school-room," a "nursery," or a "seminary"—the figure varied slightly—in which souls were educated for the "eternal state." Hence the fatal dangers of the narrowly defined, practical education offered by the state. Worse still, "the attention of ministers, churches and parents, has been turned away from home, the school where children *must* receive their principal education, to schools of men's appointment, and hireling teachers have been called in, to do that which God has imposed on parents as a solemn duty."[28]

The issue of school textbooks was largely symbolic: behind it lay a crisis of sectarianism in America. Could the evangelicals hope through struggle to dominate American life, or must they accede to the development of institutions that did not acknowledge any system of religious belief? Never in his life was Henry Wright more intolerant than in these years of attack on the infidel common school system. If Christians took a wiser view of the dangers of contamination in their towns, they would not patronize infidels simply because they were competent at their professions; Christian parents would not teach their children, by example, that getting by in this world was more important than the next. In the fight for public allegiance he took a jesuitical view of means and ends. He knew from experience that "there is hardly any heart of a parent, however hard and opposed to the truth, which a minister may not reach by attention to the children." By befriending the children and bringing the gospel to them, the church might win over their parents. He applauded a New Hampshire minister who had always been excluded from even talking about religion in a certain neighborhood until he visited the district school and interested the children in having a sabbath school. The children brought their parents to a subsequent meeting, and thereafter the minister was welcome in the neighborhood.[29]

In England the Sunday school movement led to the creation of massive institutions for the urban working classes, but its American counterpart worked differently. Wright twice addressed a Sunday school society at the Amesbury mills, but there as in the small towns on his circuit the overriding purpose was to collect "subscriptions" to support missionary campaigns in the Mississippi Valley. The immediate locality assumed secondary importance: "I have no motive," Wright told his superiors, "except the promotion of *christian education* throughout the country & the world." When the American Sunday School Union launched an invasion of the South, he recognized that the campaign in Virginia "awakened an interest in education generally—that never was felt before." In his anxiety to join the fray he mapped out "a tour through the Southern & Western states" in order "to acquaint myself with the State of society as to the means of religious & intellectual improvement." At the same time he planned "to seek out a place where I might settle with my family." Subzero temperatures and winter colds delayed these plans, however, and Wright never set foot in the South.[30]

He became a specialist in the souls of children. From his sabbath school post he moved to Boston to serve the combined Presbyterian and Congregational churches as minister to the city's children. After a three-month trial at sixty dollars a month, in January 1835 he was voted a salary of $1,000 a year to carry on this work. At West Newbury he had made $350 a year. In finding his new vocation and freeing himself of the settled ministry, he had not ceased to come up in the world. He had his own office in Boston, established a model sabbath school, and met with children in many other schools and churches. Six hundred children were directly in his charge, and he gave at least three addresses to children every week. Later he called these two years, in which he was followed around by children, the happiest of his life. He also met frequently with sewing circles and other groups of mothers and showed them their responsibility for Christian influences over the young. Infiltration of the hearts of children was the surest remedy against the diseases of infidelity and disorder that threatened to make American liberty a curse, rather than a blessing, to the world. Mothers should enforce the Christian message, and their authority should be unquestioned.[31]

Wright was, in a strict sense, a conservative. As he read news from Washington and overseas, as he listened to arguments over revivalism and Unitarianism, he lamented "a strong propensity to try new measures in civil governments & in religious matters." In view of the social changes of the previous fifty years, "the revolution of opinion" that the world was undergoing, and the distressing problems everywhere, there was an understandable temptation to think any change better than none. "But changes are dangerous; & we should be slow to admit them." In the face of this revolution his usual recourse was to wish for the unity of Christians and return of true worship. There was a practical sense, however, in which Wright, as the proponent of new measures and institutions designed to reform society through education, was an agent of the revolution he disliked. He was trapped in what modern sociologists consider "the underlying paradox of all ideologies that seek to control or contain modernity": the very idea that societies may choose different paths of development is strikingly modern.[32]

As an expert on educational reform, Wright needed more than a clergyman's background and a good rapport with children. He tried to read everything written for children, though much of it was "trash" and "poison." He attended sessions of the American Institute of Instruction, went to lectures on Pestalozzi, and read works by Combe and Spurzheim. He consulted with William Alcott of the American School Society and cornered Theodore Dwight of New York and everyone else he met who had experience in religious or common schools. Although he continued to deplore the separation of training for this world from preparation for the next, his sectarian tone softened as he clarified his views of public morality and private conscience. He began to doubt the efficacy of corporal punishment in any kind of school "to awaken conscience"—to make the child himself "feel conscious of wrong doing." He admitted that public schools, despite his disillusionment, were "the only Institution that can ever raise up the great mass of our citizens," particularly the poor of the cities. Schools were also appropriate to other classes of citizens at a time when new inventions promised to create leisure time. Education was, in other words, central to the ideological conjunction of discipline and individual opportunity; and Henry Wright was remarkably articulate about its advantages in stifling feelings of resentment against privileged classes. One advantage of infant education, he told the Board for the Moral and Religious Instruction of the Poor in Boston, was that it teaches children "the value of Social order & gives them a love & sympathy for the Institutions of social life." Left to "Street Education," children would gain "an impression that the rich are their natural enemies." Neglected in childhood, they would hate those who were better off; as adults they would regard any injury to society as "just retaliation." It was wise policy to instill feelings of social obligation as children grew up.[33]

As minister to the children of Boston, Henry Wright had many occasions to take part in the reform of society. He helped create an "Association to aid Indigent females by furnishing them with plain sewing." He held a series of meetings to persuade young men to enter the ministry; one evening he boasted eight successes. He joined two distinguished gentlemen—Rev. Dr. Justin Edwards and Lucius Sargeant Esq.—in writing the constitution of the Boston Union Temperance League. On February 24, 1835, a day when temperance meetings were scheduled all over the world, he went to Old South Church, offered a resolution and spoke in its favor. On that day he also talked two of his fellow boarders into joining the league; the entire experience was "solemn." Two days later, on February 26, churches throughout the land prayed for the colleges. He went to the Park Street Church, joined in the prayer, and offered some remarks on why the cause was good.[34] Boston was an exciting place to be during these worldwide and nationwide activities.

Boston was no holier, however, than any other city; it constantly reminded him of the ruin awaiting civilization if evangelical labors fell short. Not only were the wealthy Unitarians faithless, but the simple people of the Jackson party succumbed to the allures of atheism as practiced by that notorious woman, Fanny Wright. Charles Follen, who taught German literature at Harvard, made the horrible recommendation that the irreligious Gibbon should be read "in every Hamlet in the land." A "notorious—crazy Enthusiast" named Matthias received a sentence of only three months for murder. A rumseller hit the Rev. George Cheever of Salem at midday on a downtown street. Moreover, a "tide of Catholics" poured across the city; without stiffer immigration laws foreigners would shortly control the United States.[35]

There were many new things to think about during these happy years in Boston. Attending a lecture on water, Wright wished the lecturer had emphasized temperance as much as science. After lectures on phrenology by his Unitarian nemesis, John Pierpont, he wondered whether this fascinating art of analyzing character by feeling the contours of skulls led inevitably to materialism. Day after day he attended the trial of twelve pirates. His feelings oscillated between romantic interest in their cutthroat lives and solemn reflection on the certain punishment for their crimes. When he went to the execution, however, and saw the jeering, inebriated crowd, he was appalled and felt some sympathy for the pirates. He left before the hanging.[36]

Because his family stayed behind in Essex County, Wright resided in a boarding house with other stalwart Christians, some from Andover, some with old distinguished names like "my chum" Solomon Stoddard. Over the meals they discussed the churches, the moral state of the union, the progress of benevolent societies and reform movements. Some guests stayed there for short periods while they had business in Boston: one who especially impressed Henry Wright was Elihu W. Baldwin, who had made a "great sacrafice" by leaving a large church in New York City to become president of Wabash College. They talked about the prospects for evangelical faith in the Mississippi Valley, about the mistakes often made by ministers in selecting their wives, and about "the folly of young men while at Andover."[37]

Amidst all his successes, earnest conversation, and good comradeship, Henry Wright continued to doubt the cosmic significance of his career. After paying ten dollars to have his teeth cleaned and five fillings put in, he noted in his diary: "Have long debated whether to give my money for this—or to the spread of the gospel." Because he was close to the Boston docks he could see off missionaries to the Pacific or the Zulus; on these occasions it was clear that something was wrong. He had not given up enough in his profession. In a sense he was a missionary in Boston rather than a settled minister; he complained that the city's clergymen were too jealous to share the esteem of their audiences (even though he was embarrassed by signs of ambition in himself). He made proposals to the board that paid his salary in order to improve his position and enlarge his work, but the board rejected them. In April 1836 he finally asked for dismissal. On his thirty-ninth birthday, August 29, he paused as he did each year to reflect on the miracle that he was not in hell on account of his accumulated sins. He prayed to begin a new life dedicated "entirely to the promotion of God's kingdom in this world."[38]

Conversion

By revising his opinion of William Lloyd Garrison and the abolitionists Henry Wright broke through his vocational doubts. To understand this conversion, we might begin by examining his attitudes toward slavery before coming to Boston. Although slavery was scarcely a burning issue to him in his days as minister and Sunday school agent, there is no reason to believe that he ever condoned human bondage. In fact a vaguely defined opposition to slavery was entirely consistent with the civilizing intentions of Andover evangelicalism and the anti-Southern prejudices of Essex County Federalism.

It was in spring 1823, his last term at Andover, that Henry Wright had, in his words, "my attention distinctly called" to the problem of slavery. There was "considerable stir all over the country about colonizing the free negroes in Africa," an interest that was quickened at Andover by the martyrdom of a New England minister who died in the course of a mission to secure land on the African coast. During that term the Society of Inquiry, Andover's chief support of missionary work, commissioned and approved a passionate report on the "black population" of the United States. The report noted the growing numbers of slaves in a nation that vaunted freedom; it reserved its sharpest language for Northern bigotry that condemned free Negroes to a separate caste. Even the purpose of Christianizing Africa received less emphasis than the relief of an impoverished, reviled, and dangerous people.[39] After this report the American Colonization Society asked the Society of Inquiry to appoint two New England agents, and Wright's classmate Leonard Bacon commenced his long career as one of the most formidable advocates of colonization.

Bacon later became an enemy; the colonizationist program of removing Negroes from America was later denounced as ineffectual bigotry. As an abolitionist, Henry Wright denied that he had ever supported Bacon's cause. This may perhaps be true, but in 1823 colonization represented the logical expression of humanitarian sympathy for Negroes coupled with evangelical concern for the social order. From that time on Wright "hated the word [slavery], as meaning injustice and oppression." His difference from Bacon and colonizationists was that they devoted much time to the relief of free blacks, while he "was so absorbed in study" and his subsequent chores that he lost sight of antislavery until he was jolted in Boston twelve years later.[40]

The urgency of antislavery was restrained by evangelical beliefs concerning the transcendence of the soul and the authority of Scripture. As agent of the American Sunday School Union, Henry Wright recommended education for the afterlife, not only for its own sake, but also as a source of good discipline in this world. A similar position was taken in a poem on slavery that appeared in the first volume of the *Sabbath School Visiter* during Wright's agency:

A tawny slave whom grace had chang'd,
  Was ask'd, with scornful voice,
"In what religion did consist,
  And why he should rejoice?"

"*Massa,*" he cried with simple tone,
  "In my poor way I'll tell,
"Tis only *ceasing to do wrong*
  And *learning to do well.*

"And when poor black man feels his heart
  Fill'd with the love of GOD,
He can rejoice,—give thanks, and sing,
  Though smarting with the rod.["][41]

Without some recognition of the immortal significance of the black man's soul, even in this trite form, few American hearts might have opened to antislavery arguments. There might well, on the other hand, have been unexplored contradictions in sentimental prayers such as one Wright recorded during this period of his life: "The African is dark in skin but we shall kindle a light in his heart that shall light his soul to God. O Lord let the poor slave go free."[42]

Occasionally Wright revealed a sensitivity to the indignities suffered by black people that was unusual for his place and time. He predicted divine wrath on America after traveling from Newburyport to Boston with several wealthy men who forced another passenger—a well-to-do colored man—to ride outside in freezing weather. Inside the coach conversation turned on the contentment of Negroes in slavery. Although his sensitivity was unusual, it is probably significant that Wright recorded no vigorous protest on his part. He disliked breaks with the society he served.[43]

As a minister and a specialist in education, Henry Wright was inconvenienced by the tendency of certain issues to divide Christians and prevent them from joining the good work he recommended. Slavery was not the only issue with this power. In one town it was opposition to masonry that impeded any cause "unless it is made antimasonic"; to the traveling agent this smacked of idolatry, worshipping a single opinion more than God. This kind of divisiveness was also reminiscent of Unitarianism. In one New Hampshire town where Wright tried to enlist support for Sunday schools in the South and West, his listeners declined to commit themselves without knowing his opinion of the American Colonization Society. He refused to take sides, simply insisting that Sunday Schools would benefit the slaves. Eventually "all parties" welcomed him and gave support. "Three brothers made themselves life members [of the Sunday School Union], one a strong abolitionist—another as strong a colonizationist—& another indifferent."[44] This was his first meeting with Nathaniel Peabody Rogers, later to rival Wright's own reputation for radical extremism.

Some Northern Negroes had long been critical of the American Colonization Society, but it was the emergence of white critics that forced choices on men of benevolent disposition. William Lloyd Garrison's *Thoughts on African Colonization* (1832), a masterpiece of denunciation, called colonizationism impracticable, proslavery, and anti-Christian. Garrison continued the assault each week in the *Liberator* (begun in 1831), often quoting the leaders of the Colonization Society to show their hypocrisy, bigotry, and antirepublicanism. The American Anti-Slavery Society (formed in 1833) declared that slavery must be abolished *immediately*—that is, without compensating masters and without deporting the liberated.

Thereafter, "immediatism" joined in strenuous ideological competition with older styles of antislavery humanitarianism. And men like Wright had to choose. Although Henry Wright would not have accepted Garrison's characterizations of his friends and associates, he was drawn toward immediatist argument from the start. In June 1832 he observed that the Colonization Society could never return all slaves to Africa; in June 1833 he complained that the British plan for emancipation in the West Indies by giving compensation to former masters and holding freemen to periods of apprenticeship required the slaves to pay for their freedom. In both instances he stated that slavery must be renounced at once, without qualification or hesitation. Yet he accepted the logic of immediatism with important restrictions. In the first place, he regarded the time and money spent on schemes to remove Negroes as competitive with worthier missions. He was committed to the "nobler" project of exporting Christianity, presumably by means of white ministers, to "benighted" Africa. He even questioned the wisdom of missionary efforts to convert adult heathens: "If all the Heathen Children now in Africa & Asia—under 10 years old—could be educated in christian schools—in 20 years Idolatry in those continents would be overthrown."[45]

In addition, he could not contemplate slavery's abolition without a program for educating the bondsmen and preparing them for freedom. Otherwise, his fantasies of disorder might as easily have justified slavery's prolongation. In March 1834 he wrote: "Should the slaves of the South be released—*as according to God's law, they ought to be tomorrow*—while they are totally uninstructed in any knowledge human or divine & while there are no means to instruct them in the South, what would be the consequence? The poor ignorant slaves would rush into the New England states & bring a curse & a blight on them & fill them with robbery & murder. I believe this will be the way in which N.E. will be punished for her share in this crime."[46]

His main objection to Garrisonian anticolonizationists was that they were too "bitter in spirit"—too hostile toward slaveowners and toward Northerners who failed to share their opinions. They declaimed in their own circles, impeached the motives of others, and excited angry feelings everywhere. The North could not, in his view, end slavery "by talking & disputation," but only by earnest missionary endeavors aimed at "piercing the heart of the slaveholder with the sword of God's spirit," which was irreconcilably antislavery. How could Southerners be expected to bow to "wrong & unchristian feeling"? The proper means for antislavery action were roughly the same as the plans of the American Sunday School Union to spread knowledge of the Bible in the West and South with money collected from orthodox Northerners. Not only were the anticolonizationists callous to the spiritual growth of the masters; they also had "no plans for the religious & intellectual improvement of the slaves. . . . They propose no plans to prepare the slaves for freedom." When Wright read in the newspapers about the mob violence and arson directed against Lewis and Arthur Tappan, prominent New York merchants and leaders in the American Anti-Slavery Society, he assumed the trouble was "occasioned by the spirit created by the speeches of Abolitionists." Without revivals of religion and widespread education, New York was doomed to mob rule.[47]

Few abolitionists in 1834 would have dissented from Wright's views of revivals, education, or mob rule. And Wright had not tested the radicalism of the means he called going "to work the right way—i e—to thrust the sword of the Spirit into the heart of the planter." He seemed surprised to discover that one anticolonizationist whom he met on his travels held the same "moderate" view of tactics.[48] Wright was typical of many Northern ministers and benevolent reformers whose careers were menaced by the way in which "the subject of slavery seems to be swallowing up all others."[49] In his mind the subject had to be kept subordinate to education; for others it might have been the status of the clergy or the dissemination of Bibles that took first place. Surely Wright was not the only evangelical who regarded political disruption as disastrous and who hoped to perpetuate the union by "spreading religion & intelligence in the South & West."[50] Despite all this caution, he hated the word *slavery*, regarded the institution as antigospel, thought of the South as benighted, bridled at scenes of racial discrimination around him, and nursed plans for the Christian education of blacks. We may count it part of the tragedy of the 1830s that many in positions similar to his, and close to him in opinions, could not bring themselves to immediatism; they show some of the cost of "bitterness of spirit." But Henry Clarke Wright is a case study in a type of conversion that took place in the 1830s and provided essential leadership for antislavery radicalism in the decades ahead.

In January 1835 a new association addressed itself to men who felt, as Wright did, "that Colonization was not enough & who objected to the *Spirit* of the *American Anti Slavery Society*." The American Union for the Moral and Intellectual Improvement of the Colored Race was an attempt on the part of Joseph Tracy of the *Boston Recorder* and other guardians of Congregationalism to bank the fires lit by the Garrisonian radicals. These men recognized the impossibility of continuing to favor colonization: it had been too seriously damaged by Garrison's attacks to remain consistent with their advocacy of reform and social progress. They were equally determined not to be associated with anticolonizationists who challenged their authority and whose religious orthodoxy was suspect. It was embarrassing that Garrison came to the founding of the union with some disruptive comrades, including Amos Augustus Phelps (who had a good Andover background) and George Thompson (whose associations with English evangelicals made it hard to shut the door on him); they tried to force discussion of whether a new organization was necessary. They had no business, in Wright's opinion, at the creation of a new society which accepted their contention that slavery was sin but tempered it with concern for social order. In abolishing slavery, it was necessary to "pursue such measures as shall be adopted to the best good of all concerned. In doing our duty, we are not to cause great evils by the manner of doing it." Wright joined this union stressing "the improvement" of the colored race. The margin of his diary bears this afterthought: "(Deeply lament it 1842. March 10)." But his initial reaction to joining was different: freed of colonizationism, "I feel my mind at rest now."[51]

To this point in his life Christian reform had been synonymous with education. One crucial step toward the crossroads was the decision that it was impossible for slaves to be educated and Christianized prior to emancipation. This decision shook the evangelicals' tricky balance between antislavery and antiradicalism; it altered his sense that slavery must be abolished slowly, without rending the fabric of the union. He discussed education with James G. Birney, an Alabama slaveholder turned abolitionist, who lodged with Wright and his evangelical chums during the week of benevolent society conventions in 1835. Some of the boarders complained that abolitionists were pretending to be interested in other reforms so that they could invade good orthodox homes. But conversations with Birney helped Wright clarify his attitude toward the education of slaves; they prayed together, and Birney explained that it was a contradiction in terms to expect a master to enlighten his chattels. The next week Wright went to the meetings of the New England Anti-Slavery Society and offered the resolution that "every system of means to Christianize the slaves, *while slaves,* must, of necessity, be in great measure inefficient." In advocating this resolution, which passed, he was joined by Birney and Amos Augustus Phelps.[52] For a man of his views, to see education and slavery as irreconcilable was prerequisite to immediate abolitionism.

Wright's course toward abolitionism was marked by fluctuating perceptions of two groups of acquaintances; he was leaving one circle and entering another. On the one side stood the ministers of Boston, graduates of Andover, companions of his boardinghouse; on the other side waited Garrison, Phelps, and Thompson. He wavered between those who represented respectability and those depicted as bitter incendiaries. Defined in this way, the conversion clearly had vocational implications, and not surprisingly, it marked a dividing line in his career. The conversion permitted him to pass judgment on the ranks of powerful men he had spent much of his life in reaching. He was freed to expose their sanctity as a sham and to express resentments that had never before surfaced. When he was told that colonizationists were wealthy and talented, while abolitionists were poor and ignoble, this no longer seemed an argument in favor of the former. It was an occasion to join his name with abolitionists as "their Brother." After making the leap he became venomous toward titled "Gown-men" and D.D.'s, and was proud to be counted as the friend of those called "nigger." Most of all, he was happy to befriend Garrison, "the poor printer" scorned by the rich and titled just as "the fisherman of Galilee" had once been scorned by priests.[53]

Because the issue of conversion was cast in terms of group loyalties, it was terribly important that abolitionists in person did not match their boogieman reputations. First came James Birney, who was neither bitter not fanatical. When he proposed to New England abolitionists that they should avoid "all harsh personalities," Wright seconded the motion. Garrison, Phelps, and Thompson spoke strenuously to the contrary—why would sinners desist unless made conscious of their personal responsibilities?—but Birney and Wright's motion finally passed with amendments.[54] Next, George Thompson turned out to be gentle and kindly when he dined at Wright's boardinghouse. The two spent considerable time together after Wright confessed his previous misjudgment and asked Thompson's forgiveness. [55] That left Garrison, about whom Wright was already torn: he saw too much zealous vituperation for the movement's good, and yet he would rather have had Garrison's standing before the bar of God than that of any cautious minister. Then he saw that Garrison, too, had a "warm heart," and Garrison's closeness to children induced him to believe that the aspersions against him must be untrue.[56] While discovering that these men were pleasant in private, he was also studying their views of "personality" and "vituperation," and learning that there was nothing uncivilized in expressing hostility to sin. That was how society progressed. While changing his personal allegiances, he was learning to publicize hatred. He soon changed his attitude toward harsh language, and won his own reputation for bitterness.

As his perception of abolitionists was softening, his view of Boston's ministers hardened. He thought many of them were persuaded by Garrison but lacked the manliness to admit previous errors. He was increasingly dissatisfied by the terms of his employment. Benevolent societies seemed to hedge their commitments to worldwide reform because the ministers wanted each reform movement "*to benefit the people of the place where it meets.*" The clergy also preferred vague attacks on sin, and were unwilling to attack specific problems like drunkenness, prostitution, pride, or slavery. They feared that if they specified one sin too closely, then "that sin will assume such an importance that every body will think nothing is necessary to make them christians but abstinence from that particular sin."[57] This was a fair summary of an important argument. Protestant theologians had long guarded against idolatrous, ceremonialized notions of sin that were devoid of awe of God. Some may have felt their concerns were borne out in the subsequent history of abolitionism, in which avoidance of one sin often constituted a politicized, surrogate religion.

Wright's disengagement from the ministers came in large measure through conflict with Rev. George Washington Blagden of the Salem Street Church, an influential leader who held an early antislavery commission in Essex County but was already a vehement foe of Garrisonism. Blagden marshalled theological distinctions that Wright, with his Andover training, might have recognized as forceful: "Brother Blagden thinks the whole tendency of the Anti Slavery movement & of the Temperance & Moral Reform & Peace movement—is to lead men to make all religion consist in breaking off from *external sins. Seems to think it wrong to urge men to break off from external sins till their hearts are changed & the fountain is purified.* He forgets that one of the best ways to conquer an evil *propensity* is—to cease to indulge it *outwardly*."[58] There was nothing absurd in Blagden's position. Modern psychologists disagree sharply over the sufficiency of modifying behavior without entering the depths of personality. But Wright's rejection of that position did not depend simply on intellectual processes. He thought Blagden was using theology to camouflage his real preference for colonization. He hinted, further, that Blagden must have had "some *special* reason" (today we would say, some hidden agenda) for becoming so excited and irrational during their discussions. (Abolitionists later charged this prominent clerical antagonist with being a slaveholder.)[59] Through such discussions Wright became aware of his disaffection from the ministers and his growing desire to be part of a movement fiercely combatting external sins like slavery.

Important discussions also took place with his landlady and the other lodgers. Although one was an abolitionist and none defended slavery, they all disliked Garrisonism. What was striking to Wright was their nasty racism; he was now struggling with his own feelings on this score and so watched his fellow evangelicals closely. Mrs. Bliss objected, for example, that abolitionists encouraged "amalgamation." Wright, who not long before had felt that the Negro race, when freed and educated, would be "lost by amalgamation," now contended that antislavery was more likely to prevent amalgamation than slavery. Which was worse for a black woman, he asked his landlady, living together with a white man in marriage or outside? Neither, she answered; they were equally bad. He had never before seen her show such "moral obliquity" before the entire family at table. His friend Noyes then regaled the other boarders with the story of "a spruce young man" in Philadelphia who saw a carriage tipping over and ran to aid the passengers. When the first one out was a well-dressed colored woman, he said "O you are a black nigger are you?" and let her fall on the pavement. The whole company laughed, according to Wright, and yet these antiabolitionists all pretended "they are the best friends of the grieved [and] oppressed Negroes."[60]

Perhaps the most important incident occurred when he accompanied a Negro schoolteacher to visit the parents of her pupils. It was a wintry night, and he offered her his arm. At his boardinghouse he was teased for being seen arm-in-arm with a colored woman (and he reproached himself for feeling the sting of disapproval). A decade later he told an English friend that this incident caused his conversion to antislavery.[61] Actually neither this nor any other single event effected his conversion, but he may well have remembered it with special intensity as summing up the entire process of withdrawal from the prejudices of the circle in which he lived. His evangelical chums helped him set his sights for self-reform. In 1836 he invited a Negro girl to stay in his Newburyport house during an antislavery convention. At first he was torn by internal conflict over what people would think. "The moment I said I *will* do it, all my fear of man vanished & at once I felt a better man—that I was *free*"[62] Overcoming prejudice took a longer haul than joining the abolitionists, but it exemplified his views about eradicating evil propensities by ceasing to indulge them.

His encounters with prejudice played against the perodic encounters with black children that were part of his Boston job. They helped him with the step-by-step decision that immediatism was the proper course for antislavery, and that he must join the Garrisonians whom he disliked and repudiate the powers of benevolence and evangelicalism with whom his lot had been cast up to now. He might have been taken off the hook by plans for merging the American Anti-Slavery Society with the American Union, but they came to nothing.[63] Wright wavered for months over whether to join the Garrisonian organization, and criticized his own lack of resolution. Finally he "got so wrought up about it—the debate in my mind was so violent I started & ran to the office to [sign] my name." No secretary or book was there, and he had to wait. But his mind was settled and he felt at peace. This was in May. By July he had paid fifteen dollars to become a life member of the Massachusetts Anti-Slavery Society.[64]

It took until autumn, however, to iron out all the jangling dissonances between old life and new commitment. In this process of changing values and defining a new career, it was useful to observe how opposition to immediate abolitionism turned to violence. He was away in Newburyport in October when Garrison had to be rescued from a mob. Though Wright went to the *Liberator* office when he returned and had exciting talk with other abolitionists, he did not meet Garrison until his return from a country retreat in early November. They mulled over the heady Christian obligation of foregoing retaliation.[65] In November he learned that George Thompson, hardy veteran of mobs that he was, had been driven from the country by the threat of hired assassins. Less than a year before, he criticized Thompson for promoting anarchy, but now he saw the departure of this man, who had forgiven him, as a terrible judgment on the rich and powerful of the land.[66] On the other hand, he was happy to see at a meeting in the Mechanics' Lyceum that working folk had more respect for the free speech of abolitionists than those who were wealthy and supposedly more decent.[67] This observation was pleasing because in all this violence Wright was reversing his old strivings and putting the ideology of Andover and Newburyport behind him.

He turned his hand to writing. First, in July he published a complaint about the *Recorder*'s hypocritical reporting of the bad manners of colonizationists. Joseph Tracy had scolded abolitionist ladies, after a noisy debate, for clapping and showing emotion in "promiscuous public assemblies." Wright maintained that colonizationist ladies had done it first (he said nothing, Tracy retorted, about it being "very unbecoming" in any case).[68] In July Wright also visited an abolition-minded lawyer, David L. Child, and borrowed a volume of Blackstone "to learn the crime of Theft." Like all abolitionists he took the law seriously and searched for a reliable definition of slavery. When the threats to Garrison and Thompson became burning issues in the fall, he sent various Boston newspapers a whole series of letters charging collusion between respectable gentlemen and the nasty mob. His pseudonyms conveyed his identification with eighteenth-century probity: he was Hancock, Cato, Justice, or most simply, Law.[69]

If the law provided a cover for attacks upon those who, in effect, still employed him, it was only a temporary identity. Before he could write as abolitionist in his own name, he made an extended appearance under one other pseudonym. As the "Genius of Africa" (where once he yearned to go) he wrote a three-part attack on William Ellery Channing that was his first ambitious venture as an antislavery author. "I would feel, think and speak as one whose body has felt the lacerating scourge—whose heart has been torn and into whose soul the iron has entered," he announced. "Africa is the country of my adoption—her sons and daughters, however abused and trodden down, are my brothers and sisters, even unto death I love them and will plead for them."[70] This theme of empathy for the slave was always central to antislavery propaganda. It was a short step, furthermore, between sentimental identification with the slave and the dramatic reversals of perspective that almost always go along with satire. In Wright's case we can see how the ability to play someone else's role could be a major breakthrough for someone wracked by uncertainty about his career and allegiances. As the Genius of Africa he approached a satiric style that would be familiar to readers of the *Liberator* for the next thirty years. Sometimes playfully he would ask his audiences to imagine themselves in another role; sometimes viciously he would turn role playing into complicity in murder or exploitation. In the fateful summer of 1835, for example, he startled his colonizationist roommate by proposing to colonize him to Africa. Wright had shown little penchant for irony to that date, but now he countered each protest with the standard arguments of the colonization movement. Though his roommate wished to stay, he didn't know his own good and would fare better in Africa. Later examples of the same spirit are numerous. In 1837, for instance, on a stage from Lynn to Boston he attacked his friend Amos Dresser's views on slavery and peace for some time before unmasking his deception of the other passengers. And in 1848 he imagined himself to be "a slave on Zachary Taylor's plantation," and contrived dialogue to show that Zachary Taylor was no better than men who hired an assassin to get an inheritance.[71] Empathy and satire, together, liberated Wright into a new vocation.

William Ellery Channing was fairly irrelevant to the Genius of Africa's taunts. His major fault, besides being a prominent Unitarian (an old hate) and a man of some standing among respectable Bostonians (a new hate), was that he held Wright's own rejected position: *"I love the principles of the Abolitionists, but I detest their measures."* In a sense, all the Genius of Africa claimed was that if one identified with Africa one could not be a gradualist. But his argument was carried by a skillful rendition of the empathy theme, switching back and forth between imagined scenes of uncompensated work and unprotected chastity. What would Dr. Channing do if a master took his daughter as property and left her lacerated and dishonored? Would he refrain from vituperation? In the end the annihilation of the marriage institution appeared to be the salient feature of slavery. Slavery allowed a man or woman to desert a spouse at will; men were unable to defend wives and daughters from ravishers. Wright had moved, almost instinctively, from the empathy theme to another mainstay of antislavery propaganda: the erotic South.[72]

By the end of 1835 he had begun to conquer racial prejudice and fear of others' judgment. Although he occasionally claimed "a deeper & deeper interest" in the schools he visited "every day," actually his diaries were absorbed by the slavery question. In what may have been wishful thinking, he wondered in May 1835 whether the ministers' displeasure with his abolitionism would cost him his job. Actually he held it for another year before resigning. By that time he was an abolitionist who had added a new note to his old millennialism. God's judgment was hanging over the land, and a "fearful time" was nigh because of "our sins towards the Indians & Africans." As it turned out, Wright had little to say about Indians during the remainder of his life, but his interest in slavery persisted. Slaveholders claimed, he said, that the intelligence and virtue of the North were on their side; if so, then he had no wish to be counted among the intelligent and virtuous.[73] He passed the crossroads in his career.

The Philosophy of Slavery

After resigning his Boston position Henry Wright landed a commission to work for the American Peace Society. At least in private, he had long been a pacifist. In two books he later attributed his pacifism to a casual encounter with a Quaker in Providence, Rhode Island, in 1831. The old man supposedly teased him that if he were going to kill even the most wicked assailants, and if he planned to be true to the Bible, he would have to kill "with love."[74] This memory must have summed up his struggles to reconcile aggression with the spirit of love he identified in the New Testament; it may also have been a source for the ironic style of argument he made his own. But like the memory of being teased for walking with a Negro schoolteacher, it could not have had quite the formative effect he later recalled. At most it may have fortified his desire to speak out on peace like a Quaker, for his private views on peace were already quite radical. In his approach to peace, there is no evidence of trials similar to those he experienced in converting to abolitionism.

In 1830 he purchased a small notebook and outlined his thoughts on peace and war. He believed that Jesus' commands not to injure other men, even in retaliation, should apply to governments as well as individuals; he was well aware this meant radical revisions in the nature of government. It also meant that until governments were made subservient to the laws of God, Christians could not participate—even by voting—in existing governments of force. He copied down quotations to show that the seventeenth-century Anabaptists had held the office of the magistracy to be an encroachment on the spiritual liberties of Christians (with his divinity school training, he was not venturing into heresy without a sense of history). He added a quotation from Joseph Warren's oration of March 5, 1775, commemorating the Boston massacre: "Even *Anarchy itself,* that bugbear held up by the tools of power—(though truly to be deprecated) is infinitely less dangerous to mankind than *arbitrary government.*"[75] In a creative reading of history, Wright was yanking sources out of context to fashion his own view of uncoercive, even anarchistic government.

He did not let this bugbear out of his diary in 1830 or preach anything that might be mistaken for radicalism for several years thereafter. But his private inquiries continued. In 1833 he attended the meetings of the American Peace Society in New York, and on the steamboat from Newport he met the society's greatly respected secretary, William Ladd. He was much impressed by Ladd, who spent the first half of life in gathering a fortune and the second as a tireless itinerant in a good cause. In his diary Wright asked himself: "Is the belligerent spirit in man directly opposed to Christ? *Is any kind of war private or public justifiable on Christian principles? I am satisfied it is not.*" He vowed to preach and pray more often against war. In September 1834 he met Ladd again, with renewed admiration, and sharpened his irritation at the narrowness of local ministers in contrast to this great internationalist.[76]

Further visits with Ladd were bright moments during his Boston assignment. Here was a man as radical as Garrison, but without his incendiary reputation, a man who was acceptable to good evangelical folk, but without their parochial caution. At several dinners with

Ladd, Wright argued that the American Peace Society must proceed to more radical ground: it must repudiate personal violence under all conditions and all wars, not just aggressive ones.[77] While he was vacillating with regard to abolitionism, references to peace, a subject on which he knew his mind, were means of recapturing self-assurance. At this time, as we have seen, arguments over vituperation and aggression were very important. In his meditations he pictured slavery and war as deadweights dragging down church and nation. In April 1835 he participated in a public meeting on whether Christian principles would justify slaves in an armed uprising. He identified himself as "a peace man—a quaker if you please"—and argued that slaves could rightfully go no farther than a passive refusal to work. A thousand pacifist martyrs would bring about total emancipation.[78] As "Wickliffe," he wrote the *Liberator* in October 1835 that if critics of abolitionism could point out one among their ranks who proposed vengeance against slaveholders, they would expel the offender and send him to join "menstealers, kidnappers, and pirates. Our glorious motto is—Non-resistance."[79]

He welcomed a new assignment to work for the American Peace Society. Though he was sent to Cincinnati, however, he got only as far as Rochester; and this commission lasted only from June until September 1836, when he resigned. The assignment would have taken him farther from his wife and family in Newburyport. His missionary yearnings may have tempted him to welcome this deprivation, but his family was unhappy. Not yet ready to make a clean break to the itinerant life, Wright returned home, once again in search of vocation. In Newburyport he met a new minister who was a good abolitionist and peace man, but whose "family relations are all against him. . . . Poor man—he begins to reap the bitter fruits of rich family connexions. Deliver me from such a servitude."[80] It was Elizabeth Wright's wealth, of course, that gave her husband the luxury of still looking for a career as he approached the age of forty. For the time being, he hoped for an agency where he could take his family along.

Family considerations did not, however, really explain his resignation. It was quickly obvious that his relationship with men at the top of the American Peace Society was bound to be conflict-ridden. Under Ladd's leadership, the American Peace Society belonged to the empire of benevolence, held its meetings alongside the other educational and missionary societies, and enjoyed the support of prominent ministers and laymen. The society included conservatives like Ladd's protégé George Beckwith, whom Wright knew from Andover days. These men preferred the relatively uncontroversial ground of opposing aggression while conceding to governments the right of armed defense. They felt that efforts to build a broad popular base for the cause of peace were jeopardized by a faction of radical pacifists who charged that opposing only aggressive wars was meaningless; governments always pretended to act in self-defense. In the mid-1830s there was little peace in the peace society, and hiring Wright, whose views placed him in the radical faction, aggravated the tension. Ladd tactfully suggested that, in his capacity as agent, Wright would make more converts if he proceeded more slowly. The executive committee flatly told him they disapproved of his arguing that all wars were wrongful. The new agent turned around and went home.[81]

Fortunately the American Anti-Slavery Society, after three years of existence, was shifting tactics from the distribution of tracts and pamphlets to the dispersion of speakers and organizers in the North. The society had been sorely disappointed by the failure of clergymen to take charge of the antislavery message in the North, and its hope of converting the master rather than coercing him seemed increasingly naive without strong expressions of public disapproval of slavery, which was thriving on the ignorance and bigotry of the Northern public. Wright was hired as one of fifty to sixty new agents (whom the society, following scriptural inspiration, called "the Seventy"). After working briefly in Rhode Island, he joined the other agents in New York for November training sessions to trade experience and "harmonize" doctrine.[82]

These wonderful days promised to be the culmination of his long search for a useful place in the hosts of reform. He stayed at Nicholson's Temperance House with some of the other agents, dined at the homes of New York abolitionists, shared a merry visit to a phrenologist who read many of their skulls, and had fun with Lewis Tappan's daughter Georgianna. When she heard he was a "Peace man" and was going to lecture in Pennsylvania, she told him, "I hope you will *Piece* them all to *pieces*." Mostly, however, the sessions were hard work, morning, afternoon, and night. Besides listening to speeches clarifying their own doctrines, the agents tried to face every objection to abolitionism, every defense of the continuation of slavery, and find definitive responses. Some of their methods resembled psychodrama or the coaching of witnesses by attorneys. On the first topic, for example—why agitate the slavery question in the North—

"Brother Ray Potter took the ground of a Slaveholder to urge objections," and four others responded. Their purpose was not to acquire sympathy for the masters, of course, but in the lengthy notes Wright took at every session he frequently imagined himself in the exercise of guilty power. The sessions probably heightened his fascination with role playing and reversals of perspective.

The agents did not always reach agreement. Wright regretted some "flinching" over possible dangers to the Union; he would have no part of the strategy dissociating abolition from demands for racial equality. The most protracted disagreement occurred over the definition of slavery. Both in the executive committee, of which he was a member, and in open sessions the agents labored over a dispute between Charles Stuart, a retired British army officer who had far-reaching impact on antislavery movements, and Theodore Dwight Weld, Wright's distant cousin[83] and the man who personified successful speaking and agitating in the minds of most of "the Seventy." Stuart favored a simple definition of slavery as involuntary, uncompensated labor. But Weld carried the hour, and the Americans chose a definition based on a divinely ordained, hierarchical scheme. Slavery was, in effect, sinful intervention in God's disposition of persons and things. Another note taker, Angelina Grimké, grasped Weld's distinction as "the philosophy of slavery." She wrote: "I never heard so grand & beautiful an exposition of the dignity & nobility of man in my life—his description of the creation of man was sublime, the distinction which God had made between all other beings & this best great result of the counsels of Divine Wisdom, this immortal creature made only a little lower than the Angels, crowned with glory & honor, the sceptred monarch of the world. Under his feet all other creatures were placed, & they were all made subservient to his use [as] they were things." Slavery was a sin, Weld taught the others, because it "with an iron grasp seized this God like being, [and] wrested the sceptre of dominion from his hands." It erased a distinction fundamental to God's government.[84]

Weld's distinctions reminded Wright of radical views on peace that he held since 1830. As he sat at the training sessions he jotted down reflections on the parallels between slavery, war, and arbitrary government. All three interfered with divine sovereignty. His thoughts also turned in other directions, less abstract and theological.

The definition of slavery was almost inevitably an exercise in self-definition, especially for someone who had spent many years looking for a legitimate vocation in a fluid society. As Wright listened to

Weld he imagined himself a slave and disowned traits that he described as "passive," as compliant with the sinful work of others. One of the disadvantages of Stuart's English view, he noted, was that by stressing labor it neglected to condemn a man who held another for pleasure: "If a man holds a fellow as a thing & decks him out & places him in his parlour & looks at him as a beautiful toy, this is not *sin*."[85] The dispute between Weld and Stuart disclosed psychosexual meanings of commitment to antislavery, a movement deeply concerned with the proper spheres of God and man, of men and things, of men and animals, and of men and women. In his notes Wright was setting boundaries for his independence and his own masculinity.

While rejecting the English definition of slavery as too narrowly economic, the Americans were also commenting, at least obliquely, on the changing economy. Wright took it for granted that work has moral and psychological implications, and he was well versed in new educational theories that confirmed the assumption. Theodore Weld, prior to abolitionism, had served the cause of introducing manual labor into the routines of college life, a cause which took the Swiss educator Philipp Emanuel von Fellenberg as its hero. Listening to Weld expound on the decadence of Southerners, Wright noted: "*Industry the great moralizer* (Fellenburg). Industry—habitual industry necessary to tame the human passions. Slaveholders are educated in a community where industry is disreputable."[86] The masters' motives were not normal economic ones; their passions were undisciplined, and their incentives to drive others to work were sadistic pleasure and a rage to obliterate the humanity of other human beings. Wright was trying to identify ways in which economic power might be wielded guiltlessly and love of neighbor might be rendered consistent with the practices of the marketplace. He explicitly denied his personal responsibility, as slaveholder or abolitionist, for misfortunes that might befall the slave from sudden independence. The antislavery distinction between a man and a thing had this implication for economic life in the nineteenth century: A true man was a worker, neither passive nor dependent, unwilling to submit to another man's care. On the basis of some ancient-sounding distinctions Wright learned to reject some of the protective attitudes toward the welfare of others that had been features of his benevolent evangelicalism.

Although most of the agents were to go west, the committee on agencies of the American Anti-Slavery Society assigned Wright to Maine. Then they decided that he should form juvenile antislavery societies in New York City. ("Thus I am arrested once more," he noted in his diary, "on my way westward.") But it was a good assignment, making effective use of his previous experience. It was a pleasure to write in children's publications like the *Slave's Friend* and to speak to children, who were "born abolitionists." All that was needed was to keep them from developing "the *martial spirit*" by which men were enslaved. In this work he made good use of the training sessions on the philosophy of slavery, as was shown in his report of catechizing more than 100 children and parents. How much lower than the angels did God make man? Did he give man dominion over anything? Was anything given dominion over man? Were men given dominion over one another? "But, dear Garrison," he concluded in the *Liberator*, "what a scene this earth presents! One continued bloody struggle of man to gain dominion over his brother—to hurl God from the throne, and trample his brother beneath his feet!"[87]

Reassigned to Essex County, Wright gravitated from children's spirits to women's rights. Angelina Grimké and her sister Sarah were powerful additions to "the Seventy" because they spoke from the experience of having been brought up in a South Carolina slaveholding family. They caused a sensation by speaking to men as well as women. Censured and scolded by powerful New England clergymen, Angelina wrote: "our *womanhood* is as great offense to some as our Abolitionism." But they searched for courage to endure the storm, "if we can only be the means of making the breach in that wall of public opinion which lies right in the way of woman's true dignity, honor & usefulness."[88] It was one of those startling moments of change that historians can appreciate but scarcely explain. The sisters knew that their battle had to call into question the clergy's power. They were tested more severely by protests from abolitionists, notably Weld and John Greenleaf Whittier, against their moving so swiftly. For support in this war they called on the Garrisonians—and especially their friend from the training sessions, Henry C. Wright.

His Newburyport home served as their headquarters in the midst of their exhilarating tour of Essex County in the summer of 1837. He watched over their health, and supplied the encouragement and guidance that Angelina especially needed. While they sometimes felt frail and uncertain of their direction, Wright was a veteran of combat with the Boston clergy and bore scars from earlier efforts to vindicate an agent's right to speak on diverse subjects. He issued regular reports on what he called (some thought ludicrously) the women's

"LABORS." His supposed hegemony over the Grimkés became an issue in the nasty atmosphere hovering over abolitionism that summer. Quite likely, his powers over them were exaggerated by many contemporaries who wished to see the Grimkés as impressionable women led astray by a sinister Svengali. But clearly he tried out on them his radical views of peace and government, and they were thrilled. In preparing a dear friend for Wright's visit, Angelina promised "he will tell thee all about his views of civil government & be not afraid to be converted. I can truly say that until I embraced them I never understood the full extent of that Liberty wherewith Christ makes his followers *free*."[89]

The Grimkés enjoyed "the green pastures of christian intercourse & the still waters of peace in his lovely family."[90] For his part, Wright used friendship with these celebrated (or notorious) women to announce some of his radical conclusions. Under the title "A Domestic Scene," he recounted a conversation with his family and these women. Its publication provoked much furor; yet we may wonder what seemed so frightening, where lurked the alleged danger of anarchy in the first paragraph:

> There is one school that I believe was founded by God, and that is the Domestic Institution. In this school of God's appointing, man is to be educated for two worlds—for time and eternity. This school is peculiarly fitted to educate man for the whole of his existence. It receives the immortal spirit from the hand of God as it first starts in its journey of endless being; and here God designed that it should be trained to meet all the vicissitudes of an eternal progression. In this school are we all cast to be educated to become the associates of angels, and to be priests and kings unto God. But how often is this institution perverted and made a school of vice and infamy, to prepare us to become associates of devils and damned spirits! Let God preside over this school as the great Teacher and let his pure and living oracles—the Bible—be the great textbook, and how soon might this whole world be subjected to his holy will.[91]

Why the furor? Part of the problem was his evocation of scenes of intimacy with the Grimkés in a context that hinted at some alteration of marriage. The "Domestic Scene" raised the standard by which Christian radicals traditionally attacked existing social arrangements: "*The state of man before the fall.*" Once upon a time, nobody had pretended to hold dominion over anybody else as they all were entitled to lord it over beasts, birds, and fish. Each man, woman, or child had "a right of ownership over all the earth, but himself [was] owned by God." Then came the Fall—and the spirit of usurped authority that characterizes every form of slavery. "From the day in which Adam began to usurp dominion over Eve to this hour, man has been struggling for dominion over man." The countervailing "spirit in man" that resists domination had yielded a long history of chaos and conflict. The goal of Christian reform, then, was to restore order and peace, which meant to eliminate the struggle to enslave one another, which in turn meant to revive divine ownership of man.

The Wrights and Grimkés inquired which earthly institutions currently pursued that goal. Which led to subjection and conflict, which to liberation and peace? They were disappointed in the old bulwark: "Our school system, from the infant school *down* to the University, as now constituted and managed . . . tended to enslave the mind of man to man, to alienate the soul from God and bind it in chains of human servitude." Similar conclusions were reached concerning the sinfulness of existing churches and governments. Moreover, the family, which had unlimited potential for God's work, was usually instead "an engine to crush the soul and subject it to man." In the "gentle service" of God there was no place for human dominion, "not even parents over their children," nor man over woman.[92]

One can begin to understand why some readers of the "Domestic Scene" heard not the obeisance to God but the overthrow of existing lines of authority. For example, Rev. James T. Woodbury (brother of the secretary of the treasury) attacked the "Domestic Scene": "I had as soon my son should be taught that the Bible is not true, as that I have not the right, under God, to chastise him; for he now understands that if done it is done by the direct sanction of the Almighty."[93] Wright was indeed challenging traditional patterns of control, though he took second place to no one in professing respect for truly divine sanctions. He was beginning to enjoy scenes of controversy in which, while being charged with sedition, he could insist on his orthodox, conservative intentions. Here, at one of the most controversial moments of his career, he was identifying liberation with self-restraint: If one is owned by God—and therefore free of usurped, coercive authorities—controls are internalized. He was elaborating a simple logic set forth years before in a peace notebook: "The action of each human body must be controlled by a *power within it*—or by a power without it—by An *Interior* or by *an* Exterior *power*."[94]

This logic became even clearer in a second "Domestic Scene," composed without the Grimkés but still set in his home. The party searched for a "rule of life" that would rid the earth of such curses as the Inquisition, despotism, and slavery. In this search they talked exclusively about the family and its two systems of instruction. First came "*physical means*": "the system of scolding, threatening, cuffing, beating, whipping," and all efforts to "make children hate and avoid sin, and love and practice holiness, by the infliction of bodily pains and injuries." This system was self-defeating; it encouraged sullen feelings of revenge and half-hearted attempts at external reform. The second, more effective system relied on "*moral means*": expressions of affection, consistent examples, and conversation about the dignity of man and the sovereignty of God. Animals might be whipped, because they were placed under man's ownership. Children should not be beaten because it hardly could be done in "the spirit of Christ" rather than with excitement, anger, and shouting. Wright referred to parents who were "often surprised that their children turn out no better after they have scolded and whipped them so faithfully. . . . Had parents trusted less to the rod and more to moral influence *to instill good principles into their hearts* and lead them to virtuous practices, the results might have been far different." The internalization of "good principles" was, then, the social meaning of what otherwise sounds like otherworldly preaching. In stressing obedience to the divine will instead of following one's own will, Wright was indeed urging some reorientation in social arrangements, though it is easier for us to see implications for social control than it was for some of his contemporaries. One minister thought he "had the mind of old Nick."[95]

Wright had entered the service of the American Anti-Slavery Society at a time of increasing divisiveness. Although his first months of service were apparently happy enough, he was soon at the center of extremely unfriendly conflict. He did not mind being attacked in furious antiabolitionist handbills, or sought by a mob, after he called New York's district attorney a manstealer. This kind of threat had been endured by Thompson, Weld, and other heroes.[96] Some abolitionists, however, had taken offense at his catechism of children: was not government, they asked, a form of man's dominion over man that God had ordained?[97] Although Garrison vouched for Wright in this instance, the charge that Wright advocated "no human government" became more disturbing as more of his opinions slipped into print. When he was sent away from New York, he became identified with the Grimkés and made things worse. By August 1837 he was uncomfortably aware that the New York board disliked his work. They felt he should be more guarded when representing the society; they might even drop him from his agency. Instead, they assigned him to Philadelphia. He moved his family there, and listed Philadelphia as his "home" for the remainder of his life. In late September, however, he received formal notice that he would not be reappointed agent of the Anti-Slavery Society. The happy atmosphere of the training sessions was shattered.[98]

According to two distinguished scholars, Wright was sacked because he "proved to be incompetent as an agent and a trouble-maker in the county societies where he labored."[99] On closer examination, we may discern two different tracks leading to the board's action. In the first place, his intimacy with the Grimkés was galling to Theodore Dwight Weld, who had also met the sisters at the training sessions and was secretly in love with Angelina. A magnetic leader, Weld had problems in expressing intimate feelings. Wright foolishly hoped that, having brought the Grimkés to his views of government, he would soon hear of Weld's conversion. Weld fretted, instead, as he read accounts of the sisters' "LABORS," and sent numerous long letters to warn them against the course they were taking. He accused Wright of having an incurable "itching to be *known*." Wright's cleverness in attaching the Grimkés' reputation to his "Domestic Scene" and his habit of sending signed letters to hosts of newspapers indicated to Weld that the publicity available to reformers had turned his head. Eventually Weld voiced his love, Angelina reciprocated, the lovers were married and set up household with Sarah, and Wright saw little of them thereafter.[100]

Besides depriving him of famous and intimate friends, the significance of the Weld-Grimké romance for Wright's life was that Weld infused his employment by the American Anti-Slavery Society with undertones of enmity. Weld's standing among abolitionists was very high after the training sessions; he had the reputation of a brilliant, unselfish strategist. After straining his voice by speaking so long on the philosophy of slavery, he had been forced to give up itinerant agitation; thus he had more time to spend with Elizur Wright, John Greenleaf Whittier, Lewis Tappan, and others who manned the New York office. It was Weld who pushed them to reassign Wright to Philadelphia, thus causing the Grimkés to feel the loss of a pillar of support.[101] At the time of his firing Wright was stung by Weld's charges that he was "*vain*—& desirous to make a display & to seek popularity." Weld charged that "I was continually speaking in the *Convention* of Agents last Fall. (Brother Weld did *four-fifths* of the talking in the Convention.) Brother Weld . . . Begged me to cease thus to make myself public—to keep unknown—lest I become vain & ambitious." Since Weld had not yet confessed his love for Angelina Grimké, perhaps even to himself, Wright was hardly conscious of the origins of these accusations. He never developed Weld's nervousness over the snares the open society of the nineteenth century spread out before hungry egos.[102]

There is no doubt that some abolitionists believed Wright was hurting the cause. "A man may be a good man but a very pernicious agent," concluded James G. Birney, who feared "H. C. Wright would bring some evil on us by his multiplied writing and violent spirit." Others were less charitable. Wright was the target of complaint by clergymen, some of whom Birney characterized as "the *Conservative ultra party*," and others, like the old Garrisonian Amos Augustus Phelps, whose views could not be dismissed so easily. The questions facing the board were whether the best of these complainers could be kept within the antislavery movement and whether the worst could be deprived of the convenient target of Wright's radicalism. Whittier wrote to Phelps (who was lost anyway) that Wright would be dismissed as he had recommended.[103]

In November Wright went up to the antislavery office in New York and argued with Weld, Birney, and the others—especially Lewis Tappan. Wright ignored the practical question of how to hold onto conservative clergymen. He insisted, as a matter of principle, that antislavery must allow its representatives perfect freedom, that one divine truth could not be harmed by linkage to others, and that antislavery urgently needed to be identified with peace lest it be charged with stirring up bloody slave revolts. But Tappan was adamant: agents should not preach their beliefs on any subject other than antislavery, except in private. In Wright's view, he was fired for advocating peace. This view afforded some self-righteousness with which to salve unmistakable signs of hurt. Remembering the uneasy entry of abolitionism into the empire of benevolence, he saw certain ironies: "So the Abolition Society—after denouncing the narrow, one-idea-exclusive Policy of the Temperance, Peace, Missionary, [and] Bible Societies in refusing to say anything against Slavery & join Abolitionists for fear of loosing [*sic*] influence & becoming unpopular—is now that it has become popular adopting the same policy. Abolitionists have been spoiled by flattery—stones, rotten Eggs & Brick bats have done us more good than soft words of flattery." Wright was loyal to Garrison, furthermore; and he felt the New Yorkers, with their outmoded view of reform, were courting the Andover-Boston circle from whom he struggled to win independence.[104]

Wright, unemployed for a year, relied once more on his wife's wealth. Then in 1850 the American Anti-Slavery Society split apart over the issue that Wright had dramatized as its agent—whether abolitionists should take radical ground on subjects like peace and women's rights. Most of his antagonists departed and set up their own short-lived American and Foreign Anti-Slavery Society. The Garrisonians, after managing to keep hold of the "old organization," continued to invite women's full participation. But on the peace question they expressed their opinions through the New England Non-Resistance Society, and by the same logic they resisted motions that would have committed abolitionists to support third-party political action. Wright was a leading actor in these quarrels that had the effect of limiting antislavery organization while creating new fields of action. He found employment again as traveling representative of the New England Non-Resistance Society.

Several factors played into the creation of this organization in September 1838. It gave Garrisonian abolitionists a separate forum for anarchistic views that were stirring up rancor within and against abolitionism. It provided a haven to radical pacifists who finally gave up on the American Peace Society. It also turned out to be a place of discovery for individualistic, prophetic voices searching for ways of imposing religious authority in a loose, secularized society. Many of these prophets went on to experiment with Christian communities. John Humphrey Noyes, the perfectionist founder of the Oneida Community, had great impact on Garrison's nonresistance, though he refrained from joining the new society. Bronson Alcott, best remembered as a Concord transcendentalist and founder of the Fruitlands Community, emerged in the Non-Resistance Society as an inspiring advocate of primitive Christianity. Adin Ballou, the most dedicated and thoughtful leader, founded the Hopedale Community, which kept nonresistance alive.[105]

Generally speaking, nonresistance was associated with rectitude and sobriety, but it could never shake off images of eccentricity and heretical prattle. Not all of these images originated in the minds of accusers. Once Wright came across Adin Ballou and the highly respected Unitarian minister Samuel Joseph May, arguing with Alcott and "his *apes.*" One of Alcott's disciples approached May and said mysteriously, "I am *God!* What do you think of that?" May answered, "I think you are a false God." When asked his opinion of Jesus, another disciple replied, "*Damn* Jesus." Wright recorded their sorry applications of the widespread millennial teaching that all men have it within them to become perfectly holy: "These poor silly men hold that *theft* is no crime. That each has a right to take whatever he wants—wherever he can find it. They swear like pirates—under pretense of giving outward expression to their souls—an old doctrine, & made use of to excuse all indecency, vulgarity, outrage, blasphemy, & wickedness."[106] It was indeed an old heresy, precisely what churchmen predicted would be the outcome of blasts against authority under the color of holiness.

Most nonresistants, of course, deplored theft, crime, swearing, and other symptoms of disorder. They opposed all wars and all acts of personal violence. They disagreed among themselves over borderline instances of force such as the restraint of madmen, over the duty of obedience to the state, and over the holiness of the violence-filled Old Testament. As a result, they spent much of their time in clarifying doctrine. Although critics charged that their "no-governmentism" would bring on chaos and anarchy, they were firm in their belief in order. In renouncing violence, they were renouncing slavery and anarchy. They were men of peace in a fluid, anarchical age. Wright had a major role in hammering out this position which he had been working on privately for years. "A novel and *harmless* anarchy," he called it, "in which there is no violence."[107]

Nonresistance had vocational as well as theoretical importance. To the centuries-old opposition to a paid ministry the nineteenth century added the anxious belief that all occupations depended on cash exchanges instead of authentic trusts. Wright had for years been looking for a calling where he might be both selfless and successful, a problem that his bitter experience with the New York antislavery office made more acute. A sympathetic Angelina Grimké, bridling at restraints on her own expressions of conscience, told Wright that his embarrassments arose from "being paid for thy services & I believe God will break up this unrighteous selling of his holy truths." Reform now resembled the corrupt, pre-Reformation church: "Is not the whole system of religion," she asked, "the machinery of piety which passes for Christianity, a compromise with God to give us heaven for our money in some shape or another?"[108] How fully these reformers confirmed old warnings against letting reform movements stand as surrogates for true God-fearing religion! Marriage removed Weld and the Grimkés from the "machinery of piety," while Wright moved onward to nonresistance's unfettered service.

He did not take a regular salary from the New England Non-Resistance Society. The instructions of the executive committee when they appointed him general agent reflected years of controversy over conscience and vocation. They freed him to speak on any subject, since "every truth strengthens and forms a part of every other truth." They gave him full freedom of speech because effective language only flows from the individual heart: "we disparage no man's armor, because it does not fit *us.*" They expected frankness of communication and would send him occasional suggestions. But they would not give orders; "the man who yields his own judgment . . . in obedience to the will of any executive committee, is not fit for the office of a teacher of divine truth."[109]

In this exciting livery he traveled more than ever previously. He accepted the invitation to search out new applications of truth, and he chose gentle or vituperative language as the armor suited him. He printed dozens of accounts of each year's journeys and meetings. At the end of his first year the executive committee marveled at the work he had done; "were it not that he is favored with a vigorous constitution and extraordinary powers of endurance," he might not survive. They praised him in terms that must have been heartwarming:

> . . . he has performed [his task]with an elasticity of mind, an alacrity of spirit, and a firmness of purpose, which have rarely been exhibited by reformers in any age or country. . . . He has labored in season and out of season, by day and by night, . . . scorned and reviled on the right hand and the left, and held up to the gaze of the people as an object of detestation; yet has he not grown weary in well-doing, nor shrunk appalled at the prospect before him, nor evinced the slightest unwillingness to 'bide the peltings of the pitiless storm' that is raging over his head. His position is one of great peril, yet full of moral sublimity.

Whenever he spoke he gained proselytes, and future generations would "revere his memory." His accounts of his travels, a regular feature of the *Liberator* and the new society's *Non-Resistant,* would become "an important portion of the history of the times."[110]

Without quite gaining the place in history that was predicted for him, he did win a prominent role among New England reformers and was constantly at the center of controversy. Ministers closed their churches to his visits, editors attacked him as a wild "ultraist," conservative abolitionists deplored his sway over Garrison; and at the same time friends of nonresistance reported that his talks revealed divine inspiration, and homes were open to him wherever he traveled. No longer a hireling of church or board, he lived on donations and acts of kindness. According to the *Liberator,* he often had barely a subsistence but was nonetheless content.[111] He found himself as an author and never used a pseudonym. Besides the endless stream of reports, letters, and arguments, he wrote a book on nonresistance that proved to be one of the durable achievements of the movement. *A Kiss for a Blow* (1842) went through many editions for decades to come; even the American Peace Society praised it, hoping children would not be kept away from its instructive tales because of the author's heresies on other subjects. The abolitionist Wendell Phillips called it "the best book for children ever written. It will always be popular."[112]

Now that he had found his vocation, Wright completed his independence of the churches and benevolent societies that had detained him for a decade. To antislavery and nonresistance he added a message of venomous anticlericalism. Many other abolitionists eventually turned to the belief that the churches were the main protectors of slavery; that view attracted even old adversaries like Birney. Some antislavery New Englanders left their churches, and others, like Stephen S. Foster, disrupted church services to call attention to slavery. While never imitating this tactic, Wright became the chief spokesman for the view that the professional ministry polluted the pure spirit of Christianity and that the sabbath was a priestly invention to distract souls from the obligation to live a blameless daily life. No Garrisonian—not even Nathaniel Rogers, a master of invective—surpassed Wright's furious denunciations of ministers. He publicly withdrew from the ministerial association to which he had belonged, calling his friends and colleagues sinners on the path to hell. All proper callings were sacred. He was proud to be counted among *"poor, despised, obscure, untitled laymen"* rather than among the pretentious, professional misleaders of the people's consciences.[113]

The Wide Universe

While toiling for nonresistance, Henry Wright began to express publicly the motto he reiterated, with variations, throughout the rest of his life. Sometimes it defined his atomistic approach to morals: "*I am alone with God in my responsibility*," he told the ministerial association as he resigned. "I am an isolated being, a recluse, in perfect solitude, absolutely and forever cut off from all social sympathy and aid, in my *responsibilities*." In this period he consistently preached an individualistic vision in which society could give no help to the lonely regulations of private consciences. To the extent that ministers retained affection for older, organic visions of a society with capacities for nurture and forgiveness, they were unlikely to be impressed by Wright's motto. But the atomistic vision strengthened his sense of vocation, as was clear in his sketch of "A Christian Reformer." It was terribly important to be seen as free from selfish considerations of rank, power, or place. Wright's torn feelings about making his name known were not so different from Weld's, after all. Christian reformers "feel ourselves alone with God in the wide universe, seeing nothing but his glory, fearing nothing but his frown, and desiring nothing but his approbation."[114] Wright's metaphorical reclusiveness was, in fact, part of his sense of calling: even if he did not stay put in a local pastorate, he certainly proposed to be of service to universal mankind. With time he learned to speak of God less, and the universe more.

Wright felt, as others did, that the name of the *New England* Non-Resistance Society was absurdly parochial. He joined others—particularly Alcott, Garrison, and the strong-willed organizer Maria Weston Chapman—in planning for a "World's Convention for the discussion of all wrong" (with invincible parochialism they assumed it should occur in Boston, where great historical movements always commenced). This convention of humanity would escape the strife over women's rights that marred an 1840 world's antislavery convention in London. Committees were appointed, meetings were held, and many took up the idea of a congress of right-minded individuals working "to move the hearts of man to the attainment of a higher civilization." How much better this would be than a pretentious congress of the representatives of "governmental machines." It was all "as A.B. Alcott said a *great talk*"; as agent of the Non-Resistance Society Wright was in the thick of it.[115]

In March 1842 the executive committee of the Non-Resistance Society changed Wright's assignment. Garrison pointed out that the "Public mind in Great Britain and Ireland is, at present, in a singularly plastic and reformatory state, and therefore prepared to receive right impressions." This was the right moment to send their agent there. Donations of money to support his travel were urgently solicited: he had to leave on short notice to reach London in time for the 1842 benevolent meetings.[116]

His mission was not uncontroversial. Whittier was caustic about wasting money to give the English the advantage of Wright's long-windedness. Wouldn't it be better to send food to starving families in Manchester and Leeds? Friends of nonresistance regularly asked whether Wright wasn't needed more in the United States (they rightly predicted the cause would decline in his absence). But it was hard to admit that this glorious cause depended on the work of one man. At a meeting of his friends Wright expressed his thought that "we ought to overlook all national feeling; and mingle with different nations." Nathaniel Rogers had doubts about the practicality of the mission, but hinted that Wright might be close to burnt-out anyway. "He needs respite," and the voyage would make him slow down, even if he started rushing again when he stepped on shore. "The scenes of the old world will entertain him, and refresh his over-labored spirit." Having made his own journey to the 1840 antislavery convention, Rogers felt the English would benefit from hearing Wright; and his work would hasten the world's convention in New England. But Wright would undoubtedly be missed: "He is the beloved of abolitionists. The little children exult and bound when he comes in sight, and weep aloud when he departs. They will pray for him on the deep—and talk of him to their mothers and among themselves, at night. The clergy here will exult. . . . God speed him, though we cannot part with him."[117]

The world's convention never occurred, but Henry Wright spent five years overseas. He set the same exhausting schedules for himself in Britain as he had in New England. He lectured widely on peace, although the London Peace Convention immediately warned against him and disclaimed any connection with him. "Well, I tell them," Wright told the *Liberator*, "I mean to be *a most belligerent non-resistant*," sparing none of the venerated military institutions of the kingdom. He gave hundreds of lectures on peace, sold thousands of copies of *A Kiss for a Blow* and other writings, and distributed even more free tracts calling for the abolition of the army and navy. During this period he also wrote one of the most comprehensive books on nonresistance by an American, *Defensive War Proved to be a Denial of Christianity and of the Government of God* (1846). There were glorious conflicts, such as the day in Bolton when "tories" laid rough hands on him while his friends resolved that the clergy should be employed as hangmen. When some Americans pressed him to come home in 1846, two Scottish Garrisonians—John Murray and William Smeal—totaled up a balanced estimate of the value of his labors. England had its own temperance advocates and a steady supply of American abolitionists. Peace, however, was "*peculiarly* H.C. Wright's question"; if he left, no substitute could be found and the door to future reform would be closed. Interest in peace had dwindled, to be sure, after the rising excitement of Wright's first arrival, but now it was welling up again. Didn't it make sense for the premier peace agitator to stay in Britain, as fitting a place to strive against war and nationalism as America was for antislavery action?[118]

It was agitation against slavery, nevertheless, that gained Wright the most fame and notoriety in Britain. He showed a knack for stirring up controversy even over his identity. In Glasgow he charged, for example, that John Tyler sold his own colored children. One American paper, the *Madisonian,* picked up the charge and denied it. The *Philadelphia Mercury* said Wright was not an American but a disgruntled Scot whom Tyler had refused a consulship. The *New York Express* repeated that story. It remained for the *Boston Post* to say, no, he was a hypocritical, heretical Congregational minister who had become an ultraabolitionist, nonresistant, and "advocate of the self-marrying system." Then, of course, the *Liberator* could recapitulate the controversy, defend Wright's honor, and send the matter back across the Atlantic with Wright better known and the original aspersions on Tyler forgotten.[119]

His antislavery work reunited him with George Thompson. He also traveled frequently with two American abolitionists, James Buffum and Frederick Douglass. Many British abolitionists found, as white American friends had previously, that the ex-slave Douglass could be vain and testy. But Wright steered clear of that kind of conflict. He professed to find Douglass "full of fun & frolick—in the *Zip Coon* way." Douglass had the capacity "to accomplish any amount of good," although there were many who wished him ill. Therefore Wright adopted a simple strategy: "I get along with him by leaving him to himself, never interfering[,] doing just what I think ought to be done, leaving him to join me or not as he is disposed. This is my only way to go with him."[120]

Wright did not travel randomly in Britain. He spent much more time in Dublin, Edinburgh, and Glasgow than in London; more in the north of England and the Midlands than in the east or south. He lectured in towns throughout the Lowlands and Central Highlands of

Scotland but only in Dublin, Belfast, and a few scattered locations in Ireland. Everywhere he enjoyed squabbles over his credentials as an abolitionist. He was not the first Garrisonian to visit Britain (John Anderson Collins had made an equally contentious tour in 1841) nor the last; and he went with considerable knowledge of what soil was worth tilling. In the provinces antislavery people tended to favor American Garrisonism; they were at odds with the Broad Street abolitionists of London who sided with Garrison's critics. The provincials may not have understood all the issues in the American schism, but their own resentments prepared them to welcome notes of bitterness and rivalry. In looking for antislavery battles to join, Wright usually stayed with persons who dissented from the prevailing religion of their locality. This was true of Quakers in Ireland; it was also true of the stalwart Garrisonian in Lancashire, Philip P. Carpenter, who was a Unitarian. Nor were his Scottish associates members of the Church of Scotland; some were Quakers and Unitarians, others had come out of the newborn Free Kirk.[121]

In Scotland Wright discovered an issue that activated his severest detestation of the clergy and made him the focus of anger over the sundered condition of true religion. Numerous churches had withdrawn from the Calvinist establishment in 1843 in order to defend congregational control over the choice of ministers. The product of this "Disruption" was the Free Kirk, and to help solve its financial problems one leader brought back a donation of $3,000 from a visit among American Presbyterians. Much of this money was collected in the South, some presumably from slaveholders. To abolitionists this was blood money squeezed from the slaves' bodies. Its acceptance linked the Free Kirk to bondage, and made a mockery of its defense of religious freedom. Henry Wright has been called "the key figure" in the early years of the campaign to force the Free Kirk to "Send Back the Money."[122] He darted all over Scotland to arouse intense interest in the subject of slavery, and gloried in the exchange of charges and countercharges. This uproar was magnified by the concerted work of a team of Wright, Douglass, Buffum, and Thompson. The "Send Back the Money" campaign was the best opportunity Wright ever found to lash the churches for condoning slavery.

Antislavery is sometimes regarded as a link in transatlantic Christian cooperation, and Wright's travels reveal some of the evidence for this view. But slavery also destroyed hopes of Anglo-American cooperation. The Free Kirk dispute was only the loudest of several similar explosions in the 1840s. Wright likewise tore into a proposed

Evangelical Alliance including American churches that gave fellowship to slaveowners, and he criticized Irish Quakers who in their concern about famine relief accepted money from the American South.[123] In these disputes Wright followed British leads, for in the lingering competition among sects in Britain, where there was extensive agreement on the iniquity of slavery, the issue was useful when one religious group wished to isolate or embarrass another. Angry disputes over institutional connections with American slaveholders might have their actual basis in British sectarian rivalries.

If there is one salient theme in the visits of American abolitionists to Britain, it is the stirring up of old-fashioned *odium theologicum.* No one orchestrated religious hatred more zealously than Wright, no one leveled more dramatically phrased charges, no one occasioned more fury. Even Garrisonians might have hesitated before the zeal which he attached to religious controversy. But it is doubtful that antislavery lost anything because of his actions, and in Scotland it very likely gained a good deal, at least temporarily. Even a caustic analysis suggests that Wright acquired great influence there by his speeches, the sale of his writings, and the prominent attacks on him. Many who were not ordinarily antislavery joined his assault on the "blood money" in the Free Kirk's coffers. But the irony to be stressed is that the bitter foe of parochialism found his greatest influence in a conflict of primarily sectarian significance: some who joined him did so in reprisal for the "Disruption."[124]

Wright had come to Britain with his own dreams of transoceanic cooperation. Although he ceased talking about a world's convention in Boston, he still imagined a conference of the world's peoples, perhaps in a Highland glen, overcoming the artificial barriers of nations and denominations. In his mind, however, alliances between the Scottish Free Kirk and American Presbyterians or between the varied denominations of the proposed Evangelical Alliance were the dishonest gestures of the American churchmen who scoffed at all his dreams. They were disheartening forms of ecumenicism because they were based on the preservation of sects. Therefore he blasted them, probably without recognizing that he was being pulled into sectarian competition. He was licensed to use invective against particular denominations and clergymen in a way that was impermissible in America, where denominations effected a closer and more vigilant alliance. He could portray the distinguished Dr. Thomas Chalmers of the Free Kirk with hands dyed in blood; he could ask "Is Mamon or Is Not Mamon the Divinity of the 'Free' Church Folks?" and accuse specific ministers and laymen of being tipplers.

One such salvo caused acute embarrassment. In Hawick, Wright's charges about a local minister, supposedly based on a letter from a local currier, landed in Deacon's Court, where the informant, who had no recollection of saying what Wright attributed to him, was forced to demand satisfaction. Wright then had to admit "with grief and astonishment . . . that my own *running notes,* apart from your letter entirely, are by the printers inserted as part of your letter." Several Free Kirk pamphlets publicized Wright's "*Acknowledged Slander.*" For Wright this was the low point of a campaign where he himself sold tens of thousands of pamphlets, and a pamphlet accusing him, Douglass, and Thompson of infidelity reportedly sold 6,000 copies in the first six days. He was not usually careless but he was always controversial. One can understand why some abolitionists, notably Frederick Douglass, became reluctant to be associated with him.[125]

In a *Farewell Letter* Wright said that despite being diverted into antislavery work he left Britain with a deeper commitment to nonresistance. He had learned that love knew no national boundaries.[126] This theme runs through letters to American colleagues while he was in Britain and to British friends after his return. The ocean was no obstacle to the loving unity of mankind. It seems clear, nevertheless, that he had pared down the universalist mission on which he had originally crossed the Atlantic; he had tacitly given up the millennial hope of a world unified by the collapse of denominations. A denomination on one side might call its cognate on the other shore to conscience on the slavery issue; sectarian rivalries in Britain might be exploited for antislavery purposes; but there was no evidence that the strong religious institutions of Britain were ever going to crumble, whatever stand they took on America's peculiar institution. More and more, then, the letters passing between Dublin, Glasgow, Lancashire, and Wright on his travels resembled those of "a people among peoples," if I may borrow Sydney James's term for the Quakers after they surrendered millenarian purposes for lives of exemplary distinctiveness.[127] They were letters of a closely interknit network of friends for whom slavery was a point of contact with worldly power. It was no accident that Wright began to adopt the Quaker thee-and-thouing in these years. Amidst all the rancor and vilification of his stay in Europe, he was taking steps toward agitation as a profession rather than a calling.

The more vehemently Wright denounced existing institutions in the name of God's sovereignty, the more he was isolated as the roving representative of a tribe—Murray and Smeal in Scotland,

Richard D. Webb and James Haughton in Dublin, Carpenter and a few others in Lancashire, Garrison and other nonresistants in Massachusetts. He was at the same time gaining in literary ability and becoming conscious of an audience for *his* work. Besides venomous criticism of the clergy, one of his most characteristic forms of writing consisted of little "domestic scenes" among the families he visited on his travels. He also experimented with travel literature, giving Americans his impressions of Macbeth's castle, for example, or of Highland lochs, while also reminding them of his identification with the international concerns of humanity. His best writings were a nearly endless series of "Letters from Henry C. Wright" carried in the *Liberator* in 1844 and 1845 and publicizing his responses to the monuments, cathedrals, and battlefields of Europe. Later he sold to American audiences pictures of a Scottish girl who figured in these letters. Thus his peculiar identification with a tribe and his contacts with a wider audience were mutually reinforcing. We should notice, furthermore, that service to God was transformed into familiar genres of popular literature and that his quest for a world's convention began to reflect middle-class habits of tourism.

In Europe he took one more step toward the secularization of his calling: he began to write on health reform. Wright had for years been interested in dietary reform; this was a natural result of the temperance movement's fascination with bodily self-control. Like other speakers and travelers, Wright was plagued by colds, scratchy throats, indigestion, and diarrhea. Staying in different homes and choosing the fare of different inns made him conscious of links between his actions and his health. In August 1836, when he was troubled by the temporizing of many reformers, he recorded a triumph: "This morning much tempted in my appetite. Very hungry. Determined to live on vegetable food. Some good fish & meat set before me. Was enabled to resist. Now I feel all the better." But he was unlikely to persist in vegetarianism, if only because his views of "the philosophy of slavery" stressed the right of human beings to use animals as they wished. There were many defeats to record on his travels: in January 1837, for example, he was feverish "in consequence of eating grease in Newark." At the home where he was a guest he had eaten a fatty roast goose. "I have no doubt that animal *Fat* is at the bottom of all my trouble.[128] Vegetarianism was not in any case one of the extraneous issues on which he spoke out as an antislavery agent. These were simply the private reflections of an uncomfortable itinerant.

His voyage to Liverpool in 1842 was a torment. He was sick for twenty days, could not hold food down, and lost twenty pounds. From Liverpool he went to Ireland where humid weather seemed to worsen his debility. He soon developed a chronic cough and propensity to fever that were aggravated by the wearying lecture schedules he set for himself. His illness caused great concern among other reformers; some feared that he was dying of consumption. Finally he was prevailed upon to give up his chores. With financial assistance from Richard D. Webb of Dublin and Elizabeth Pease, a wealthy British abolitionist, he was sent to the most famous health center in the world—Vincent Priessnitz's cold water establishment at Graefenberg in the Silesian Alps. There were excellent water-cure establishments in England, Webb reported to Wright's American friends, but none could compare to that run by the Silesian peasant whose genius had made him "the Hippocrates, the Jenner, the Graham, the Thompson of cold water." As an aside, Webb wondered why reformers in the United States had paid so little attention to hydropathy.[129]

Wright was publicly depressed about this side trip. He preferred to lecture in the Orkney Islands and die at once if such were his fate. There was work to be done, and he bore a commission for a world convention. But these protests quickly diminished, in part because the journey to Silesia would permit a nonresistant inspection of important parts of the world. Priessnitz's fame and the novelty of his methods also gave the trip a reform purpose. In numerous letters to American papers and his book on *Six Months at Graefenberg* (1845) Wright gave public accounting of his journey to restored health.

He described the instruments and procedures of the water cure, the various kinds of douches and baths, the hearty dosages of cold water taken internally, the techniques of massage and enclosure in wet sheets, and the experience of cold air and icy walks during an Alpine winter. He acquainted American readers with the reserved character and rapid intuitions of the miracle-working Priessnitz, who had discovered laws of health. These laws, like others favored by nonresistants, were not the arbitrary impositions of human governments; they demanded submission as laws of divine majesty. Graefenberg was an obvious scene for other travel books besides Wright's, and Priessnitz was sometimes criticized for the harshness of his methods. The novelist John W. DeForest, for example, described dismal tortures. But Wright apparently had greater tolerance of discomfort in pursuit of a restored constitution, and he was cured because of, or, in the words of an Irish friend, "in spite of his horrible treatment at Graefenberg." Even Wright could see comedy in a miniature world where wretchedness served as prelude to cure. "I am fast recovering my strength," he wrote in "the dialect of the Water Cure"; "that is to say, in plain English, I am growing weaker every day." He complained to Richard Webb that when Priessnitz saw a painful boil that "laid the bone nearly bare" on his wrist, he "chuckled and exclaimed, Schon!" A cure was on its way! There was a kind of penance in getting well. It was no wonder that his diagnosis had included the side ailment of "hydrophobia," or fear of the cold water.[130]

But the exciting fact was that Wright recovered from his much publicized illness. He returned to England hardy enough to endure the pace he set himself for peace and antislavery. On his travels he regularly poured cold water over his body and consumed it by the quart. And he had located a new specialty on which to lecture: the laws of health. The uneducated Priessnitz worked from genius; Wright could speak from professional experience. He never opened his own establishment or boasted of curing others; instead, he lectured on the preservation and recuperation of the body. This theme became a feature of his repertory after returning to the United States in 1847 (a trip that he postponed out of dread of renewed debility). Although he still spoke of himself as alone with God, there were several respects in which he now had a secularized career. The most important was that he now gave supposedly scientific advice to audiences concerned to learn about good living. In his supreme moments as an agent of nonresistance he had preached the necessity of submitting to suffering and death rather than violating God's moral laws. The new Wright who returned from Europe was ready to teach that by obeying God's scientific laws one could escape pain and deformity.

Professional Itinerancy

Two images may help us understand Henry Clarke Wright's life as an itinerant reformer. First, there is the Christian image of the pilgrim, expressed in a long tradition of wandering friars, scholars, and preachers. The metaphorical links between spiritual quests for knowledge of God and actual journeys on land or sea can make a settled life seem imprisoning and a life of unencumbered travel attractive. Because of his disinterestedness, the wanderer may disregard the material concerns of other human beings; on the other hand, as modern Catholic Workers continue to remind priests, the religious person who has no narrow interests in a competitive society may take to heart the larger interest, including the material interest, of all humankind. The traveler may be a teacher and an advocate. In the history of New England, however, the settled minister had always been praised as spokesman for Christianity; religious itinerants were generally troublemakers. There was one escape: missionaries to unfortunate heathens could merge their own pilgrimage with a life of concern for others. It was this exception to congregationalist views of the ministry that Wright and many other Christian reformers exploited in developing new careers of disinterested benevolence.

The second image is that of the commercial traveler using modern modes of transportation to cover wider and wider markets. In his study of Engels, Steven Marcus looks at mid-nineteenth-century descriptions of commercial travelers who carried ideas, especially Balzac's comic portrayal of "traveling salesmen charged with presenting skillfully, *urbi et orbi,* in Paris and the provinces . . . announcements and prospectuses." Ideas became negotiable property, and no sooner was a scheme cooked up in one place than it was being brought to market someplace else. These "philosophical commercial travelers"—to borrow Marcus's term—played a welcome role in societies where the division of labor had created uncertainty of judgment; the traveler had a new perspective to peddle.[131] In America the lives of antebellum reformers furnished numerous instances of men and women, some of whom had once actually been Yankee peddlers, skipping uncertainly from one nostrum or enthusiasm to another before finally presenting themselves commercially as experts on peaceful minds and healthy bodies.

As Wright shifted his stress from being alone with God to being in the wide universe, his travels changed from those of a pilgrim to those of a commercial traveler. Unlike commercial representatives, however, he was not in anyone's employ. Soon after his return to America, it was announced that he was "the voluntary, unhired agent" of the New England Non-Resistance Society; thus he was free of the "restrictions imposed by the relation of a paid agent." He was expected to revive interest in the movement that had become moribund during his absence. He made his headquarters at the Hopedale Community, actually buying a one-half-acre lot there in 1849. He issued cheerful reports on the expanding audiences for his lectures on peace, and his letters to friends praised the festivals at

Hopedale as worthy alternatives to the warlike rituals of Christianity. But this relationship died out by the end of the 1840s. Hopedale folk found him too hostile to Christianity; the nonresistance movement was not revived by his increased success as a lecturer; and he went on to become his own man. While living at Hopedale, in fact, he completed his autobiography, simply called *Human Life* (1849).[132]

After this brief unpaid agency, he fell into a fairly consistent pattern for his remaining twenty years. He traveled more extensively than ever, from Maine to Pennsylvania, from Minnesota to Missouri, with occasional stops at his family's house in Philadelphia. Usually he stayed three or four days in a town, though he might rest longer at the home of dear friends. Favorite towns came to expect a visit every couple of years with lectures on three or four related topics. Not only did he collect for admission to lectures, but he had books and pictures to sell. The scores of letters that he continued to send the *Liberator* and other reform papers became, in effect, publicity for his act, letting his audiences know what he was doing and giving them a sense of themselves. He learned the value of regular changes in what he had to say, preferably keeping a step or two ahead of public opinion, since his audiences identified themselves as "progressive." But keeping a step ahead meant keeping track of public opinion as well. Wright no longer met angry mobs or locked town halls; he made himself known through controversy over his heterodox opinions. He was always reticent about how much money he took in for his labors, and there is no evidence that his proceeds were ever much greater than his expenses and needs. But he made enough so that he no longer depended on his wife or any executive board for his living.[133]

Health was the issue that carried him into this new territory. One of his favorite lecture topics was "The Abolition of Death." From nonresistance he extracted the judgment that men should not be killed by others. He added the notion that death by disease was unnatural; it resulted from ignorant human transgressions against laws laid down by God.[134] Though presumably following natural laws during his lengthy lecture tours, he suffered periodically from fever and coughing and resorted to the water-cure establishments cropping up in Ohio, Michigan, and elsewhere. But the pursuit of personal health no longer detracted from his mission.

The abolition of death did not mean that bodies would endure forever. If a body passed away after a lifetime of proper use, the spirit moved on to a higher sphere. Wright did not count that natural process as death. Though never a medium himself, he bore the news transmitted by others. He told of asking one magnetized woman to send the spirit of Nathaniel P. Rogers from the other side of the veil; all who were assembled heard the music of a horn. Wright recalled that Rogers and he had listened to a hotel keeper in the White Mountains play a horn in the same way. Although he knew some mediums were fakers, in it for the money, Wright was never publicly involved, as were some of his friends, in trying to separate true from false spiritualisms. It was enough for him that spiritualism vaguely signaled the new dispensation of which his lectures bore early tidings. Sometimes he contrasted spiritual communications to the religion of the Bible. The spirits never imitated the God of the Old Testament in sanctioning disease, slaughter, and sexual crimes.[135]

His new trade required Wright to have a fresh book or pamphlet to sell each time he made the tour. Although all his writings touched on war, slavery, health, and spiritualism, his major books developed a distinctive approach to another subject: the family. He explored the origins of healthy bodies, the proper role of sex and marriage, the sorrows of unwanted pregnancy, the growth of the child in the uterus, and the influence of mothers on history. The titles of these books were the same topics that drew audiences to his lectures: *Anthropology; or, The Science of Man* (1850); *Marriage and Parentage; or, The Reproductive Element in Man, as a Means to His Elevation and Happiness* (1854); *The Unwelcome Child* (1858); and *The Empire of the Mother over the Character and Destiny of the Race* (1863). The books revealed his success in defining himself as an expert on domestic matters: they were packed with letters from worried wives and mothers who were grateful for his help and whose experience verified his teachings. He also gained some reputation as an advocate of "free love."[136] Although the charge was not strictly true, he was a critic of conventional marriages; besides, it was not harmful publicity.

Henry Wright had always been particularly concerned with children. He had been a sabbath school reformer, children's minister, and even children's abolitionist. "His great *forte*," Garrison had written Elizabeth Pease in 1842, "lies in addressing little children, over whom he exerts complete mastery. Place him in the midst of a crowded assembly of children, and he never fails to produce a deep impression upon their minds." That same year he claimed to have lived with "over one thousand families" and to have addressed "more than fifty thousand Children"; in ensuing years that pace hardly slackened.[137] He was, in short, well prepared to present himself as an expert in domestic problems. But as his proficiency shifted from training the young to sex and marriage, he made a shift—not always acknowledged openly—from religious to physiological perfectionism. He no longer professed that all children were born abolitionists. Instead of denouncing adults for persisting unnecessarily in sin, he promoted the idea that the lives of well-born babies would always go well. Evangelicals, it now appeared, had mistakenly urged an eerie second-birth for nearly grown-up beings. What was needed instead was a proper first birth that would make second thoughts unnecessary. The secret of progress, in this view, was happy, healthy mothers.

The reformer who turned physiological perfectionist gave at least implicit recognition that human nature had disappointed his fond hopes. Emerson had reformers like Wright in mind in writing about "Fate": "In our first steps to gain our wishes we come upon immovable limitations. We are fired with the hope to reform men. After many experiments we find that we must begin earlier,—at school. But the boys and girls are not docile; we can make nothing of them. We decide that they are not of good stock. We must begin our reform earlier still,—at generation: that is to say there is Fate, or laws of the world."[138] Wright, however, had no interest in Emerson's gloomy tone. Rather than reading signs of defeat, he celebrated notes of progress. Reformers, after taking on many evils one by one, had moved on to the larger work of advancing society and abolishing death. The laws of the world caused liberation, not resignation.

Although I have been stressing disjunctions in the character of Wright's work and in the messages he carried, it is important to observe that he conceived his life as one of unfolding unity. One theme of each of his books was his steadfastness. He was a living example of the logic of the nineteenth century. By speaking freely on what had once been decried as "extraneous issues," he had explored the margins of reform. But with each new doctrine he was still opposing slavery, rebuking false authority, defending divine law, advocating peace, searching for salvation, alone with God. When he raised a new slogan as the unifying plea of his life—"Institutions for men, not men for institutions"—this was a measure of how secular his appeal had become. Usually, however, he headed straight back to the "philosophy of slavery," as in this passage from *The Empire of the*

Mother: "'God gave to man dominion over the beasts of the field, the fowls of the air, and the fish of the sea,' but to whom did God give dominion over man? Not to kings and queens, nor to presidents and potentates; not to parliaments and congresses, nor to priests and politicians; not to church and state, nor to armies and navies; not to pulpit and press, nor to the school and the college—but to the mother."[139]

Wright's life as a commercial traveler challenges us to rethink the political biases of our history. The saga that historians tell most frequently about abolitionism concerns the growth of a dissenting minority to political power. It assumes that politics is the truest gauge of public opinion and that antipolitical movements are at best eccentric, at worst harmful. This is the saga, supposedly, of the Whittiers and Welds who retired Wright from his antislavery agency (although their lives never fit the saga very well under careful examination). The best it can say for radical Garrisonians is that their agitation ultimately translated into political influence. Without questioning the importance of politics, however, we may wonder whether the antipolitical attitudes and extraneous enthusiasms of the Garrisonians were hopelessly out of touch with antebellum public opinion. I am not referring to fashions in cynicism about lawyers and politicians, interesting as those fashions are. The problem, instead, is the audience Wright discovered for his talks, an audience found at water-cure establishments, progressive villages, spiritualists' conventions, and at various institutes and lecture series on marital and health reform. This is not to mention little communities of utopians and nonresistants.

Exact measurement is impossible. A goodly number of Wright's audience were excluded from the franchise. How many persons who did vote in those years did so with reservations of different kinds and energies? How many persons went to water-cure establishments solely for their health, and how many thought they were dipping into a new period of historical progress? Were there really eleven million spiritualists in the 1860s, as some tallies claimed? What did spiritualists believe about the political state? How did people really feel about motherhood, marriage, improved offspring, and "the good time coming" of their songs? The point is simply that Henry Wright discovered a sizable audience that is not, and scarcely could be, familiar to us from political history. He was not the only one tilling these fields; a host of other progressives and experts were making the same discovery. He helped define a cultural place for domestic advice and scientific approaches to progress in the nineteenth century.

But the political saga, though a selective telling of history, is not exactly a distortion. No longer the hired agent of antislavery or any other cause, Wright nonetheless remained a loyal abolitionist. He appeared regularly at conventions of the American Anti-Slavery Society. (When he missed one in 1853 and Frederick Douglass said he had been asked to stay away so as to shield the society from charges of infidelity, the Garrisonians were indignant.) He was also a regular under the big tent used by Ohio abolitionists for their meetings. In fact, it is doubtful that anyone else spoke to antislavery audiences as extensively as Wright.

Loyalty to nonresistance was more problematical. As he toured the Midwest in the 1850s, Wright reported excitedly on preparations for violence. He was cheered to believe that citizens were mobilizing spontaneously against slavery. Each man must combat slavery by whatever means he favored; those who were not pacifists must turn to violence. Though a nonresistant himself, Wright did not hesitate to shout, *Aux armes!* While the news of John Brown's aborted coup d'état at Harper's Ferry initially confused other abolitionists, Wright from the start saw it as a splendid act that would stir up Northern hatred of slavery. When Brown was put to death, Wright's praises became extravagant. Brown would be the central figure in a new man-centered religion; it was not Christ crucified but Brown hanged who would emancipate humanity. When war came Wright put aside "nonresistance" altogether and recommended instead the "self-abnegation" shown in the lives of Christ, Brown, and dying union soldiers. All the families he visited had boys missing on the battlefields. Wright spoke passionately in commemoration of one of his nephews who died in Tennessee; he was glad another had enlisted to fill his place.[140]

During the war Wright lectured frequently—at times exclusively—on antislavery themes. He was booked more solidly than ever before and pushed himself to new feats of travel. His knowledge of a broad lecturing territory equipped him to give notable service to the Republican cause. From the outset of hostilities he enthusiastically supported Lincoln against his antislavery detractors. When Stephen Foster told Massachusetts abolitionists, for example, that without an emancipation proclamation they could give the government only obloquy, Wright was angry. "Our business is to get the people to regard the government as an anti-slavery government," he replied, "not to heap opprobrium upon it." Already Northerners regarded the Constitution as antislavery, and the South joined battle on that understanding. The war, in his view, would inexorably take an antislavery turn. Years later Garrison's sons tried to account for the fact that the vaunted anarchist Henry Wright had "clearly perceived the irresistible tendency of events, the difficulties surrounding the President's Administration, and the duty of sustaining the government." They attributed his clear-sightedness to his itinerancy. Because he traveled more than any other abolitionist, especially in "the Great West," he had the best command of public opinion. Not only was he certain of antislavery sentiment pulling the president in one direction, but he was not tempted, as eastern editors might be, to underestimate the dangers posed in states like Indiana and Illinois by the Knights of the Golden Circle.[141]

All his hostility to the American government vanished with secession. For fifteen years he had been advocating Northern withdrawal from the Union; now he undertook to explain to Northern audiences the superiority of their civilization to that of the Southern renegades they were destined to defeat. He told workingmen that the slave power, in league with fiendish representatives of capital, had plotted to enslave them. He praised majority rule, and claimed that the secession had placed the South under European-style despotism. He portrayed the Union as "the Messiah of freedom and salvation to earth's toiling millions" and the Confederacy as "the Barabbas of Slavery and Piracy." In short, he turned his hand to the blend of religious and free-labor rhetoric in which Northern Republicans discovered the purposes of war. One of his set speeches was on "The Star-Spangled Banner as the Symbol of Liberty"; it linked the Union cause to "planetary redemption." He stood firm, however, when pressed to emphasize the Union or economic matters and to forget the Negro. War revived the Genius of Africa; and to his audiences he announced, "the crushed and crucified Negro has become the sole arbiter of the nation's destiny." He often ended his performances by "singing the John Brown song—the audience joining in the Hallelujah chorus."[142]

When news reached him of the passage of the Thirteenth Amendment, he hailed the vindication of Garrison's prophetic stance of long ago. He, too, had fought for many years: "Whether my name shall ever be mentioned in connection with this great victory, I care not." The triumph would last. Wright joined Garrison in calling an end to the work of the antislavery societies and resisting the suggestion that abolitionism entailed a continued obligation to look after the Negro. Some limitations of the old "philosophy of slavery" became evident: "We have labored for the redemption of the slave from his condition of chattelhood, where he has been left to feel after God and immortality among beasts and creeping things, and to place him on the platform of humanity; and I maintain for one, that so far as that is concerned, the labor of this Society [in this case, the Massachusetts Anti-Slavery Society] draws to a close."[143] But more was at work than ideology. He had exhausted himself during the war, and retailored his understanding of his own life to make it consistent with military necessities and political approaches to abolishing slavery. He was now sixty-eight years old, and wanted his labors to be over.

Although he did not stop traveling and lecturing after the war, he did not find things quite the same. He observed that some women he knew "*snarl & growl* at all Men"; he suspected that the "Inquiry Meeting" he held on "Domestic Relations" would not be forgotten in their town for a long time.[144] He stayed out of the limelight on such stormy public issues as suffrage for women and blacks. When he did speak, however, he favored a broad stand that would give the ballot to intelligent whites, blacks, and women and deny it to all the ignorant and immoral. The old nonresistant now spoke with feeling, though a little vaguely, about "a national movement to give the ballot its true place and value as a means of redemption to earth's toiling millions from oppression, and of progress to the world."[145] He also appeared at a few nostalgic, lightly attended meetings of old-time pacifists.[146] But his preferred lecture topics in the late 1860s included "The Institutions of Europe," "Obstacles to Progress," "Christ the Reformer," and "The Destiny of the Republic." He also spoke widely on marriage and the family. He played on old themes like "The Curse of the Drunkard's Appetite" and themes of widening popularity like "Spiritualism and Progress." He was barely a controversial figure any longer. Some parts of his old message were fast becoming ensconced in subcultures that posed little threat to politics or the churches; other parts had been absorbed into a widespread, if unsystematic, religion of health and spiritualism.

Henry Wright died while staying with friends in Pawtucket, Rhode Island, in 1870. Because of his wandering life there was some uncertainty over where to bury him. Then Mrs. Rockwood, a Boston healing medium whom Garrison consulted for his own ills, told him of Wright's spiritual presence. His spirit described in detail the plot he wished in Swan Point cemetery. When no such plot seemed to exist, Garrison chanced across another medium who confirmed its existence. Then the site, which the Swan Point staff had forgotten, was located. The exciting story of the choice of Wright's resting place was often retold by John Bright, who had known him in England. It was the first instance, in Garrison's words, "of a departed spirit signifying the precise spot where he desired his earthly tenement to be deposited."[147] On top of this tenement was placed an impressive eight-foot monument given by a friend of his later years named Photius Fisk, a retired naval chaplain who used his pension to erect a series of monuments in memory of neglected antislavery heroes. The speakers at his funeral were great names of Massachusetts abolitionism: Garrison, Wendell Phillips, and Senator Henry Wilson. The monument is still erect, praising this "steadfast advocate of anti-slavery, peace, temperance, and human brotherhood" as a brave adventurer against powerfully entrenched opinion.[148]

Like many abolitionists, Wright was forgotten by postbellum chroniclers of the Civil War. It was particularly the divisive, heterodox side of Garrisonism that was submerged from view, so that only in recent years have historians noticed Wright's importance.[149] His reputation has gained from the rise of women's historians who give some of his "extraneous issues" a more sympathetic hearing than antislavery scholars often did. He was a key influence on Garrison, to be sure; but he was also a widely known traveling agitator in his own right. In an age when all orators took to the road, probably no one surpassed him in miles logged and audiences addressed. When we consider his numerous books, tracts, and letters to periodicals, it is doubtful that many reformers published more (and he kept a massive diary besides). The career he carved out for himself on both sides of the Atlantic was regarded as a singular life of reform; there were times when his friends predicted for him a prominent niche in history.

I do not claim that Henry Wright was representative of his age in the sense of striking an average of the views of others. He had the knack of moving from one concern to the next a bit more rapidly than most contemporary reformers and of stating new convictions more forthrightly than would make them comfortable. Yet that makes him significant: it is easier to observe some processes of change in his thought than in the thinking of most contemporaries. He struggled openly with certain fundamental issues of nineteenth-century culture; the secularization of religious values; the competing claims of

God and society over the individual will; the place of women in a transformed political economy; and the hope that new sources of orderly improvement might be found in spiritualism, introspective science, and physiological perfectionism. "My life has been a conflict," was his summation. He had lived through the triumph of fact over fiction, of realism over ideals that failed to serve humanity; and he expected "a crown of hearty approval" for his earnestness on the field of combat.[150] There is a wonderful chasm to be observed between his youthful religious orthodoxy and the romantic excitement he conveyed as a lecturer. Unlike many contemporaries, he transcribed the painful steps by which he crossed that distance.

Two

The Living Present and the Dead Past

How pure at heart and sound in head,
  With what divine affections bold
  Should be the man whose thought would hold
An hour's communion with the dead.

In vain shalt thou, or any, call
  The spirits from their golden day,
  Except, like them, thou too canst say,
My spirit is at peace with all.

Tennyson,
In Memoriam (1850)

Family and Aggression

Henry Clarke Wright's two most striking preoccupations were the family and aggression. Through all the shifts and crises in his career he was always an expert on children. He was also a belligerent nonresistant—a combative, divisive figure urging mankind to be calm and harmonious. Whatever reform happened to engage him, his theme was always discipline over violent impulses; and he was constantly traveling away from his own family in order to address mothers, fathers, and children on the importance of the family to the peace and improvement of humanity. The root of social evil, he taught, was man's attempt to transgress upon his brother. In the self-denying, protective relationships of the ideal family he discovered the secret of world order.

There was a long tradition in political theory that stressed analogies between good arrangements in the state and in the family. But Wright's preoccupations with the family and aggression had a more immediate source in his passionate self-analysis: he searched out the origins of violent feelings in his own boyhood, then extended his findings to all mankind. He composed an autobiography audaciously entitled *Human Life,* a compilation of memories that took its cue from Emerson's dictum, "There is properly no history; only biography."[1] He belonged unmistakably to the generation Emerson described as "born with knives in their brains, a tendency to introversion, self-dissection, anatomizing of motives."[2] Yet he surpassed many of his contemporaries in recognizing how fixed his responses to experience had become in early childhood. *Human Life* is an unjustly obscure book, comparable to the best introspective autobiographies of the century, and a great assistance in understanding men's motives in an important period of transition in American life.

Human Life was nearly contemporaneous with Max Stirner's *The Ego and His Own* (1844), which began with a discussion "Of Human Life." It is extremely unlikely that Wright even heard of Stirner, who was not translated into English until 1907, and then was familiar only to a small circle of individualists and iconoclasts.[3] But their works shared a common view of Western history and individual psychology. Both opposed the reappearance of authoritarianism in the postmonarchical era, an opposition that won both some reputation as precursors of anarchism. Wright's *Human Life,* moreover, can be read as a Stirnerian quest for emancipation, commencing with birth, in which the individual, whipped and propagandized, struggles to create a hold over his own identity quite apart from the definitions of reality that others seek to impose. Wright's antislavery pronouncements often intimated goals of unfettered autonomy that bring to mind not only his German contemporary but also some radical psychologies of the twentieth century. And yet his life illustrates just how illusory the promise of "self-ownership" usually is, how powerful—even in the life of an emancipator in a fluid society—are the commands imposed by those who conceived, protected, and punished him. *Human Life* illustrates the allure of Stirnerian, liberating goals at the cultural moment when it appeared; it may also be read as a step in the direction of Freud's codification of the mechanisms of repression.

Because of his discoveries in self-analysis, Wright stands as a distant predecessor of Freud. As a belligerent nonresistant, however, he also resembled one of those "walking contradictions" whom Freud liked to analyze.[4] He was known, on the one hand, as a joyous man who liked to sing, play the fife and flute, and romp with children; his life was crisis ridden, on the other hand, and he passed through sloughs of personal depression and caused bitterness around him. Sometimes he struck acquaintances as "itching to be *known*," and he himself expressed desires to shout to thronged conventions from mountain tops. At other times, however, he was confused by the emergence of "ambition" from the back of his mind and tried to deny the slightest impulse toward self-assertiveness. "The *excellence* of music in a Choir," he observed, "is to have every voice so combined that no individual voice shall be distinguished."[5]

Sometimes Wright even sounds like one of Freud's patients, preoccupied with some bit of information about himself but unable to decode its meaning. With some self-recrimination he wrote to himself: "I have been on terms of greatest intimacy with thee during all my life; yet my knowledge of thee is slight. The time I should have spent in cultivating an acquaintance with thy physical organism, and the capabilities of thy nature, I have spent in trying to learn the ways and doings of others. . . . I have sought to solve the mysteries of thy surroundings, rather than the deep secrets of thy nature."[6] When he asserted that "H.C.W." perused the record of his life and sat in judgment, it was not clear that he met his own approval. "Oh Henry! I fear thee and no one else. . . . I am in thy power."[7]

The limits to his self-analysis can easily be seen by looking at his interpretation of his dream of accepting a challenge from a famous boxer. "Is it true," he asked, "that our sleeping thoughts take on the hue of those which occupied the mind when we fell asleep? Then why did I not dream of peace—instead of inflamed and angry looks and angry blows? Yet in thinking of peace we naturally think of its opposite[,] war."[8] The association of peace with war *is* natural, of course, but modern analysts would not conclude their analysis by simply noting the association. We surmise all too quickly that the enthusiasm for peace concealed unresolved feelings about fighting and anger. We suspect that nonresistance was, among other things, Wright's way of living with powerfully belligerent feelings. Since control over violent impulses is an essential part of civilization, however, we realize that we are not judging the validity of Wright's pacifism when we probe its sources.

He recorded another dream from his early thirties, one that haunted him for days. It displayed no terror or anger, but perfect calm. In this dream he saw himself lying in his coffin, dressed in a black silk robe, with his family seated around him. He felt perfectly serene, and hoped his real death would be equally composed.[9] This is not a surprising vision for a man who later sought communication with spirits and advocated the abolition of death. In imagining himself dead, and the center of attraction, he was translating into his own experience the deaths of his mother and his closest fraternal rival. The serenity of his own imaginary death stood in contrast to the torturing guilt that hovered in his memory. In this dream we catch glimmerings of the psychological sources of his lifelong quest for a world in which children would obey the laws of the divine Father and venerate the life-giving powers of mothers and in which brothers would cease to act like Cain. If we ask for confirming evidence from Wright's family history, we find passionate records of anxiety concerning losses he had suffered and felt he might have caused.

Although historians should be careful in bestowing pathological terminology on their subjects, Wright often brings to mind Freud's view that neurotics "cannot get free of the past."[10] Not that he didn't try. One of his most self-revealing books was called *The Living Present and the Dead Past.* One of his watchwords was that mankind should not kneel before institutions hallowed by the past. One of his obsessions in Europe was to tally the costs in human lives of the irresistible tourist attractions, battlefields, ruins, palaces, cathedrals, and other historical sites. He later argued that the new martyr John Brown was worth much more than the "dead failure" Christ of tradition.[11] He was at war with history.

To consider Wright's professional life in the light of themes persisting from his childhood is simply to continue the decision Wright made in *Human Life*—to stress the historical importance of the little dramas that take place within families. This approach leads to the view that the career of a reformer, with the style of conflict it legitimized, defended Wright against disturbing threats from the past that were regularly revived by persons and issues he confronted in the present. Since the historian's purpose is not therapy, there is no need, as there is no way, to measure the healthiness of the protection this career afforded. We can take notice of both the endlessly reduplicated symptoms and the ability to function in society.[12] We can even begin to appreciate Wright as a carrier of modern attitudes toward such subjects as sexuality and death. After all, it is his unsparing discussion of himself that allows us to document links and associations that in the lives of other men would require conjecture and unsubstantiated analogy.

Thanksgiving to Thee, My Loving Mother

Henry Wright's earliest memory was of his family's migration in 1801, when he was four years old, from Sharon in the Housatonic Valley of Connecticut to Hartwick in "the Western country," near Cooperstown, in New York. He faintly recalled parting from old home and friends; he clearly remembered the ice of the Hudson cracking under the horses and the near-drowning of his mother and the "younger children." It was a move from civilization to "comparative wilderness," as he recalled it. Dark woods, with Indians inside them, surrounded his new home.[13]

Besides mobility, early recollections dealt with broken attachments and unrepaired loss. Shortly after the move west, his brother Miles was born, his parents' eleventh child, the tenth still living, and Henry's replacement as the youngest. Shortly before Henry turned six, his mother, Miriam, died. His father, Seth, remarried "after some months . . . and brought another woman [Polly] into the house, whom I was told to call mother; but it was long before I could do so." Seth and Polly had three daughters before her death when Henry was seventeen. He received this loss with echoes of his old sorrow. After he went away on apprenticeship he welcomed an opportunity to return home unexpectedly. He found that his father had married again and he had "a second step-mother." But he seldom, if ever, referred to her again. It was the death of his own mother that counted.[14]

Many of Wright's contemporaries lost parents during childhood. In trying to understand the particular impact of his loss of Miriam, we should note how closely it followed the family move and Miles's birth. Then we may listen to the words in which, years later, he described his mother's death. What was most memorable was its suddenness:

> It was evening. My father had just come home from his labor abroad. We were all seated around the supper table. The scene is fresh in my mind. One of my sisters anxiously cried out, "Mother, what is the matter?" She answered, sweetly and calmly, "Don't be alarmed about me; all is well." This called the attention

> of my father and all to her. She was carried to her bed, and never spoke again. In a few hours she was dead. She died of apoplexy. I stood by her bedside, frightened to see her so pale, silent, and motionless. My heart was heavy, for I was told that she would never look at me nor speak to me again. The neighbors came in for miles around. They took away my mother, to bury her in the ground, as I was told. All the family went away with her, except myself and a younger brother, who were left in charge of a kind neighbor. I looked out of the window, and saw them carry her away. . . . My mother was buried at the foot of a high hill, or cliff, amidst some beech and pine trees, in a solitary spot, which in after life, was often visited by me.[15]

Seldom did Henry Wright use the simple sentence so consistently. But these memories had been endlessly rehearsed, and they fell heavily into place. On one occasion when he wept at her grave, he told his diary that he had not understood she was gone forever until the coffin was carried away and he was informed (perhaps by the kind neighbor) that he would never see her again. He praised her fairness and kindness, and promised never to forget her last kiss.[16] How much of this is fantasy it is impossible to say. Clearly, the loss came terribly suddenly, without preparation or much explanation. What few memories he had or manufactured were treasures to be polished by frequent, fond handling.

"I brooded over my feelings in silence," Henry recalled; his desolation was akin to the withdrawal and despair that very young children pass through when mothers disappear. But he was neither so young nor so unfortunate. Help was available: "into the bosom of an older sister, who became to me as a mother," the boy could "pour my aching heart." This sister "talked to me of my mother, and called out my sympathies."[17] In the long run Polly seems to have been an effective mother substitute, too: she taught him further lessons in how one woman could stand for another in his affections. In talking things out, furthermore, Wright went beyond the mourner's typical daydream conversations with the dead; he learned that dramatic expression of his feelings supplied a form of mastery over them. Rather than withdrawing from unpleasant experiences, Wright tended to deal with them, as he did with his mother's death, by drawing up a little scene, in an enclosed space, with himself as a central figure, but with a full cast of other characters around. "A Domestic Scene" were the words that sometimes headed his essays. He denied his own aggression, in short, by the expressiveness, the dramatic flair, the populousness, and the domesticity of his imaginary world.

It is possible to add some guesses about the meaning of the dream in which he lay still in his coffin. Clearly, it was another version of the domestic scene, another reenactment of his innocence. In addition, the dream indicated his lifelong search for renewed communication with his mother. May we guess that the serenity of his death scene is partly due to its recapitulation of hers, with the implied promise that they may now talk without even the intermediary older sister? Enclosure in the box was also a serene return to the uterus. Or is the affair more ambiguous? Wright's later writings often discussed unwanted pregnancies, and sometimes he assumed that a young child in a large family must be an unwelcome child. Possibly the dream builds on the feeling that his death in the womb would have been welcome. It may merge an incestuous wish for communication with his mother and a yearning that his birth had been more hospitable. It may also refer to his brothers and sisters, as we shall see.

Besides his recurrent coffin dream, how else did Wright endeavor to restore dialogue with Miriam?[18] In an age of famous diary keepers, no one kept diaries more relentlessly than he. More than one hundred are extant, and there must have been at least one hundred more, written in repose and on the fly, some utterly private, some used as notes for public writings, others sent as intimate records to female friends. He did not think of his diary as separated from his life. He liked to quote from it in his published writings. Often he wrote while he was among other persons, at a reform convention, for example, at dinner table at the Graefenberg water cure establishment, or while listening to children's answers to his catechisms. At Graefenberg he was urged not to write so much: it made him too serious and retarded the cure. But this was impossible advice. He wrote in the *sitzbad* as he soaked in a tub of freezing water. On a nearby mountain, "when alone, I have frequently thrown myself down in the snow . . ., my body from head to foot wrapped about with the fleecy covering, and now and then a portion of it falling into my open neck; and whilst thus reclining, I have often taken out my journal, and, pencil in hand, endeavoured to describe the sensations produced by the surrounding scene of enchantment."[19]

To whom were these journals addressed? Some were missives to loved ones, with instructions not to throw them away; some were stiched together and returned. Almost all were for Wright the author to use as jogs to his memory and insertions in his books. They were shared, except for the most intimate ones, with friends. "Just take a peep into his diary," Garrison advised Elizabeth Pease, "or get him to read from its pages, and you will find many things of a curious and an instructive nature."[20] Often they were addressed to the general reform public, however they might happen to find their way into print. Distinctions between private and public, between diaries and published writings, meant little. Just as Theodore Weld protested against Wright's parading his "domestic scenes" in the press, we may be surprised at the paucity of private correspondence. Wright's expressive style meant that he was unceasingly on stage.

The diaries also laid out his experience for the perusal of an intelligence outside of time. Sometimes he noted in the margins his changed sentiments so that he would no longer be held accountable for old ones. In one of the notebooks he kept as a student at Andover we find this notation: "The preceding remarks I regard as the offspring of a mind—in a state little better than that of an entire infidel. Henry C. Wright July 14, 1834." In another notebook he wrote: "I hereby discard and recall all this which is inconsistent with the idea that Christ by his death, made it consistent for God to forgive us. Calvin and Edwards and the Orthodox hold the only just view of the Attonement [*sic*]."[21] We have previously seen his marginal criticisms of his tardiness in coming over to Garrisonian abolitionism. The journals express the reformer's conviction that there will be an accounting of one's beliefs and actions. They are a kind of metaphor in paper and ink of the life itself. "May I be a living Epistle of thee," he prayed on one New Year's Day; while seeking blessings and forgiveness for family and friends as well as himself, he reiterated the self-image of being "alone with God in the Universe."[22]

In the 1820s and the 1830s, so long as he was religiously orthodox, his external audience appeared to be male—God the father. Thereafter it was clearly his mother who read over his accounts. At least once he traced the origin of his diary keeping to childhood fantasy. *The Living Present and the Dead Past* consists of letters addressed to his "wiser, better, and nobler self," by whom he had been attended since boyhood. He described this self in terms familiar to any student of the role of the antebellum mother. The other self's—and the mother's—"mission has been to control and keep in subjection the animal man. With this second, wiser and better self have I been in the habit, for forty years, of constant intercourse, by *spoken* and *written* words often, and more frequently by silent thought and soul communion." If anyone could be more intimate with him than this split-off self, he asked, "where is that one to be found? Among the Living Present, or the Dead Past? By my side in living form, or among the dead, in the sepulchres of the past?" These rhetorical questions supposedly favored the present, but they ineffectively denied interest in the tombs of the dead.[23]

Echoes from the grave often threatened him with disorientation and confusion. A good example is a public letter to Garrison commenting on his reactions to loving letters received in Britain from his wife and other "precious inmates" of his home: "I saw them, heard them, *felt* them all, and for about half a day I felt much as a little child, who on waking up in the morning, and finding himself in a strange place, called out, 'Ma, I can't find me,' Really, I could not find myself; I did not know myself for a few hours. My soul had left the body, and I moved about a *soulless* body."[24] It is not surprising, perhaps, that his disorientation reminded him of the plight of a lost child, especially given the familarity of themes of family separation in contemporary literature. But the cry—"Ma, I can't find me"—also suggests private dimensions of his unending search for a legitimate vocation. He had an infirm grasp of who he was, who others were. He told an English woman with whom he was deeply in love that his soul was knit to Garrison's "as to a brother . . . [obliterated intimacies]. . . .If ever human beings were united in one I think thou and Garry thus united."[25]

In one of the most bizarre passages in *The Living Present and the Dead Past,* he parodied lover's assignations by taking the state room on a steamer, going to bed with his nobler self, and enjoying "the most intimate and ennobling of all relations," a phrase with a clear sexual meaning in his other writings. "I feel that my destiny is entirely in thy hands," he told himself. "As the steamer glides over the waters, in silence and darkness, lying in my berth with thee, I am passing the night in most intimate communion with thee, and with that loving, anxious one that hovers around thee or nestles in thy heart to shelter thee from harm. Full of hallowed beauty and glory is the night, and never to be forgotten; because of the vitalizing and ennobling intimacy I enjoy in the loving, gentle, and just one, who is ever present in thy [his other self's]bosom *to welcome me to my home in Heaven.*"[26] There can be little doubt that this complex fantasy evoked the presence of his "Ma," once again with overtones of confused identity and guilt. Whether he transferred feelings from one intimate to another or split himself into different personae, his mother was never far from mind. The diaries mediated between a profusion of selves and the sepulchral Miriam, barely known to him and idealized through early daydreams and conversations with the sister who talked him out of his sorrows.

Wright may have tried to recapture distant experiences in the womb. The manuscript survives in his handwriting of "Ante-natal History—or History and Education before My Birth." Of course it records "no conscious recollection of my experiences, my sufferings or my joy," in that state; but it expresses confidence that "from the hour of my birth to the present, my character, my health, the tone of my spirit and my happiness have been deeply affected by those influences." Probably this manuscript copies the "memories" of a psychic with whom Wright shared intimate experiments.[27] In any case, it shows the direction of his curiosities.

Whatever Wright did to learn more about himself—in his view the only learning required to understand human nature—was a way of approaching his mother. Sometimes he explicitly inferred knowledge of his mother from the facts of his life (falsifying those facts as he did so). He praised his mother for the health and happiness introduced into his constitution by "the pulsations of thy gentle, loving heart, and . . . materials derived from thy blood." He pretended that "during his sixty-five years of experience in life, he has not been called to one week of suffering that deserves the name," and the slight discomforts of his life had been "easily and speedily rectified by the energetic, living, ever-present and ever-watchful Recuperator or Redeemer thou didst organize into him. Thanksgiving to thee, my loving mother! and the voice of melody will ever fill my heart for the life of almost uninterrupted health and happiness thou didst organize into me."[28] On the contrary, he was often ill, nearly died in Britain, exposed himself to harrowing cures, and endured recurrent fever and coughing thereafter. Shortly before this apostrophe to his mother, he described a case of consumption that resembled his own history; this he blamed on the exhaustion of the sufferer's mother during pregnancy.[29] Whose was the guilt for his own illnesses? By his theory his mother should also have borne responsibility for his agonies of religious doubt and excruciating loneliness—his was not a contented life. By idealizing mothers in general, however, he denied feeling unwanted by the mother who left him too early, absolved himself of guilt, and approximated conversation with her.

His curiosities drew him to living mothers. First he married a mother of four children, a widow forty-three years old when he was twenty-six. Second, his early reform work took him to Sunday schools, sewing circles, and maternal associations, and gave him the unusual privilege of frank conversation with women about child rearing. Years later, he boasted that he had inquired into every "physical and psychical" dimension of pregnancy, including the "rights of children to a love origin." Some mothers kept for his perusal intimate diaries of their experiences and feelings during pregnancy.[30] Actually the journals do not entirely confirm these voyeuristic boasts, but the purposes of his interrogations of mothers in his own system of curiosity is still plain.

One of the advantages of the agent's itinerant life was the entry into numerous homes that it afforded—over one thousand by his count in 1842 and presumably thousands more in the following twenty-eight years. Besides board, room, and balm for his loneliness, he gained further opportunities to watch mothers and talk with them. He was virtually adopted into many of the families he visited. Thankful Southwick's daughter recalled that Wright came to their house in 1835 to apologize to George Thompson for his previous antagonism; "from that day our house was one of Mr. Wright's Boston homes, where he would come for weeks at a time."[31] More than any other reformer, he had the liberty of Garrison's house. At Mrs. Garrison's funeral, Wendell Phillips testified that Wright had verged on tears when speaking of how the desolation of his life was remitted in her home; Wright himself stated, with some exaggeration, that it was "the centre of my life so far as a *Home* is concerned."[32] Hannah Webb was a surrogate mother in Dublin. Because of her displays of love and forgiveness, he called her a "perfect and living interpretation of my own conception of God and heaven." Her death threatened to ignite painful old memories. Twice he wrote: *"I cannot make her dead."* In his view she still lived and reigned "as one of the earth's truest saviors, and most loved and honored queens."[33]

Wright was not consistent on the question of saviors. Sometimes the only savior was mother, sometimes a wife, sometimes children, sometimes an inner voice, and sometimes any life devoted to the cause of humanity. But idealization of the mother was predominantly his approach to human salvation. In many of his writings he discounted the importance of any influence on children once they left the womb. If they were born of loving parents, they would be well created, healthy in body and soul. He may have felt that he was alone with God, but he yearned for the empire of the mother. His search for renewed dialogue, in other words, explains more than his personal quirks and his itinerant style of life. It helps to explain the views of health and spiritualism that he codified as "the Abolition of Death."

Father's Whip

Occasionally Wright's God sounded as though he owned the womb and breasts of the mother. One wonders what the wealthy New York reformer Gerrit Smith and his wife thought when Wright introduced himself to them as a person whose "rule of practice [was] that I may unbosom myself to any one who loves the Lord Jesus—who sits at his feet as a little child—to drink in wisdom from him." His sole desire for the Smiths was that they too should be "entirely swallowed up—*drowned*—in the ocean of his [God's] everlasting love." These comments may betray some confusion in Wright's own sexual identity. If so, it was a confusion he used creatively in trying to understand his age's softening of patriarchal religious images. In one of his books he urged his readers to regard human beings with "the same loving, tender, and holy reverence that we feel for the good and gracious Father and Mother, God."[34] As religious concerns made room for secular ones, adjustments in the sexual images of God might be dared.

Generally, however, Wright thought of God not as woman or hermaphrodite, but as a man. Thus he wrote the Smiths that "our true course" was not to trust in human sympathy, but "to learn to stand alone with God on earth as we must in Eternity—to lay our hand in his and let him lead us as a Father a little child." He was preparing them for his flinty, atomistic version of nonresistance. But he was also giving a rather accurate rendition of his own life history: mother was dead, and he was alone with father in the wide universe. It was too wild a dream to expect communication with mother without appeasing father. In describing the Christian reformer, he expressed hope that loyalty to paternal authority would unblock the gates of heaven. It was Christian reform, moreover, that licensed aggression.[35] Our interpretation of Wright's career must come to terms with the father with whom he lived as well as the mother for whom he longed.

Henry recorded very little concerning his father, Seth Wright, either in his books or private journals. He was evidently a good farmer and a skilled carpenter. Henry remembered him as a just man: he refused to charge high prices for his corn during hard times; all he wanted was a just remuneration.[36] But if this detail suggests a consciousness of the market that was far from modern, his work as a house joiner gives a contrary impression. He took part in a great moment of innovation. Primitive board cabins in which children could see sky through the chimney openings were fast replaced, throughout the Cooper country, by framed houses suitable to the ambitions of men who had moved their families from New England. Nor did these houses follow traditional patterns; instead, carpenters at the end of the eighteenth century found complicated ways of blocking entrances and creating intricate walkways. There was so much demand for this work—and Seth was in this sense responsive to a market—that he was often distant from home. He was away so often on business that the role of head of household was commonly played by brother Erastus, nineteen years Henry's senior. "Thou wert as a Father to me," Henry wrote when he learned of Erastus's death in 1834.[37]

Seth Wright also seems to have been distant in another sense. There was a frightening aloofness in his punishment. Though asserting that his father was naturally lighthearted, Henry stressed that his father was "stern, prompt and determined. In the government of his children, he allowed but little familiarity on their part towards him, never allowing us to speak to him or of him, as thou, or you, he or him; but only by the appellation of father, or by a word of equivalent meaning. When in his presence, a look, or a tap of his foot on the floor, was enough to guide us and keep us quiet."[38] Perhaps we might borrow Freud's description of another nineteenth-century father who ruled by eye movements: "Such a father as this was by no means unsuitable for transfiguration into a God in the affectionate memory of the son."[39] We may begin to understand how Henry conceived of himself as alone with God and conversing with phantom selves.

His father was linked in memory to several customs and institutions that Wright the reformer repudiated. He kept whiskey around the house and thought it healthy to drink with work. He was a veteran of the Revolution. Henry's first remembered impressions—and therefore very important ones—caught Seth in regimental array; and he ascribed to his stern, disciplined father the temperament of a "warrior."[40]

Seth was evidently a dutiful Presbyterian. All of Henry's recollections of his religious upbringing were paternal and negative. Father required the memorization of Bible verses without discussing their meanings. Father sat in the center of his children, eyed them coolly, and made them repeat the Westminster catechism "as a parrot repeats words." Praying, which he called "doing duty," was a regular, dreadful family exercise. He called Bible reading conversation with

God, but took no care that such conversation should be animated or intelligent. Seth adjusted his spectacles and read, not caring whether it was the Sermon on the Mount or slaughters from the Old Testament. Then he prayed, always the same prayer in the same deliberate manner; and "we at once became as usual." Henry sometimes admitted that in his youth he was not critical of these observances. When he was not distracted, "I regarded my father with a feeling of awe. . . . There he stood, his back towards us, his face to the wall, leaving his hands on the top of a chair, talking in a solemn, deliberate and earnest tone of voice to a 'Being' whom I could not see."[41]

It was Seth's attitude toward the sabbath that Henry later repudiated most bitterly. Others referred to these customs as the Puritan Sabbath. It was an unhappy day with what Henry recalled as a great deal of unpleasant role playing. "The whole family assumed a Sunday face, a Sunday dress, a Sunday tone, a Sunday step. . . . It was to me a day of gloom; many a time have I been rebuked on that day for looking out of the window, or for a merry word or laugh." When the sun set at last, "we lived and breathed again, nature resumed her cheerful looks, and joyous sounds again burst from all creation." Apparently Seth had a reputation for singular strictness regarding the sabbath, for Henry recalled an incident when a Quaker who owed Seth money tormented him by choosing Sunday to stop by with the payment. Henry was critical of the Quaker's intolerance. He was even more critical of his father's religion for stressing observances and ceremonies rather than educating him to see the distinction between sinful and rightful conduct. In 1845 he still felt that his father's idea of the sabbath was impressed on his mind "so firmly . . . that to this day it is not completely eradicated."[42]

Seth Wright was, then, an absent father without much chance or ability to help his young son understand his guilt and hostility. Probably, Miriam's death both confused and intensified Henry's rivalry with his father. The laying aside of that rivalry and the development of a conscience (or superego) in the years after Miriam's death were a puzzling and painful process. Henry held his father in awe, even though he did not lastingly incorporate all his values (he preferred to think he imbibed his values from mother's blood). He made a God of Seth in his most characteristic, frightening role: the God was that figure whose punishment was terrible when a child plagued his siblings. The guilt arising from his mother's death and the awful fear of his father merged in the preoccupation that he made the center of his religion and his career: that children should not fight or even feel the desire to fight with one another. This was the least they could do for the dead mother over whose attentions, in a large family, there had been great competition. The father-God demanded it.

A recent study of another period of American history speculates that large families with closely spaced children lessened the severity of the "generation gap" as we think of it today.[43] In Wright's case this was not true. The chasm between father and son was enormous: Seth was remote, frightening, just, and good. There was no flagrant conflict because Henry converted his father into a distant object of obedience instead of competing with him; but we can feel the intense emotion with which the chasm (the wide universe in which he traveled alone) was filled. In his pre-Freudian family there were few ways of dealing with competitive triangles except as religious parables. His throat was endlessly vulnerable to Abraham's knife. His brothers were endlessly on the verge of discovering that he was Cain. It took him many years to learn to repudiate the entire Old Testament and everything in the Bible inconsistent with Jesus' injunction to turn the other cheek when struck by one's brother. During those years he worked out obsessive ceremonies to show his hands were unbloodied.

In his own selective memory, his touch had been destructive. He does not mention his mother in this regard, but he reports that because of his bad temper he had taken out the eye of a bossy pig and hurt the cow that supplied his favorite milk. He also recalled feeding a family of sparrows and becoming "familiar" with them. When he picked up one of the babies, however, the mother caused a commotion; impulsively, he threw a stone and killed her. After a similar experience John Woolman—a prophetic figure in the history of nonviolence and antislavery in America—had reflected that the tender mercies of the wicked are cruel and killed the orphaned birds. Wright feared the judgment of his heavenly father who heard every sparrow's fall. He convinced himself that the cock-sparrow would assume the maternal role, but the next morning all the young were dead. He wept and gave them a funeral, remembering the spot long afterwards. "This was the first feeling of deep remorse I remember to have experienced," he wrote, seemingly oblivious of how many issues of his boyhood this parable summed up.[44]

Henry Wright was very fond of his brothers, sisters, and half-sisters, as he tells us repeatedly in *Human Life*. He kept in close touch with them throughout his life; in fact, one advantage of itinerancy was that he could visit regularly the dozens of siblings, cousins, nephews, and nieces scattered across New York, Pennsylvania, Ohio, and Indiana. Towns where the Hartwick Wrights moved were not long without a traveling agitator on nonresistance, spiritualism, or the rights of unborn babies. In 1857, while bragging to the *Liberator* how many of his siblings were radical abolitionists, he paused to wonder why children couldn't be brought up as naturally as swallows in a barn, without beatings or correction.[45] His autobiography shows how confused he was by feelings of hostility and acts of aggression that he could not reconcile with his professions of love. He had no concept of ambivalence. Even after learning that such conflicts were universal, he could not think of them as "normal" or natural.

The next oldest child after Henry, a boy named Milton, died not long after their mother's death. His death also came swiftly. Henry recalled watching him die, seeing him in the coffin, being told that God had killed him, watching his burial beside Miriam, hearing his father calmly thank neighbors for their aid, and preserving Milton's toys as precious mementos. It must have been hard to sort out the various meanings of these experiences: guilt over rivalry, jealousy that someone else was with mother, reawakened grief at her death, fear of his own peril, dependence on father and resentment of his distance, attempts to see himself as an uncompetitive playfellow. We may well believe his report that "perplexities were in me." Not only was Wright astonishingly modern in the details he chose to record, but also in the lessons he drew concerning his perplexities. "I could not avoid them; and if I had had someone to speak to me affectionately and cheerfully, to bring them out and explain them, it would have given me relief, and spared me many sad hours, then and afterward."[46]

With his other closest rival—his younger brother Miles—Henry remembered a happy, affectionate relationship. He was Miles's protector and educator. His longest and most specific recollection concerning Miles, however, was an episode in which he nearly killed him—by mistake. He led Miles in some play that got both boys caught under a crushing load of hay. As in so many memories, "father was from home." Henry squirmed free and realized the entire weight then rested on Miles. He ran and cried for help. When Miles was extricated he did not breathe at first, but was successfully revived. The memory sparked many denials: "I thought not of myself; my concern was for my brother, whom I had led into danger. . . . I could not shed a tear while he lay under the cart, nor when I saw him lying in my mother's arms as dead; but when I saw him open his eyes . . . I cried for joy, for I felt that the weight of his death was taken off from me."[47] There is reason to doubt the accuracy of this memory, since his mother died when he was five, but not its importance. It belongs in the same category as the details he selected to show his fondness for his younger half-sisters: during their illnesses he experienced "indescribable anxiety," so severe that he could not eat or sleep.[48]

Memories of school blended the same themes of tenderness and competitiveness. He liked games of competition for "mastery over my playmates"—wrestling, racing, ball playing—and had a joyous sense of being able to accomplish whatever he wished. In later years, however, he reflected that sports had excited selfish, warlike feelings in him. He retained a guilty memory from his competitions, ending in symbolic self-mutilation. He won a contest (ironically, by memorizing a sentimental poem about the grief of mother and father birds when their young are harmed), and his prize was a penknife that was desired by a girl friend whom he loved and who loved him. Despite her sorrow, the teacher forbade him to give her the knife as he wished. Before long he cut one of his fingers "about half off," and got rid of the knife.[49]

School not only set him in competition for mastery over other children, but also confronted him with adults who aroused complicated, angry feelings toward authority. One was Elder Woolcutt, a terrifying drunkard as Wright recalled him (and he did so recurrently) with a long whip. Forcing the children to pray, "he would go on telling God what depraved little creatures we were; how we were more inclined to be unkind than kind, to be cruel than gentle, to hate than to love, and to injure than to do good to one another." Another was so abusive in punishing Henry that the boy cherished fantasies of revenge when he became a man, though at the time he "entered no complaints to my father." When he returned to Hartwick as an adult, he searched out this teacher (or so he claimed), and asked whether "he was ready to be operated upon by the spirit which his conduct towards me in the school had excited in me." He had fonder recollections of a woman who controlled the children with a "calm, collected, affectionate, but firm and undeviating" tone of voice.[50] We might recall at this point the distinction Wright later stressed in his "Domestic Scene" between two systems of instruction, one of which yielded sullen desires for revenge, the other, internalized moral values.

The most arresting passage in *Human Life* suggests, however, that the whip played its part in the development of Henry Wright's conscience. It recapitulated his childhood struggles over issues of competitiveness with his brothers and submission to his father; it ended in some feeling of control over the hurtfulness he saw in himself. "It was a rule in my father's discipline," he recalled, "that, if his children pushed one another into the snow in winter in going to or returning from school, he would whip us." Yet Henry was tempted irresistibly to do whatever was prohibited, and he constantly teased Miles. After one ducking he tried to brush Miles off, but Miles ran home with snow on his clothes. Though protesting he had ducked Miles "in fun and frolic, without a thought or feeling of unkindness," he got his whipping. The next evening he reenacted the episode:

> I suddenly tripped my brother, and tumbled him head foremost into the snow. I then fell upon him, rubbed the snow into his face, his hair, stuffed it into his neck and bosom, and filled his pockets and his hat full of snow. I then let up, and again he ran home and told my father. I walked resolutely and deliberately home, my mind being fully made up and prepared for another whipping. My father met me, and spoke to me kindly, but in a manner so cool, deliberate and measured, that I saw that I had no hope of escape. Though not one word was said to me about the matter; though my father seemed very particularly kind to me, and my brother and I were on as good and loving terms as ever, yet I seemed to see the whip in my father's eye, and to hear it in his heart.

He did not get his whipping that night. He felt "irresistibly" drawn to his father and was "officious" in helping him pack for a journey the next day. In the morning the family followed its routine of chores, breakfast, Bible reading, and prayer. As his father prepared the horses for his trip, Henry wondered if the whipping had been forgotten, but gave up the hope "for I saw too plainly the whip in his calm, determined face, and in his decided though kind voice." Taking the reins, his father said simply, "Henry, I'll settle with you when I come back," and left him to suffer for two weeks.

> A thousand actual whippings would have been as nothing compared to what I experienced in the certain prospect of one. At length, the earnestly longed-for day of his return came round. I watched with feverish excitement his coming. . . . [T]he first words I spoke to him were to entreat him to whip me. Soon as convenient he did so; not sparing one jot or tittle of the sum

> total, out of regard to what I had already suffered. These were the last blows my father ever struck me, though he lived many years, to see me come to man's estate. But it was not the violence that did me good; it was the mental anguish and mastery acquired over my own spirit by those two weeks' suspense and expectation.[51]

This is by far the most impressive, passionate reminiscence in *Human Life*. It tells much about the energies in Henry's relationship with his father; it is a passage that almost gets out of control in a book that is supposed to illustrate the futility of violence and the efficacy of love. Note well: though Wright by the time he wrote *Human Life* was an opponent of coercion, this punishment was clearly presented as just and salutary. He "mastered" himself by watching the whip that lurked in a kind, determined face. He no longer was whipped by father because he took within him his own lacerating conscience. He had taken the critical step toward the view he later articulated as being alone and judged by God. Later he also taught that hell was not a state of future punishment; it was the pain and remorse men suffered here and now as automatic consequences of guilty behavior.

Competitiveness was, then, a grievous problem for young Henry. We may guess that both the boxer and the coffin dreams, if we had sufficient associative material, might turn out to share this subject matter. There is no mystery in his dreams of combat after daytime wishes for peace. Perhaps his serene corpse in the coffin replaced that of a sibling whose death he wished; more likely, he wished to replace dead Milton, thus being cleared of guilt and gaining mother. In any case, his memories of childhood featured scenes of rivalry, death, and remorse—scenes placed in association with the wish to renew dialogue with the mother and fear of the awsome, righteous father. His solution to this problem was a style of dramatized conflict through which he could present himself as a man of peace. This solution was elaborated during his apprenticeship and perfected in relation to his fellow students at Andover and his brethren in the ministry. Once it was perfected, he had stifled the conflicts of childhood and his calling was that of a reformer.

Wright learned to cope with the conflicts of his childhood during what we would call his adolescence, what he called his youth.[52] In 1814 his father took him to be apprenticed to a hatter in Norwich, about thirty miles from home. Now that he "had left the paternal roof," he was besieged by guilt. "Every remembered instance of disobedience to my father; of cruel vexation to my younger brother;

or of want of attention to any of my brothers and sisters; all . . . appeared like heinous crimes that never ought to be forgiven."[53] He was not yet a journal keeper; the clarity with which he recalled past stages of his life is remarkable.

Living among a new set of brothers, the apprentices, in the hatmaker's attic was a time of agony. He hated his master, David Bright, though his wife provided some solace. He was appalled by temptations to drink. Probably some of the agony was sexual, though he wrote only vaguely of "the shock to my moral feelings, and my loathing and disgust at certain things." It would not be surprising if he went through some anxiety and self-accusation over repeated masturbation; grief over "solitary indulgence" was common among young American men and Wright would have taken this experience very hard. Perhaps there was some degree of homosexual activity among the apprentices, or even with the vile master, but American reticence on that subject would not permit even vague discussions. Had his father known of "the moral crucifixion" he was suffering, Henry speculated, "he would have cut his right hand off" before letting him remain. But he told Seth nothing.[54]

Wright called this the loneliest period of his life. He was divided against himself, wanting sympathy and fearing it, hating food and shamming enjoyment of it, avoiding amusement and fearing exposure of his unhappiness. After five months of suffering, he walked home, found his second stepmother, inspected all the scenes of childhood, and learned how much he had already changed. He returned to hatmaking as an independent young man, and though his loneliness was unquenchable, the dreadful pains of homesickness passed away. He was able to show a kind of love for his brothers once he had accepted the reality of his departure from home. Life among the apprentices "with our discordant tempers and dispositions" became one of the most satisfying and fondly recalled interludes in his life, in part because of successful experiments in self-mastery that linked his childhood to a future career outside of hatmaking. He learned to control and redirect his anger:

> I determined that I would never be betrayed into an outbreak of anger towards those young lads; I have no recollection that I ever was. Whatever of anger I might feel I kept it to myself, and never did I speak to them when I was excited, except in a deliberate, cool tone and manner [like Seth with the whip?]. So disciplining myself . . . I became cool and deliberate in outward speech and demeanor. I then acquired a calmness of voice, and a coolness and self-possession of manners, that have stood me in stead

> since, in many a stern encounter with men of violence and blood. It has been of infinite service to me in public debates, on Anti-Slavery and Non-Resistance.[55]

This is as close as Wright came to locating the significance of his style of reform in the issues of his childhood. His conviction that in the homely details of his life lay answers to universal questions about human life almost allowed him to see his pacifism as a form of self-discipline and a sign of self-worth. He also uncovered belligerent forces that the pacifistic style kept at bay.

When he reached Andover in 1819 he faced a new circle of brothers—his fellow students—who provided his last tests before adulthood. Perhaps it was his professors' knowledge of the issues of his personality that gave him this topic to address at the 1821 annual examinations: "the evils of indulging a disputatious spirit."[56] Certainly his student notebooks show repeated distress over failures to get along with others. This anxiety appears in scribbled, scarcely decipherable comments, resembling automatic writing, in the margins and on the covers of notebooks on serious theological subjects. He berated himself for associating with "a certain vile, fat man." He taunted a student named White. He observed that others were "down as flat as a pancake" because of sickness, but must pick themselves up. Hints of self-criticism for inadequate sympathies were amplified in a tortured and partly obliterated note. It may be the draft of a letter about whether sending something will cause "uneasiness." After some reflection: "I love to see folks *miserable; you I don't.* I should be distressed to see that innocent sick —— [deleted; may be James] made unhappy." The faint pattern may be clarified if we notice two quotations on the first page of his Andover commonplace book. First, this maxim: "He that considers how little he thinks of others, will know how they regard him." Second, he copied two hymn stanzas on approaching God's tribunal to be judged for "all the crimes that I have done."[57]

Human Life did not analyze his relationships with Andover classmates as closely as those with the apprentices. He did seem amused by one man's dyspepsia. He was rather isolated from another whom he described as a perfect roommate (or "chum"): "he let me alone," wrote Wright, "and I let him alone." He was also made uncomfortable by the analogies that the "Divines" made in order to distinguish between authentically religious emotions and human counterfeits. What difference was there between a true shift in affections and the mere transference of a "character we already love to the person whom we hated"—in this case, God? "A curious quibble indeed." Suppose someone who hated his brother violently were persuaded by a third party that he was wrong, and was therefore converted to love. Wouldn't that count as an authentic change? Wright simply did not like logic chopping about the uses of altruism to conceal aggression and about projections from loved to hated objects. As he was learning to control strong emotions, it was no time to be too closely analytical.[58]

Despite self-discipline gained among the apprentices, Wright carried from childhood profound feelings of unworthiness as well as a flair for personal assertion. In the years ahead he reflected often on his inability to sympathize with others, on his wish to bury himself in Christ, and on the persistence with which selfish ambition crept forward even when his ministry was most ardent. "It seems to be written on my memory," he wrote on his thirty-fifth birthday, "that I have never done one thing with a pure desire to glorify God. . . . When I have attempted to do anything for Christ—self has mingled in all." If we take a final look at the coffin dream, we discover its origins in the interplay between childhood experience and the dilemmas of professional self-assertion. That dream occurred on "*Thursday* night the 8th, of August 1833," but he recorded it only on the eleventh after it kept recurring in his mind. He had previously described the eighth as "a day of great wickedness in my heart," a day in which he had "been dissipated in my mind." One of the day's occurrences may have released sexual fantasies: he was "alone at home," dreaming of accepting a mission abroad, and praying to be reunited with "my dear family" (a richly ambiguous term) later on, in his "home in heaven." He had noted one other occurrence on the eighth: A Captain Simpson asked him to preach at Federal Street Church on Sunday schools—a request that led him to pray for "prudence, simplicity" and to dread the assertions of self infiltrating his devotion to Christ. The serenity of the coffin reversed confusing adult experiences of ambition and desire.[59]

The ministry could not elaborate a view of society or history licensing Wright—at least persuasively enough—to express his feelings and live out the consequences of his past. It was Christian reform, instead, that eventually afforded the liberation and control that he required of professional life. From the late 1830s on, he was able to forget himself, to express himself and to carry out his work with a style of cool, deliberate anger that universalized his father's punishments.

Kisses and Blows

Wright's most enduring work was a little book he wrote for children to show them "how to prevent quarrelling." *A Kiss for a Blow* was his first book, though he had been thinking about it for ten years. In composing it he gleaned anecdotes about children from his journals; he also included fragments of autobiography. He probably did not anticipate its success with adults and the profits that covered much of the cost of his travels. He thought, however, that children would recognize the book as factual and find it "a moral mirror, in which you may see your hearts, as you see your faces in a looking-glass."[60] In truth he did focus on an aspect of reality infrequently emphasized before Freud except in the most general proofs of infant damnation—conflicts among children. While inspecting this nether side of childhood, its jealousies and resentments, he suggested it was easily vanquished. The result would be a passive character avoiding angry responses to aggression or, in some instances, responding with love and consequently winning the day.

A Kiss for a Blow consists of little stories, supposedly about children Wright had known, which make three general points. First, conflicts among children spring up easily and are usually over trifles. Second, they can have horrible costs, not only in the sorrow provoked in parents and the children themselves, but also in nasty wounds and dismemberment, intended or accidental. Third, fighting can be prevented if children will not retaliate when attacked. The remedy for fighting, in other words, lay in the hands of injured parties, such as the girl in one of his Boston schools who kissed her brother when he struck her, thereby of course reducing him to tears of penitence. Wright taught children that anger was wrong and, when felt, ought to be smothered. The trifling occasions of conflict would pass right by if children genuinely preferred the enjoyment of their siblings and playmates to their own and their own death to that of others.

Many modern readers would find that this book holds children to a standard of unselfishness amounting to an absence of healthy self-regard. Why shouldn't boys and girls try to be happy and protect themselves so long as they do not harm others? The popularity of *A Kiss for a Blow* shows that Wright's view was not idiosyncratic. We may note, nevertheless, that he offered an ideal of conduct as far removed as possible from the rivalries that awakened guilt in his own boyhood. He did not mention his struggles here, for he was posing as kindly expert (and one of the points of the exercise, I think, was the purgation that came from identifying himself with purified ideals). But nothing was ever uncomplicated for him. In several stories he intimates that returning a kiss for a blow was really a tactic in competition for mastery over others. "Thus he conquered his angry sister again, without any fighting," is the summary of one anecdote; elsewhere, children are "overcome" and "vanquished" by the same innocent means. There are slight indications, at least, that sometimes benevolence may be a mask for spite.[61]

A Kiss for a Blow could be purchased as a simple, helpful book for families—a nice pious gift from a father to a child perhaps. But Wright saw the significance of his stories in terms far grander than simply easing family spats. For one thing, he insisted that warfare among nations was exactly interchangeable with children's fights. Either might be deployed to illustrate the folly of the other; the remedy for each is the supremacy of love and martyrdom over revenge and conquest. In addition, he warned children again and again of the sadness and disapproval their fighting aroused in their fathers (almost never did he add their mothers). If such was the reaction of their earthly fathers, how much worse must their heavenly Father feel to see his loved ones fight. How pleased He would be to see them contending instead "for the right to give up the best of everything to the others."[62] This is not simply a rhetorical embellishment. Worship of a great judge and governor who was also an emotional father was fundamental to Wright's understanding of reform.

The idea of the government of God was basic to American Protestant theology in the early nineteenth century. It facilitated the quiet introduction of Enlightenment attitudes toward morality and the natural world into Protestant thought with relatively little doctrinal conflict. To think of God as a governor whose rules made sense and were applied fairly, rather than as an arbitrary sovereign, was a dilution of the Calvinist world view. It succeeded, however, in retaining belief in God as judge of the backslidings and revivals of republican virtue, and it held individuals to strict accountability for their actions. The idea had important implications for reform, and helped to explain the sinfulness of slavery. It was wrong for men to play God by exercising mastery over their fellowmen. Rather than confiding in institutions to restrain and guide, some reformers, of whom Wright is a good example, placed their hope in self-control.[63]

It is easy to see the necessity of some myth or schema of the family to shore up their confidence in internalized restraints. Wright almost invariably preferred familial imagery for his discussions of God's sovereignty. When men exercised mastery by enslaving, killing, or governing one another, the results were murderous competition among siblings and violation of paternal prerogatives. In Wright's mind, all situations of conflict and authority reenacted triangles in the family of origin. He advocated "a tender and affectionate recognition of a common brotherhood and a common paternity"; only with this recognition could civilization be reformed for the better.

Not surprisingly his own fantasies surfaced frequently when he adopted this familial schema. Often he was the innocent son absolved of guilt and preferred over his brother-enemy at father's tribunal. "Suppose that I am on board the same boat with an enemy who attempts to kill me," he wrote," and that the boat happens to upset." Neither can swim, but Wright manages to catch hold of an oar to keep him afloat. His enemy fights for it. It will not hold two men. Wright happily lets go and says: "My brother, take the oar, and may heaven forgive you and speed you to land." He sinks and dies, but wins the eternal applause of "our common father," who will be "pleased to see his children thus willing to die for their enemies." In keeping with this fantasy, Wright offered this definition of nonresistance: "Father, spare and forgive my enemy, and let me die."[64] He nearly reversed the customary view that the Lord's government was just and that He demanded no sacrificial victims. Nonresistance did not logically require this reversal. Other pacifists, then and since, have stressed the practical uses of nonviolence in reaching goals of reconciliation unattainable by other means. Sometimes pacifists have stressed New Testament injunctions against returning evil for evil or in favor of returning love for hate. But few have gone so far as Wright in proclaiming a desire to suffer or die. The reason, I think, is that the vocabulary of nonresistance in his mind always referred directly to the psychology of childhood.

Sometimes nonresistance authorized another image: as a father, he could enjoy power and mastery with an easier conscience than in the competitions of childhood. In one anecdote in *A Kiss for a Blow* he sits on "a high throne, made of pure snow," and talks to "my devoted, happy subjects"—fifty boys in a schoolyard—about the rights and wrongs of making war against the United States.[65] A Glasgow reporter similarly caught Wright playing father-God in order to illustrate the blasphemy of military prayer. "I have two daughters, Mary and Hannah," he began this little drama. "I divide my parlor into two divisions by means of a line, and call Mary's part Great Britain, and Hannah's the United States." Eventually one desires a bit of carpet across the line. They argue, declare war, collect weapons, "and before they begin hostilities they come to me, and Mary says—'Oh, father, help me to kill Hannah, for my cause is a righteous one!' And Hannah says—'Oh, father, nay; but help me to kill Mary, for *my* cause is a righteous one!'" He elaborated the same divisive fantasy in *Six Months at Graefenberg,* this time imagining two sons asking his assistance in killing one another. His point was, of course, that everyone would condemn him if he acceded, but that armies regularly put God in an analogous situation.[66] But besides identifying military combat with sibling rivalry, he had lifted himself into the position, impermissible under the "philosophy of slavery," of playing God.

Nonresistance was a new use of the discipline Wright had learned from watching his father's face and practiced on his fellow apprentices. The more aggressive he felt, the cooler he would appear. One reason for his mystification by the recurrent charge that nonresistance threatened the country with anarchy was his personal knowledge that it was a form of restraint as well as a form of expression: it represented his own victory over murderous feelings. Clearly, his aggressive wishes were not abandoned; that would have been impossible. But Wright placed high hope, as the ministers of Boston learned, in reforming the external symptoms of sin. His behavior was modified by nonresistance, even though he continued to struggle with his brothers in more cunning ways. The craftiness of this discipline could be seen in his letter to the *Liberator* hailing the formation of the New England Non-Resistance Society. His imagery was drawn, inevitably, from the family: "A brother actually wrongs me, or threatens to injure me. I remonstrate with him earnestly and perseveringly—show him his guilt—let him see that I care more for him than for myself—that I would bring him to repentance, that he might be saved." He assures this brother that he will never call earthly authorities to punish or restrain him. "But I cite my erring, heaven-defying brother to meet me at that bar of sure, impartial, eternal justice, on which is seated the King of Kings. There an all-seeing, all-wise, and omnipotent God shall judge between us. He shall be our great umpire. He knows the exact nature of the wrong, the motives of the wrong-doer, and the precise amount of penalty to be inflicted."[67] In the role of nonresistant, in other words, he was empowered to show the blood on his brother's hand and to prove his own innocence. Although Wright spoke frequently of love, sacrifice, and self-abnegation, his language constantly carried overtones of vengeance.

Wright misconstrued the point of a story he liked to tell concerning two brothers who informed their father that they fought because they loved each other.[68] He thought the point was that the children's remarks were nonsense. The story echoed his conversion to nonresistance by a Quaker who kidded him about fighting with love. The merger of fighting with love was, however, exactly what nonresistance meant to Wright. He was, as he well knew, a belligerent nonresistant, and his Jesus was "the great captain of agitators in aggressive warfare, as well as the Prince of Peace."[69]

Wright gave some thought to the reservoir of aggressiveness feeding energy to his pacifism. In his autobiography, which was too close to inflammable memories, he speedily denied the theological doctrine of innate cruelty. Whatever depravity appeared in his or any other life resulted from bad training (later he would say, from the environment of the womb.)[70] In *Six Months at Graefenberg,* however, he was far from home and his analysis ranged more widely. In one of the most honest, probing passages in all his writings, he saw that "combativeness and destructiveness are essential parts of our nature; that our guilt lies not in the possession, but in the abuse of these propensities; and that they are to be regulated and not destroyed." His words merit close attention:

> Let these powers be controlled by that love to enemies which thinketh and doeth no evil, and I care not how largely they are developed. Combativeness and destructiveness may find sufficient employment in combating and destroying evil principles and unrighteous institutions, without the use of violence. The more perfectly these powers are developed, the better, while they are under the guidance of love; for they give energy and courage to the character. A man needs great combativeness to be a nonresistant. . . . But surely no provision was made in our nature for warring against our brethren.

Seeking vengeance was not, in his opinion, "an innate propensity." There were better outlets for aggressive drives that were innate. The key was to single out principles and institutions, rather than persons, as his foes. The key was to see love as a tactical control.[71]

These are admirable insights, further testimony to Wright's sustained self-examiniation. It would have been easy for him to take a benign view of human nature, as anarchists and pacifists have often done. It might have suited covert purposes for him to have maintained that neighbor and brother, but not self, exhibited aggressive drives. Instead he developed the soundest answer to questions about human nature that are unavoidable for those who are committed to nonviolent strategies for social change. Nonresistance was a displacement of aggressive feelings, but a witty, skillful one. It liberated the will and intellect from seemingly necessary connections between aggressive feelings and violent acts. This was not simply sublimation, for the ends served were not accidentally useful to society but involved decisions to seek a more fraternal world.

In general, writers on pacifism and social change have overlooked the insidiousness of spite. When Christians speak of confronting hate with love, for example, they often assume that one party can adopt an affectionate condition independently of the party he seeks to influence. One simply puts oneself in a condition of love, thus being right with God and exposing the hatefulness of the other person, who will be mysteriously cured. In other writings we encounter an abstract world in which love inevitably subdues wrath. The slaveholder does not really want to be a slaveholder, the war maker does not really want to make war. Once shown an example of unresisting love, the evildoer's conversion is irresistible. An adequate account of nonviolent tactics must recognize, however, that significant elements of ill will and aggressiveness support the mildest poses of peaceful witness. It is infuriating when one party appropriates the manner of love in a situation of conflict. Part of the importance of Mohandas Gandhi in our century is that he demonstrated the powerful spitefulness of nonviolence in a way that offsets the Christlike model of unselfish love. (He also knew the importance of gentlemanly accommodation after conflict.) Nonviolent tactics depend on a willingness to fight. They create explosive situations, often taking the form of dramas that tease the guilt of the antagonist. Henry Wright anticipated these disciplined, ritualistic aspects of nonviolence.

His interest in nonviolence did not stop with little stories about childhood or hypothetical looks at human nature. Disciplined aggression was basic to the style of controversy he developed as a reformer. It is not always clear that he cared about his effectiveness in converting others to his views (though he succeeded in discovering a wide audience). By maintaining his single-minded allegiance to the Father, who would supervise the consequences, he was freed to tease, satirize, and infuriate others. When tempers heated up, he insisted on his innocent motives.

There are surprisingly few descriptions of Henry Wright as a speaker—we should not say *orator* although this was an age of oratory. But they make it clear that he disciplined his provocations and kept a calm demeanor. To judge from a friendly remark by Wendell Phillips, he may have carried calmness and deliberation to the point of caricature: "If I were H. C. Wright I should reply . . . in his mild, slow way, if I could:—Mr. Pres-i-dent. . . ."[72] Others marveled at his ability to stand through storms of controversy with "calmness and serenity." Garrison observed that it was not eloquence that made his speeches effective, but the plainness of his manner, his obvious sincerity, the novelty of his doctrines, and the tenacity with which he advocated them—he was "a man of childlike simplicity." Wright spoke and carried himself so that he could state the most offensive points to his audiences while appearing to be perfectly lamblike. He spoke extemporaneously, preferring to debate or receive questions. He liked to announce his position in words that made it seem extreme, then to defend it simply by identifying it with love, human needs, and obedience to God. His antagonist was depicted as antihuman and anti-God.[73]

This style became satisfying and natural to him. We can see how admirable, even lovable, he appeared to reformers who agreed with him and audiences who disliked his antagonists. A Nantucket woman was converted to nonresistance by "the very countenance of this benevolent man beaming raidient [*sic*] from the influence of the Godlike principles within." But it is also easy to see some justice in conservative opponents' complaints about the irony of his nonresistance: "like many of his brethren, while professing his unwillingness to *resist*, he seems to be always on the watch for an opportunity to *attack*." James G. Birney gave this reaction to his style: "And Wright's calmness too! Why if I did not know he was a good man he would provoke me beyond bounds."[74]

The most famous example of the revulsion that his style could inspire came from Henry David Thoreau. He saw Wright as a repulsive, feminine, anal creature who threatened his own independent action. His blows were preferable to his kisses. "It was difficult to keep clear of his slimy benignity, with which he sought to cover you and took you into his bowels. . . . I do not like the men who come so near me with their bowels."[75] This reaction tells much about Thoreau, but it may also indicate snares with which the Christian reformer encircled others while professing to have no concern for earthly reputation. The radiance with which he converted one person to pacifism appeared to another as sanctimonious encroachment.

The family backgrounds of Wright's strategy as a reformer

emerged clearly in a series of personal conflicts during the fateful years of insurgent nonresistance and antislavery schisms. Always working through public letters, he assumed the role of the guiltless child accusing his brothers of despicable crimes. At the same time, he insisted on his own humility, good intentions, and personal insignificance. This strategy combined the Christian duty of rebuking sin, a duty taught everywhere by the revivals, with a Dickensian obsequiousness suggesting his awareness of a world outside reform where men competed for profit and advantage.

To Orange Scott, one of the bitterest antislavery opponents of nonresistance, he issued the warning, "You may be found fighting against God." Though obviously stung by Scott's criticism of him, he protested that the principle of peace is "as far *above,* as H. C. Wright is *beneath,* your scorn and contempt."[76] He warned Gerrit Smith not to be too cautious to join the nonresistants. "When slaughtered billions shall arise from their gory beds in earth and sea"—what an unfriendly family he imagined!—"may no brother's blood be required at your hand." Though admittedly excited, he professed to feel only "affection and esteem" for Smith.[77] Amos Augustus Phelps met similar treatment for criticizing Wright, who counterattacked by accusing him of "departing wider and wider from a simple child-like adherence to principle," advocating the virtual enslavement of women like the Grimkés, and acting as "the prime mover" in divisions among abolitionists. If the liberation of the slave were impeded, "the guilt, I believe, must rest primarily with you." Yet his own feelings toward Phelps, who had always treated him well, were innocent; "I have no personal ill-will to gratify."[78] We might almost say that he had an impersonal ill will to gratify. The point is that Wright acted out of competitive feelings without appearing personally responsible for them. He was responsible only to his Father.

In departing from the ministry he revealed the same strategy—professions of innocence, projections of guilt onto his confreres, expressions of love, and admonitions of God's punishment. After leaving West Newbury Wright continued his membership in the ministerial association of Essex County North; and his notoriety became something of an embarrassment to them. Ultimately, they withdrew fellowship from him and he "excommunicated" them, a process that required a series of bureaucratic letters on their part and wounded replies from him. He accused them of hardheartedness toward the slave, indifference to the teachings of Jesus, and erroneous views of the ministry. They sanctioned the worst atrocities of battlefield and plantation. But these vilifications hid behind words of meekness and fraternity. Over and over, he professed his love for the ministers, his hope that they would forgive any injuries he caused them. Their conduct toward one another should be "tender hearted, gentle, easy to be entreated, forgiving." What justified his harsh language in letters he brought into print? It was the fact that he was alone with God and cut off from society "in my responsibilities."[79]

This strategy was not applicable solely to verbal antagonists. Wright endured his share of rocks, snowballs, and angry crowds. When he returned to West Newbury to discuss slavery, for example, he gathered a large audience, but "a large number of men and boys, with clubs and sticks," waited outside and around the door. Wright prayed, championed "free discussion," and invited questions and comments as he proceeded with his argument that slavery was unchristian. According to one report, he was interrupted first by an inebriated laborer and then by a succession of other men trying to work up a mob through "slang and ribaldry" and accusations that his wild charges endangered the Union. There can be no doubt that the discipline imposed on his retaliatory impulses served him well in this kind of tempest. He could calmly describe the experience to his audience as "a demonstration that slavery at the South, or liberty at the North, must die."[80]

It seems likely, however, that Henry Wright sought out tempestuous scenes more avidly than many other abolitionists and braved them with a mockery that his solemnity failed to hide. When asked for an example of the efficacy of nonresistance, he discussed the 1838 riots when Pennsylvania Hall, a new building designed for antislavery meetings, was burned down. Presumably there is a kernel of truth in his story, but there are unmistakable hints of fantasy as well. Because of his remarks about George Washington's soldiering and slaveholding, as he told the story, the mob searched for him. On five occasions he escaped from violence by promising not to injure anyone who struck him. Would-be assailants became his protectors once they had sounded the depths of his peaceful intentions. He humiliated one man with a lover's charade: "He then caught me by the waist, endeavouring to trip me; whilst I held him round his neck, to keep myself up; and thus we walked along in such a very loving attitude, that a great laugh was raised at my companion's expense." The rioters threatened to lynch this man if he did not leave Wright alone. Another assailant was reformed by Wright's suggestion that he would later regret having killed someone who loved him and preferred death to injuring him. Like a stage drunkard, he burst into tears, embraced Wright, and declared: "Had I always been thus treated in my angry moods, I should not have been what I am now."[81] The fantasy left Wright safe, his innocence dramatized, sinners rescued, and good publicity garnered for his cause.

In *Six Months at Graefenberg* a similar interpersonal strategy was revealed as Wright's characteristic way of approaching others. Throughout that book, as always in his reform career, he pondered the ironies of being called subversive because he would not fight while other persons were accorded respectability because they believed in fighting. This was an effective point for him to score on public platforms and in the reform press. But Graefenberg was an isolated spot in the mountains of present-day Czechoslovakia; he was there in midwinter with fewer than two hundred other men and women. The social circle in one's daily life was even smaller. Their debilities and the remedies being equally unpleasant, the patients tried to maintain, especially at mealtime, a gay atmosphere with music, dancing, and light conversation. Wright approved of all the festivities, particularly the joyousness of the German Sunday that was so different from his gloomy boyhood memories. He also contrasted the patients' election of a master of ceremonies to the oppressive sham democracy of America. Although there was much to approve, he was a spectator: "My own mind has been too much absorbed for many years past, in the earnest realities of human woes and wants, to mingle readily in scenes like these."[82] It was difficult for him to behave spontaneously among adults. These six months were probably the longest period he spent in one spot with constant companions from the day that he left the settled ministry. In this company he followed routines that had served him well on the road and acted out the ironies of his subversive innocence and the others' respectable belligerence. Not surprisingly, some patients disliked his company.

In the book he made his isolation public. No doubt he improved the following conversation to his own advantage, and in doing so clarified the way in which he wanted his relationships with others to be seen. He revealed a quest for exoneration that culminated in blocked affections and enhanced loneliness. At first he was assigned a dinner table at Graefenberg made up mostly of Germans, but then "a seat was vacated in an English mess, and I gladly accepted an invitation to occupy it." When he sat down, however, a man given the name Wise, with whom he had "frequently carried on the war of words," objected: "Now I suppose we shall have a perpetual storm."

Wright. Oh! as to that, it shall not be my fault if the whole season do not present a model of good humour. I pledge myself to keep the peace, and never harbour resentment against any one, no matter what he may say. I forgive all injuries and insults, past, present, and to come. I shall be quiet as a lamb—emblematic of peace as an olive branch.

Wise. You promise fair, but you will fail in the performance, for the tempest is in your heart. You are for ever agitating our quiet waters, and creating disturbances. . . .

Wright. . . . Talk of agitating the waters! The object of our being here is to agitate the waters, and I am willing to admit that I agitate them thoroughly, to the great annoyance of my poor badediener, as his dripping hair and garments sometimes testify.

Wise. It would be better for us all if you would confine your agitations to the waters in your bath, and let the saloon enjoy a calm.

Wright. I do not agree with you. Shut out, as we are here, from the world, we must have some excitement, and you ought to thank the man who raises the billows now and then. But I do not feel excited myself; I try to keep my mind composed.

Wise. But you keep the rest of us in commotion, and that hinders the cure.

Wright. You should learn to keep calm, and not allow yourself to be thrown into such a feverish state of mind.

Wise. How is this possible, whilst I daily hear my most dearly cherished opinions denounced as heathenish and wicked?

Wright. Recollect that others have as good a right to think for themselves . . . as you have; and that they should be equally free to denounce your opinions as unchristian, hateful, and hurtful, as you are to denounce theirs. . . . You are altogether too sensitive about such matters.[83]

From this point, of course, Wright monopolizes conversation and creates something like the disturbance Wise initially feared. Without questioning the importance of free thought, we can see in this dialogue a politics of manipulation and teasing. Though he professed to scorn governments, there is a sense in which Wright converted all his relationships into diplomatic haggling over anger, death, and innocence.

Patterns reminiscent of Wright's life can be found throughout modern analyses of neuroses. The clarity of these patterns is not marred by the disagreements over theory and clinical practice between Freudians and post-Freudians. To give one example: I am struck by Karen

Horney's description of "the self-effacing type" who grew up "*under the shadow*" of someone else, perhaps "a benevolently despotic father" or a favored sibling. There may also have been "a long-suffering mother who made the child feel guilty at any failure to give her exclusive love and attention. . . . And so after some years, in which the wish to rebel struggled in the child's heart with his wish for affection, he suppressed his hostility, relinquished his fighting spirit, and the need for affection won out." According to Horney, this type of neuotic, like all others, "solves the problem evolving from his early development by self-idealization." He creates an ideal self that combines "'lovable' qualities, such as unselfishness, goodness, generosity, humility, saintliness, nobility, sympathy" and places a premium on feelings—"feelings of joy or suffering, feelings not only for individual people but for humanity, art, nature, values of all sorts." To live up to abstract loyalties and sustain an idealized self require labors of self-abnegation; he must be careful not to admit pride even in his idealization of himself. This "exclusion of pride from awareness" leads him to identify himself readily with other downtrodden people.[84]

In certain respects Wright's life as a reformer might be compared to a neurotic obsession. We have noted his labors to keep hold of an idealized mother and the consequent obligation to build a pure, spiritual image of himself. There is considerable evidence, furthermore, that after his mother's death young Wright came to think of himself as destructive, and one of the issues of his life was fear of his own powers. The distance—even the uncommunicativeness—of a father whom he thought of as just and who punished his "cruelty" to his brothers deepened this fear. He developed an ideal self which served in various roles, including that of victim to be protected from vengeful authorities and pure soul to furnish protection from self-gratification. In protecting this other self and trying to live up to its requirements, he worked out rites and strategies that he repeated in one situation after another, so that in his contacts with other human beings he would be seen as selfless, nonaggressive, devoted to great causes. His style as a reformer—the ways he managed to be seen, to show himself—was as important as the testimony he gave for nonresistance, the empire of the mother, and the government of God. It displayed him always as the innocent brother, beloved of woman, and dutiful son, though it isolated him from persons whom he met in his travels.[85]

It is ironic that we can discuss Wright's career in terms of play-acting and repeated rituals, for he was an uninhibited critic of the mummery of churches and parliaments and tried to act from the impulses of spontaneous human nature. He enjoyed a reputation, too, for originality and unconventional behavior. Other reformers of his day joined him in heightened consciousness of theatrical elements in social relations and a resolve to find authentic alternatives.[86] But spontaneity may be a will-o'-the-wisp even in the luckiest lives; it is an impossibility when a life takes off from the memory of irreparable loss and proceeds under the shadow of an ideal self. The goal of spontaneity may itself be taken as evidence of where his problems lay.

Yet there are limits to this analogy with neurosis, the first of which is that Wright analyzed himself with remarkable freedom. We would have to strain the facts, moreover, to recognize in him the alleged conservatism of obsessives and neurotics generally—the preference for established routines for going about life over openness and redefinitions of self. Clinical case histories are always problematical guides to understanding instances of creativity, and the problems are intensified when the analogy stretches from twentieth-century therapy to nineteenth-century reform. In explaining an obsessional side of Wright's career, it would be unfortunate to explain away the flexibility and versatility his style of reform required.

There is an additional problem with the analogy: it is prejudiced toward explanations going back to childhood. This is not simply the tyranny of psychological notions of our day, for in *Human Life* and other autobiographical writings Henry Wright anticipated modern notions and ruminated on the determinative influence of petty histories of childhood. Wherever he traveled, he was aware of taking his bearings from the farm at Hartwick; and he recognized that the discipline he acquired among his apprentice brothers set some of the terms for the career he chose in agitation. To attribute determinative power to bygone experiences may, however, be a screen against analyzing closer and more difficult ones. Henry Wright may have been less willing to analyze his luck as an adult. In the next two chapters we will examine his training for the ministry, his marriage, and his evolving views of religion and sexuality. In this examination we may pause to wonder why he remained preoccupied with issues of childhood—why he carried on the battle between living present and dead past.

Three

Dethroning God

John Fiske, *The Idea of God as Affected by Modern Knowledge* (1886)

The human soul shrinks from the thought that it is without kith or kin in all this wide universe. Our reason demands that there shall be a reasonableness in the constitution of things. This demand is a fact in our psychical nature as positive and irrepressible as our acceptance of geometrical axioms and our rejection of whatever controverts such axioms. No ingenuity of argument can bring us to believe that the infinite Sustainer of the universe will "put us to permanent intellectual confusion." There is in every earnest thinker a craving after a final cause; and this craving can no more be extinguished than our belief in objective reality. Nothing can persuade us that the universe is a farrago of nonsense. Our belief in what we call the evidence of our senses is less strong than our faith that in the orderly sequence of events there is a meaning which our minds could fathom were they only vast enough. Doubtless in our own age, of which it is a most healthy symptom that it questions everything, there are many who, through inability to assign the grounds for such a faith, have persuaded themselves that it must be a mere superstition which ought not to be cherished; but it is not likely that any one of these has ever really succeeded in ridding himself of it.

In the Mountains

In October 1833, while passing through a rainstorm in the New Hampshire mountains on his chores for the Sabbath School Union, Henry Wright became angry with God about the weather. "I was in a most rebellious unsubdued state of mind," he told his diary at the end of the day; he resented the discomforts of the storm and the lack of a mountain view during the journey. When the thought occurred that God might be pleased to commit to him "the government of this world for the remainder of this day," he recoiled from his own presumption. "I was horror-struck. . . . I felt that I had desired to dethrone God Almighty & seat myself on his eternal throne!" He got down from his carriage and knelt deep in the mud to beg for forgiveness. "O I felt that not for ten thousand worlds would I take the government of this world for a moment. O God—my Father—my adored Sovereign—forgive me for that dreadful thought." His apologies evidently were accepted, his distress eased, and when he got up from the mud he experienced serenity of mind.[1]

There is no other passage quite like this in Wright's journals. Although he frequently assigned God the role of his father in rather obvious disguises, the thought of supplanting Him rarely found overt expression. His control over the troublesome themes of his childhood kept that ambition in check too. But the passage beautifully illustrates the personal meaning of the "philosophy of slavery"—the renunciation of wishes to interfere in God's government. It illustrates as well a stagey quality typical of Wright's mature life: even alone in the mountains he felt himself being watched and he attended to details, such as posture in the mud, emphasizing the dramatic point he chose to make, in this case the usurper subdued. He had populated the universe with emotions assembled in childhood, and it was the unquestioned dominance of the Father that kept things in order. The passage gives us, furthermore, the motif that colligated his religious life with his efforts to make a career. Throughout his early manhood, evangelical religion furnished rituals of filial submission that freed him to leave home and become a pastor. As his career turned away from the church in the late 1830s and 1840s, he tried to negate his early religious indoctrination without seeming to dislodge Father from his heavenly throne. Even when advocating woman-centered and secularized versions of religion in the 1850s and 1860s, Wright was wary of the "dreadful thought" of becoming God's substitute.

In thus defining the central theme of Wright's religious life, I am alert to the dangers of too dogmatically applying Freudian doctrines to a Christian upbringing on the American frontier. Religious impulses cannot be reduced to illusions yielded by a "father complex," and devotion is something more than a mechanism to repress guilt. Religion does not simply point backward to storms and trials of childhood in a particular life history; religious experience reaches beyond the horizons of family, locality, and society and expresses feelings that are not easily conveyed in ordinary discourse. Such feelings may arise from consciousness of the beauty or horror of elements of nature that defy human control, from acknowledgment of the brevity of life, from perceptions of the vastness of the universe. Such feelings might overcome anyone during a storm in the mountains. To complain about comfort and scenery and then to turn to gestures reenacting childhood experience may have been a poignant effort to get religious experience under control. There are, of course, anxiety-provoking and serenity-providing mysteries in growing up; but the power of the analogy between earthly and heavenly fathers does not flow from only that source.

Nevertheless, Henry Wright's religion was relatively homebound. It seldom inspired him to speak of beauty in nature or terror caused by the unknowable universe. The scenario of religion, especially in the first forty years of his life, did not stray far from a few closely related themes—death, guilt, ambition, submission—so much so that even the remark that he was operating within a "father complex" sounds plausible. Yet he did not devise this scenario on his own. He was, rather, adopting a ritualized view of the universe that his community furnished young people as they stepped from childhood to independence. The importance of submission to the father was sociological as much as psychological. It helped individuals to locate meanings in the organized society they entered, and it shored up society's confidence in the prospects for responsible behavior in a shifting world where men acted on their own.

Henry Wright lived through an era of far-reaching social change: at the end of his lifetime no institution—church, government, work place, family—bore close resemblance to its eighteenth-century predecessors. The vehicle through which corresponding changes in personal feelings were expressed, more than any other, was the Christian religion. In Wright's life those changes took the symbolic form of struggling to demote the masculine God who commanded the deferral of self-gratification and to elevate mother to the throne. With that accomplished, and with an appropriate measure of self-control, there sometimes appeared to be no limit to the pleasures and security all brothers and sisters might enjoy on this earth.

Wright eventually preached the self-sufficiency of every man and woman—a far cry from his youthful Calvinism and from the renunciations of the "philosophy of slavery." Each human being was its own system of law, he taught; men and women were their own saviors and gods. If they followed their true instincts and took care of their bodies, salvation was theirs. In summarizing his message after he was dead, one radical publishing house advertised a large selection of his works by stressing that they upheld the immediate happiness of the body over the remote heaven of theologians. His writings were "truly religious, in the best sense, . . . manly and pure, frankly addressed to the real wants of men and women, to their present condition, to save their bodies and minds."[2] It would be hard to conceive a message more alien to the religious system in which he was brought up. The purpose of this chapter is to cover the distance, which many contemporaries traveled with him, from the revival—through seminary, ministry, and reform—to recognition of "the real wants of men and women."

Rebirth, Intimacy, Mission

In later years Henry Wright complained that the Calvinism in which he was brought up had always warred with his nature. But his early religious life appears to have been fully congruent with the experiences of his youth and similar to the lives of his contemporaries. In fact his account of his conversion is a valuable record of rural revivalism (which is not quite the same thing as Calvinism) when it was working effectively.

The revival in time became well adapted to public anxieties about the control of uprooted populations in booming cities. In the days of Wright's childhood, however, the revival gathered in those who were experiencing a different kind of mobility. The revival played a key role in giving shape to a long period of divergent and uneven expectations. It was a ritual occasion for young people whose lives were broken up by seasons with differing purposes (from school to fields, from apprenticeship back to school again), by fluctuations of authority (from father to teacher to master, perhaps to an uncle, then back to father again), during a long period of "youth" (extending even into their thirties) before they unambiguously enjoyed the status of manhood. Despite a long period of ambiguity prior to independence (for example, Henry's oldest brother remained home to run his father's farm), young people were urged to think of their lives in terms of fateful choices. The revival, which was the most emotion-laden of these turning points, caught Henry away from home, living with a "boss" he disparaged as profane and wicked, reevaluating his prospects in the career he had chosen, and traveling back and forth between the homes of his father, his master, and a brother who lived in Pennsylvania.[3]

Although every day in his Presbyterian home began and ended with religious ceremonies, these were of passing importance. Following the Puritans' belief that God's elect could be identified on earth, a belief which hopeful generations of frontier Americans had transformed into the institutions of revivalism, children were taught to believe they were sinners until they were "converted," until they underwent rebirth at a particular moment and place. For Wright this moment of permanent importance arrived during the winter of 1816–17 "in my little chamber," the one shared with the other apprentice hatmakers, "on my bed, reading and thinking over my calamitous state. . . . At length, as I thus lay brooding over my condition, there was an instantaneous revolution in my feelings; from deep anguish I passed to great joy." It was a wrenching process like any birth, "a sudden revulsion," a "deliverance." He was twenty years old, about average for a second birth.[4]

Although we can speak of averages and rituals, a crucial aspect of a successful revival was that everything about it seemed extraordinary. Today's student can observe how the Puritan belief in God's power to effect conversions at any moment of time was turned by revivalists into a collective routine, but the young convert still watched for spontaneous promptings within his own heart and for miraculous happenings around him. From his bouts of heightened self-consciousness, Henry Wright cherished warm memories of two older women—Mrs. Bright, his master's wife, and Elizabeth Snow, "a kind of mother to all in the pretty village, having seen it spring up amid the wilderness." Taking a special interest in Henry, the latter woman asked Mr. Bright's permission to spend hours with him, probed the condition of his soul, and gave her opinion of the truth of Scripture. "I know it is [true], for I *feel* that it is." She led him away from the abstract Calvinism he associated with his father and revealed that religion could be a "living principle," a practical element in daily life. Her vital religion, as recollected years later, depended on acknowledging masculine authority: Mrs. Snow directed him "to God as an ever present, ever controlling Guide to my youth—taught me to look to Him as a little child to a father."[5] If we recall Wright's turbulent reflections on his father and little Miles when his apprenticeship began, we will see how ripe he was for this earnest woman's influence.

Wright had less to say about the men of Norwich. David Bright evidently paid little attention to religion, his wife's domain. But he bought his apprentice a good flute, just as he furnished books, and tolerated time spent directing church musical activities. Wright's musical talents, in turn, imposed various religious pressures on him. Church members decided it was unseemly for an unconverted youth to sing in meeting and therefore forced him to resign the directorship he enjoyed. He also encountered a music teacher, a "sweet singer" who played harp to his flute and pried into the state of his soul. This man's school was turned over to Wright.[6] The leadership he showed in music, his rank as the oldest apprentice, and his disciplined reading habits must have singled Wright out as an unusually promising member of the community and consequently as a key target for conversion before a revival could be counted successful.

Although Wright's rebirth took place in privacy, its context was the public excitement of a revival. Later in the century revivals occurred under the captaincy of touring professionals, and men like Dwight Moody and Billy Sunday played capital roles in American cultural history. But Wright was converted before the organization of grand evangelical circuits: the revival in Norwich was a church-building episode on the frontier, and the magnetic figure in his transformation was the obscure son of a Spanish indentured servant, Rev. John Truair. As minister of the Congregational church in the neighboring town of Sherburne, Truair had preached the dedicatory sermon when Norwich's Presbyterian church opened in 1815. Lacking a minister, the new church relied on lay sermons, prayers, and songs (hence the consternation over having an unconverted music leader). But interdenominational cooperation was taken for granted on the New York frontier, and Truair was on call to help the new church through its initial years. Wright remembered Rev. John Truair as a dashing figure, though a bit "foppish," a spellbinder with "piercing black eyes." Once the revival was under way, Truair worked unstintingly for several weeks in Norwich, visiting families in their homes, holding nightly meetings, employing his gifts at arousing emotions, and raising the question throughout the village,

"Who are the elect?" When he was done, Presbyterians and Baptists reaped a harvest of new members, as they did again, with his help, four years later.[7]

Some immediate effects were divisive. Christians handed notes to the minister, seeking organized prayers for unconverted relatives. Rumors spread about townsmen "under distress of mind." There was a sensation when "a sedate, influential lawyer," David Buttolph, came to grace; there may well have been another when Mr. Bright's smart apprentice came around. One night scoffers held a dance, and a revival meeting was pitted against it nearby. Zealous young converts rejoiced when few went to hear the fiddler. But the divisiveness was not as memorable as the signs of heightened community awareness. There was pleasure during a cold winter in a remote corner of the world "in seeing a whole community thoroughly aroused: in seeing them look, speak, and act in earnest, as if urged forward by some irresistible impulse to the accomplishment of some great end."[8]

At first Wright restricted himself to enjoyment of the rousing hymns and the "whirlwind" of excitement surrounding the minister. Then he discovered that he too was laboring in anxiety and entering a rhythm of emotions that he had seen and heard about but never experienced before. He veered between extremes of wretchedness and self-confidence, hopeful that he might secure peace but fearful of the requirement of an actual time and place when he was assured of his conversion. Conversion was not something he could work up in himself; it had to *happen* to him. His pleasure in the public excitement gave way to brooding private calamity as he finally sat on his bed and cursed Adam for exposing him to the tortures of hell and mourned that his parents had given him birth even though they knew the penalties of existence. Suddenly he was "brought out" and knew he had found religion. A few evenings later he stood before a revival meeting and "to use the language which all used, related 'what the Lord had done to my soul'—a phrase expressive simply of the process of being 'under distress of mind, and of 'being brought out.'" Soon afterward he joined the Presbyterian church, satisfactorily narrating his experience once more, and was reinforced in the identity he retained for many years that he was unmistakably a blessed Christian.[9]

In retrospect Henry Wright attributed his distress of mind to the false estimates of man he had acquired in a Calvinist upbringing. His authentic self fought against false images he had been given of himself. Even as a critic of revivalism, however, he could not elude the terms it posed for his life. He continued to remember his distress as something that had happened just to him: collective ritual remained consistent with autobiography. In narrating his distress he turned to one of the grand themes of nineteenth-century American culture—the romantic warfare between the head and the heart. Although he meant thereby to repudiate the revival, he was actually orchestrating a theme that drew much of its emotional power from revivalism, which urged suspicion of the ruses of the intellect and surrender to vital religious impulses. Here is his account of the conflict: "My *heart* was at war with my *head.* My theology said I was under the wrath and curse of God. My heart said No to that. My head said, I had lost all communion with God. My heart said that I loved to be close to him, and to feel that I lived and moved in Him. Thus was I sorely distressed; my heart an utter infidel to my head, and my affections pouring contempt on my theology."[10] The protest that he described in this passage was a central mechanism of the revival. The doctrines of original sin, the puniness of man, and the majesty of God surpassed mere intellectual assent; and many converts, just like Wright, wrestled angrily with them before an emotional submission gave them peace.

Wright mistook the goal of the revival to be the theological ascendancy of Calvinism, while he provided one of the most vivid accounts of the meanings of evangelical distress in one young man's life. The goals of the ritual he describes were to chasten the headstrong will and let loose free-flowing emotionality. The result was a change of heart. In the eighteenth century this ritual of submission might have reinforced respect for the visible authorities in a stratified provincial world, but in a newly created town like Norwich that form of submission was meaningless. There were great advantages, however, in the periodic upsurges of communal earnestness that revivals provided; more lasting advantages were possible if individual young men took hold of a new conception of themselves as submissive to the moral law. The convert was to go forth with the feeling that he was accountable to the Almighty Father for the record he left on earth. Bearing this sense of himself on public view, his emotional life would not be wild or carnal, but sentimental and socially responsible.

The warfare between head and heart, ending in reconciliation with tough intellectual doctrines, belonged to the conventions of revivalism. Wright's anger at Adam was a customary stage. Because religious awakenings, like most ritual approaches to manhood, included a revised accommodation to paternal authority, there was also no surprise in the other emotion Wright suffered as he thrashed on his bed before being "brought out"—sorrow that his parents conceived him. Forty years later he refreshed his memory of that emotion by revisiting Norwich scenes. He saw himself again beside the Chenango River at midnight, crying and cursing Adam; and this time he was explicit about the way in which his anger turned to the primal scene, the "*voluntary* relation" of his mother and father that brought him into the world. Struggling against a deterministic version of sin that necessitated a second birth, he resented how unfairly "a voluntary act on the part of my parents" corrupted him. Anger at his earthly father's knowledge of his mother and his heavenly father's condemnation of a poor wretch blocked him from prayer. He knelt again and again, but each time his body involuntarily popped back up—until he finally brought it to submission.[11]

Of course his memory so many years later may have improved the scene. By that time he was a well-known fugitive from Calvinist theology, one who regarded his youthful anxieties as impairments to the needs of the body. But only his conscious utterance of distress at his parents' sexual union—not his experience of it—would have been unlikely in 1816. The revival was a ritual of submission and its imagery was starkly masculine; at the same time, it was an expressive ritual in which the young man began to prize his value as a human being and to form a relationship with a proximate community as well as a distant God. As he was encouraged to explore feelings of distress, it would have been odd if material had not emerged that, in our age of different rituals, would be regarded as therapeutically lively. This might have been true in the case of virtually any young man; it was almost inevitably true of Henry Wright, whose mind frequently raced through scenes of juvenile conflict and loss.

Despite his protests in later years, the revival succeeded in reconciling Henry to a new division of paternal authority. It helped him address his father with a new blend of obedience and equality. After his conversion he wrote a solemn letter to his father, "giving him an account of the process through which I had passed in conviction and conversion, and of my joining the church." He had been away from home more than two years, but this was the first letter he ever wrote and his first attempt at "original composition." He was certain his father would be consoled by learning of God's work on his son. In turning to God he had at first feared public opinion, but his independence was secure when he saw that "this world is nothing but a prison, and that death is the only door out of it." A postscript told his siblings of his good wishes for them to end their rebellions against God the Father. It would help if they too could see the certainty of death. "I pray that your days may be prolonged," he wrote them, "and that you may not be cut off in your mad career till you shall have repented of your sins."[12]

Later in 1816 he left Norwich, "feeling for the first time . . . I was a MAN." There was sorrow in bidding farewell to the other apprentices and to the circle of young people with whom he shared the bonds of conversion. One consequence of rebirth, however, was to put ambition in manageable form; and Wright was anxious to further his education and, more specifically, to learn to write. His parents and brothers, impressed by his intellectual and spiritual growth, offered a different plan: they wished him to train for the ministry, with their backing. Instead, he went back to school for four months, "confining myself to English studies," keenly aware of the incongruity of "a man" at school. Then he took to the road as a hatter, but hit a lull in that trade and was a failure. When he returned home once more, he was prepared to become a clergyman by following the old-fashioned custom of moving in with a settled minister. During his residence with Rev. Henry Chapman, the well-educated Yale graduate who served the town of Hartwick, he learned many things: most important, how to read and write in Latin, Greek, and Hebrew; more fascinating, perhaps, how to derive pleasure from arguing the fine points of Jonathan Edwards and other New England theologians. Wright's progress must have pleased Chapman and the dignified colleagues who passed through Hartwick, for at the end of two years he found himself with three options. He could enter straightway into the ministry; he could spend a year at a mission school for Sandwich Islanders in Cornwall, Connecticut, as preparation for an assignment in their homeland; or he could pursue a new-fashioned theological education at Andover Seminary. He chose the latter course.[13]

Clearly his family ties were very close after his conversion and during his residence with the Chapmans. He returned home on weekends and for a month in the summer to help with the chores; during these stays he experienced the most "poetic" feelings of his life. He stayed with several relatives on his way east to Andover. His father accompanied him as far as Cooperstown, and told him they would never meet again. There was a scene of tears, anguish, and a long handshake—but no words—as they parted. "Stern, inflexible, just, but loving author of my being! I cherish thy remembrance with deep-felt, undiminished filial love and respect."[14]

Wright did not record his reasons for rejecting a missionary appointment, and the matter is slightly puzzling. One of his earliest writings, entitled simply "1818 Address," was delivered before the Ladies Missionary Society of the Presbyterian Church in Hartwick. He praised the value of benevolent societies in God's scheme, which left the extension of His kingdom to human labors. Would it be possible to establish a general benevolent society in Hartwick? One task would be the recruitment and subsidizing of young men who were eager to become ministers if they could only afford to study; another would be to support missionaries in Africa. Echoing the millennial rhetoric that the revival spread across New York, Wright told the ladies: the moment for the conversion of the entire world was drawing nigh. One could scarcely ask for a sharper illustration of the way in which isolated American communities, heated up by revival fires, forged their identities by projecting missions in exotic lands.[15]

Millennial hopes burned even more impetuously in five letters he wrote in the summer of 1818 to Laura West Hartwick, "*Respected Juvenile Friend.*" These letters are the first evidence of intimacy with any woman. Though he preserved the letters, his published writings, which pretend to offer a detailed account of his coming of age, are silent about this relationship. Here is the earliest indication of his tendency to keep his intimacies secret and, at the same time, hide his emotions behind grand public purposes. What he wished to tell Miss Hartwick, and to keep from all other eyes, was his decision to become a missionary in far-off, dangerous places. His heart had been stirred by hearing her express concern for benighted heathens. Probably she had seen his writings on the subject (these have not come down to us), and so he wondered whether "this female so young, my Christian friend, would she, I say, who is now in the bloom of life . . . be willing to act a part in that great drama, even of turning heathens from their bigoted superstitions and bringing them to embrace her religion?"[16]

As the correspondence increased in ardor, the imminence of Christ's kingdom inspired more dramatic expression; and as it did so, Wright anticipated the contrasts between innocence and bloodshed that played an important role in his adult Christianity. "With ecstasy I hail the approaching day of our Lord," he confessed. "My heart bursts with heavenly transports at the downfall of Anta-

Christ [*sic*]. I am pursuaded [*sic*] that his dwelling will soon become the habitation of silence. But a few more struggles & his work is done. God will soon shake the nations . . . & gather from the four winds of Heaven, all his elect into the Holy Land & then he will drench the planes [*sic*] of Palestine with the blood of his enemies, while his children sing Alleluias to the Lamb."[17]

Wright placed his ardor in the context of reforming a sensual world. While this was a normal result of the rituals of conversion through which he had recently passed, it was also a premonition of his subsequent view that marriage should be synonymous with self-abnegation. In the most moving letter to Laura Hartwick he tried to equate their intimacy with the Christian vision of a divided and imperfect world. Man was a rational creature, he reminded her, who had let his carnal nature divorce him from the favors of God; the remnant on whom God showed mercy were inevitably out of tune with society. But there was hope of a better future, which the two of them might exemplify. With his Latin studies proudly evident, he asked: "Do we live as though we expected soon to join a society where there is [*sic*] no discordant passions, no parsimonious or malevolent feelings, no malific intentions, no contumacious will to contravene our happiness, no contumelious language to exasperate our minds, in a world where perfect love & harmony, peace and virtue predominate?" He longed for Jesus' direct rule over the world.[18]

This correspondence is the best evidence that Wright's youthful religion meant much more to him than he later liked to admit. Together with information about his acquaintances in Norwich, his family's help as he backed out of unpromising work and took off in a new direction, and his successful residence with Rev. Chapman, it suggests that Wright's young manhood was a time of warmth and self-confidence. He had been lucky in the friends and overseers he had met; his conversion in the revival had marked a fortunate turning point in his life. He had paced his accelerating ambition to the needs of the community in which he had grown up. He was on good terms with everyone he knew, and beneath the Latinate prose of his intimate letters there were clear signs of pride in his own newly found abilities. He was headed toward success in an institutional network of churches and missions whose importance he took for granted. Whatever satisfaction he felt in his late-blooming talents was tempered by an urgent interest in the transformation of society. It was true that in the short run he had declined a tour of duty in the

Pacific, but by attending Andover he would become even better equipped for sacred and distinguished service.

"My Head Is an Atheist; My Heart Cannot Be"

Unfortunately, Henry Wright did not record his observations during his Dick Whittington journey from Cooperstown to Albany, through the Berkshires to Northampton where he stayed a fortnight, then on to Boston, and finally twenty miles north to Andover. It would be interesting to know more of his first impressions of a Christian, civilized world very different from the familiar one where he had previously done so well. In this world he had a new sense of himself as an outsider, struggling to make his way where everyone else had a head start. Andover offered him a splendid range of educational experiences, however, and his years there were the most open-minded and intellectually intense period of his life. During these years he was encouraged to think systematically about philosophy and psychology as well as biblical and pulpit-oriented studies. Fortunately, Wright preserved student notebooks which reveal how well he was prepared for a life of service to international Protestantism and how this preparation set the intellectual terms for most of his religious life. The notebooks also reveal spiritual agony more severe than the ritualized distress he had known in Norwich. His progress toward the ministry was not deterred, but years later he looked back to his Andover years for foreshadowings of his career as an anticlerical reformer.

Founded in 1808 to counteract Harvard Unitarianism, Andover Seminary grew in reputation as its well-trained graduates took their positions around the world. All of Wright's classmates had college degrees; his professors—especially Leonard Woods and Moses Stuart—were literate, famous men. Trustees and visitors to the seminary included prominent clergymen and wealthy New Englanders. The seminary had educated a formidable list of ministers, professors, and missionaries. Because the latter category was the greatest source of pride, the Society of Inquiry respecting Missions played a vigorous part in student life. In addition, several of the "benevolent" societies designed to promote education and distribute tracts in America were conceived at Andover; others, such as the American Temperance Society, were created by Andoverites. In its purpose of training a learned ministry to oppose liberal influences in America the success of the seminary was unmistakable. Modern scholars see Andover and other early divinity schools as models of the specialized graduate schools of the future; in contemporary eyes it was more like an evangelical fortress.[19]

Wright came there to work hard. He subjected himself to a daily sixteen-hour regimen of study, scorned the laziness of his better-prepared colleagues (as some of the professors did too), and joined the Society of Inquiry. He was in impressive company, and met many lifelong acquaintances in the worlds of religion and reform. One of his roommates was Thomas Cupples Upham, later a well-known professor of mental and moral philosophy at Bowdoin. One of his contemporaries was Edward Robinson, whose subsequent research in the Holy Land earned him praise as the "foremost Palestinologist of his day." His contemporaries who became prominent reformers included: Beriah Green, first president of the American Anti-Slavery Society and a key figure in the Liberty party; Leonard Bacon, a colonizationist who was a stalwart critic of William Lloyd Garrison, Henry Wright, and other radicals; George C. Beckwith, who served as a pastor, returned to Andover as an instructor, then became secretary of the American Peace Society and a stern foe to Wright and nonresistance; and Sydney E. Morse, editor of the New York *Observer* and, in Wright's words, "the deadly and untiring foe of Anti-Slavery, and the staunch defender of the honesty and Christianity of American slave-traders." Also at Andover were several of Wright's future associates in the Essex County and Boston ministries. At least one student's unorthodox career faintly resembled Wright's own: after becoming a nonresistant radical, John Smith was expelled from the Presbyterian ministry in western New York, and Wright often stopped at his Ohio farm in the 1840s and 1850s.[20]

Unlike Harvard's Divinity School, Andover was not adjacent to college or city (though it was housed at the well-known boys' academy). There were few distractions from the code of piety and intensive study. Professor Stuart's daughter gave an entire chapter of her memoirs to the "Puritan Sabbath" at Andover—the day was observed at least as gloomily there as in Wright's boyhood home. She also recalled a program of manual labor, designed to take care of the students' bodies, in which one student employment was making coffins: here was "a theological consistency worthy of John Calvin himself!"[21] Since Wright complained of too little vigorous exercise, he must have preceded this reform. But his mental labors never strayed far from concern with mortality and sin.

When Andover was founded, Calvinist "orthodoxy" in New England was itself disorganized. On the one hand, those who liked to be called the orthodox would brook no modification of the Westminster

Confession, wrought so carefully in the seventeenth century. To alter the great doctrines of original sin and predestination—even for the purposes of making those doctrines more acceptable or comprehensible—was in their view to invite further effronteries from Unitarians and other liberals. On the other hand, some of the most learned ministers followed Samuel Hopkins of Newport in restating those doctrines for an age of revivalism and Christian progress. They felt free to assert man's natural ability (even though his moral decisions unerringly made him sinful), to praise a benevolent disposition as a sign of grace, and to clarify God's intention to use sin not for man's destruction but for the greatest good of the greatest number on earth. Both the orthodox and Hopkinsians were planning new seminaries to combat the perfidious influence of Harvard over the training of ministers. After mistrustful negotiations, and despite the opposition of powerful ministers, the two factions were induced to cooperate at Andover.

Divided at its origins, the new seminary was ever watchful against heretical opinions. One of the pioneer historians of New England theology concluded that the "struggle to unite these irreconcilable positions is the tragedy of that institution [Andover]." The professors periodically had to assent in public to both a Hopkinsian creed and the Westminster creed with its assertion that Adam's sin was imputed to all his heirs. Distinguished boards of visitors kept track of doctrines being taught. Leonard Woods, whose career was virtually identical to Andover's for half a century, regretted that the visitors had not forced him to retract careless passages in his writings. While Wright was a student, a professor named James Murdock was impugned for preaching that Christ's atonement was not a propitiation of a sovereign God but took place instead through human agency—that is, by individual men and women forsaking sin. Students were sorely divided on this issue (and some besides Wright may have observed that they had not reflected sufficiently). Woods and the other professors eventually hounded Murdock from the faculty, partly because of departmental rivalries and partly because he wished to strengthen ecclesiastical history in the curriculum—an emphasis consistent with his view of the atonement—while they feared that historical perspective might weaken the would-be minister's assurance of the true religion.[22]

United in deploring Unitarianism, Andover professors were uncertain in their responses to the liberal Congregationalism taught by Yale's controversial Nathaniel Taylor, who granted extensive concessions to man's ability to escape sin. Moses Stuart came close to accepting this view. Woods attacked Taylor in print, but one historian concluded that he was so busy juggling the Hopkinsian and Westminster tenets that he could not really understand Taylor.[23]

Wright had entered a world in which intellectual missteps were easy, bitterness ran deep, and the rules for avoiding heresy were undefined. How unfavorably this world must have contrasted to the vital piety of rural New York—and yet entering this world had tremendous occupational consequences. Its confusion is well illustrated in George W. Blagden's celebration of Woods's theology, given at one of the frequent occasions when the seminary congratulated itself on its attainments. This example is especially appropriate because its author was Wright's nemesis among the Boston clergy. The "great characteristic" of Woods's theology, according to Blagden, was that "it emphatically exalted *God,* and humbled *man.*" But how emphatically?

> By humbling man, I do not mean that he divested him of his prerogatives as a free, accountable agent under the divine government. He held to the distinction [taken from Hopkins and ultimately Edwards] between natural and moral ability and inability, clearly, fully, and habitually. And he therefore ever pressed the obligation of man to obey perfectly all the commands of God, both under the law and gospel, unreservedly, affectionately and faithfully. . . . .
>
> Nor, did he hold to any views of regeneration, and of the sovereignty of God, which did not include the full and even accountable activity of man, in the change of character which makes him a Christian.
>
> But . . . when we approach that very difficult, and well nigh inexplicable point, that *locus vexatissimus* in theology, at which the divine and human agency meet and coöperate,—he exalted the divine agency supremely, clearly, and most carefully. He never hesitated for a moment, from the fullest declaration of the *truth,* that it must precede that of man . . . that we love Him, because He first loved us.[24]

The dense adverbs, the balanced disjunctions, the assertions of carefulness and inexplicableness in this tribute indicate one of the central features of the dogma taught at Andover and reigning over New England—its fundamental lack of clarity.

Wright's Andover was, in short, a serious environment linked to vague—and contested—conceptions of orthodoxy; at the same time, no one could doubt its success in training leaders for non-Unitarian churches and missions. If Wright came to Andover with a certain rustic awe and determination to do well, he might well have concluded there was no basis for his awe except the power and social standing of some of the people he met. He might also have been frustrated as he looked for a clear-cut intellectual system to which to apply himself and succeed. The uncertainties of the Andover world—that acme of presumption with regard to heathens everywhere—probably contributed to his immediate crisis of faith and to his eventual conclusion that organized religion was a sham.

One other fact may be relevant to understand Wright's state of mind at Andover: the seminary was remarkably open-minded in its methods of instruction. It did not propound acceptable doctrines, give out safe reading lists, and reward cautious reiterations of approved views. Moses Stuart introduced first-year students to German biblical scholarship despite the unsavory reputation of the higher criticism among western churchmen. Leonard Woods's reading lists included deists and free thinkers. The new learned ministry trained at Andover was expected to know how to use the adversaries' weapons. One of the most admirable qualities of Andover evangelicalism is this confidence that it had nothing to dread from free inquiry. Furthermore, the professors urged students to have frank conferences over problems that were disturbing them. Wright never qualified his gratitude for Woods's patience and sympathy with a student in crisis. And yet his unhappiness resulted, in large measure, from the subversive effects of critical methods and theological dialectic on the simple views of the Bible and God he had borne with him from rural New York.

When he came to Andover in the fall of 1819, first-year students concentrated on the Bible, not in English translation in order to learn how to marshal prooftexts in the manner of American ministers in preceding centuries, but in the "original" languages. Professor Stuart stood at the head of those contesting the scholarly hegemony of the Harvard liberals who had initiated philological and historical study of Scripture.[25] Although there may have been some original hope that such study would reunify Christianity under the banner of Christ the messiah, with diminished attention to the Old Testament themes of vengeance and sin, biblical criticism became little more than a pawn in battles over the Trinity. At the time of his call to Andover in 1810 Stuart knew relatively little about his field (such appointments were not uncommon), but he loved the professorial role, taught himself thoroughly in both ancient languages and German, published vastly, and became one of the most erudite biblical scholars in America.

A modern historian, while praising Stuart's thorough scholarship, criticizes his inablility to examine evidence or weigh hypotheses foreign to the Andover line. Jerry Wayne Brown also explains Stuart's failure to have more lasting influence by noting his repeated insistence that the Bible was totally consistent with orthodox doctrines and that its truths were confirmed by common sense. Why, then, bother to learn difficult languages and master arid scholarship? What appears a shortcoming in our day, however, was a virtue in Stuart's own. "It requires a fusion of a German and American to constitute a perfect scriptural expositor," said one of his pupils (who was Wright's colleague in the Essex County ministry) in describing Stuart. The mentor possessed two qualities hard to combine: "unlimited latitude of inquiry, in conjunction with the most childlike and humble deference to the authority of Scripture." This was praise, not satire. Stuart's life was seen as refuting the charge of incompatibility between "orthodox opinions" and "freedom of research." Presumably he encouraged students to imitate his "mind so bold, and yet so childlike, so free, and yet so acquiescent in just and rational authority."[26]

Nevertheless, his partner Leonard Woods reported that "for several years previous to 1825" the trustees and outside "religious community" were "disturbed . . . by the degree of attention which students gave to the writings of lax and infidel writers and commentators, and by the unhappy effect which had, already, in some instances, been produced upon the religious opinions of individuals." The trustees appointed an investigating committee, whose report was adopted. After noting that modern German theological studies generally "impugned the miracles of Scripture, its peculiar doctrines, at large, and even its claims to a Divine Inspiration," the report admitted their superior standing "on many points of science and literature, of philosophy and natural history" and agreed that they "impart, to the biblical student, much valuable information." It was especially unfortunate that students encountered these studies during their first year, since that was the period of concentration on the Bible. "If in the familiar and ardent perusal of those writings," the report continued, "the most matured and informed minds have sometimes been shaken, not to say contaminated and poisoned, it cannot surely be expected that minds comparatively immature and unfurnished, should pass through the process without injury." Indeed, the faculty had been candid that "in various instances, the unrestrained cultivation of German studies has evidently tended to chill the ardor of piety, to impair the belief in the fundamentals of revealed religion, and even to induce, for the time, an approach to universal scepticism." The remedy entailed more caution in using German authorities, more frequent reminders from the faculty of the dangers of books on their reading lists, and the development of new study aids free from Teutonic infection but saving what was useful from those quarters.[27]

Possibly Henry Wright was one of the victims of careless reading lists that worried the committee; in any case, this episode suggests larger dimensions of his crisis at Andover. It reveals the shaky foundations of orthodox learning long before the assaults of Billy Sunday and Elmer Gantry. If Stuart had no difficulty in being both widely curious and childishly submissive, Wright's was one of those "unfurnished" minds for whom intellectual training was subversive. He simply could not reconcile new methods and old beliefs any more than the young transcendentalists at Harvard could be faithful to both continental scholarship and their Unitarian fathers. Like Wright, Ralph Waldo Emerson and George Ripley proceeded from their tutelage in higher criticism to the argument that humankind required no teachers or gospels other than the intuitions all persons shared. Like Wright's, their teachers favored an educational perspective that was somewhat cosmopolitan, but not too much; it was a hard line to draw. The episode at Andover typified the jittery reception of European culture in America. It was one of many little shocks out of which an American orthodoxy was created.[28]

Wright was impressed by Stuart's teaching of hermeneutics, the science of interpreting language rather than bowing to whims of sect or party. He read German commentators and developed a "passion for the Hebrew language." So profoundly did his first-year studies affect his approach to life that he continued until 1843 to translate a passage from Greek and another from Hebrew in his journal every day before any other comments or reflections. He enjoyed Stuart and complimented his ability to transmit zeal for his subject. Yet he wrote that Stuart's character would have "peculiarly fitted" him to a criminal career! It was exciting to be near a Byronic figure, fearless, surviving without settled principles; but too often students recognized that their teacher's opinions were unsettled. One day he would present a viewpoint or author as "unquestionable"; the next he would ridicule that position and give another as "undoubted." This kind of biblical study introduced Wright to linguistic pleasure and spiritual doubt.[29]

Why was biblical study dangerous? What did it have to do with unsettled principles? Perhaps Wright was headed for crisis in any case, and perhaps Stuart's personality had the uncommitted quality that remains an academic stereotype. But the answer went beyond personality. As historians know only too well, it was not only in religion that German critical methods imperiled the confidence they were supposed to shore up. The influential historian Leopold von Ranke believed "diplomatics" and other methods of closely scrutinizing documents would lead to scientific accounts of past actuality, but one consequence was the realization that historical truth, no matter how scrupulously one studies texts, can scarcely be detached from subjectivity. The resulting "crisis of relativism" still leaves lingering echoes in the historical profession. Similarly, in biblical studies it was hard to sustain the balance sought by Stuart and the Andover trustees: to take the historical and linguistic methods of German scholars but to eschew the "innovations" in theology associated with them. Once one entertained suspicions that certain parts of the Bible were apocryphal, added at different times, varying in literal meaning, distorted by the customs of the culture in which they were composed, or in any other way relative to language, time, and culture, then it was awkward to insist that the gospel was a canon of God existing outside human limitations. For all of Stuart's fidelity to orthodoxy, it is no surprise that one of his most passionate students should have come to believe, after a period of confusion and doubt, that the only reliable revelation was given inwardly to everyone and that all men and women must measure the Bible against their personal convictions.

The idea that students could use new methods while leaving old beliefs unchanged was nonsense. How could one's attitude toward the Bible differ from the uses made of it and operations performed on it? Ends are reflected in means, meanings in forms, beliefs in actions. The Bible, on the day when Wright arrived at Andover, was the awesome book his father read aloud in his childhood home, irrespective of significance or understanding; even the long lists of *begats* in the Old Testament were holy. It existed in familiar English, heard everywhere in the same words. Things could be proved from it, and one's attitude toward it could be a test of worth. This was the book the apprentice Henry read alone in the heat of the Norwich revival, and about which Mrs. Snow had confided her feelings. Under Stuart's instruction, the Bible became a book in foreign languages which the student rendered into English with careful attention to the linguistic and historical obstacles to exact translation. Furthermore, students were expected to justify veneration of the Bible despite problems of authenticity and internal consistency by using the same methods they would apply to any other controversial text. The Bible now became an object, the scholar an agent. Like any other text from an alien culture, it might even require a suspension of judgment. Wright began his Andover commonplace book with Hume's motto, "Judge not the conduct of one age by the maxims of another"—a far cry from his struggles in the revival to rise above culture with the Bible's aid![30]

Stuart's course at least strengthened Wright's growing confidence in his own literacy, even if it endangered his rustic veneration of Scripture. The study of Christian doctrine under Professor Woods brought mainly torment and self-doubt, as his notebooks constantly reveal. The trouble was not that he was given sceptical writers to read, for he judged their arguments as "futile" as the theologians' defenses of God. But his teacher's insistence that God could not be understood in ordinary, familiar terms disturbed him. The simple act of making the existence of God a question to be settled by human reasoning contradicted all the experience he brought to Andover. In one hour's lecture, he wrote, Woods demolished all the arguments on which his belief in God was based; the new arguments Woods supplied were unconvincing. Meanwhile he was assigned the gamut of authors from sceptics to Catholics as he devised his own proofs of God's existence. On January 1, 1820, he wrote in his notebook concerning two of Woods's lectures on God: "So far as his arguments go, as addressed to my *intellect*, he has made an *atheist of me*. My *Head* is an atheist; my Heart cannot be. God is *Love*, not *Logic;* is a *Heart* & not a *Head*—experience." This formulation, which had sources in the revival, now helped him endure his studies; it was a formulation he would never forget. God is "a law of life," he wrote, "to each one what he conceives him to be."[31]

Wright was apparently undismayed by the relativistic implications of this view. He quickly rejected the theologians' view that the existence of God could be inferred from the fact of the creation but that man could have no direct acquaintance of God. Instead of theology he began to praise—as early as 1820—what he called anthropology. This term had none of its later associations with the study of non-

Western peoples, even though Andover's missionaries frequently brought home reminders of cultural diversity. Anthropology was little more than a word coined in contrast to theology, and Wright probably assumed that the most important human characteristics were universal and constant.

His notebook covers are coated with antitheological scrawls. "Theology is the way to hell[,] leading down to the chambers of death," one of them begins. "It is hell-fire—where there is weeping & wailing & gnashing of teeth. At least I have gnashed mine here." The back cover of the same notebook announces: "The true theology is Anthropology. The science of man is the science of God. He who best knows, loves, respects man—best knows, loves, & honors God. To love man with all the soul is to love God with all the soul. To hate man is to hate God. Let the professors say what they will, this I say in the Lecture room in 1821. There sits Doctor Woods. What would he say were he to see it? I [reckon?] it will [blow] his theology to the moon." Another notebook denounces the "theological God" as a "Monster—a Phantom," and goes on: "Poor Philosophy! I pity her," for she is "at war with the facts of human existence."[32]

Taking notes afforded a private control over what he was taught. Some of Woods's remarks on divine powers were set down as "a humbug." "God never operates on mind or matter except in a natural way—according to fixed laws. Dr. Woods may speculate about decrees and divine influences, it is only by the operation of natural laws, not by miracle, that God regulates the physical and natural universe."[33] Sometimes Wright showed the independence—even the cockiness—of a self-educated, older student testing his powers.

More often, Wright's notes on anthropology and natural law originated in anguish. He was critical of his inability to agree with Woods, whom he deeply admired. The front of his first notebook for 1821 reads: "Woods is a man." Thirteen years later he wrote his professor a letter professing gratitude for his help and apologizing for being a problem. Showing no sign of anthropological defiance, he simply said he had adopted a doubting spirit for purposes of study and lost his faith temporarily.[34]

It was perplexing to question his own orthodoxy, although one notebook asserted a trifle too bravely: "Don't be afraid, for it is an honerable [*sic*] thing to be downright, good honest *Heretic*." On another occasion he wrote that Spinoza had been denounced as an atheist after asserting "that God & the universe were the same thing." Wright called himself a hypocritical liar because of a sermon he had given. On another cover he stated: "some men's heads are like a hemlock swamp Just in the edge of evening. Wonderful dark." Then he added:

> Your brains are muddy,
> If you did but know it
> I'm sure you would be less dogmatick.[35]

This was not the spirit in which he had accepted help from friends in Hartwick to come to the seminary. This was a sad departure from the unflinching missionary role he had described to his juvenile correspondent. These anxieties explain why he took a year off before returning to Andover for his senior year.

His flirtation with anthropology, his view of himself as a heretic, his confused looks into his "muddy" unconscious—these signs of trouble appear mainly on the covers and in the margins of his notebooks. They furnish a counterpoint to his lecture notes and essay drafts, which seldom point ahead to his later beliefs. But even these pages were not easily done. At one point he congratulated himself on escaping Woods's review of his essay on regeneration with little more than ridicule, "at least with an unbroken head." He was overjoyed to finish an assignment on the Lord's Supper: "I have done,—done,—*done;* the whole, *all alone, alone, alone.* My strength is weak, my patience, gone—For I this work have done alone—!!!!" Despite such edgy asides, however, the body of his notebooks suggests an earnest effort to make sense of Christian doctrine for himself, not to place himself outside it. When his biblical studies turned up no reason to believe in the Trinity, for example, he observed that it was "important to believe it, not because I can see its use, but because it is revealed."[36]

Wright had no trouble, furthermore, with the version of psychology he was given at Andover. Although men spoke of various properties of the soul as if they were distinct faculties—reason, understanding, will, conscience, feeling—the student disavowed the existence of a faculty as "something which is antecedent to actions." It was, rather, the observation of mental actions that led men to speak of these attributes as faculties. Moral principles, similarly, did not have real existence but were attributes which men classed under one heading. According to Woods, even the basic distinction "between moral & natural attributes does not exist in fact, but from considering the tendency of some action we make the distinction."[37]

This kind of Lockean empiricism was rampant in the New England orthodoxy, which derived so much of what passed for philosophical wisdom from the writings of Jonathan Edwards. Its distinctions made it possible to reconcile morally inevitable sins with the natural ability not to sin; they provided rules for inferring the attributes of the Creator from the variety of nature; and they made religion consonant with the protocols of science. On the other hand, these intellectual procedures harbored threats of relativism as yet scarcely seen. What guarantee was there that all persons were furnished the same perceptions and would subscribe to the same classifications of attributes? For the most part theologians soft-pedaled this question by asserting, despite the absence of faculties or independently verifiable moral truths, the certainty of self-evident laws, such as the golden rule and the sum of two plus two. Only in a manner of speaking did conscience decide the former and reason the latter; they were identical mental acts "put forth toward different objects," as Wright jotted down in his notebook. The appeal to "consciousness" or intuition that upheld these laws was a Scottish elaboration of Locke's discussion of "reflection," and because it gave indisputable status to moral as well as logical principles this elaboration dominated American orthodox circles.[38]

In 1834 Wright chanced to travel by stage with Dr. Woods, and the two men had a good talk on the same old subject. They examined the folly of trying to prove what Wright loosely called "innate truths—or truths resulting from our constitution—by a process of reasoning." Some examples were "free agency, dependence on God, the existence of God, immortality of the soul, sin against God," each of which was "an elementary principle of our nature—resulting, not from any process of reasoning—but from *instinct* or from our constitution." It followed that "the child of 2 years old knows as much about free agency as the greatest Philosopher—& more—because its feelings are not perverted. The more clear & distinct a man's feeling of dependence—the more perfectly will he feel himself a free agent." Here was a charming portrait of teacher and student concurring in the most pejorative view of academic discourse. It shows how the psychology taught at Andover reinforced appeals to the feelings such as Mrs. Snow used in urging him to accept the gospel and how it aggravated conflicts between head and heart that were axiomatic in the revival.[39]

Neither Wright nor Woods was much of a technical philosopher, and the Edwardsean system by their day had more ideological significance than analytic sharpness. Their opinions and terminology were crude but functional. The psychological views they shared fit well with evangelical religion's admonition to young people to explore their hearts and embrace the emotional truths of Christianity. These views, though adopted from Scotland and the Continent, easily corresponded to rhetorical occasions when republican Americans paid homage to the moral discriminations of farmers and simple folk (without detracting from the merits of those who succeeded at college). This psychological system could splinter off into romantic idealism and radicalism, and many studies of American intellectual history have discovered a succession of nineteenth-century idealists and mavericks—a succession in which Henry Wright has his place. But that is a history of unintended consequences. The ideological purpose of the psychological system in which Wright was trained was the control of instinctive forces by society. The psychology of "the heart"—which was both a personal and collective attribute—melted away sharp distinctions between autonomy and control by others, and it did so under the aegis of natural law and "instinctive" truth. The religious psychology of Andover offered Wright the opportunity to dispose of the issues of evil motivation and inexorable death which he carried as his individual burden. It invited him to merge his individual feelings into the interests of Protestant America.

Wright's notebooks reveal his intense desire for order and dislike of conflict. He deplored the crusades as vicious wars glossed over with holy talk. The controversies and warfare of seventeenth-century England drew the simple comment that if all sides had sincerely tried to make "a christian conduct & orderly life the bond of union," there would have been no bloodshed. (The pacifist Wright added at this point: "Good. Monday Sept. 6, 1849—though written in 1820–1.") He preferred Melanchthon to Luther, because the former was gentler, less inclined to fight out points that could never be settled, less dogmatic on difficult passages of Scripture. It was unpleasant to observe that some controversies—over free will, original sin, God's role in regeneration—had vexed the church for fifteen hundred years and were still raging. And not a ray of light had been shed on them, so blinding was man's combative spirit, no matter how piously disguised. Christians, he reflected, should restrain their taste for controversy because it results in "unfriendly feelings & a disunion of all the bonds of social intercourse."[40]

These student attempts to deny belligerent feelings play off ironically against his subsequent radicalism. "The more ridiculous anything is the more important it appears to the mind [of] an enthusiast," he wrote of the Anabaptists. Their folly extended to the notions that the church should be "exempt from sin," that every Christian was rightfully a preacher, and that civil government was unnecessary. Why wouldn't they retract ideas that were so obviously pernicious? "It must be accounted for [by] a principle common to our nature; that the more we become attached to them; & the more important they appear."[41]

The goal of submerging combative feelings sometimes made a pre-Lockean faculty psychology more attractive than the modern views espoused in the lecture hall. It tempted him to lower the value of emotionality. He would have liked, in old-fashioned terms, to impose restraints on the imagination and delegate power to the reason so that the passions might be directed wisely and the will might receive good counsel. But that was nearly impossible for a man whose heart was changed in a revival and who was learning psychology in the school of Jonathan Edwards. He was obliged, a bit sadly, to accept limitations on man's ability to rise above nature and history. For a good illustration of his dilemma, consider his notes on Bishop Bossuet, whose rationalism he admired, and Madame Guyon, whose pretensions to supernatural guidance Bossuet denounced. Guyon and her followers exemplified "the influence of feeling in forming religious opinions" and thus raised the danger "that every one, who felt any thing to be true; i.e. was prejudiced in its favour, embraced it as an article of faith." Wright continued:

> We should be surprised, if we know how much, not only enthusiastic, but men of clear & enlightened minds, are influenced by this feeling. Not a few at the present day interpret Scripture, more by feeling than by just principles of *reason*. As it is impossible to convince a man of defects in an object that he deeply loves; so neither can a man be convinced of the falseness of a doctrine to which he is strongly attached. . . . It is a principle of our nature that arguments have the greatest influence when they are on the side of the affections; & orators know how to take advantage of it.

Religion and morality were in a "sad predicament" on account of their dependence on "whims and passion," but the fact was undeniable.[42]

The Quakers, of course, welcomed the influence of the feelings. In addition, overtures had been made to the feelings in New England's hallowed past: Cotton Mather had delighted in spiritual meditations, and Jonathan Edwards had praised the "sense of the heart" as a sixth sense heightening the saint's appreciation of traces of God in the universe. As Wright browsed over these examples, they suggested a universal religious trait, just as the Quakers said. The same "spiritual feeling" for which Mather was esteemed could be imitated by "an Arab or South American Negro, if they would turn their thoughts inward a moment." Introspection intensified feeling and diminished attention to "sensible objects," but Wright resisted its allure (and for the time being resisted racial egalitarianism too). "Let those who prefer such abstract meditation pursue it, but let my heart be warmed with the incomparable loveliness of nature; with the exhibitions of Divinity in his works & words; with sympathizing with my fellows, & studying their passions and conduct."[43]

Wright's later career followed that course quite faithfully. In his life the evangelical tradition led toward the scientific study of man and a carefully contrived appreciation of nature, always honoring the practical over the ecstatic. Although his feeling of being alone with God was intense, and although he stressed individual liberation, he was in fact always concerned that his thoughts appear useful to man in the aggregate. He frequently stopped for introspection and appealed to consciousness, but only so long as it took to prove socially useful propositions. It was easier for him to accept Edwards's interest in general human nature than his followers' invocations to explore private feelings. And he balked at their fundamental tenet—the belief that sin was synonymous with the human predicament and that virtue remained outside the sphere of human relations. He was more suited to a view of man bound in society and striving for "self-abnegation" by identifying with particular others.

To understand his student musings on sin, it is necessary to recall the disturbed feelings about mother's disappearance, brothers' deaths, and father's anger that he brought from home. The first entry in his first notebook, a meditation on man's fated return to dust in consequence of Adam's sin, raised those memories to the foreground. He pictured death not as a blessed haven but "an unhappy gloom." In his vision he enters a cemetery and points to the grave of a seventy-year-old man, once proud and handsome but now "putrid & loathesome." Next he sees a young man cut off before he had time for God. As his "kindred youth," Wright pauses before the "breathless corps[e]" and observes how ugly it is. "I call, and would convers[e] with thee, but no voice responds to my call." (In later years the spiritualist Wright interpolated, "I am sure thou dost" hear.)

Approaching the grave of a baby, once briefly loved by all but now decayed, Wright grasps the reality of his own doom, but he protests: "Oh my God why is it that I must groan & gasp & die?" Then he surveys "with horror" the future prison below earth, resembling a cave, its inhabitants cold and speechless, where "no genial ray of yonder Seminary" can penetrate. Death weighed so heavily on his mind as he began his studies that he heard a voice announcing he would soon join the horrid specters in the subterranean world where there were no wars or social distinctions. He prayed for strength to remember the inevitability of death, strength which would "wean" him from "this worthless world."[44]

Years later, as he traveled the Midwest as an expert on maternity, Wright denied the reality of death and the need for exculpation. The body, he taught, housed its own sources of preservation. At Andover, however, Wright depended on a more traditional religion of the Father for courage to face death and comprehend the guilt he felt so strongly. If Andover had offered an undiluted Calvinism, it might, temporarily at least, have found a willing devotee. But the vacillations of Andover's Calvinism served him poorly, as is evident from his notes on "divine decrees" for individuals and nations—what we would call predestination. In the margins he rejects this doctrine as part of the claptrap of theology, but his adult negations, as in so many other cases, cannot hide his youthful struggles to assent.

The power of God was one of those ancient controversial questions that Andover straddled, thereby leaving one student confused and uneasy. The great divines, including Calvin, believed in predestination, while more recently "verry [*sic*] able theologians" dismissed it for encouraging "absolute fatallity" (*sic*) instead of moral exertions. No doubt close study of the Bible would clarify the issue, but predestination held too much personal significance to be left to hermeneutics and reasoned analysis. And so Wright turned to his own consciousness rather than the Bible:

> When we consider the evils which befall mankind & which it is impossible to avoid, that man must sicken, groan, & die; that the fury of the elements are [*sic*] let loose for his destruction, that the earth opens her ponderous jaws to swallow up *Cities,* & that the raging pestilence converts fine and populous Countries into places of dessolation [*sic*] & solitude, the reflection that all these, though apparently unnecessary, are ordered by infinite *Wisdom* & goodness, satisfies all our doubts & puts to rest all our anxieties.

> Though now things appear in confusion, & contrary to what we deem our happiness; when we consider this doctrine; we can say to ourselves; wait patiently for all will be well.[45]

Remodeled theories of evil and benevolence, however impressive to the faculty, took away the cold comfort one student gained by thinking all adversity was willed from above. Under the new theories personal "anxieties" were less easily explained, and individual propensities to sin could not be attenuated by analogies with the plight of kingdoms.

Wright's notebooks include numerous scenes of a student floundering over the distinctions of Edwardsean theology, grappling with a system that did not hold together very successfully. It was puzzling to view man as a free agent, yet without control over his decisions. "Dr. Woods thinks the mind is as really a machine as a *clock*," he wrote with a trace of incredulity; "the one he calls a physical machine, the other a moral. The mind is under the controul of certain laws; as much as a clock." Woods also held that man depended on God for "the continuance, as well as for the beginning of our existence," lest the metaphor of the clock should suggest that man held the slightest autonomy. Nevertheless, man was a free responsible agent whose conversion depended on human exertions (even though Woods thought it "best to preach up the doctrine of general dependence"). No doubt other students, dulled by years in college, had fewer questions and jotted down their notes with fewer signs of uneasiness. But Wright, with his rural earnestness, could not bypass the most vexing questions of Protestant faith—why was there evil in the world? was not an omnipotent God really its author?—and his jumbled answers revealed how slippery Edwardsean categories had become. He admitted, to be sure, that "God, in some sense, is the *cause* of the actions of our minds" and thus, to some degree, "the cause why creatures have broken their conversion to him." But turning to consciousness, as he always did at a sticking-point, he could trace the evil in his own thoughts no farther than his own agency and thus he regarded man as "the author of moral evil." Accordingly, the existence of evil could not be blamed on God.[46]

The learned approach to benevolence was similarly troublesome. Despite the many secularizing influences on Andover, the theologians exposed their students to Jonathan Edwards's portrayal of divine goodness in abstract, aesthetic terms: God watched over the beauty of all creation in a way that was invisible to ordinary human eyes. The student Wright, however, simply posited in his notebook that God's benevolence expressed itself in concern for "the happiness of his creatures"—a utilitarian inference which might have been drawn from lectures on Hopkins and which afforded welcome reassurance of paternal love. Wright was even less pleased with the received definition of the saints' benevolence. Edwards had taught that affections, to be counted virtuous, must extend to being-in-general rather than persons to whom we are attached, but Wright simply noted that he was "not satisfied" with this low estimation of private affections.[47] In time this discordant emphasis on the creatures' happiness gave heart to a new religion of which Wright was an ardent apostle, a religion that stressed affectionate relationships—real or fantasized—and virtually dethroned the heavenly Father. Through the scribbled exclamations in his notebook, Wright shows something more than the moodiness of an exceptional student, more than the contradictory strains to which Calvinism was repeatedly subject. In his notebooks we see premonitions of new evaluations of creature comforts and familial emotions that gave a different shape to American culture.

Despite the careful checks and balances in Andover's constitution, most of Wright's teachers favored Hopkinsian theology. The student plainly was taught that Adam's sin was not "imputed" to all subsequent persons, as the Westminster Catechism would have it, but that sin followed historically unavoidable, endlessly repeated, freely willed choices. This view alleviated the resentment of Adam's and his parents' bad faith that had tortured him on the eve of his rebirth. Although sin remained inescapable, it provided a logical exculpation of human nature that could be psychologically important. In any case, Wright's protests against the aridity of theology referred to the picky distinctions that Woods and Stuart wielded rather than to the issues of guilt and death they addressed. If it really could have lightened the burden of original sin and infant damnation, Hopkinsian Andover would have been a happier place.

When contemplating the powers of God Wright leaned toward the comforts of strict, old-fashioned views, but when the time came to study human nature he was open to a more generous theology. He disliked President Porter's orthodox argument that Adam did not have a sinful nature and therefore might have avoided sin while our incapacity to avoid sin, distinguishing us from him, indicates that our nature is sinful. Was this not an invalid inference of attributes from acts? Woods's view made better sense: "man has no depravity antecedent to actions; . . . his mind must act before he can be guilty."

From this standpoint Adam's sin was just like ours, only happening to be the first in "a course of conduct" that we continue. Since "moral circumstances" were worse in modern times than in Adam's, Wright reflected, our sins were more understandable. Certainly it was "ridiculous" to say that we "derive from Adam a moral taint & infection" and foolish to think nothing else explained the bad conduct of children except that sin was "infused" into them. Wright's conclusions on whether dead infants went to heaven or hell cannot be deciphered. It is unlikely he thought they went to hell, but until he disposed of his conventional images of heaven and hell as actual places, inhabited by ghosts, the question was inevitably painful.[48]

How was sin forgiven? The Andoverites' answer to this crucial question raised further puzzles. Unlike Unitarians they insisted on Christ's essential role in the process of redemption, and unlike Universalists they denied that all men were saved in Christ. Christ's death was not a sacrifice to propitiate a wrathful God, but Wright found it hard to distinguish the professors' teachings from this pagan image. Christ's suffering could be regarded as meeting God's requirements as moral governor of the universe. When Professor Murdock took this ground and proceeded to argue that the atonement took effect through moral decisions on the part of individual men and women, he was fired; he went too far toward the Unitarians' demotion of Christ and faith in man. Yet it was hard to see how Murdock's theory of atonement varied from some conceptions of history and psychology nourished at Andover. When Professor Woods averred that sin could not be forgiven on the basis of repentance, for that would undermine God's sovereignty, Wright balked: he doubted the "good old Dr" could demonstrate his case.[49] He paid too close attention to Hopkinsian lectures to assent to this feeble reassertion of the independent majesty of God.

It is doubtful that Woods persuaded many students to downplay moral choices and repentant feelings. Most of Wright's future colleagues in the benevolent empire of evangelical Protestantism shared a sense of mission that led them to talk in terms of earthly laws and human sentiments. Although few imitated Wright's hostile attitude toward the theology of Andover or scoffed at its efforts to fuse eighteenth- and nineteenth-century outlooks, he was not alone in stretching the elastic notions of benevolence and morality taught there and emphasizing that God's government legislated by the people and for the people.

Wright's years at Andover covered painful conflicts that he characterized as warfare between head and heart, between theology and anthropology. In part his problems were familiar ones of students in young manhood. He was overwhelmed by a combination of long study hours, brooding introspection, and anxiety to make good. In part his problems followed inevitably after the leap from a frontier conversion to an academic course of study, particularly one in which God's existence became a problem in logic and Scripture the basis for linguistic exercises. These problems were exacerbated by the uncertain compromises wearing down nineteenth-century Calvinism, despite the vigilance with which Andover reminded students of heretical pitfalls. These years were filled with promise, of course, as well as problems. The heterodox voices of anthropology—of natural laws arising from society and confirmed by his consciousness—unified much of his life's work. The academic side of Andover—its intuitive psychology, its rehabilitation of human nature—proved to have the enduring strength of an orthodoxy, while the theological structure, which the professors hoped to modernize, dwindled in importance.

But that was not clear at once. Intolerance for theological disputes was hardly unusual among practicing ministers, their studies behind them, and Wright managed to suppress the heretical side of his Andover conflicts fairly effectively for the next dozen years. In one Andover notebook he had looked forward to the way in which professional responsibilities carry men beyond their youthful turmoil: after probing inconsistencies between God-given grace and the all too human excitement of revivals, he reflected, "it is well for us that our speculative notions & doubts do not have much influence on our conduct; & that difficulties, started in the cloister, vanish in active life."[50]

Wright left Andover after his second year, supporting himself as a schoolteacher in Newburyport. Then he returned in 1822–23 for most of his senior year, though withdrawing near the end. Such moves were not unusual, since the seminary did not award a degree; and Wright clearly was given good credentials and recommendations. He took various temporary pastorates in New Hampshire. After marrying a Newburyport widow he served a church in nearby West Newbury as a supply preacher until receiving a formal call to that pulpit. There had been *Sturm und Drang* in his Andover days and nights, but the institution had not failed to turn a rather ill-prepared young man into a learned clergyman. It conducted him toward an active life where the anxieties of the cloister would vanish.

In his safe, orthodox position Wright sometimes perused his student notebooks on the divinity of Christ, human depravity, and the atonement—the notebooks on which my analysis is based. Some of his words he obliterated; more often, he repealed old phrases with new comments in the margins, acknowledging "with shame that my mind was captious. . . . I know my heart & mind were not in a proper state to investigate the subject." His was a variorum life, however, and later on the reformer Wright laced the same pages with applause for whatever pacifistic or anticlerical substance they yielded.[51] These glosses overlaid the tension between margin and text that had characterized his notebooks when first written. Wright could never succeed in making the rich, tangled meanings of his Andover experience lead to a single conclusion.

Professional Priest

Henry Wright returned to family ground in New York for the formalities certifying his new status. Although there were ludicrous aspects to his examination by ministers whose proficiencies, especially in languages, were inferior to those he had reached at Andover, nonetheless his "License to Preach" from the Hartwick Presbytery obviously meant a great deal. He was not required to go back there to get it, and he never lost the sheet on which it was written. Besides certifying his education, the license said he had experimental knowledge of religion, a good character, and orthodox beliefs.[52]

New England was the actual scene of his ministry, which was one of the calmest, least eventful periods of his life. He described himself in West Newbury as a bookish minister, determined to spend much time studying and little on house calls. The fruits of long hours at his desk still exist—copious manuscripts on the Book of Job and the Hebrew Prophets, for example, formal treatises that came close to research for its own sake and that could scarcely have edified the farming village he served. His love of languages also was apparent when he translated Virgil and Ovid with his children. By polishing the linguistic abilities in which he had been schooled, he could leave other seminary subjects behind him. He wanted his congregation to regard him not as a Calvinist, Hopkinsian, or Arminian, but rather as a man preaching the gospel as he understood it.[53]

This bookish flexibility may have served him well. Despite the anticlerical fulminations of his later years, it is clear that his flock appreciated his manner and that he was comfortable as a pastor. He gave almost no signs of impatience or intransigence in this role until 1832, when he began to thirst again for a missionary post.

There was some controversy preceding his ordination. According to Wright's account, on the day he was ordained a council of ministers from churches near West Newbury questioned him on religious and scriptural points. The council deliberated a long time because some felt his views on regeneration leaned too heavily toward good works. Since the town was already assembled for his installation, the ministers were caught up short by the reflection that, whatever they said, the people were going to have him as a minister anyway. Another account, written by a West Newbury successor who disliked Wright, substantiates this point: the council was swayed by evidence that "the people had set their hearts upon him." The same account reveals that his chief opponent was Rev. Luther Dimmick, in whose house he had boarded during his year away from Andover, who had been his wife's minister, and who officiated at his wedding. Since his opponent knew Wright very well, it is unlikely that mistrust arose solely from his answers to the council. When the church members voted on the new pastor, there was only one negative. Dimmick maintained that even this token dissent gave the council enough pretext to refuse Wright; "but as this member was a poor man, and as all the wealthy and influential in the Parish were in favor of the settlement the objection was not made."[54] Perhaps this comment means that his wife's standing in nearby Newburyport saved Wright some conflict.

Even the later jaundiced account praises the successful relationship Wright developed with his congregation. "It would seem that he did not concern himself most with theological questions but preferred preaching in an easy familiar manner upon the duties of common life. His social hearty intercourse with the children & his interest in the schools completely enlisted their affections; and through them, he found access to the hearts of such parents as might perhaps secretly mourn for more of the substantial food, wh[ich] the gospel provides. All seem to have loved and esteemed him." Wright, who frequently credited his pastoral experience with teaching him that children were the most "influential" part of the community, would surely have been cheered if he knew of this narrative of his years in West Newbury.[55]

His success was still more remarkable because the church had been in serious decline. In an earlier day it was large and important: Leonard Woods preached in West Newbury before Andover called him, and the village was the prospective site of the seminary before the Phillips Academy adopted it. But membership had dwindled to twenty, only six of whom were males, when Wright settled there.

The situation was ripe for a revival, as his jealous successor reported. "Mr. Wright's susseptable [*sic*] spirit being enlisted" by news of awakenings in other Essex County villages, he energetically carried on "the work wh[ich] was operating in the hearts of many of his flock. . . . [T]he instincts & early impressions of his mind & heart favoring, he was ready to help all such as were inquiring how they might be made better & do better; and in 1831 & 2 seventy four were added to the church. Eighty-eight, received during his ministry [into the church] have for 30 years proved themselves to be emenently [*sic*] worthy." Not only did membership grow under his tenure, but also many institutions of the church—especially the sabbath school—were put on a firm basis.[56]

After Wright's departure the First Church of West Newbury sank back into its problems. The next minister, also an Andover man, preached "after the old models" and hard Bible doctrines; parishioners protested his ordination and opposition remained intense until he resigned. Unfavorable comparisons with his predecessor must have been a grating experience, though a familiar hazard of the profession. Observers began to wonder whether an orthodox man could survive in West Newbury, and "some of the fathers in the ministry felt great anxiety lest this church should be controlled by another faith." It lost members and finances and went pastorless for seven years. From this antipathetic account, it is clear that Wright was justified in thinking of himself as a bulwark of evangelicalism against Unitarian heresy, even if his doctrinal soundness was suspect in his own camp.[57]

In spite of controversy and suspicion, as long as Wright resided in West Newbury, he enjoyed meetings with brother clergymen and the chances they provided to emulate the habits and values of his Andover teachers. Wright was host at more than his share of the periodic gatherings when the Essex North Association of Congregational ministers met for public religious observances and *in camera* scholarly discussions. As one of the most active participants, he read dissertations on Hebrew tenses, Augustine's controversy with Pelagius, Philo the Jew, and other esoteric subjects. Years later, when his ex-colleagues called him a heretic and even an imbecile, they conceded his abilities as "a good Hebrew scholar." Probably few others kept up their linguistic training so adamantly as Wright. There is every reason to believe they were sorry to see him quit the county for a larger arena. For his part, though he eventually denounced the "priesthood," he seldom criticized its collegial, scholarly side.[58]

The strains beneath this good life were apparent during a curious 1828 trip "to rest from my ministerial labors." In Rhode Island he visited scenes from Indian warfare and romantic fiction, mused on his taste for dark forests and craggy rocks, and jotted down Byronic reflections on the romantic side of his nature, entrapped within his profession, that "sympathizes with any thing terrific, daring, desperate, and energetic." But travel appears to have allayed resentment that his smooth transition into the ministry had stifled a reckless, exuberant inner self. While recalling an old prophecy that he was destined for a roaming life, he found himself glad to get home to parish, family, and pets.[59] There is no other evidence of personal crisis during his ministry.

Some parishioners complained, several years later, of their minister's harshness during a season of revivals, and Wright agreed he was less "liberal" than before. We should make no mistake on this point: he had always detested the "liberal" contentions of Unitarians. But he had followed the decision of many other ministers in an era of ecclesiastical conflict that it was best not to push too hard on divisive doctrines. The revival aroused his sense of a pastor's obligation to chastize his flock even at the cost of their friendship: he exposed the ruses of postponed conversion.[60]

In other words, besides avoiding vexatious dogmas, his ministry lived up to positive goals, including the personal desire to be earnest, useful, and independent. He also was concerned to obey God, notwithstanding recent struggles at Andover where God nearly receded into private consciousness. As a minister, who had the power to conduct revivals, Wright restored the faith he had experienced by the Chenango River, bobbing up and down until he finally knelt in obedient prayer. An 1829 journal entry spoke of waking up at three, walking by the Merrimack River, and crying into the void that he was a child who wished to be nearer his "kind Father." Confined on earth, where he could see only himself and other creatures, he was desperate for the sight of God. During his ministry this scheme of values warned against excessive attachments to other people and held in check his student passion for anthropology.[61]

The minister's secular responsibilities have been previously recounted.[62] Rev. Henry Wright conducted numerous activities showing more regard for social order than for an unmediated glance at an otherworldly God. But in temperance work, lyceum building, supervision of education, and other programs of social improvement, ministers like Wright denied that their attention wandered from God to man. Indeed, by imposing order and winning the loyalty of children they longed to find authority to censor secular tendencies in society. When Unitarians infiltrated the school system (as the ministers saw it), the message was obvious: serviceable public institutions might prove indifferent to worship of God. Wright's response was to attack "infidels" and mobilize parents to demand the centrality of Christ in their children's education.[63] This issue, ironically enough, turned out to be Wright's bridge away from the clergy and toward reform, first in the cause of sabbath schools, then in causes that were steadily more secular. Protest against secularization turned out to be a form of accommodation.

There is considerable evidence of the routines filling Wright's clerical life, from guiding a revival to officiating at weddings, from founding a lyceum or temperance society to composing treatises on history or Scripture. Except for occasional remarks on God's invisibility, however, we have few indications of his religious beliefs and feelings in the years after he left Andover. It is as though a search had been suspended. As he had hoped, release from the cloister and the Congregationalist strategy of avoiding offensive doctrines helped him revive the naive faith of his youth. But this suspended search, welcome enough in the short run, appeared different in retrospect when his quest for his authentic self resumed and the ministry appeared to be little more than a paid role. Subsequent visits to his old haunts awakened unpleasant memories of days when religion was "too much a matter of *profession*" and he was "a paid, proud, and ambitious, professional priest."[64] When life became real and earnest and he roamed as an exponent of great ideas, it was nettlesome to recall studious days when his writing was dry as dust.

But this view lay far in the future. When Wright left his pastorate, he had not yet perceived the ministerial role as dry or hypocritical, nor was he aware of the secular drift of his own commitments. He did not embark on a course of romantic self-exploration, but criticized, instead, his reluctance to wean himself from a comfortable post. Mired in a local perspective, like his sluggish townsmen during the revival, he too was postponing service to God. He received a girl of eleven into the church on the day he bade farewell, "the most solemn & affecting day of my life."[65]

His ministerial years were not terribly at variance with the mainstream of that profession. In fact his life exemplified crucial transitions in the history of the New England clergy.[66] When Wright entered the ministry, memories lingered of better times when well-settled men expected to stay put for a lifetime. Trained by living with an experienced minister, these men had kept sensitive watch over the needs of localities. In return they had been accorded high social standing, addressed as "Reverend Sir," deferred to as public officers. Like all such officers, living off public moneys, they had been hard to remove. Those times had long since disappeared, however, and public office now rested on the support of parties or factions. The ministers' defense was to isolate themselves from the unseemly risks of politics and to locate themselves in a freshly defined "moral" sphere of operations. Trained in seminaries instead of pastors' homes, they altered the public image of the minister: they identified him with a translocal, professional class moving freely without loyalty to parish or community. As revivals came to depend on professional specialists, they also diminished the stature of local pastoral work. While some ministers felt increasingly insecure in transactions with congregations, others drew toward a new system of values in which local service ranked lower than posts in the national, moral, professional empire of reform.

Henry Wright was typical of the new class of ministers who, unlike the majority in earlier times, were neither the children of ministers nor the intellectual sons of well-to-do parents—they were not born to the cloth. These new men required financial assistance for their education. They were unlikely to think in terms of ascribed social standing; they measured themselves against a professional ladder of success. They were not bound by local affections. Wright was a good pastor who was unscathed by diminishing deference toward the clergy (though his keen sense of cultural trends cannot be discounted in explaining his leap away from West Newbury). He left the ministry not as a failure, but out of awareness that reform, or "benevolence," was a more promising field of endeavor. Except for the shrill blasts against the priesthood which became his specialty, his movements were in tune with those of other ambitious men in his profession.

All that was unusual about Henry Wright's ministry was its calamitous end. Many of his contemporaries managed a seamless progression from pastorates to reform posts and increasingly human-centered concerns. As we have seen, however, Wright's 1835 conversion to antislavery took the form of a tense competition between old attachments and new ones, concluding with rejection of "D.D.'s" and "gown-men" and with love for unpretentious fellows like Garrison. Attacks and counterattacks over his vociferous radicalism helped him resolve whatever dissonant loyalty he felt toward old colleagues.

In 1839–40 he wrenched free. The Essex North Association treated him in the best traditions of "watch and care" over a brother. Clearly, they resented many of his actions, including agitation in the Amesbury mills, abuse of one local minister before his parishioners, and generalized indictments of the clergy; moreover, his notorious association with radical causes, particularly during the Grimkés' tour of Essex County, embarrassed the fraternity. They were not an easy group to ignore. Besides his enemy Dimmick and a few bitter conservatives, they included Gardner B. Perry, an early Garrisonian and Wright's loyal advocate, Leonard B. Withington, a decent friend whose judgment was widely respected, and several other well-intentioned moderates like Henry Durant, later president of the University of California, who had shared the work of creating lyceums and temperance societies. Their unpublished records show none of the public acrimony of the late 1830s: insisting that this was a private concern, they did not reprimand or expel Wright, but "inquired" whether he had treated them justly and whether he felt that he ought to withdraw from the band. Theirs was the most infuriating possible response to the style of reform that Wright was perfecting, and it elicited some of his goriest pictures of Death and Judgment. But he was unable, despite several highly public efforts, to get himself tried for abolitionism and nonresistance; in the end he adopted the expedient of "excommunicating" the ministers from his faith.[67]

Ex-clergyman Wright participated in an 1841 "anti-ministry" convention, thus making his extrication from Essex North a sign of the new order. On this occasion, Amos Augustus Phelps, an Andover man and erstwhile Garrisonian, offered "statistics, showing that . . . [ministers] have been several hundred per cent. in advance of the people in the anti-slavery reform"; but the avant-garde were not placated by demonstrations of relative sanctity. Wright proposed a root-and-branch standard, abolishing the ministry in the form to which he had been educated. "'The ministry,' said H. C. Wright, 'is not a profession or a calling, as is that of a physician or a farmer, but a duty. Every Christian is a heaven-ordained minister of Christ. The spirit of Christ is his commission. If he has that, he needs nothing more—no course of study—no process of mental discipline, except that which God gives in the great school in which he places us. I would have every man his own minister, and his own church, and his own state, under God.'" In the same mood he examined the Greek words translated as "church" to prove that they meant nothing more than assembly: all who lived with the spirit of Jesus belonged to his congregation. Although he had assured the Essex North fraternity that he had not deviated from the theology of "trinitarian Congregationalists generally," he swiftly discovered, in private, that Quaker principles were most Christian. In short, he dissolved the ministry.[68]

Wright was correct in identifying professionalism as the hallmark of the nineteenth-century ministry, but it was hopeless to expect rhetoric taken from radical reformation to overturn the processes of change. The universal standard—"every man his own minister"—temporarily signaled Wright's allegiance to God's government and thus permitted his secession from a profession that no longer interested him. After earning a reputation for uncompromising radicalism, however, he set off toward secular professions that diminished God's importance.

The Millennium and Beyond

When Henry Clarke Wright departed from the Christian ministry in West Newbury, his labors assumed a this-worldly cast. Taking up collections for Amherst College, establishing Sunday schools in New Hampshire, and supervising missions and schools in Boston, he put his talents to good works in the intersecting worlds of education and benevolence that beckoned many other ministers away from obscure localities. In his life these were first steps toward a decidedly secular career as a lecturer and author—a career defined by slashing denunciations of the religious apparatus that had once been his own.

Departure from West Newbury was not intended, however, to be an anti-Christian or self-assertive move. It was one of many turning points when Wright felt he was weaning himself of earthly attachments—in this instance, parishioners and family—so as to be free to carry out what God the Father asked. This was the time of his life when he wished for the anonymity of one voice blending in a grand Christian choir and when he knelt in the mud of the mountains to beg forgiveness for a blasphemous thought. In the early

1830s, furthermore, he thought about missionary service overseas as passionately as in those intimate letters to Laura West Hartwick more than a decade before. No doubt an assignment to savage isles or dark continents could fulfill multiple purposes, especially for a young man, with an anthropological bent, who had mused on the matrimonial customs of Andaman Islanders as a student, and who had toyed with the idea in his West Newbury study that someone who knew the "experience & devices" of two nations would enjoy great advantages over those who knew but one.[69] Nevertheless, the allure of missionary service was that curiosity and sensuality were suppressed in the name of Christ. As Wright frequently admitted, nothing would have blocked him from securing a missionary post if he had genuinely sought one; but the aspiration sufficed to indicate his selflessness as he turned to increasingly secular and ambitious enterprises outside the clergy.

The opening up of new markets for ambition caused many of Wright's contemporaries to have knife-edged self-consiousness. Viewing themselves as actors and peddlers could be disconcerting, but even the most practiced postures of self-denial gave way to surprising moments, seized on by novelists and essayists, of "getting out of one's self" and observing "one's eventual and moral self, as if it were another person."[70] As Henry Wright set forth in new directions, after climbing so long to reach the ministry, his journal abounded in devotional self-abasement, and he showed more interest in Jesus than at any other time of his life. "O my soul pants to be with yours," he wrote, despite the knowledge that he deserved to go to hell. On his thirty-ninth birthday he repeated what became annual reflections on his sinfulness and his hopes to start a new life of unselfish loyalty to God's kingdom. In such moods he depicted himself as a child, not as spontaneous and free, but as an infant requiring tutelage. "The world is my *nursery*. . . . Shall I pretend to be guided by my own understandings?"[71] To the extent, then, that Wright caught glimpses of himself as another person, he did not brag about a nobler self but tried instead to cast himself as submissive, uncalculating, and still growing.

Reversing the traditional image of the ministry as a calling devoid of ambition, Wright struggled to leave West Newbury as though it were selfish and competitive to linger. Stifling any sense that agencies of benevolence emancipated him, he meditated on global responsibilities to God's kingdom. When he ran across evangelicals, like those in the Maine Missionary Society, who planned to keep their resources in their own vicinity rather than subsidizing work far afield, he was indignant. They were ignoring the logic of anonymity and disinterestedness.[72]

Despite his enlarged views of missionary work and distant service to the Lord, Wright did not minimize the importance of America. For the evangelical in America it is always the best of times, always the worst; as the nation teeters at the verge of perdition it still has the opportunity to inaugurate the millennium. Wright's personal self-abasement and his criticism of narrow-minded state organizations coincided with extravagant reflections on the vital importance of America both to the cause of political liberty and to "the prosperity of the Redeeming Kingdom."[73]

The political conflicts of the Jackson era helped an ambitious evangelical in mid-career to sort through the implications of shifting values. South Carolina's efforts to nullify the tariff—the major clash between old localism and the new wave of centralization—magnified his nationalism, as his journal recorded: "Had solemn & interesting thoughts on the relations which we as a Nation sustain to the Kingdom of Christ in the world. I believe they are important as Eternity. May God avert from these United States civil wars & bind these states together in the bonds of Christian love. . . . Once let this Country be agitated by measures of disunion & none would care for their souls." How his antagonists of later years might have laughed to see these reflections! Their significance was that he was discovering difficulties in the ministers' hearty attempt to locate a "moral" sphere: this national work could not be divorced from partisan strife. Revivals and sabbath schools depended on "*peace* & . . . the preservation of our Union." There were radical implications, too, in the emerging fear that slavery might call down God's wrath, thus ending America's millennial hopes.[74]

What tied together these divergent themes—self-abasement, missionary zeal, nationalism—was a fervent belief in the approaching millennium. Taken literally, the millennium referred to a thousand years of God's direct rule promised at the end of history; but Wright, like others who became reformers, believed the millennium commenced "silently in the heart," not waiting for noisy trumpets or a day of wrath.[75] This belief had caught fire after his conversion in Norwich, smoldered throughout his Andover days, built up again during his ministry, and now blazed freely while he journeyed as a Christian reformer. Millennialism began with personal submissiveness. "I love to look at God as a universal King [,] a Sovereign Ruler over all the world & myself as a subject of his righteous dominion," he wrote in 1834. "I think I feel a comfort & joy in feeling that I am a member of such a government." This was an acceptable form of self-regulation, echoing Jonathan Edwards's famous account of how he came to love ascribing absolute sovereignty to God. Problems arose in applying such personal feelings to collective action: what was the relationship between God's government and man's? Few Christians would have quarreled if Wright had shown them a list he compiled, showing the properties of God's kingdom in one column and Satan's in another. Light was balanced against darkness, love against hate, holiness against sin, the moral against the physical, turning the other cheek against returning evil, divine punishment against human punishment. These were nice pieties, respected almost everywhere, controversial only when they led to categorical judgments on imperfect earthly institutions.[76]

It was all a question of keeping things in perspective, the cosmic struggle on the one hand and earthly business on the other. But how was one to do that, when millennialism implied imminent change, when revivalists and missionaries strove to extend God's kingdom, and when fealty to the Almighty was supposed to be a transforming rebirth? Under those conditions obedience to the Heavenly Father might overspill the boundaries set in the revival and weaken the edicts of worldly fathers.

Wright had been forewarned that millennialism was a Pandora's box. Although the Hopkinsian system rested on a vision of the millennium, it was dedicated to gentle support for social improvement, not to radical scrutiny of the familiar arrangements under which men lived. Students at Andover read about misguided enthusiasts during the Reformation, another era of heroic evangelicalism, about fanatics who made immoderate demands of the Bible and forgot the chasm separating God's perfect realm from the temporal world. He may well have heard Moses Stuart preach on the text, "My kingdom is not of this world"; if not, almost any other preacher would have given the same warning. The standards of Christ's kingdom, said Stuart, were not transferable to this one. Only a misreading of the text could lead Christians to refuse obedience to civil powers, especially in a land where they formed a democratic majority. "Any thing in word or action," he concluded, "which tends to excite civil discord, & foment a seditious spirit, is hostile to the precepts & the spirit of Chr[istian] religion."[77]

Wright was not impervious to such considerations, as his remarks on the nullification controversy made clear. In the long run, however, his allegiance to the millennium inspired precisely the cries for perfection that Stuart warned against: he demanded full-scale realization of the virtues belonging in God's column and denounced the coercive human law that belonged in Satan's. If civil discord hampered the work of redemption, then it was time for Christianity to turn its attack on political institutions. Going further back, the simple categories of the millennium provided a formula in which he could be submissive to paternal authority and devoted to his brothers' welfare, while at the same time displaying contempt for frustrating authorities. His conversion to abolitionism in 1835 brought these possibilities to the surface. His best known contribution to reform was the "no-government" idea that obedience to the kingdom of God precluded support to slaveholders, rulers, armies, and other embodiments of human force. He influenced Garrison to blend a version of Christian anarchism with opposition to slavery; he caused other abolitionists, like William Goodell, to downplay their own perfectionism lest they further embarrass the cause of the slave; and he furnished a useful target to conservatives who wished to draw boundaries around the permissible range of evangelical belief. He got a lot of attention, in other words, in the anonymous role he played in behalf of the kingdom of God; and all his uncertainty on matters of theology was past. He had placed himself on long-sought ground, detached from selfish and local interests. To his own mind, his position seemed impregnable: if charged with disrespect for order he could answer that he was escalating respect for the supreme authority; if charged with heterodoxy he could insist on his total submission to God.

In his early years as a radical abolitionist and nonresistant, Wright stifled the "anthropology" of his student notebooks. He dwelled instead on the familiar millennial themes that had covered his transition from local ministry to itinerant life, and discovered in his own life history a general imperative for mankind. Fashioning a sort of politics out of what previously had been kept at the level of private devotions, he advertised dependence on God as a solvent of more immediate dependencies. Viewed in this way, Wright's emergence as a radical abolitionist was not the abrupt break from what had gone before that conflicts over Garrison and George Thompson made it appear.

The late 1830s and early 1840s furnish hundreds of illustrations of Wright's quasi-anarchistic rendition of the millennium, all of them proceeding from stark assertions of God's absolute sovereignty rather than from libertarian views of human potential. For example, in his earliest tract he offered this basic definition of "DIVINE GOVERNMENT":

> A government of divine will and divine penalties. The divine will is the rule of action, or the governing principle, and the divine power the sanction. The Deity prescribes the rule of action, defines crimes, annexes penalties in kind and degree at discretion, and executes them by such instrumentalities as He sees to be just and right. The legislative, judicial and executive powers are in him. GOD IS THE GOVERNMENT. Non-resistance assumes that this is the only *rightful* government in the universe, and that entire and instant obedience to it, is the duty of all moral beings.[78]

To a remarkable extent, Wright's nonresistance can be read as an assertion of his undeviating orthodoxy in a time of headlong vocational change and, beyond that, as a protest against the compromised Calvinism in which his generation of ministers had been schooled. The submissive nonresistant made claims on God's behalf that his dons had not dared.

Even some sympathetic readers might have wished to have answers to obvious questions—such as whether human government was not the "instrumentality" God had chosen. But for Wright this was beside the point; what mattered was unexceptioned fidelity to the divine power. As reformers repeatedly said, men should obey God's law and He would supervise consequences. Yet their appeal for sinners to "come out" of political institutions took for granted the possibility of new lives and remodeled careers, and their antagonism to slavery, in particular, carried with it the exciting prospect that no enlightened man was obliged to endure oppression. There were, in other words, promises of release in the nonresistant movement for which Wright was spokesman, and its opposition to slavery required courageous nonconformity. But even when he was most stridently at odds with "the powers that be," Wright never failed to show aversion to unregulated human behavior, as this 1840 extract from his journal may illustrate: "*Human Authority*—is a nullity. Man never did & never can have any *authority* over man—to say what he shall & shall not do. God alone is invested with authority over man. No man is free & fitted to be a christian & a Reformer till emancipated entirely from all human authority of Church & State, & brought under the authority of his God. Slavery—subjection to *Man*—Liberty—

subjection to God—& the more absolute & entire the subjugation—the more perfect the Liberty."[79]

His psychological stance as innocent brother had merged with his vocational stance as self-abasing innovator to create the style of Christian reform, rebellious and yet orthodox, that nonresistance epitomized.

Negations

As late as 1844, while defending himself against charges leveled by Scottish churchmen, Henry Wright maintained that his religious views were "in substance—in all essential particulars—like unto those held by John Calvin . . . and the views that are now taught at Andover." All that differed were his opinions of war and slavery. Christ was still his God and sole lawgiver, and "I need no other light than my own experience and observation, to teach me that man is a sinner, and must be born of God, before he can see the kingdom of heaven."[80] Similar protests cropped up throughout Wright's life: whether they were sincere or merely tactical, his reform commitments did in fact work changes in Andover's teachings, which were already modifications of Calvin.

Submissive nonresistance proved to be a temporary, though important, stage of Wright's religious life. As professional confidence grew, it was no longer essential that he seem more orthodox than the seminarians. His role actually became that of an emancipator from ecclesiastical tyranny and a bearer of modern, sensible teachings. The importance of nonresistance was that it allowed him to dissolve old allegiances before moving on. If at first he insisted on his perfect loyalty to a celestial government, as time passed he was emboldened to emphasize his repudiation of the paraphernalia of church and theology; and, still later, he could lecture forthrightly as the champion of a new era of human relations. It was by turning Christianity against Christian institutions, however, that he escaped old masters and launched the search for new sources of authority.

Modern, sensible teachings often amounted to little more than a nullification of what he had once been taught. Perhaps some persons can depart from a religious system and never think in its terms again, but not Henry Wright, whose flight from theology was conducted as an antitheological enterprise. If his "experience and observation" dictated a modification of traditional doctrines, he was notably unsuccessful in describing the process. Antitheology, no less than its opposite, relegated human experience out of sight so relentlessly that the only period of his life that he examined thoroughly, in writing, was the pretheological, pre-Andover years discussed in *Human Life*. Nor were his occasional appeals to "consciousness" convincing explanations of his changing system: when he turned inward, his thinking was imprisoned by terms set at Andover, though now contradicting what once had been affirmed. His radicalism was, in short, fixed in dialectical relation to his orthodoxy; and we can follow his professional emancipation as a sequence of awkward negations—first of traditional views of sin, then of the Bible, and finally of the sabbath.

No matter how strongly Wright proclaimed the orthodoxy of nonresistance, it drastically altered the equations regarding original sin that he had studied at Andover. Emphasis was redistributed from questions of will and inevitability to questions of authority and obedience. In the winter of 1837–38, after being fired by the American Anti-Slavery Society, he mused more than ever on the Kingdom of God. His journal for January 8 describes Christ as chief magistrate of a kingdom with no human underlings, and then gives this sketch of history: "(1) Man before the fall. Under the dominion of God. No power given to man over man. God all in all. (2) From the fall to Christ. All the efforts made to reestablish the dominion of God over men. Penalties executed by men only as God directed. (3) Christ came to set up the Kingdom of God fully again. All who come into the Kingdom, are to be as, Adam was, solely under God's dominion."[81]

This eschatology was basic to nonresistance. Government, it indicated, was "just as necessary as human wickedness—no more so"; the duty of Christians was to annul allegiances to every authority except God and thereby "to change this field of blood into a paradise of love."[82] This logic proceeded from a traditional view of government (both *Common Sense* and the *Federalist* had commented, for example, that government resulted from original sin, without calling for its dissolution) revised in light of the revivalistic hope that some men and women could escape sinfulness. Why should they be bound by institutions suited to the unredeemed? Despite its sources in recent evangelical excitement, this question was bound to remind theologians of some of the oldest delusions in Christian history. They were certain to hear the simple logic of separatism that church fathers had steadily denounced since the time of Augustine, the logic that seventeenth-century Puritans had ingeniously suppressed in their endeavors to balance the needs of an orderly society alongside the individual aspirations for holiness that Protestantism released.[83] Wright's teachers may well have snorted when they heard that his eschatology was as orthodox as Calvin's, or that his beliefs had not altered since leaving the cloister.

Wright's goal was not the segregation of pure Christian communities (though he did live for a while at the little venture at Hopedale). An altered view of sin was essential to the generous approach to human needs that he was developing: he sought to remove the traditional taint on human nature and offer Adamic perfection to all who took care of their bodies. Spiritual perfection was, in other words, a useful step toward its physiological successor.

Although human nature was the ultimate target of theological revisionism, and the topic on which the grandest alterations took place, much of the fight took place elsewhere. The antitheological struggle concentrated on the Bible—the evangelical symbol of assent to divine authority, the token of the liberating (and confusing) knowledge Wright had acquired at Andover. Here, too, Wright showed the subversive potential of unmodified obedience, as he began by asserting that his faith in the Bible motivated nonresistance and concluded by attenuating, if not destroying, that faith.

In the first place, nonresistance appeared to be a strict-constructionist Bible religion because of its assertion that everyone but a pacifist violated Christ's reiterated teachings. The nonresistant Wright quoted the Bible constantly and scanned historical literature to find the political opinions of the earliest disciples. But what about the voluminous records of violence in the Old Testament? This question deterred potential recruits like Sarah Grimké from joining the nonresistance society and gave enemies like Theodore Weld ammunition against it. Probably most nonresistants believed in some scheme of changing dispensations, such as Adin Ballou's complicated system of shadows and substances in which Old Testament law was transfigured into pacifism, or the less elaborate view that the Jewish law was outmoded by Christ's sacrifice. Wright's statements on eschatology hold to the latter view. When pressed, however, he stated categorically: "ON NO QUESTION ON WHICH THE OLD TESTAMENT DIFFERS FROM THE NEW TESTAMENT, IS IT TO BE REGARDED AS OF THE LEAST AUTHORITY."[84]

This step was more radical than it first appears. Moses Stuart, for example, could admit no conflict between his namesake and Jesus. Much as he appreciated advanced scholarship, he insisted on the unbroken unity of Old and New Testaments and hid the few inconsistencies he saw under the rubric of progressive revelation. Although his students supposedly interpreted the Bible by the same methods as other books, they were notified that its authority was exceptional.[85] From this perspective it was clear that nonresistants like Wright, who regarded half the Bible as at best irrelevant and more likely erroneous, were heading toward a religion based on human judgment.

The next step was to deny Old Testament institutions even the status of a historically necessary dispensation between Adam's fall and Christ's coming. In the late 1840s Wright specialized in abrasive lectures on the errors of the Old Testament. The titles of reports he sent the *Liberator* are self-explanatory: "Is God Unjust and Changeable, or Men, the Writers of the Old Testament, in Some Things Mistaken?" (four times in 1848). "The Bible, If Opposed to Self-Evident Truth, Is Self-Evident Falsehood." "Must We Reject Christianity, or Believe the Old Testament Writers to Be Infallible?" "Seventy Children Beheaded to Punish Their Dead Father for Sinning." Such provocative titles appeared so frequently that parodies were nearly inevitable. "Is the Bible a Lie, or Is Henry Wright Mistaken?" asked Henry Grew. "Is Henry Wright Wiser and Better than Jesus of Nazareth?" asked William Goodell. Even Wright's dearest friends in England were offended by his implacable assault on the Bible.[86]

But the assault had its uses. For one thing, Wright drew large audiences, especially in Ohio, and won considerable newspaper space with his monotonous assertions that the Old Testament was filled with barbarous and immoral acts which the nineteenth century could not condone—acts allegedly done by command and approval of God. The Bible was, moreover, a useful pretext for scanning modern fields of violence. In denying that scriptural carnage could be tolerated as safely "past," Wright drew upon lively fantasies. He answered Goodell, for example, with this analogy: "The three million slaves in the South combine under Frederick Douglass, as the Jews combined under Moses, and march upon New York, take the city, and slaughter every man, woman, and child in it; and then spread over the State, and kill 'infants and sucklings,' and 'every thing that breatheth in it;' and take possession of the gold and silver, the horses, lands and cattle for themselves." Obviously Northern white abolitionists were supposed to shudder at the thought, not rejoice in it, but what a strange vision for an unequivocal pacifist![87]

Conflict between Andover and Wright was long-lasting, but in curious ways unacknowledged. From the seminary flowed recurrent attacks on Garrisonian abolitionism, often stressing Wright's heretical opinions, but none mentioned its education of this fallen angel. Similarly, Wright kept his Andover ties to himself even when periodically scolding Stuart's reluctance to call slavery a sin. His tact was especially dramatic when he denounced the seminarians' role in banning antislavery activities at Phillips Academy because it outweighed his pride in his stepson, one of forty students who resigned in protest against the ban.[88] There was but one occasion when Wright publicly traced the anti-Bible cause back to Andover: he produced a letter from his former classmate John Smith, who had a farm in Mecca, Ohio. Smith's student notebooks proved that Dr. Woods had justified Old Testament atrocities as part of God's moral government in which human agents were commissioned to kill the iniquitous. Confronted with genocidal murders of children, Woods found them no harder to accept than modern epidemics. Equivalent casuistry, Smith believed, could be found at all theological schools, and the task of reformers was to rehabilitate a God hostile to human interests. "Let us have a good God," he wrote, "if we have nothing else, not even a scrap of a book left."[89]

It would be a mistake, however, to let Wright and Smith appropriate this plea to their camp. They were simply voicing one radical version of sentiments that had been swirling about for a century: deists had preceded them in compiling lists of Old Testament atrocities, and Thomas Jefferson is only the best remembered of scores of commentators trying to salvage the pure teachings of Jesus from the wreckage of superstitious despotism. The necessity to have a good God, acknowledged more or less openly for decades, was as clear when Woods pondered instances of genocide or Stuart struggled with the question of slavery as when Wright vilified them. One of the most important functions of the seemingly interminable nineteenth-century disputes over the biblical status of slavery was the reinterpretation of gospel in a liberal age. When Stuart decided slavery was condoned in the Bible, he went further than Wright gave him credit: he also declared slavery contrary to the spirit of Jesus and therefore destined for ultimate extinction. In other words Stuart, no less than Wright, abandoned Calvinist confidence in God's unvarying judgment and, at least covertly, appealed to notions that anticipated theological modernism. By imagining that God worked slowly through time, he continued to admire the inspiration of all of Scripture. While urging society to go slowly in carrying out God's will, he was no stranger to the desire for a good God.[90]

To men like Stuart the survival of Christianity depended on the sacredness of Scripture. They defended the Old Testament largely because of their concern for the New: if critics dislodged the inspiration of the Book of Genesis, then Jesus' stature also shifted. This fear was not simply a conservative reflex, but resulted from long-standing struggles with interconnected problems of biblical interpretation. Henry Wright proved to be a good example of what they feared—that is, of critical attitudes toward the Jewish dispensation that culminated in subjecting Jesus too to human judgment.

Wright published his final view in *Errors of the Bible* (1857), which began with references to twelve years once spent in studying the Bible in "the languages in which it purports to have been written" (but not mentioning where). Beyond question, his views had changed dramatically from those of his teachers, and all pretension to orthodoxy was now doffed. Whereas Stuart regarded the Bible as implicitly involved with history, in Wright's view history left the Bible behind. The Bible was a document from ancient times, admirable enough in its way, but it was "absurd to suppose that human beings have made no improvement in their conception of God and immortality since the days of Moses and Jesus." The New Testament contained a defective notion of "the superior state," currently being illuminated by spiritualism. Furthermore, Jesus was neither husband nor father and, despite the brilliance of his nonviolent teachings, these "imperfections" blurred his understanding of love. His celibacy and that of several apostles represented an "error" threatening the most important social institutions. It was possible, therefore, to praise Jesus as a great teacher and renegade, but he deserved worship no more than Garrison, Fox, Parker, or Emerson. More than an attack on Jesus' authority, *Errors* was an exorcism of the routines of Andover and the theological style of thinking, a scornful reminder that biblical interpretations generally mirrored contemporary opinions. Wright ended with a parody, probably unintentional, of his professors by including a lengthy extract from a German tome proving the Bible's vulnerability to human influence.[91]

Wright showed no wistfulness over the loss of an authoritative Bible, but he could scarcely tolerate the idea that truth was relative to time and place. Like many contemporaries, notably Theodore Parker, he searched for methods to establish the permanent and discard the transient—a search leading Parker and other transcendentalists to intuition and Wright, beyond that, to a science of the body. While the transcendentalists were responding to a cold moment in the Unitarian dialectic, Wright was still reacting to Andover's fusion of the higher criticism with orthodoxy. There are ironies, to be sure, in the capacities of both Andover and Harvard to yield similar offspring, but they are ironies that reveal centripetal forces in nineteenth-century American culture. As they pondered timeless authorities and temporal human needs, erstwhile antagonists shared too many assumptions to stay apart: by the century's end Andover and Harvard theological schools were merged (until courts ruled the match unnatural).[92]

In *Errors of the Bible* there was no diatribe against Jesus like that sometimes aimed at the Old Testament. Wright simply renounced the custom of regarding a book as authoritative—what mattered were human needs. But the fact that his reasoning began with the Bible, though with criticisms and negations, meant that he never strayed far from the essential spirit of Protestantism. Much as he honored social institutions like marriage, he could not shuck the belief that man in his quest for salvation stands alone. Even in a series of rather derisive pamphlets appearing at the end of his life and arguing that the Bible had no more authority than Mother Goose, he repeatedly stressed that one man's needs cannot atone for another's. Christ's goodness redeemed Christ—and no one else.[93]

That Wright had broken from Calvinism was made clear by the psychological insight that "an angry God exists only in the conscience-stricken soul of the theological sinner." There was accordingly no need for a propitiatory sacrifice, and the effort to picture Christ as such was pure myth making. People were not defiled by sin, and it was preposterous to think of nine-tenths of the earth's children on an irreversible railroad to destruction. While this analysis seemingly liberated mankind, however, it did not relieve the burden on individuals. The point should be stressed: sin was real, and imposed its own heavy punishments. In Wright's calculus the individual had no chance of atoning for major sins, like Booth's assassination of the martyr president. The lesser sins that typified ordinary lives exacted pains of anxiety and physical deterioration, and none of these costs could be explained as predetermined signs of God's glory.

Wright's attitudes toward the sabbath followed a pattern similar to his treatments of the Bible, sliding from obedient devotion to flamboyant disregard. Emotionally, this was a transition away from his father and unpleasant memories of the "Puritan Sabbath": for this reason, he frequently expressed antisabbatarianism through images of romping, childlike freedom. Since it was also transition away from his first starts in adult life as a minister, he was quick to denounce sabbath observance as a relic of priestcraft. But the fundamental significance of the sabbath went beyond family or ecclesiastical history. As Wright had given witness when he worked for the Sunday School Union, sabbath institutions aimed to regain religious control over the pace of secular life. Because the sabbath had accumulated great symbolic importance as an occasion for resistance to the business of a commercial age, antisabbatarianism inevitably appeared to bow before secularizing influences.

It was not simply the church that Wright and his comrades opposed: they were caught in a basic conflict between reform movements. The empire of benevolence took up the preservation of the Christian sabbath as an emblem of its conflict with the noisy party system and grubby new economic alignments, and in doing so benevolent men called attention to business transactions occurring across vast distances. Why, it was asked, should the government run the mails on Sunday, and why should Christians patronize canal lines that worked seven days a week? First-day observance, though justified from Old Testament texts, took its impulse from the ministers' recent segregation of the moral realm from the workaday world. It derived strength from the fervor of many busy men to demonstrate that they kept some space in their lives for old-fashioned devotion, but it also caused bitterness among those it pressured to suspend money-making operations. The sabbatarian movement is an excellent example of the way in which reform movements retailored the signs of good character; it illustrates, at the same time, how they could be regarded as repressive and unpopular. The movement's lobbying and petition campaigns set influential precedents for other reforms, and its recurrent disappointments intensified suspicions that the party system was inherently corrupt.[94]

The sabbatarian emblem meant the most to constituencies that Wright was leaving behind: a preliminary Sabbath Union was led by Lewis Tappan, the New York merchant who turned into the most grimly anti-Garrisonian abolitionist; its successor in the 1840s, the American and Foreign Sabbath Union, was led by Andover's president Justin Edwards. Although these men wished to impose sabbath observances as their rebellion against secularizing forces, their campaign struck others as the worst of modern interferences in private life. Sabbatarianism met opposition from a sizable anticlerical population, some agnostic and others deeply pious, scattered and poorly organized—a population that was bound to attract Wright and anyone else at odds with the species of orthodoxy termed "benevolent." The sabbath was, in sum, an unusually promising issue for redefining philosophical allegiances. Antisabbatarianism drew its symbolic potency from the same sources as sabbatarianism—the need to adjust religious conceptions in accordance with the puzzling contours of social change.

Boundaries between sacred and profane, between first day and the other six, were important to those who drew them, but they could easily seem arbitrary and illusory. Wright's employers at the Sunday School Union, for example, breathed hopes that in a short time the majority of American voters would be graduates of these holy environments and thus revealed the extent to which their sabbatarianism had solidly political objectives. It rankled lecturers on antislavery and temperance, therefore, to hear that these causes were secular and could not be advocated, in meetinghouses at least, on the Lord's Day, the one time when most citizens had leisure to come and listen. From the mid-1830s on, sabbatarians, who were already at war with freethinkers, confronted other reformers who regarded first-day observance not as an antisecular defense of holiness but as a retreat from the transforming obligations of Christian faith. To their eyes, church services and restful activities on one day compensated inadequately for the escalation of unholy business on the other six—what had happened to the Christian goal of a second birth leaving no aspect of life unchanged? The question could be raised in unison by persons agreeing on little else. After attending a highly publicized antisabbath convention at a hall on Boston's Chardon Street in 1840, Ralph Waldo Emerson captured the ambiguity of the moment: "the most daring innovators and champions-until-death of old causes sat side by side."[95]

As he rose to prominence as an antagonist of the sabbath, Henry Wright blended old-style Protestantism with new-style acceptance of social change—the kind of concoction that typifies his religious life. Consider his diary report of conversing with English friends in 1846:

> I denounced the idea of consecrating days & places to God as heathenish & said I cared not how they kept days, sundays or other days provided—*they kept themselves pure & holy;* that the 1st day of the week was no more holy, no more the Lord's day than other days—all days were his; that churches were no more sacred than barns or theatres; that the Clerical profession was no more sacred & pleasing to God than the profession of a Merchant, a Shoemaker, a carpenter, or farmer; that praying, reading the

> Bible, going to Church, Baptism, the supper, singing, preaching, were no more *religious* exercises than baking bread, knitting stockings, cooking a dinner, sweeping the room or the streets; that the *duties* that regard the purity, comfort, health & happiness of the *Body*, were as binding, as important, as sacred, as christian, as the duties which relate to the purity, comfort, health & happiness of the soul.[96]

At first glance this message repeats themes that had been circulating since the Reformation—the uselessness of intermediaries between the individual and God, the superiority of faith over ceremonies, the right of private judgment, and the sanctity of honest callings. Viewed more closely, however, it verges toward the irreligious conclusion that good deeds are completely redeeming.

Wright had stayed away from the Chardon Street convention, and Garrison had kept surprisingly in the background, perhaps out of concern for reputation that contemporaries—and later historians—failed to notice. But strategies changed while Wright was in Europe. He wrote one antisabbath tract while sitting in Rosneath Castle (when he lost it in a Glasgow storm, he was amused to think that ministers would point to this as a sign of God's anger); a second version finally appeared, with variations for English and American audiences, as *First Day Sabbath Not of Divine Appointment* (1848). Taking Justin Edwards as its target, the tract turned the methods of ecclesiastical history against the institutions of the church. When Wright returned from Europe late in 1847 he dashed to Ohio, where Garrison was in a sickbed, to propose "an *Anti*-Sabbath Convention," and found his old friend's mind already set in the same direction. They swiftly laid plans for meetings that were eventually held at the Melodeon in Boston in March 1848. While Wright had urged those who attended the 1840 convention to enjoy "free meeting," allowing many opinions and avoiding votes, he joined Garrison in devising stricter rules for the new venture, framing numerous resolutions, and planning to evict any lunatic, like the ubiquitous Abigail Folsom, who took advantage of their forum.[97]

The convention proceeded with a minimum of conflict or lunacy, though it would be hard to say that participants spoke from a shared perspective. Charles Calistus Burleigh, whom the press depicted as a long-haired eccentric, made several able presentations of what today would be called a First Amendment viewpoint: sabbath-enforcing laws violated the rights of Jews, Quakers, Seventh-Day Adventists, free thinkers, and others who made up a disorganized majority in a diffuse country. Theodore Parker, who regularly preached at the Melodeon, introduced resolutions assuring the public that the sabbath would still be devoted to instructive, moral purposes when put on a voluntary basis; other speakers envisioned bucolic excursions out of the cities. Many stressed the Old Testament origins of the sabbath, but there were subtle differences between those who simply regarded it as a custom outpaced by time and those who saw Jesus' coming as an emancipation from the law—differences between a genial outlook on existing society and hunger for a new dispensation. While the millennium inspired some speakers, others turned to science to challenge the six-day story of creation.[98]

Probably the most unexpected development was the convention's preoccupation with labor problems. There do not appear to have been many working-class people present, and neither sabbatarians nor their antagonists showed much concern for the effects of secular change on labor. But the charge was made that sabbatarian laws were all that prevented a seventh day of grinding toil; in answering it, antisabbath speakers were hard put to demonstrate their liberality toward labor. Some argued, plausibly, that the sabbath actually reinforced the hurried-up sense of time fashioned by the industrial revolution. It announced when clocks should stop and begin again. Others contended that forthright legislation concerning hours of labor was preferable to customs supposedly based on God's commands. Garrison, however, showed a tin ear to the concerns of working people when he spoke of the "priestcraft . . . and the rabble . . . joining in common persecution" of men like him.[99]

Wright mostly stayed out of the fracas, which may not have interested him. He stuck to the main line that brought him to antisabbatarianism: the denial of the sacred/secular distinction that nineteenth-century clergymen had delineated. There was one extravagant moment when he declared: "The drunkards, the adulterers, the thieves, the robbers, the French revolutionists, and the authors of all the violence and all the wickedness in Christendom, are generally men who believe in the Sabbatarian principle, and who have been educated under the influence of that principle."[100] This list of transgressors underscored the point that his real interest was in secular morality. Through exegesis he showed the modern sabbath contrary to the beliefs of great theologians, including Luther and Calvin, who appropriated more time and space to religion. But his goal was less the restitution of ancient Christianity than adaptation to a new era. Edmund Quincy, Wendell Phillips, and others in the Garrisonian crowd missed the point by protesting that antisabbatarianism was a "*Theological* rather than a *Moral* reform,"[101] when for Wright it was escape from a theological world view that the movement symbolized. They missed the simple assertion that earthly morality was centrally important to human life.

There is no evidence that Wright was disappointed in the antisabbath convention, although unfriendly newspapers threw taunts that Garrison overshadowed him. (He walked "with the air of one who affected to 'boss the job,' and pass himself off as master-workman," according to his old nemesis, the *Boston Recorder;* but still remained "chief train-bearer to Garrison.")[102] Never a flashy speaker, he exhibited what the *Recorder* called "tedious pertinacity," what his friends saw as uninhibited quest for truth. So far as we can tell, he was pleased that so many voices sounded in the well-planned convention, as the *Liberator* reprinted the speeches for months thereafter. Possibly the holding of the convention was more important than anything that was said. Antisabbatarianism had become solid ground and remained in his repertory for the rest of his life, but it was not an area in which new explorations could be made. Having turned the corner toward the religiosity of ordinary secular life, Wright was free for other kinds of work. "The inevitable result" of the sabbath system, he had decided, was "to leave the child without the moral and religious restraints upon his passions, his words and actions on other days."[103] Now he could turn to a new system of seven-days-a-week controls, the system of spiritual authorities and intuitive anthropology.

One further negation was virtually inevitable. After his concerns had become flagrantly secular and he had overturned his youthful opinions of sin, gospel, and sabbath, he took a new look at the *philosophes* of the eighteenth century—the bugbears of his teachers and ministers. The *philosophes* had tried to disentangle a true religion, implicit in the teachings of Jesus and consistent with the needs of modern man, from superstitions and repressions accumulated during the intervening centuries of priestcraft. They had tried to rescue religion from the church. In the United States they were rewarded for their pains by cries of infamy that gave them considerable symbolic importance. In the bitter conflicts of the 1790s the Enlightenment was assailed as inimical to the religious welfare of Americans; in the succeeding decades Voltaire, Rousseau, Hume,

Paine, and their friends were denounced from pulpit and revival platform as enemies to freedom, piety, and the millennium.[104]

When an orthodoxy depends on vilifying unread authors, it takes the chance of making them more attractive to rebellious young men. The danger is that someone will open forbidden books and find them less odious than advertised. Traveling to Switzerland in 1844, Henry Wright recalled: "Voltaire, in early life, became an object of deep interest to me, in consequence of my hearing him so oft and so bitterly denounced as an infidel and atheist. To my early imaginings, he stood out from his kind, conspicuously wonderful—as Mt. Blanc stands out among Alpine Glaciers. . . . [W]hen I came to read his works, I was surprised to find him feeling, thinking and talking like other men." Voltaire's shortcoming was that he reacted excessively to the corrupt ecclesiastical institutions; had he seen the example of practical Christianity, as taught by Wright and nonresistants, his life would have gone differently. "The infidelity of Voltaire, Rosseau [*sic*], Volney, Hume, and Gibbon, and the blood and horrors of the French Revolution," he reflected, "are directly chargeable upon the popular churches and priesthood of France and christendom. . . . In *spirit* and *practice*, Voltaire was nearer the kingdom of heaven than the slaveholding clergy of America."[105]

Wright's stance with regard to Voltaire was still a distant one, though it afforded a welcome perspective on the clergy. When he first read Paine's *Age of Reason* in 1852, he felt strong affinities to the dishonored hero of the Revolution. All his life his mentors had calumniated that book; now that he was making it a point to read the works of other men who were branded as infidels, he discovered that Paine's actual purpose had been "TO VINDICATE THE CHARACTER OF GOD." This fellow antagonist of clergy and Bible had exposed Old Testament violence and New Testament supernaturalism in a manner that Wright applauded. Ecclesiastical Christianity had sanctioned violent habits that finally took the form of the terror of the French Revolution, as Paine in his dungeon had well known. Nothing Paine wrote was so derogatory to God as the churchmen's defenses of violence, Wright concluded; certainly God was more abused by the justifications of slavery that Moses Stuart had carried to his deathbed.[106]

As this salvo against Stuart indicated, Wright was fitting Paine into his system of reversing old orthodoxies. In 1868 he turned out a sharply worded pamphlet on *The Merits of Christ and the Merits of Tom Paine* that converted a deeply Protestant interest in individual salvation into a denial of Christ's efficacy as savior. Christ's deeds saved only Christ; Paine's only Paine; and every child could anticipate a "self-made destiny." The pamphlet had little to say about Paine, except to speculate that if Christ returned to earth he would be vilified, like Paine, for heretical ideas on violence and for excessive sympathy with the poor. But Paine had become a vivid symbol of underground religion in America, a tradition resisting the compromises of the institutional church and liberating the conscience from misguided superstitions; and by identifying his writings with those of Paine and the Enlightenment, Wright gave his personal negations the security of a tradition.[107]

Although others pursued this tradition in the direction of "free thought," there were limits to Wright's interest in freedom and his confidence in reason. A follower of the Paine who wished to vindicate God, Wright searched enthusiastically, as we shall see, for new religious authorities.

Communications

The victim of a compromised theology passed off as orthodoxy during seminary days, Henry Wright labored to repudiate the old system and offer mankind a new one. Since the positions that he advocated on lecture platforms and in the press had been discovered mostly through a process of negation, they often equalled their predecessors' ambiguity. Just as Andover's Calvinism was riddled with secular compromises, Wright's religion of human needs hedged its bets on the ultimate authority of God.

The challenges of an agitator's life help to explain inconsistencies running through Wright's doctrines. Attacked for heretical opinions when his task was to promote antislavery, he exaggerated his obedience to God during the "clerical controversy" in Massachusetts in the 1830s and declared his unadulterated Calvinism in Scotland in 1846. When speaking on his own hook as a public lecturer, however, he was tempted to overstate the novelty of his beliefs. In addition, his public style emboldened him to make *ad hominem* thrusts at his opponents' hypocrisy, thereby diverting attention from troubling religious issues and postponing demands to clarify his own stand.

Even when the give and take of an agitator's life is fully considered, there remains an unmistakable note of hedging in Wright's religious beliefs. Profound uncertainties seethed beneath excessive protests that his arguments were not unchristian, beneath the sophistry that despite his personal faith in God's existence other men must obey their own convictions, and beneath the reiterated claim that satisfying one's own needs is a way of pleasing God. Wright's religious views were especially fuzzy from the mid-1840s until his death—precisely the period when he lectured most confidently on human nature. He remained caught in the same old dilemma he met at Andover: horrified at even the self-accusation of atheism, he still could not find much content in the idea of God. No matter how adroitly he presented himself as an expert on human concerns, he could not constrict his thoughts to earthly horizons.

His confusion was most pronounced when he thought about the inescapable experience of death, so difficult to reinterpret in terms of human "needs," so difficult to reconcile with visions of unbounded self-sufficiency. The antinomies of death-as-murder and death-as-fulfillment defined his public life just as certainly as the contrasted systems of raising children through external coercion or internal discipline: he could not be expert on early stages of the life cycle while ignoring its end. But death had been explained poorly to him as a child, and Andover during his residency transmitted blurry pictures of sin, the soul, and the afterlife. Although images from the grave invaded his fantasies, he was compelled to face the horrid possibility, seldom addressed in his day, of sheer pointless annihilation.

Disbelief in survival after death was a latent issue in Garrisonian reform. According to "the philosophy of slavery," as we have seen, masters interfered presumptuously in the sacred connections of accountability between man and God. This claim weakened some traditional meanings of the afterlife, for immediatists had no patience with the idea that slaves might faithfully serve human lords in this nasty world and expect relief from individually unmerited woes in the next. There is no way of knowing how many abolitionists actually doubted the existence of an afterlife, but the nonresistance movement made such an implication stronger. In working out the logic that assigned war (and all physical coercion, including government) to the same category as slavery, Wright refashioned Theodore Weld's argument that the master reduced his man to a thing, an item of property, thus sundering his ties to God. Wright contended that war also rendered man an object and was blasphemous by the same reasoning that condemned slavery. One of his abolitionist critics, William Goodell, underscored the dread of death implicit in nonresistance: "You say that to *kill* a man, is to 'abrogate human nature—to sink MAN to a *thing,* by making him a corpse—to annihilate all his relations, rights, and responsibilitis, as a human being.' This statement cannot be strictly true, unless the death of the *body* be the *annihilation of the soul,* which you cannot intend to *imply*. Death does not reduce men to chattelship, nor contradict nor suspend their moral agency. *This* God never does."[108] It is surprising how seldom abolitionists dared to discuss eternity openly. Few of Goodell's allies wished to make careful discriminations on the subject of death (eventually he was known as an eccentric among reformers because of his theological orthodoxy). For their part, Wright and the other Garrisonians preferred to speak portentously of undying allegiance to God, while confessing only indirectly the place of the horrible finality of death in the logic of nonresistance. But the problem was serious and could not be evaded forever.

As nonresistance waned in the late 1840s, Wright became attached to spiritualism, an exciting new movement that lightened fears of annihilation by conducting tentative discourse with souls who had passed "beyond the veil." It would be mistaken to regard spiritualism as Wright's peculiarity or as a passing craze: it was a major episode in the endeavor of literate Protestants to comprehend the transformations of nineteenth-century America. In the lives of many other reformers, wisdom communicated by spirits helped to replace the eroded authorities of their youths. As a lecturer in "advanced" thought, furthermore, Wright could not ignore a religious movement that raced from Barnumesque controversy over the authenticity of rapping noises in eerie rooms to widespread faith in solemn messages received from loved ones and famous men in "the superior state." Spiritualism attracted too many charlatans, as Wright and other reformers glumly admitted; and showmen inevitably got into the act. But imposture was an accepted risk of nineteenth-century existence and could not squelch Wright's serene conviction of the truth of some mediums' performances.[109] In any case, the movement's greatest importance, as reformers saw it, flowed from the aspirations of its audiences: would improvements in individual consciousness keep up with the rush of material progress? Spiritualism was a movement that looked benignly toward the future without necessitating specific social changes, that encouraged Christian devotion without demanding faith in musty theologies, that had numerous adherents and yet managed to be "progressive." Spiritualism was reform made popular and shorn of its divisiveness, and it was crucial to Wright's career. Many of his books appeared under spiritualist auspices; many of his talks were given at well-attended local conventions of the movement.

The thrill of spiritualism stemmed from the hope that mediums were harbingers of a new dispensation. In one sense, the movement continued the work, begun when reformers denied the Old Testament's authority, of freeing the future from chains of the past. In another sense, it was an instance of a muted, respectable millennialism—favoring evolutionary change instead of violent antagonism—that became the shared faith of middle-class Americans in an industrial age. Wright was an observer of spiritualism, not a medium; but he left no doubt about his own thrilling hopes that the spirits inaugurated a new era of reform. He hailed the seer of Poughkeepsie, Andrew Jackson Davis, as "a Jesus of this day." He furnished eyewitness accounts of miraculous events in the upstate New York home of the Fox sisters, who introduced Americans to the spirits' abilities to speak through rapping tables. He testified to the remarkable powers of the abolitionist-turned-alienist, La Roy Sunderland, whose house was a scene of occult visitations. And he rejoiced when the deceased abolitionist, Nathaniel Rogers, recreated the sound of a horn they had once heard together in the mountains.[110]

Wright was a favorite of mediums, perhaps because he retained a pose of scientific detachment while conveying the spirits' private communications to large audiences. Mediums helped him in various ways. No doubt he welcomed the prophecy from Nathaniel Rogers (who visited many seance rooms), as conveyed by the medium "Annie" in the *Liberator*, that Wright would go down into Hades and bring woman up from prostitution and sensualism to a higher plane of love and purity.[111] In 1862 other voices encouraged him to drop plans to return to Britain to publicize the union message. He had his bags packed and tickets purchased when "news" arrived, as he put it, to change the decision. The "news" came to William Lloyd Garrison from Julia Friend, a Gloucester medium who had clairvoyant visions of Wright suffering. Garrison approached the problem objectively: though a believer in spiritualism, he advised that no good plan should be vetoed because of their messages. But in this case, he pointed out, various mediums, unknown to each other and from scattered parts of the North, bore the same testimony; Wright's debility after his previous voyage and the value of his services at home gave additional reasons for heeding the spirits. He did not go.[112]

The relationship of spiritualism to reform was ambiguous. Though occasionally inspiring visions of destruction, the spirits typically heralded an impending order when the peaceful teachings of Jesus would be amplified by new sources of guidance. While forecasting the eventual triumph of most reforms, spiritualism might justify withdrawal from political struggles in an imperfect era. As a result, not all reformers listened to the spirits with kindness. There was criticism of La Roy Sunderland's transtition into mental science. And the militant Parker Pillsbury had sharp words for the spirits' fatalistic attitude toward black slavery: "Apologies for slavery, everlasting twaddle about 'different spheres for different races,' (or sexes,) in Heaven's name, when shall we have done with them?"[113]

Henry Wright managed to avoid charges of defection, and he never allowed the fatalism inherent in spiritualism to stifle its "progressive" implications. When he was persuaded, for example, that bankers and copperheads were plotting to get the first national convention of spiritualists to endorse Clement L. Vallandigham for President in 1864, he campaigned to build raucous majorities for Lincoln and he attacked those whose pacifism struck him as a mask for treason. To one bitter participant it seemed that Wright was either employed by the Republicans or else let "the foul virus of his political animosity" distort the position of conventioners who simply argued that their joint purposes were spiritual, not political. "Nobly done! Generous reformer! A kiss for a blow!" Wright's cohorts turned this great meeting into a "Babel" of clapping and dancing that concluded with "the 'doxology' in honor of the murdered murderer, 'Old John Brown.'"[114] This was an exceptional episode, but it illustrated how important it was for spiritualism to elevate its view of reform beyond the divided realm of politics. Spiritualism revived the clergy's notion of a moral sphere, with its own laws; when it brushed too near the political issues on which men and women disagreed, it lost its powers to heal and reassure.

Spiritualism owed much of its allure to substituting family ghosts for distant gods: word came directly from father and brother instead of a transfigured sovereign. Since Wright's religious life depended on fantasies begun in Hartwick and Norwich, it was almost inevitable that he should try to lay aside theological vexations by communicating in public with essential influences from home.

First, let us consider a remarkable test that Wright proposed for the authenticity of spiritualism. In 1853 he reported in the *Liberator* on an evening in an Ohio farmhouse with his friend Joseph Barker, several other come-outers who had emigrated from England, and a medium—an occasion he used for a spiritual prediction of his brother Chester's death. The medium was silent when Wright tried out wrong information and then produced three raps when he wrote, on paper that she could not see, the (presumably) correct state, county, town, and date of death. None of the English reformers at the table knew anything about his family, according to Wright, and he had supposed Chester alive at sixty-six until he got this message. As he sent inquiries whether his brother had indeed died of apoplexy on July 7, he promised that *Liberator* readers would hear the news. The accuracy of the other information was striking, he thought, even if Chester survived.[115]

What is more striking is Henry's failure to report sorrow or alarm: spiritualism allowed a curious distancing from bereavement. By opening communication, however awkwardly, with those who were gone it overcame the finality of death. At the same time, because of the quasi-scientific controversies and operational sideshows associated with spiritualism, communicating with loved ones took the form of experiments to be reported with suitable expressions of detachment and doubt—and thus with control over real or imaginary grief. Joseph Barker learned through the same medium that his brother had not perished from the cause the family had long accepted; with clinical detachment he recalled evidence to support the spiritual diagnosis. What about Chester? When the *Liberator* published no report, readers asked: was brother indeed dead? No, Henry was obliged to answer, there has been "a mistake, somewhere," because spiritual knowledge was still inexact. But his confidence that spirits could identify truth and dispel error was unshaken, though "hunkers" scoffed at new ideas. Even this imperfect communication with the spirits renewed his aggressive faith in change. "Every reformer's mission is, not to bring peace," he concluded, in what was not really a non sequitur after this experiment in self-control, "but the sword."[116]

Chester's response to the test is unknown. When he finally died, ten years later, brother Henry relied on the Gloucester medium, Julia Friend, to transmit a long questionnaire across the veil. Some queries arose from the brothers' disagreements, others from Henry's efforts to lighten the grief of the widow Patience Wright. In this experiment Mrs. Friend, without having read these queries, collected a return letter taking them up in order. Henry swiftly relayed the answers to Patience in order that she might share three messages: that Chester now saw how right Henry had been on theological matters; that Henry had done well in consoling his sister-in-law; and that Chester's current status could not accurately be called death, for his soul was still united with Patience's.[117]

In providing Henry with vindication and Patience with reassurance, spiritualism plainly served useful purposes in the family's experience of death. Moreover, these fraternal letters showed that spiritualism held interesting implications for divorce and remarriage. The idea of an everlasting love match probably comforted Patience, but how could it have untangled Henry's complicated memories of his parents?

In his most important venture into spiritualist controversies, Wright conversed with Jesus and enjoyed reconciliation with his father. In this episode publicity went to the New York *Tribune,* and the medium was Ann Leah Fox Fish, eldest of the Fox girls, later accused by her sisters of having instigated the rapping hoax.[118] Upon arriving at her house "to obtain whatever evidence I could to elucidate the question of social intercourse between this and the next sphere, now being discussed in all social and domestic circles in this nation," Wright laid the scene as he had so many others, his mother's death, for example, or his dialogues with the Grimkés: he described the room, the table, the persons seated around, the woman at the center. As soon as he arrived knockings began; "three emphatic raps" assured him of a spirit's wish to speak with him. After secretly writing eight names—Paul, Peter, John, Jesus, Isaiah, Matthew, Luther, Calvin—and concentrating on each in turn until further rappings occurred, he learned of Jesus' presence. How he knew the visitor belonged to that exclusive company is unexplained.

> Then by a mental operation, without moving a muscle, I asked, "How did Jesus come into being? Was it by the same process by which other men enter this world?" Instantly three loud raps and an earnest call for the alphabet—five raps being the signal for that. . . . As I thought over the alphabet, my face was turned from Mrs. Fish, and my eyes and lips were concealed from her. . . . [and] she could not see the letters at which I pointed, and raps were made. . . . I then began to *think* over the alphabet, and in answer to my unexpressed thoughts letters were designated by raps which make the following sentences: . . . "I was mortal like other men." . . . "Jesus is a pure and holy spirit." . . . I then asked, mentally, "Is all true that was written by Matthew, Mark, Luke, and John, respecting the birth, life and death of Jesus, as it is recorded in the New Testament?" No raps—silence being, as I am informed, equivalent to negative. I then asked again, mentally, as before, "In what light ought the death of Jesus to be regarded? As the death of other martyrs to truth, or as having something peculiar in it?" Instantly three raps and . . . soon the

following sentences were spelled out. "Many misconceive the secret. There are things for you to know hereafter. The time has now come when prejudice and superstition must cease."

To Wright (who had been concealing his other self for years) it seemed improbable that Mrs. Fish could divine his thoughts, especially since she pointedly ignored him. It was more consistent with his hostility to the priesthood, which for centuries had frowned on continuing revelations, to believe that "the author of the raps [who] could read my thoughts" was Jesus. Not only did this revelation revise arguments encountered at Andover, but it also showed how exegetical problems that he liked to characterize as deadly were in fact tied to the most pressing emotional issues. The question of being "born like other men" had often distressed him (once beside the Chenango River), and by altering the Christian balance between the soul's immortality and death's finality spiritualism gave public currency to longings he had privately cherished since the deaths in his childhood home.

Returning to Mrs. Fish the next day, Wright heard from a spirit whose name was not on the list. The rappings solved the mystery: "I am your father. My son, I keep watch over your daily occupations, though you are not aware of the fact at all times." Without giving away a trace of cheer or sorrow, Wright tested the spirit's knowledge of his father's name, age, and "the disease with which my father died" (a burst blood vessel)—all information which no one else in Rochester knew. When the spirit scored perfectly, Henry asked whether father approved "my course as an advocate of Anti-slavery, Non-resistance and other radical reforms?" This answer was spelled out: "Yes! I speak to your mind, my child, when I see you laboring in the cause of humanity. I will go and prepare the way for you. Your way leads onward. You will wear the crown of honor among the blessed!" No longer need he humble himself in the mud at the thought of rebelling against his father's rule.

Even at this news Henry betrayed no emotion, but instead submerged his individual feelings beneath hopes for general reform. In fact, after all the rigmarole that apparently validated the mysterious communications, he affected a lack of interest in them: "It would be very pleasant to feel the presence and sympathy of loved ones who have gone before; but I care not for the matter unless they can instruct us as to *what* and *how* to do to elevate our condition in this state." Wright's version of spiritualism, unlike some others, focused on the comforts of the current hour, the blessings that fear of death could undermine. Discourse with his father was subordinated to his lifework of reinterpreting the Calvinism of his father's generation: he hoped the spirits would "add value to man as man" and "divest existence of its great Trinity of Theological horrors, DEATH, JUDGMENT and ETERNITY."

And yet spiritualism revealed an undertow of religious concern that Wright's secularized comments about present human needs should not obscure. It was his religious critics who insisted on a this-worldly explanation of the rappings. A doctor at the Hopedale Community, for example, believed Wright to have telepathic powers: he must be "a *medium*, (let him test it,) and get his thoughts rapped out, as any medium can. The sentiments look like off-shoots from his theology."[119] Clearly, his messages involved what we would call projections, and it is easy to see how readers who knew Wright took offense at messages attributed to Jesus. Nevertheless, a critic who saw only the irreligious side of Wright's spiritual adventures ignored the boundaries being set around secular life. Spiritualism was important to him, as to others, because he wished to believe in its otherworldly provenance: the transience of earthly life in a period of rapid material change intensified hunger for knowledge of the permanent. Historians of the "middle period" frequently say that old orthodoxies succumbed because they clashed with the period's tendency to regard man optimistically, but the terms in which optimism expressed itself could be gravely religious. Spiritualism was the clearest instance of an opposite tendency to fear annihilation—everlasting silence—in a last-chance world where nothing seemed certain.

Wright often lectured on "the Abolition of Death," a topic synthesizing the spiritualists' claim that death was merely passage to a superior condition with the Garrisonians' opposition to unnatural deaths such as those caused by war or capital punishment. He added a theological twist that was becoming nearly synonymous with modernity: if God's will, rather than man's acts, were responsible for disease and disaster, then God was "exceedingly malevolent or exceedingly ignorant." His point was not only to liberalize old-fashioned conceptions of God's determinism but also to elevate good health to a religious duty. The clergy were wrong, he preached, in preparing men to face death; it was better to abolish death by adhering to natural law. The kingdom of heaven was "engraven on every nerve, muscle, vein and artery of our physical nature." Wright published modernistic slogans denying both the permanence of death and the existence of the Christian afterlife, but still testifying to the force of fundamental religious impulses. "HEALTH IS HEAVEN, AND DISEASE IS HELL," he told audiences frightened by the body's frailty, life's brevity, and the uneven distribution of pain.[120]

With some plausibility, Wright saw his work as a response to the old religious question, "WHAT SHALL WE DO TO BE SAVED?"[121] But his answers were astonishingly incomplete and evasive, in view of his prolificacy: although he advocated "anti-Death societies" and criticized death as an erroneous idea that ought to be discarded, he stopped short of "mind cure" or any other reform subordinating the body to powers of will or fantasy. His interest in the proper care of physical nature, at least on this side of the veil, included such temporary expedients as pure diet and water cure as well as long-range hereditarian defenses against illness. Spiritualism merged with practical earthly concerns in the reassuring formulation that man had no reason to perish. Wright sometimes made it clear, nevertheless, how cold his vision of existence could be. He was occasionally criticized, in fact, for cheerless funeral discourses resembling a secular restatement of Calvinist prescriptions for bereavement. It was illusory to think that the child had to die, or that it rested happily in God's bosom. Death was unnecessary, a violation of law, an imperfection that could have been abolished. These discourses may strike us as just one more instance in modern history when the grief of parents was forced to serve as a test-case in the fabrication of adult intellectual systems. But Wright's words were not always unwelcome and could furnish control over emotions that death threatened to evoke. An admirer named G. W. Madox reported on Wright's 1860 visit to a Maine community that was "sufficiently enlightened" to hear twelve of his lectures and "pay him for telling them of their own crimes and sins." One lecture treated the death of Madox's child, an event that Wright discussed "in his own peculiar way, saying he had no consolation to offer, only this: 'You did the best you could.' A kind Providence had no hand in it."[122]

Quite apart from these formal uses, spiritualism gained in personal importance in the last decade of Wright's life as loneliness wore on, death drew nearer, and old habits of splitting his identity were aggravated. He resided much of each year with the medium Julia Friend, and after one dialogue at her home—his "home" too, as he imagined it—he confessed: "When shall I be at peace with H. C. W.? Never—I fear—in *all* things." Unconcerned about charges of religious infidelity, he was wearied by his "disloyalty to H. C. W."[123] In the same period he invited Gerrit Smith and his wife to visit the Garrisons and him in "our *Home*, our *Hearts*, the *Holy of Holies* of our life"—what a sweet reunion for reformers who had been estranged too long. There were also, he hinted, "special reasons derived from *my* Religion—the Religion of Spiritualism"—compelling their visit, especially if Nancy Smith would come. Awkward gestures toward this-worldly domesticity pointed to a more precious domicile beyond the grave. The *"Holy of Holies"* assumed different meanings when he informed Smith, not long after, that he was prepared to welcome death as the long-sought transition to *"the Inner Court."*[124] Despite sorrowful origins in his personal history and fraud-ridden surroundings as a public philosophy, spiritualism appeared to give Wright impressive serenity as he faced the end.

Ultimately, however, there was a vague, compromised quality to the religion that meant so much to him. Even when faulting the Bible's conception of "the superior state," Wright typically failed to give his own conception for purposes of comparison. Jesus alluded to "a fixed state . . . holding out no hope that the mistakes and sins of this state can be remedied there," while Wright felt it "more natural" to suppose a state of continuing self-examination and correction. It was "more rational," too, to believe human beings were "free agents there as they are here; that they progress in knowledge and goodness there as they do here. . . . The social relations and sympathies will exist there as they do here, only in a higher and purer form." His inferences were "natural" and "rational" because they were fitted to human needs.[125] Even after death, it seemed, history would be a fluid process without a given end, carrying on the best and worst of nineteenth-century life, only in a vaguely heightened fashion. Instead of furnishing a coherent body of doctrine, spiritual communications merely relaxed the requirements of logical discourse that had dampened the inspiration of the Bible. The outstanding feature of the new philosophy, which stiffened Wright and his followers' courage to face death, was that it formalized uncertainties that could be taken as signs of philosophical incoherence and gave them the dignity of a faith. After all the negations of a mobile lifetime, the one thing certain was that life would constantly unfold.

Wright's religious odyssey may be summarized by looking at another reflective letter in a series he sent to Gerrit Smith. In 1865 an entire generation of abolitionists sensed a climax to their careers, and Wright was touched by some antitheological musings that Smith published in the *Liberator.* Glimpsing a common logic in their careers despite frequent clashes over tactics, Wright asserted that ever since 1826, when he first took a stand on temperance, he too had found theology a major obstacle to human progress. He and Smith both knew "there is a God," but did not forget that the more one loved man, the better one served God. Although he wished to stress the unshaken faith in God that unified their lives, his summary of their common principles was embattled: *"Man above Theology! Conviction above Authority! Nature above Art! Self-evident truth above Bibles!"*[126]

Beneath the jangling oppositions and the pose of romantic self-confidence, we catch hints of inability to pin down a shifting faith. For one thing, there was falsification: Wright's ministerial colleagues had pressed him to relinquish the fashionable drinks to which his *arriviste* status among Newburyport's elite accustomed him. Although his expectations of religion had been frustrated in the dusty academic world of New England Protestantism, service in reforms like temperance had taken him further from his juvenile faith. Similar commitments carried theologians along the same path. Opposition to theology, in short, gave only a superficial unity to his memories. Second, his protests that humanitarianism had not altered his belief in God were strained and unconvincing. Once humiliated at the mere thought of God's sovereign judgment, he had gradually persuaded himself that it was theology, not God, against which he bridled. But he spoke, significantly, of arraigning theology *before the human soul,* an awkward metaphor reflecting a covert shift in the locus of ultimate judgment. Third, the insistence on his unvarying belief in God meant that the needs of earthly existence, to which Wright gave so much attention, required higher justifications. Spiritualism was the appropriate religion for a traveling expert on human needs not simply because old-fashioned theologies depreciated those needs, but also because to defend them too exclusively was self-defeating. If the death of the body was man's final end, then human life was more confined and degraded than the old school ever imagined. "My soul recoils from Materialism," Wright told Smith. "God & Immortality are the deepest, holiest & most potential demands of my Nature."

Anthropological Science

Wright's audiences accepted the balances he struck between body and mind, between temporal needs and the alleviation of death. Where we observe the persistence of religious emotions that the new age supposedly had outgrown, they subscribed to an emancipating philosophy whose truth was certified from the "inner court." But they asked something more of him than the sleights of showmanship to connect religion and culture, something more than the debates over "new measures" tying together the world of revivalists and mediums with that of actors and magicians. Wright was an expert on human life who explained to modern audiences what to make of basic experiences, like death, that religion once had eased. He was expected to present truth in systematic form—and the less discussion of measures, the better. Although he allied himself with spiritualism and called it his religion, in some ways he kept his distance from it and relegated it to a subsidiary role—somewhat like the place of miracles in the corpus of Christianity—in the systematic view of the world that he called anthropology. While bestowing unearthly significance on the spirits, he adjusted their messages to the canons of science.

It is hard to know precisely what Wright meant by "science." He almost never referred to the writings of college professors, doctors, or any other group of professionals; and it is by no means clear that his audiences recognized an organized community of scientists equivalent to the clergy. Rather than giving way to forces outside religion, Wright came to science as part of the internal process of negation that commenced at Andover when his imagination created anthropology as an alternative set of values to pitch against theology. The authority of science also flowed from the necessity of portraying himself in new guise after breaking with the ministry: at times science connoted little more than a willingness to receive wisdom from new quarters. But if science implied open-minded approaches to the study of man, it also revived the immutable divine laws that Garrisonians contrasted with the arbitrary acts of human governments. Science was, in sum, a way of enveloping tensions between man and God, change and permanence, and mortality and immortality that always characterized Wright's religious and intellectual life.

Wright's central maneuvers are visible in *Anthropology; or The Science of Man* (1850). In his day the term "anthropology" ordinarily referred to study of physiology and physical properties of the brain—to man as an animal[127]—but he altered it to fit the study of man as an accountable moral agent, thus creating an unusually theological science and blurring distinctions that other men sought to preserve. His science restated the traditional view of man situated higher than the animals and slightly lower than the angels, or spirits. Although Wright gestured in the direction of physiological causes of moral behavior, such as diet and heredity, his mind recoiled, as he put it, from materialism. His chief goal was to place man systematically under the hegemony of the soul.

There is no doubting his interest in the body. "To learn the nature of the human body," he wrote, ". . . we must go to the body itself. This is the only authoritative teacher in the science of physiology." Instead of honoring the work of specialists in that discipline, however, he headed toward a do-it-yourself method undermining every profession but his own. Three years before, in Dublin, he had bragged of getting the best medical advice in the kingdom, "for I have been to myself, and I think I am my own best physician"; it was not surprising, therefore, that *Anthropology* shed suspicion on all book learning untested by immediate observation of nature. Because he showed utterly no interest in scientific experiments, there would have been no point in replying that scientific books contain not only information but also procedures for defining and verifying information. Indeed, in Wright's hands "science" sometimes meant little more than that certain statements were self-evidently true to all men, others false, and that no one should follow the Bible or any other preceptor in violation of common sense. No intermediaries were necessary to discover the fixed laws by which God's universe was governed; and each man was an inviolable "empire within himself." Wright's elastic sense of law included analogies between mathematical laws, laws of health (such as temperance), ethical laws (such as pacifism), and much more as well: "Love, marriage, forgiveness, kindness, and self-sacrifice, are essential laws of our social nature." This kind of *Anthropology* might be described as a scientized version of anarchism: the sum of human obligation, it argued, was attention to natural law. But Wright had traveled a long way since the "no-government" controversies of 1839–40, and it was clearer than ever that political antagonisms were not his main concern. He was most vigorous when attacking biblical revelation and dismissing the idea that social relations presented complex problems once biblical authority was lifted.[128]

It should be obvious that, except for incantatory gestures, Wright was not really urging close inspection of nature. His science was dredged from his intuition, which certified the fixed truths he promulgated and which gave anthropological status to his need to believe in God and immortality. Thus the science of a new era recapitulated lifelong preoccupations.

Intuition had passed through a succession of meanings in Wright's thought. After the illumination of his heart during the revival came the "consciousness" of God that helped him weather Andover's demolition of God (and self-accusations of atheism). His professors had transmitted Scottish interpretations of consciousness that were easily absorbed and then gave incontrovertible authority to conventional moralisms. As a clergyman and educator, Wright had stressed that "all that constitutes moral character is the result of the feelings & passions of the heart rather than of cultivated intellect."[129] And as a nonresistant he reduced God's lawmaking to occurrences in the individual conscience. Wright liked to present himself as a maverick, and historians are bound to be impressed by basic cultural shifts occurring during his lifetime. The educated heart, as Donald Meyer has pointed out, resulted from compromises between an old intellectual order that derived sanctions from God and a new one deriving them from science.[130] It could be argued, nevertheless, that the ethical psychology learned at Andover interpreted and regulated the experiences of Wright's lifetime with remarkable flexibility. In codifying the cause of the heart, conscience, or intuition as a "science," Wright disowned the crisis-stricken religious side of seminary life, but reaffirmed most of the intellectual content of orthodoxy. While his teachers unquestionably deplored his anticlericalism and other radical positions, his life nonetheless illustrated the sturdiness of a system which proved to be well adapted to pay homage to science and to incorporate intellectual novelties for a century, despite stunning changes in the social contexts of religion.

This sturdiness could be exaggerated. Reliance on intuition did not leave theology unchallenged: the history of American Protestantism continued to teem with doubt, conflict, and heresy hunting. But it was probably another century before many students reenacted internal battles like Wright's at Andover, and by that time it was easier to subsume private experience under cultural malaise and to speak of "the roots of the sickness of today [the 1920s] . . . the death of the old God and the failure of science and materialism to give any satisfying new one for the surviving primitive religious instinct to find a meaning for life in."[131] Wright had anticipated this strain of thought in some ways, but never managed to believe that God was dead. He could always turn to the personal drama of head and heart to organize his spiritual life. He had entered maturity as deep-riven cultural antagonisms between religious ecstasy and rational moderation were compressed into dull, but securely orthodox formulations.[132] Consequently, once his heart was victorious and his career was launched, he was merely an extreme case of popular reconciliations of individual autonomy with the social order. Each man's heart, in this system, was a sufficient measure against which to check the claims of Bibles, governments, and all other authorities; even God could not disturb the laws infusing the universe. But the universe *was* governed by law. The relativism that theological students periodically confronted was submerged beneath faith in intuitive discriminations between right and wrong, in automatically sympathetic impulses, and in the sentimental magnetism of universal human nature. Anxieties were kept below the surface; Wright's culture resolutely expected happy endings.[133]

Ultimately, Wright's two attempts to give his faith strong foundations—spiritualism and intuitive science—referred to the same interior drama. Neither explained individual failings in terms of widespread crisis, neither afforded the slightest critical perspective on culture. Both attributed important powers to the soul, on which natural law was engraved, which decided moral problems effortlessly and faultlessly, and which harbored healing powers. The soul was in fact one of those vague notions that sometimes prove susceptible of redefinition and expansion so that little explicit change in belief has to be acknowledged. The soul, put simply, was that remnant of human life that surpassed mortality. Wright did not have to go so far as some of his co-workers in summoning wisdom from across the veil because, in his system, the identical guidance issued from honest, uncoerced dialogue with his better self—which was identical, in turn, with universal consciousness. There was nothing metaphorical about the soul. It was a birthright, compounded from materials in the mother's blood flowing through the uterus, and scheduled—for better or worse—to last perpetually.

The fact that the soul developed inside the mother became the key to Wright's confidence in life. He thought most comfortably about the end of life when he concentrated on its beginnings; he was most successful in giving substance to the ideas of God and eternity when he feminized them. The private significance of his redefinitions of the soul was clear: they amounted to a covert dethroning of God by which Wright was freed to pay obeisance to his better self and the "loving, anxious one" hovering maternally in the background. His late protests of undeviating belief in God were beside the point; they could not conceal a shift in the powers attributed to distant masculine authorities. No spiritual messages emanated from mother, a fact that will appear less surprising when we remember how awkward communication with father and brother had been. His mother was not so far off; she was an element in his soul. Furthermore, these private adjustments between masculine and feminine reflected the general deterioration of localized, hierarchical rule and its replacement by strongly matrifocal values. But we should catch more than reflections: as Wright lectured, he helped to carry out this shift away from obedience to visible male authorities and toward the inner discipline that supposedly resulted from the soft, principled guidance of women. Thus in the end we may see Wright's religious struggles as a vehicle for cultural changes in which mothers, whose wombs, blood, and hearts infused the social order with moral assuredness, were elevated to new pedestals. To consider these developments further, we must turn from the experiences of childhood and adult religious controversies. It is time to consider Henry Wright's childless marriage, his traveling, and his painful efforts to assuage his loneliness.

Four

Unappropriated Heart

Brooks Adams, *The Emancipation of Massachusetts* (1919)

. . .Each day I live I am less able to withstand the suspicion that the universe, far from being an expression of law originating in a single primary cause, is a chaos which admits of reaching no equilibrium, and with which man is doomed eternally and hopelessly to contend. . . . I take, as an illustration of my meaning, the development of the domestic relations of our race.

I assume it to be generally admitted, that possibly man's first and probably his greatest advance toward order—and, therefore toward civilization—was the creation of the family as the social nucleus. As Napoleon said, when the lawyers were drafting his Civil Code, "Make the family responsible to its head, and the head to me, and I will keep order in France." And yet although our dependence on the family system has been recognized in every age and in every land, there has been no restraint on personal liberty which has been more resented, by both men and women alike, than has been this bond which, when perfect, constrains one man and one woman to live a joint life until death shall them part, for the propagation, care, and defence of their children.

The result is that no civilization has, as yet, ever succeeded, and none promises in the immediate future to succeed, in enforcing this

> primary obligation, and we are thus led to consider the cause, inherent in our complex nature, which makes it impossible for us to establish an equilibrium between mind and matter. A difficulty which . . . has never been more lucidly defined than by Saint Paul, in the Epistle to the Romans, "For we know that the law is spiritual, but I am carnal, sold under sin. For that which I do, I allow not: for what I would, that do I not; but what I hate, that do I. . . . Now then it is no more I that do it, but sin that dwelleth in me. . . . For the good that I would, I do not: but the evil which I would not, that I do. . . . For I delight in the law of God after the inward man: . . . But I see another law in my members, warring against the law of my mind, and bringing me into captivity to the law of sin which is in my members. O wretched man that I am! who shall deliver me from the body of this death?"
>
> And so it has been since a time transcending the limits of imagination. Here in a half-a-dozen sentences Saint Paul exposes the ceaseless conflict between mind and matter, whose union, though seemingly the essence of life, creates a condition which we cannot comprehend and to which we could not hope to conform, even if we could comprehend it. In short, which indicates chaos as being the probable core of an universe from which we must evolve order, if ever we are to cope with violence, fraud, crime, war, and general brutality.

Misalliance

Henry Clarke Wright grew up in a Protestant tradition that despised hypocrisy and double-dealing. Calvinism was deeply hostile, in the historian Natalie Davis's words, "to the whole psychology of two worlds, of two levels upon which life could be lived"; it was this hostility that prompted familiar antipathies to theater, sport, and festival.[1] The proper goal was a straightforward life with no gap between appearance and reality. In the post-Calvinist world, Wright still identified rectitude with ingenuousness. One sign of society's increased complexity was the display he made of living simply in accordance with the impulses of his heart; in his solitary meditations, furthermore, he prayed for selfless transparence. But the ascendancy of the heart over the head, intended to lead the way to spontaneity and altruism, defeated these original purposes by delineating spheres of existence with their own appropriate modes of behavior. Wright's lectures and tracts, like those of other Victorian moralists, exaggerated the differences between public and private life. Not only did Wright become a proponent of the new cult of "domesticity," but he also discovered the attraction, familiar throughout the Victorian era, of secret lives in which lonely men guiltily pursued self-fulfillment.

Wright's private life is hard to recover: it falls between the vast public record and voluminous diaries. It lies buried beneath righteous self-denial and illicit suppression. But to understand his writings on marriage and sexuality, which are central to his life work, we must first examine his marriage and his furtive search for happiness.

Historians know a good deal about the spouses of other abolitionists. A few worked as teams of reformers; some enjoyed sunny marriages in which the wives stayed home; others contested angrily over domestic responsibilities. But one could read fairly deeply in antislavery sources without knowing that Wright—the indefatigable migrant—was not a bachelor and celibate. Friends referred constantly to his lighthearted friendships with children, and he conceived himself a missionary to young people all over the world. But this authority on marriage provided only the briefest glimpses of the wife and children he left behind in the interests of reform. In the early years of itinerancy he spoke occasionally of missing them, but family affections dwindled as his identity as a reformer strengthened. This celebrator of domesticity was not, except perhaps in imagination, a family man.

Henry Wright met the prominent Newburyport widow Elizabeth LeBreton Stickney in 1822 while he was on leave from seminary. That summer his father died. In October he returned to Andover and stuck out his religious doubts till the next spring, when he was prepared to assume the role of an orthodox clergyman. On June 26, 1823, Elizabeth and he were married by Rev. Luther Dimmick. On the same day they set off for the newlyweds' mecca, Niagara, and took with them Mrs. Wright's seven-year-old daughter Mary. All told, she had four children—the others were Elizabeth, twelve; Hannah, eleven; and Peter, nine.[2] Wright never recorded how he felt about the size of this family, but it was probably part of his wife's attraction. Marriage was instant fatherhood as he stepped into a new serious vocation.

Mrs. Wright was the daughter of a successful shipowner, Peter

LeBreton, who had emigrated in the 1760s from Nantes to Newburyport, via Guadelupe, where his father was a sugar planter. Peter LeBreton's ships ploughed the triangle from Newburyport to the West Indies to France. Though a well-known Mason, he was also, according to family tradition, a secret Catholic with a shrine discovered only after his death. In any case, he provided well for his children, giving Elizabeth a house and land in 1808; her portion of the estate when he died in 1813 amounted to $25,264.90. Upon her stepmother's death in 1822 she received a great deal more in rents, investments, and cash.[3] Her first husband, David Stickney, whom she had wed in 1805, continued the pattern of success to which she was accustomed. Trained as a silversmith, he inherited a fourth of the estate of his father, Captain William Stickney, and eventually he too was "styled merchant" and captain. The latter title in his case went beyond the honorific usage of this mercantile town: he became a captain in the merchant service after naval duty in the War of 1812. (His family believed that imprisonment at Halifax destroyed his health and led to an early death.) When he died in 1820, he had securely provided for his wife and children.[4]

Not only was Elizabeth LeBreton Stickney well-to-do and amply provided with children; when Wright married her she was forty-three years old—only four years younger than his mother at her death. When she had first married, Wright was only eight. Her first husband had been all of twenty-three years older than her second. In 1823 Henry Wright was seventeen years younger than his bride, unaccustomed to prosperity, beleaguered by religious doubt, and a neophyte in the sacred vocation he had chosen. In this marriage he may have mixed the emotions of both son and father, as he faced responsibilities for which his previous experiences left him ill equipped.

Because of laws and customs respecting women, marriage meant that Wright assumed responsibility for the four Stickney children. But for some reason—perhaps his inexperience with money—on the week of the wedding his wife's brother was appointed their legal guardian, and Wright had to deal with him frequently. Family records preserve Wright's efforts to keep track of the considerable sums allotted to each child; there are numerous chits to recover money for their upkeep—bonnets, boots, combs, handkerchiefs, pens, toothbrushes, schoolbooks, and tuition. One dollar per week per head he charged for board. In addition, in 1830 he assumed responsibility for another kinsman, George Washington LeBreton. There does not seem to have been deep attachment here, and it is not clear whether the boy even boarded with the Wrights. When the accounts and money passed the next year to another member of the family, Wright charged an extra dollar for his services in preparing the account.[5]

To be businesslike is not necessarily to be unfeeling. Because he arrived by marriage at a prosperous status, however, Wright had better reason than most men to see the contractual side of the institution. There was a basic bookkeeping structure to his domestic life.

Joining the LeBreton-Stickney alliance involved Wright in weightier decisions than an apprentice hatmaker or doubt-wracked theology student might have imagined. Now he belonged to the gentry. He sold a pew, he sold a house. Elizabeth and he appointed a representative to manage transactions concerning "all manner of debts, rents, arrearages and all dividends on Stocks or shares in any Bridge, Turnpike, Bank, Insurance Company or any other Incorporation."[6] This firm monetary situation gave Wright the freedom to work over Greek and Hebrew in his study; later on, it freed him of concern for his family while he traveled for reform.

The Wrights lived in spacious homes, with elegant furnishings, abundant food, and servants. The children had, by their later accounts, "every care and comfort" and "every advantage of education available at the time." Mrs. Wright's father had "indulged her in beautiful clothes," and her children learned the same habits. Her daughter Elizabeth wrote with amusement in 1851 of acquiring a bloomer costume because it made sense for the dusty streets of California; she could not bring herself to wear the new garb, however, because "the long skirt is more graceful."[7]

The tone of Wright's household may be gathered from one of his few anecdotes about early married life. When the ministerial association met at his house in 1828, "Mrs. W. prepared a dinner in her usual way for company, considering brandy and wine a necessary part of hospitality. . . . She had been trained to this from childhood in her father's family, and had no idea of setting a dinner table for company without spirits of some kind." Some of the ministers were temperance men who preferred not to have ardent spirits at the dinner table. To Wright this was "impertinent dictation"; he insisted that the brandy and wine remain though none partook. A few words with a colleague and a bit of reflection soon brought him in line with the other ministers. Although the point of most of Wright's stories was to demonstrate his independence, this one showed him leaning on wife and colleagues for instruction and correction.[8]

Even from the partisan evidence her husband left it is clear that

Elizabeth Wright's interest in reform preceded and equaled his. Like many other women of her class and generation, "she was noted for her benevolence and humanity, and her active promotion of those societies whose object was the multiplying of ministers, the spread of the Bible, the diffusion of religious knowledge, and the sending of the gospel to the heathen" (the same themes that Henry had presented to the churchwomen of Hartwick). When the American Board of Commissioners for Foreign Missions urged support of schoolchildren in India, she "adopted" a boy who was given her late husband's name. The family kept many letters to his "adopted mother" from this David Stickney, who grew up to be "a native preacher of standing and usefulness." Possibly the widow Stickney's marriage to a young, impecunious minister also expressed her wish to promote divine benevolence.[9]

When antislavery immediatism divided the ranks of benevolence she quickly embraced the new radicalism. Henry submitted to a clergyman's nervousness about the social order, but "my wife and her children at once responded" to Garrison's message. When her husband finally caught up, she delighted in meeting Garrison and walking arm-in-arm with him to church. She took care of visitors like the Grimké sisters and sat through the "Domestic Scenes" that Henry described for the newspapers. But hers was not the antislavery of conventions and denunciation: she and her daughters, especially after they moved to Philadelphia, visited the colored neighborhoods, teaching people "to read and become thrifty." While wandering in Austria in 1845, Wright sent a public letter to his stepdaughter Hannah remembering "how you and your mother and Mary used to spend your Sabbaths in Philadelphia among the scorned and outcast of that city. You would not go to hear the pro-slavery preachers of the city, nor enter those dens of wickedness called churches, where the poor and despised colored people are set up as a mark of scorn. . . . Do you still go from house to house among the poor on Sunday, instead of going to the churches?"[10]

Playful children lightened the demands of vocation and social status. After Henry's conversion to temperance, the Wrights puzzled what to do with the family glassware. This problem vanished when he was "having a joyous time" playing blindman's buff with the children and smashed the entire set to the floor. "There was silence in our merry group for a moment; then a laugh, then a shout, that our scruples about the wine glasses were all solved." It is significant that his marital family provided the first instance of the opposition between children's redeeming merriment and the cold formalities of society—a constant theme throughout his life. He did not wish to emulate his father's dour authority. And though he later turned this opposition against his marital family, there is evidence that the Stickney children remembered him as the playful comrade he desired to be. "I suppose you know," wrote Hannah to an Irish woman who had befriended her stepfather, "that Father was once a real bona fide priest and used to wear black silk gloves and look solemn! only think of that—Well one thing I know [,] he never was much of a priest to us—we used often to tell him he did not keep up the *ministerial dignity*." At times Wright condemned himself for being too giddy and playful, thereby endangering the girls' souls. Such mistrust of himself was one reason he gave to justify leaving his settled home.[11]

Few diaries survive from the period when Wright lived at home with his family. When the diaries become plentiful, they show much affection for his favorite Lizzie and the other two girls (he had a harder time with Peter). Nevertheless, he began to conceive of reform as divorce from a family that impeded his greater usefulness. Concern for three unmarried girls burdened him as he contemplated a foreign missionary post; and he spoke to Lizzie, the oldest and frailest, the one who "leaned" on him most heavily, about marriage. An affectionate letter from his wife made him pause in his travels long enough to worry that "there are those whom I love with an idolatrous attachment." He had hoped that his heart was "schooled . . . into submission to Christ," but this letter revived his misgivings and the struggle resumed. "Shall I give up my Savior or my home—my wife and her children?" Since he portrayed Christ and his wife as hopelessly at odds, there could be no question about the outcome. One "dull day" at home in summer 1834 he admitted: "I do not enjoy my home as I did when a settled Pastor. My home seems to have passed away like a dream. I look around and I find it not. I feel like a wanderer in a desert, trying every expedient to support his spirit. O my God—make me fit for a home in Heaven." Even here Wright did not voice any lack of affection for his family. He weaned himself slowly, denying the process as it occurred.[12]

The family took some time to articulate resentment of the household's missing head. He conferred with them periodically as he vacillated whether to accept an agency, for example, or whether to go overseas as a missionary. Once, coming home with his mind "in [a] *whirl-pool*," he was delighted that they were "all well and ready to eat me up." But family ties were strained by his absences, the girls' failure to marry, several changes of residence between West Newbury and Philadelphia. There was a crisis in August 1835 when Mrs. Wright and "her children" (as he called them) challenged him on the detestable topic of "money matters." "They seem to think that I have wrongly appropriated to my own use about *$200* of their money." He insisted that he had tried to do well as their guardian, and as he did not care about money they could have it all. Any mistake was inadvertent, caused by two years of absence and not keeping regular accounts. He had already settled with Hannah and Elizabeth, and was about to settle with Peter. But he was hurt—"They talked a little hard to me; and I felt as I never wish to feel again"—and asked forgiveness, in his diary, for his own harsh words. The next few days were taken up with "pecuniary business": he "sold 3 shares in *Insurance Office* for 10 percent under par" to pay off the children. Then he enjoyed a pleasant dinner with the family, if we can believe him, and headed off to Boston.[13]

The next crisis came in September 1836. It helped him escape criticism from overseers in the American Peace Society who feared his radical talks would hurt the movement. On his way to Cincinnati, where he was assigned to be peace agent, he received disturbing letters from headquarters. Then a "cold and comfortless" letter from home gave a reason to drop the new assignment. "My wife feels that I neglect her—that I don't love her nor the children—that I feel no interest in them. I feel that she is mistaken for all the love I have for any in this world I have for her and them. Wherein I have injured her, may God forgive me. I will give up my agency and settle down." A few days later he decided to go no farther unless the family came too: "I here renounce all *agencies.*" He subsequently found much to obliterate in these emotional pages of his diary.[14]

Within a month he was off again as an agent of the American Anti-Slavery Society; soon the family moved to Philadelphia. There were no more crises because all parties accepted what they probably would never have admitted was a quasi-divorce.

The children were remarkably faithful followers of their mother's and stepfather's commitments to reform. Peter left Phillips Andover in an antislavery protest against Moses Stuart (he went on to Dartmouth and became a physician). Hannah and Mary, who never married, were glad to be called "come-outers," and boasted of not having "much reputation to lose since Father became a nonresistant." Elizabeth was a friend of the Grimkés and a familiar figure in Philadelphia antislavery circles. When she married in 1839, at the age of twenty-eight, she chose Lewis Carstairs Gunn, a prominent abolitionist.[15]

Gunn's restless career resembled Wright's. He served antislavery as editor of the *Philadelphia Times* and the *Independent Press* as well as through the printing firm of Merrihew and Gunn. At least one of his poems appeared in the *Liberator,* which applauded all his ventures. He was a guiding figure in the "Requited Labor" movement, which sought to boycott slave produce, market free-labor commodities, and purify antislavery lives.[16] Outside reform he tried his hand as apothecary, doctor, schoolteacher, and farmer. In 1841 he took his family to Ohio but returned to Philadelphia when Elizabeth and he embraced the doctrine, known as Millerism, that the second advent of Christ was nigh. He wrote a tract using Greek philology, chemistry, and common sense to show that "the 2300 days [referred to in Scripture] terminate sometime between March 21, 1843, and March 21, 1844." When the Gunns gave away most of their possessions in getting ready for the end, the rest of the family was bitter. Eventually all was forgiven; Mrs. Wright took parents and two children into her house until they could reestablish themselves.[17]

The Millerite business was one of few occasions when the family turned to Henry, traveling in Europe, for his advice. He agreed with Peter that practical reform was a more important Christian duty than worrying about the second advent. "Whether the world ends this year—or next—it matters not to me—if I may but be found following after God as a dear *child* walking in Love." Henry concluded, without a trace of irony, that he longed to embrace his family but suspected they would never meet on earth again.[18]

It was an interesting step from coming-out to going-out, from giving away goods to mining for gold, when the Millerite Gunns of 1843 became forty-niners. Lewis went from Philadelphia to New Orleans in March 1849, crossed Mexico by horse, and then sailed to San Francisco. Though a nonresistant, he acquitted himself well in skirmishes with Comanches. Elizabeth and four children sailed around the Horn to join him in 1851. After poor luck in the mines, Lewis found success as a doctor, political figure, and editor. As an important California Republican who enjoyed a series of patronage appointments, he found it possible to follow his own star and yet advance the political fortunes of antislavery.[19]

The bonds in the Gunn-Stickney family were close. A collection of family documents, published in the 1920s, abounds in joy and affection, as well as supplying a fascinating account of the settlement of

California. It portrays a merry Mrs. Wright, dancing and singing even at the age of sixty—a woman who is invisible in thousands of pages of her husband's diary. Her relationship to the grandchildren was obviously loving and even indulgent as she plied them with sweets and advice. There remained a cultivated tone to the family—she spoke French with her daughters—but everyone also associated the LeBreton streak with a warm temper.[20]

Not only did Wright omit this side of his family; they omitted him. Evidently few references to him could be found in his wife's papers. One of the Gunn children dismissed him in a brief telling reference: "When the children were grown, about 1828 [*sic*], my grandmother married the Rev. Henry C. Wright, a well-known lecturer who traveled extensively in this country and Europe, speaking on humanitarian subjects. His long absences were agreeable to his step-children, and the recurring entry in their mother's diary, 'Were glad to see Mr. W. who came unexpectedly for several days,' seems rather perfunctory." This comment disposed of the chief unpleasantness in an otherwise happy genealogy. As the children forgot boisterous play with their stepfather, and as Mrs. Wright lived on without the company of her husband until she was eighty-nine, resentments came to the surface. It could finally be said, within the family circle, that they "seemed . . . not to care for Mr. Wright or to be associated with him in any way."[21]

His family's bonds of affection were immaterial to Henry. He seldom complained openly, but on one occasion he contrasted his wife's coldness with his own spontaneity. He vented all the romantic antagonisms between head and heart, child and society, and tied his wife to the religious past he had relinquished. This occasion arose when he was "*politely* and *formally* received" after returning from a long journey. "I do wish people would let their hearts out," he wrote. "Orthodoxy, *Hell-born* Calvinist Orthodoxy! It freezes the heart; makes it stony, congeals it to a lump of ice. My folks were glad to see me—I know—but *granite* propriety forbade all outward manifestation of it."[22]

Only eight-year-old Sarah Gunn greeted him with unrestrained warmth. Her father was in California, and she had "entered into" Wright's affection the previous year when he was last home. She was overjoyed to see him, "drowning my face & neck with kisses," until they came into a room with the rest of the family, at which point "her whole body assume[d] a formal, upright, rigid posture in my arms." This spontaneously loving child was caught, as he saw it, in "the trammels of cold & heartless propriety." She "has been *drilled*

drilled—drilled—but her glorious, loving, firey, *blazing* nature cannot be utterly crushed." Despite reprimands for behavior unbecoming to her age, she sneaked up to his room for surreptitious cuddling. I doubt the family was as frigid as Wright reported, though they may well have obeyed strict proprieties regarding hugs and kisses. His account covered up coldness directed particularly at him and unwillingness to let the child violate an unspoken ostracism.

After the struggles of 1835–36, home became a foreign place. Henry spoke no French, nor did he possess a LeBreton or Stickney temperament. His wife in 1841 was a sixty-year-old woman who thought of herself, however joyously, as old. The children—one of the lures of marriage—were grown up. Most important of all, as far as Henry Wright was concerned, the stepchildren were not followed by new progeny. He remained an outsider.

Wright yearned for a child, especially a son. He wrote in a Boston diary, for example, when he learned that his nemesis Blagden had a boy: "I wish I had a little Son." In 1834 he wished to raise a foster child, but Mrs. Wright and the children said *no.* This veto probably pushed him further toward the itinerant life. At that time he resolved to accept his fate: "The blessing of having children, God sees fit to deny me." Years later he indulged the fantasy of taking little Sarah Gunn as his own and raising her without stifling her loving nature. "But such happiness is not for me—in this world. I'll do better in another state" where gentility and propriety are less important.[23]

Why did Heaven deny him children? Some of Wright's traits may perhaps have been linked to impotency—his confusions of gender for example, and his dread of aggressiveness. Sometimes he seemed to fault himself for lack of nerve. Yet there is no strong reason to doubt his explanation, in an intimate 1843 diary, that the difficulty was his wife's. "No marriage love is between us. She was past child-bearing when I first knew her—we have not had intercourse as husband and wife for 15 years—it is many years since we have slept in the same bed."[24] In former times wives bore children at regular intervals as long as the physiological possibility lingered, but in Wright's day they were increasingly likely to omit children after the early years of marriage. Sometimes they accomplished this goal on their own, through marital conflict or even invalidism; sometimes their husbands collaborated in planning the omissions. Assuming it was within the realm of physiological possibility, other men might have bullied a forty-eight-year-old woman into pregnancy. That recourse was not open to Wright. He was a junior partner in marriage, and he admired his wife's benevolent disposition. As he became acutely conscious of his personal disappointment, it was typical of him to withdraw from the scene of conflict, to stylize his home as a society of stultifying rules, to carry on the battle and express his resentments nonresistantly, at a distance, in speeches and books.

Itinerancy and Propriety

Henry Wright's career in reform was grounded in frustration. If reform provided a lonely escape from frustration, however, it also satisfied positive longings for purity. Celibacy and itinerancy are ancient companions in the quest for self-improvement. Together, they had formed one of the earliest Christian definitions of the sacred life and shown monks and hermits the way to elude carnal snares. Writing may figure crucially in the kind of journeying that tests devotion, wards off earthly distractions, and proceeds toward purification. Some of George Herbert's exquisite poems reenact a journey in the pattern of words on a page. Henry Wright wrote as he rode along, but his journals and public letters are, in a sense, his wanderings toward holiness. Whether we emphasize his frustration or his quest, clearly one important function of reform life was control over sexuality. But the vantage point of reform could also disclose new forms of sexual union.

Reform life meant constantly being put up in a home. Wright did not simply pause for bed and food; he won acceptance as a beloved intimate of many families. Although he must finally have remained as much an outsider as in his own home, living in a little attic or back room and doing some writing, this was the role he preferred. An unencumbered parent who came to be loved and to observe, he was inspiring to the menfolk, inquisitive with the women, and an exuberant companion to the boys and girls. This role allowed him to share some of the warmth of marriage, to pry where others couldn't, and to depart without responsibilities. Without forfeiting his quest for purity, he could observe, at first hand, affectionate earthly institutions.

His abstract pronouncements on the kingdom of God issued from detailed study of the lives of women and children. His insistent self-publicity—no matter how loudly he cried that he was alone with God—contained oblique boasts of (philosophical) intimacies with the opposite sex. At least Theodore Weld heard risqué overtones in his conversations with Angelina and Sarah Grimké on the liberation of men and women from iniquitous controls: "Brother Wright . . . walks leisurely out before the broad eye of the three thousand subscribers and hardly less than twenty thousand readers of the Liberator, and on that conspicuous eminence spreads out his 'Domestic Scene.' There is the table, the lamp, the bible, the Grimkés, and here am *I* [i.e., H. C. Wright]; then the arguments, the premises, the processes, the inferences, the Startlings and momentary flinchings of 'some of the precious little circle', and finally the *conquest,* formally announced—'the conclusion was unanimous.'"[25]

Weld envied Wright's easy, if indirect, manner with the women before he steeled his own nerve to propose marriage to Angelina. He detected the strains of intimate exploitation in Wright's nomadic life because of his own struggles to conceal a dominating spirit behind screens of anonymity and celibacy. After working through these struggles and submerging himself in marriage, Weld believed his rival Wright was a gloomy wedding guest. Wright was less openly competitive with Weld. News of the betrothal must have been shocking (he had visited the sisters while Weld was a disguised clandestine guest), but he recorded prayers for the couple's happiness. His remarks brought to the surface the implicit antagonism between reform and marriage that all parties shared: "There is none other [than Weld] whom she ought to marry. Quere. Whether she ought to marry at all. She ought to be the great reformer of the age." The duties of marriage did, in fact, separate the Welds from the sphere of reform and confront Angelina with new struggles for emancipation. Meanwhile, Wright stayed free to tinker in his mind with the bonds of love.[26]

In controversies over nonresistance Wright frequently had to deny that he was antimarriage. He could, however, challenge the existing structure of the family by criticizing tyrannical parents who mistakenly insisted on dominion over their children rather than teaching loving obedience to the will of God. Nonresistance within the family implied a surrender of possessive feelings—it made possible the types of invasive adoption that Wright customarily practiced. In any case it was children whom he first sought to liberate from the slavery of domiciles based on force, and children first allowed him to express ardent feelings that he otherwise thought were animal and illegitimate. They figured so powerfully in his emotional life that one historian speaks of Wright's "almost pathological fondness for children."[27]

But there is no reason to disparage the fine moments he spent with little boys and girls. His correspondence is filled with their letters to one adult who paid attention to them and treasured their love. Reminiscing in 1905, a seventy-year-old Irish woman clearly depicted the "vitality" and "good humor" of his visits sixty years before. He sang songs, ranging from "The Days When We Went Gypsying" to "The Cold Water Army," with the children clustered around his knee and joining "very much ad libitum" in the choruses. He read "by the hour," never indicating that "he might be less interested than ourselves in Hop-o-my-thumb" and pausing only occasionally, "poor man, to take breath, and saying 'Now, let's think,' which seemed to us quite unnecessary." He was delightfully at odds with polite attitudes toward children: "One day while Henry Wright was walking around Stephen's Green, holding my hand in one of his, and his hat in the other, swinging along and singing heartily, an old woman stopped us and told him he ought to be ashamed of himself. Probably she supposed him to be tipsy. He answered her pleasantly, quite undisturbed." What vivid memories of a childhood love! "When Henner . . . was going back to America [in 1847], I felt as though life would not be worth living without him."[28]

Wright was still a slow public speaker, a reserved public man. With children he broke out of his chrysalis and developed intense attachments that were free of crisis. This was the other side of his mastery over children as the agent of reform movements: if he was their guide, they were his emancipator. After spending the decade of the 1830s enticing them into sabbath schools and abolition brigades, he discovered that they had taught him the difference between repression and spontaneity. Besides giving him love, they helped him find new versions of reform.

There was one special child whom he sought to convert into an international celebrity: Catherine Paton, one of "Scotia's noblest children," called in many of his writings "My Wee Darling," and in his diaries simply "Wee." *Marriage and Parentage* (1855) began with a sweet portrait of her leaning by his side. His rambles with her were probably his most popular writings, and he sold the same picture at lectures and conventions. In *Human Life* (1849) he repeatedly interrupted memories of Hartwick, Andover, or West Newbury, in order to depict scenes of his present frolicking with Wee. When she dragged him from his desk to play with shells, he drew the moral: "Would that I could ever have the simplicity, the confidence, the truthfulness, freshness and innocence of this child: It purifies, elevates and refreshes my spirit to mingle it with hers. . . ."[29]

Wee's father was a merchant named Andrew Paton who, like other wealthy Glaswegians, rented summer quarters for his family among the hills and lochs where the Clyde reaches into the Highlands. For several years Henry Wright stayed in the attics of their cottages on

Rosneath peninsula, carrying out his writing for the year, celebrating the beauty of the Central Highlands for American abolitionists, and romping through the heather with little Catherine. When he took a steamboat to his lectures and conventions, she missed him terribly: "you have a nice mouth for kissing," she wrote, wishing she could crawl into his lap and go to sleep with him. After one ardent day with her, Wright yearned to become "like a little child in the spirit and simplicity of my heart" so that he would be fit for the kingdom of heaven.[30]

Play authorized pleasures that Wright lacked in reality: he could be sovereign and lover. Children established him as a kind of godlike king or master rivaling God. In real life he fell in the mud at the thought of replacing God and denied that he would cast a ballot even if he were empowered to end slavery by that single act. In *A Kiss for a Blow*, however, his playmates elected him king and he sat high on a throne of snow.[31] With Wee he imagined himself presiding over multitudes in a world's convention: "I should like to congregate all of human kind on these mountains around, and speak to them of human brotherhood." When his playmate doubted whether his voice could carry so far, his attitude toward the natural beauty of the glens turned slightly equivocal. "'O,' I say, 'it is not over one hundred miles, and that is not much in these railway times. With the voice of an archangel, and the trump of God, i.e., the electric telegraph, I could speak to a world on human brotherhood.'" Quite simply, the innocence of children released fantasies of guiltless mastery and thus helped him pass through difficult transitions in his life.[32]

Since power was allied with sexuality, there was something furtive about his friendships with children. They were parodies of liaisons in which he could protest his sexual propriety; they delimited the boundaries of come-outerism. They gave him a secret life. But when attacked for letting go, he could rightly declare that he was not tipsy, mad, or libertine. Furtiveness and exposure were the themes of an interesting public letter to Garrison about Wee: "I am glad no mortal eyes are upon me," he began, as he experienced the kingdom of heaven in the "perfect mingling of human hearts" with his beautiful companion. He yielded his soul to her, and she forgot the "differences between us which age, size or other circumstances might suggest."

> I said, I was glad no mortal eyes were upon us in our merry rompings. Why? Not that I feel there is any thing wrong or weak

> in this affection for that child, and in throwing my whole soul into her sports and amusements. No: Heaven forbid that I should be ashamed of the best part of my nature. . . . I am not ashamed to have these lofty mountains, the bright sun, and the Being who made them, look down upon my rompings with that child of nature: why should I fear to have the eyes of my fellow beings upon me? . . . Mortals may sneer at such childlike amusements; I glory in my capacity to join in them, and I am willing the eyes of all the immortals should be upon me and my wee darling, in our wanderings by dark lochs and over hills of heather, and in our songs, our dancing, and our "round about merry-matanzas;" for they would see nothing but joyous innocence in them, and would be glad to join us, if they could.[33]

The letter exemplifies, almost comically, what Weld called Wright's "itching to be *known*": his penchant for parading his intimate life in public and boasting of his conquests. The letter was also a formulaic way of discussing sexual restlessness. He simply could not conduct the quest for perfection in hermitlike seclusion; he was ever watchful for an audience. His romps with Wee were so far from public outrage that they helped establish Wright as an author, but he used them to signal that he was grappling with secret thoughts. Wee people furnished safe pretexts for exploring how far large men could go in breaking society's rules. His romantic effusions about children dramatized two related facts concerning his British years: emotionally, he was tired of celibate reform; and professionally, he was preparing to advocate new codes of marriage.

Dangerous Liaisons

When he crossed the ocean in 1842, Henry Wright was forty-five years old. He soon considered reform an unhappy substitute for a failed marriage and began to look around for new attachments. It is impossible to be sure of the full story, for Wright and his female correspondents vigorously crossed out many key passages in his journals. The network of Victorian reformers in which he traveled simply papered over disturbing clues to scandal in their midst. It is clear, however, that there was a covert side to a series of deeply meaningful relationships with abolitionist women, including Elizabeth Pease and Mary Martin in England, and the Poole sisters and Maria Waring in Ireland. The Highlands were the appropriate site for his diversionary romps with Wee, because Scotland was the one leg of his travels on which he had no reason to fear "the eyes of my fellow beings."

Quite possibly, throughout Britain the abolitionism of wives and daughters was more radical than that of husbands and fathers. As a representative of the radical wing of American abolitionism, Wright's contacts with British women extended well beyond his customary interviews with spouses in the American families who housed him. In intimate conversations, moreover, British women disclosed a kind of restlessness that was new and exciting.

After arriving in Liverpool, feverish, coughing, weak from seasickness, he headed directly to Dublin, where he entered a circle of fervent reformers, mostly Quakers, interrelated by marriage and united by warm loving ties. The male leaders, all well known to New England abolitionists, were Richard D. Webb, Richard Allen, and James Haughton; of greater importance to the convalescent Wright were the ladies. Hannah Waring Webb (thirty-two years old in 1842) he apotheosized as the perfect mother, though thirteen years his junior. More intimate, and closer to his own level of sanctitude, were her sister Maria Waring (twenty-five years old), Elizabeth (twenty-five) and Sarah (twenty-nine) Poole of Wexford, and two sisters from Limerick—Susanna Fisher (twenty-seven) and Deborah Fisher Gough (thirty-two). Intensely interested in reform, these ladies were also playful, gossipy, and confessional; they towed up the undersides of emotions in a way Wright had never encountered among American evangelicals. Decorations in the first diary of his British years include rows of mounted soldiers, with this inscription: "Presented by Lizzie Poole as a token of her Love for his enemies." Sarah Poole once wrote him: "My heart blesses thee for the pity that is in thine, for the love, and for the *hate* too. . . . Art thou not an excellent hater?"[34]

On December 11, 1842, after illness had let him tarry a month and a half in Dublin, he recorded his impressions of Maria Waring—an important entry with a marker at the page. She had a good mind that had not been encouraged. "As to her heart—it is full of all kindly & loving feelings but her affections have budded & blossomed & *perished*, as it were, in her own bosom. She has never been accustomed to entwine them vigorously & actively around her fellow beings—made to repress rather than foster & act out the warm gushing affections of her generous & noble heart. I feel for such persons, & with my whole soul execrate the artificial system that has crushed them." A few weeks later he observed that Susanna Fisher also was "confined—she feels cramped—has not room for her soul to expand in. I wish she were in a situation to let out all the energy of her affections." But the morbidity in these lives alternated with laughing speculations: he proposed that Lizzie Poole should "invent a new creature, a machine," impervious to cold, heat, death, and drunkenness, and capable of providing "unexcited enjoyment" for the earth's dissatisfied. A new model husband, no less![35]

Maria Waring had already decided she felt more comfortable with Garrisonians than with most British abolitionists, because they were women's rights men who did not treat women as dolls. Now she made Wright uncomfortable with the shocking doctrine that "it is a sin, in itself, for a man & woman, however they may love each other, to promise each to the other to live together as man & wife for life." Much of what follows is obliterated; apparently Wright argued against her but still believed she was "pure & high minded."[36] Wright was hearing new ideas and female complaints before he had confessed, even in his journal, dissatisfaction with his own marriage.

How much advanced doctrine on love and marriage greeted Wright during his first stay in Ireland? He often conversed with Maria Waring, and someone crossed out most of the record. He also knew men who held unorthodox opinions. Lizzie Poole recalled years later that Maria's brother Thomas, who "took my fancy a good deal," was a pale esthete, well dressed and cool in manner. "Ah, poor boy! He had no moral stamina, and consumed himself in extracting pleasure from the things of sense. He died at the age of 28."[37] Then there was the intellectually gifted Joseph Poole, whose sad life nearly summed up the disturbed interior of Quaker benevolence in Ireland. According to Sarah's tragic account, Joseph had "alighted upon" Shelly's poems and they "poisoned" him. Early illnesses and career irresolution seemed on the verge of cure, until an "interesting girl" rejected him. Religious ferment excited their generation, "and this young woman romantically formed the idea of not entering into any matrimonial connexion—but still the friendship continued for some time." The problem of marriage always lay in the background of his troubles. After another wave of religious enthusiasm, for example: "He avowed an attachment to a pious young woman—All old romances seemed to be done away." Sarah also spoke darkly of "a marriage [that] took place in the family that gave uneasiness" at the same time as a potato failure hit his lands. Otherwise, Joseph's was a long story of ill-conceived business ventures, brooding over Catholic unrest, poor health (he accompanied Henry Wright in search of the water cure), attempted suicide, and incarceration for "mental weakness."[38]

From passionate Ireland Wright went to the north of England, still coughing and feverish, but determined to resume his errand of reform. In May he reached the Yorkshire home of Elizabeth Pease, daughter of a wealthy Quaker family who were bulwarks of peace and antislavery. This woman has almost eluded historical notice—partly because of her modesty, which increased after her marriage in the 1850s to a Glasgow professor. At times, however, she was the most important link in transatlantic abolitionism, and she inspired much affection. Garrison and George Thompson both named daughters after her. Wright soon found himself engaged in duplicity. When he met Samuel May in Glasgow, for example, and the Massachusetts abolitionist called Elizabeth Pease "the noblest specimen of a human being he had met in the Kingdom," Wright was secretly thrilled. But he noted in a diary that he sent to her, another one that is heavily obliterated, "so cold I *seemed* to what he said that he really thought I did not assent to his applause."[39]

Wright came to Darlington to meet Elizabeth and her illustrious family on May 6, 1843. He spent the next five days in unending conversation about reform and, evidently, in being coaxed back to health, for he often spoke of her fondly as "my nurse." At antislavery and peace conventions in London, June 1843, he spent more time with her. The precious value of one episode on a sofa in a hotel's back parlor shines through obliteration: "Wherever I wander, East or West, North or South, by sea or land, that parlor and that sofa will live in my heart." In succeeding months he felt the kind of torment regarding this attachment that he had experienced, years before, in detaching himself from his West Newbury home. In July he lamented his excessive care for worldly opinion, but it was not exactly the abstemious life of Christian reform for which he yearned. He would rather die than offend God, he protested, but he had possibly offended Him by worrying too much about the opinions of men "in a case where I feel sure I have the approbation of God." As he traveled on to Liverpool and Glasgow his diary noted more emotional convolutions. He regretted causing her "a moment's anxiety or trouble." Yet he felt sure, in between crossed out passages, there was only "one created being in the universe that could solve the present mystery of my soul"—his soothing nurse. On August 19, his forty-sixth birthday, he reflected on the crucial year just passed. He had written his first book *(A Kiss for a Blow),* taken his first Atlantic crossing, at the cost of a "shock to my physical nature from which it will never recover." He had visited many towns and studied the British character in its natural habitat. And in this "year of experience," most important of all, he had met Elizabeth Pease. "My personal acquaintance & intercourse with E. P. have formed an era in the history of my spirit. No mortal ever had that influence over me."[40]

There is no way of determining what "dear Lizzie" was to him besides a nurse. Richard Webb reported to American abolitionists: "H. C. Wright is not very strong, but he has had the best medical advice in London, through the kind and watchful attention of Elizabeth Pease, who acts as a daughter towards him."[41] We know too much today about secret lives and protective silence in Victorian England to be sure she was only nurse and daughter. But Wright's pattern, as we shall see, was to infantilize women with whom he desired intimacy (he also favored the passive role of patient). In these circumstances the women may not have suspected that any border of propriety had been crossed. When Elizabeth talked about Wright to correspondents who knew him, no false note suggested the slightest anxiety in her mind.[42] Nevertheless, we cannot see her letter that Henry vowed to keep forever, and we lack the "old letters from E. P." that he sat up reading one night before launching into obliterated musings on her "heart" and femininity."[43] From looking at his subsequent adventures we know that she raised a painful question—could he remarry?—but perhaps she ignored strange overtones during their meetings, even on that memorable sofa.

On August 18, a woman named Mary Martin sent him a "sweet" letter (the word was unsuccessfully blotted out) exhorting him to be kind to E. P. Next she sent her framed profile, and Elizabeth praised her lovingness, generosity, beauty of spirit. Was she summoning a more eligible woman to whom Wright could transfer his need for love? Or did she introduce them only because he needed a professional nurse? The relationship, in any event, quickly developed a momentum of its own. He went to a watering spot, Weston-sur-la-Mare, and met "the pet darling of E. Pease," whom he described, in an unusual burst of physical detail, as a "short, black-haired, black-eyed, rather dark-complexioned, sweet faced, rather slender framed woman." Someone marked over his observation that she was "very affectionate," and in his account of walking with her by the sea the word "dear" is also canceled. The web of surreptitiousness was more and more complicated.[44]

On his first night in Weston, fever and chills (and the discomfort of having imbibed too much hot water) kept him awake. Mary joined him on the beach early in the morning and they walked until he was able to sleep a little. She sent him grapes but he could not eat; then she returned in the afternoon to nurse him. For ten days they watched his health and walked on beach and esplanade by sunlight and moonlight. "Dear, precious Mary," we can read through patches of ink; it was "sweet to mingle spirits with such an one."[45]

In another back parlor, on September 11, he and Mary said farewell. She sat beside him and promised to return to nurse him if sickness struck again anywhere in England. In the months ahead there were frequent obliterations wherever his journals referred to this sweet nurse. In December he indicated that he was sending his diaries to her, to enjoy and censor. But we know her feeling about him only from a public letter to Garrison in which she compared her meeting with Henry to Garrison's with Elizabeth Pease (how tangled these transoceanic alliances became!). She had previously "loved" Henry "for his writings," and now she received the chance "to look in his face, and hear him talk about our relation to God and Man, Time and Eternity. . . . Oh! I do feel that week has added much to my responsibilities; for in Henry I have seen what I consider to be a model of Christian character."[46] By characterizing him as an authentic Christian, unlike men who talked without acting or who behaved like "automatons," she provided ironic commentary on the links between his earnest religiosity and the emotional frustrations he had breathed to her.

After recuperating under Mary Martin's care, Wright fell ill once more in Ireland. It was widely believed that he was dying: Elizabeth Pease and the Dublin circle prevailed on him to journey to the famous water cure establishment at Graefenberg in Silesia. His traveling companion was the unlucky Shelleyite Joseph Poole, and the connections between health and love became even more intense. There is so much scissoring and blotting out in Wright's Graefenberg diaries that I cannot establish to which of his friends he sent them. It is clear that Joseph shared his secrets, even the name of his favorite mountain to climb, Mount Elizabeth (others were Mount Maria and Mount Garrison).[47]

Wright loved Joseph, despite his recklessness, and admired his fidelity to convictions. He participated in Joe's bittersweet romance with a patient named Elizabeth Baker (who called Wright "mon cher papa" and herself "your affectionate daughter Lizzie"). Joseph's departure was a small crisis: Henry took a cold bath, climbed Mount Elizabeth, and confided to his diary that he needed someone to love.

Only by playing with children, he wrote, could he cope with his distress; they poured out their souls and his expressions of love were uninhibited. No one hollered "prudence" or "Propriety."[48]

There was obvious duplicity in his book *Six Months at Graefenberg; with Conversations in the Saloon, on Nonresistance and Other Subjects.* Not a mention is there of Mount Elizabeth or Lizzie Baker, not a breath of Joseph's views of marriage; instead, Wright presented himself as a high-minded reformer vigilant against evil and falsehood. The same duplicity typifies the long series of public letters on Graefenberg, published in the *Liberator* and frequently addressed to his wife and stepchildren, as though he longed exclusively to be with them. "It is a pleasant thought to me," he said to his American Elizabeth, "as it must be to you, that your heart is freed from all this malignant prejudice against color. Go on, to cheer the crushed and wounded spirits of the victims of American religion and American Republicanism; and God forever bless you and yours." No need to holler "Propriety" at this effusion! Nor at his wish, as sites of the Reformation renewed his anger at American religion, "Oh that you, dear wife, and all your children were come out forever from all connexion with these slaveholding and war-making churches."[49] The causes of reform once carried him away from home; now they fostered a semblance of family unity to hide new adventures he was contemplating.

The woman who most fully captured his heart after he came back from Graefenberg was Maria Waring. Before he left, on December 16, 1843, they had shared intimate moments in Mt. Jerome cemetery, where they agreed to "feel & think aloud" before one another. Such openness necessitated the deletion of many journal pages; it made them very close. Wright knocked on a tomb, and they disputed whether anyone could hear, whether the earth was indeed a dismal place. Wright's view was that the highest human energies and sentiments flourished in the wake of death, while Maria, regrettably, was an infidel who could not face death serenely. Death and the spirit life had long interested Wright, but in this instance graveyard conversation was a kind of metaphor for immediate problems of coming-out. As so often in his British diaries, Wright chided his cowardly inability to act: "Why should we ever feel ashamed of what our God has made us to be & to feel? It seems dishonest to God—to seek to conceal from men what we are willing to have known to God." He was approaching Maria's view of marriage, and wanted courage to bring his affections into the sunlight.[50]

The cemetery was never far from his struggles with spontaneity. In *Human Life* he recorded a visit, with little Catherine Paton, to the Glasgow Necropolis, overlooking the scene "where Mary fought her last battle for her throne." He reflected that he was always as happy in the cemetery as in the forest—past and future joyously intertwined in both. Yet he confessed sadness when thinking of his body—"a thing so intimately connected with all I have known of existence, so cherished, so fondled, so loved, the care of which has occupied so many of my thoughts and feelings"—dissolving in the ground. Nor was it easy to bury a loved one. "I asked myself how I should like to lay away, to become dust, the body of my Wee darling, who was by my side; a face and form I had so often looked upon and caressed, and that had so often nestled in my bosom." He thanked God for death, nevertheless, "for I felt that what constituted that loved child and companion would survive death, to meet me again." Although he presented this passage as an excerpt from his Scottish journals, the actual pages reveal that it was Maria who occupied his thoughts as he rambled among the tombs. He had, in short, slipped M. W. into his autobiography as "one of Scotia's noblest women."[51] This deviousness was all the more fitting, because Henry and Maria gained their occasions for intimacy on account of his reputation as the spontaneous friend of children and her responsibilities for the Webb nieces and nephews. At one point Wright wrote obliquely concerning "this trickery about the children." At other times he felt unable to be candid even with her. "Though I am apparently frank & open—I am desperately *secretive* about my feelings & thoughts."[52]

In late 1846 the relationship climaxed in importance. On October 27, he bemoaned "a want of one who has lived in me & for me, & in whom & for whom I have lived the past few weeks." How he wished they were "settled down" together, so that they could take care of each other. That being impossible, it pleased him to think of her coming to stay in the bed at the Webbs' house that he currently occupied. They were usually apart, and composing love letters to her became the pleasantest portion of his day, reviving his memories of "mingling our entire natures into one." If a line of these letters vexed or saddened her, he authorized her to destroy it. His yearning for a daguerreotype of her ceased when Hannah Webb secured one for him and another for "our dear Lizzie" (probably Pease). When Garrison visited Liverpool in November, Wright refused to lend him the picture. He did share a treasured letter from Maria, though he later felt guilty about this exposure and tendered an apology. "All that was said was to your praise & I confess my heart responded *emphatically* to all they said about the letter. . . . I do know you are my own . . . [crossed out] child, & therefore I cannot without pain endure to cause any feeling of sorrow to your [crossed out] heart."[53]

Wright's characterizations of her were strikingly ambiguous. She was part lover (they mingled natures); part child (like all the women he cherished). "You are my own, loving, kind father," she told him. Though she vexed him in some ways, he said, "I love you still, you are my . . .[obliterated] child—& no father's heart ever clung to a loved child with more fondness & tenacity than mine cleaves to you." In addition to such familial affections, she held abstract importance as the incarnation of the spirit of *excelsior.* "I know thy nature—I love it—I love thee . . .(crossed over) because life with thee is earnest & great, never frivolous & vain."[54] In spite of rhetorical wishes that they might live together, unattainability was essential to the relationship, which could not be allowed to interfere with the grand business of humanity through which Wright hustled to his grave. Wistful thoughts and letter writing supplied a counterpoint to the earnestness of his commitments. Theirs was a solemn affair, built on the necessity of striving and the reality of distance.

The sexual content of the relationship is uncertain. Clearly it reawakened confused feelings about his body's requirements for gratification. In some ways, Wright's tendencies toward self-denial were becoming more pronounced, verging on self-mortification in Mount Elizabeth's icy streams and on Mount Maria's snowy slopes. He prophesied the consummation of the affair when the couple *discarded* their bodies. Yet he wanted his body to be nursed and comforted; part of his learning in Britain, however conflictful, was that his body might be liked. We catch glimpses of the conflict when he wrote Maria about a coat that one of the Lizzies gave him: "I know you will admire the *coat,* if not the *body* it covers. The *coat* will be precious to you, if—I was going to say if the *body* is not, but that thought should not have entered my mind & I do not think it except as a *joke,* but I have no right to joke thee . . . [obliterated] in that way—for well do I know thou wilt care nothing about a coat except as it contributes to the comfort of my body."[55]

The point is that interest in his own body revived in a context of intimate conversations with women who complained about male lust—self-regard was tied to self-control. After hearing the revulsion several women in Maria's circle felt toward one demanding husband, Wright took the side of wives and mothers: "If I were a woman

I'd... act on my own responsability [*sic*] as to the disposal of my bodily functions. They should not be used for purposes which I abhorred."[56] His personal emancipation merged with modern ladies' usually silent discovery that control over fertility was a key to self-respect. This merger goes a long way toward explaining how his emotional turmoil in Britain contributed to his subsequent career as an authority on the home. But in the short run what mattered most were new experiences of potency and control. Maria had "worked a change" in him, he told her. It was a beneficial change, and no one else ever had affected him similarly. "I must tell thee in what [the change consists] if I can get near enough to thee to do it. You'll love to hear it, & I shall love to tell it. It is a pleasant change & makes me happier & better every way. If I can get near... [blotted out] thee again, I'll tell thee."[57]

In spite of the disembodied state to which Wright often ascribed the perfection of their love, it remains possible that their affair was explicitly sexual. Perhaps they followed one of the plans for male continence—intercourse without ejaculation—promoted by reformers of their day. This blend of birth control with restrained, spiritualized excitement was consistent with Wright's subsequent teachings on sex. We cannot be sure that the affair with its inevitable interruption by the Atlantic was not also an experiment in interrupted or prolonged sex. Or perhaps Wright developed his American sexual expertise as a denial of the frustration of a series of unconsummated relationships abroad. Perhaps he was only an awkward, beloved, embarrassingly confessional father figure in Maria's presence, just as his later lectures on sexuality evaded frank discussion of coition.

Whatever its sexual content, the affair was a source of covert pleasure. Notes of concealed excitement buzzed through his correspondence with Sarah and Elizabeth Poole, notes that were quite foreign to his usual role as a practical Christian. Sarah was the subject of rumors herself, and Henry warned Maria, at least once, that he didn't want to hear about them. Yet his correspondence with Sarah is filled with ironic, private references, particularly when she teased him about Maria and his need to be petted.[58] Richard Webb, sensing undertones in his household that he didn't understand, asked Edmund Quincy about Wright's curious indifference to his American home. In an 1857 letter he was far more direct. Wright had troubled Dublin abolitionists by "the handle he would have given [foes of reform] if his dallying with young ladies had been observed."

Wright had, in effect, been protected by his abolitionist friends' wish to avoid the hint of scandal. It was not until after his death that Webb conceded that he never trusted him and disliked his "unpleasant oily manners" with young women.[59]

Webb also provided the only descriptions of his sister-in-law. Twice he used the same words: Maria was "a silent, reserved and morbidly conscientious body." In 1849 he added that she "would go to the stake in any cause in which her conscience was involved." She was always counted one of the most generous contributors to the fairs and bazaars through which antislavery women worked for the cause. Webb also observed: "She is a staunch friend of H. C. Wrights, who, I believe, is almost her only correspondent." Maria did not marry until 1858, at which time Webb called her "a tender spirited, conscientious, strong willed young woman of forty, whose hair has grown prematurely grey & who has yet a remarkably youthful & sweet expression of countenance." She married a doctor, slightly older than herself; the family welcomed the marriage, though she had to be disciplined by the Quakers for going outside the sect.[60]

When, if ever, correspondence ceased between Henry Wright and the future Mrs. James G. Palmer is unknown. He had begun the relationship with a sense that their destinies overlapped, that they were bound to give each other "great happiness or misery—or both," and that, although they would never spend much time together, they would influence one another far into the "dark future." Then he came to expect a reunion when "our bodies will . . . be thrown aside." Writing from America in 1849, he reiterated, rather pompously, that they loved each other as manifestations of God.[61] It is not clear whether they had made any commitments to each other on either side of the veil. He evidently felt free to construct new relationships after returning to America (and before she married). There is no doubt, however, that he had found the thee-and-thouing Quakers of Britain an exhilarating group, who helped him break with his past and reintroduced him to long dormant agonies. Maria Waring in particular was equaled in emotional importance only by his mother and his later acquaintance Julia Wass Friend.

A Course of Concealment

During these exciting days Henry Wright kept several diaries; one written on the fly with a metallic pencil, a more reflective one resembling his American diaries (though dropping Greek and Hebrew), and various journal-letters mailed to his lady loves, censored, sewn together, and returned. At Elizabeth Pease's home in Darlington in 1843 he began to write intermittently in what he eventually described as "my most *private* journal—the only friend into whose faithful bosom I can pour out all that is in my soul."[62]

Sometimes, he noted, it took daring to set down his thoughts anywhere. There are blank pages in the secret journal, and the entries are not in chronological order (suggesting, perhaps, the existence of an ur-journal on these private topics). The subject of this journal was love and sexuality—or what another Victorian with a penchant for secrecy called "nympholepsy . . . or the longing for a wife."[63] Nowhere else is the pain in Wright's life more visible; nowhere else are his theological and social opinions so unmistakably connected with private trials and conflicts. In this journal, we may trace his route, during his years away from America, from peace and antislavery to marriage and parentage.

In the first Darlington entries he confessed that his heart longed "to be sought by some woman." He was a wanderer on earth, looking for a home. He must locate a woman's love, for his heart could not be "absorbed" by man; yet he had never found a woman who would take his heart. "All my heart's energies are driven back to prey upon itself, & my own bosom is the grave of my purest, brightest, most divine emotions. I die hourly," he continued, "for want of an object of adoration, in human, female, form on which to exhaust the resistless, ever-grasping energies of my soul."

> I cannot live in my self. I cannot exist in my own heart. I never wish to go there; except to visit the guests that are there—whose sweet faces are deguerreotyped [*sic!*] there. An unappropriated heart has been the bane of my life. I want to give my heart to some woman, who can enter into it, know its nature—who can treat it gently—who would feel gentle toward it, & use it lovingly & gently. I have borne a heavy load, all my days since I was 12 years old. That burden has often seemed too heavy to be borne. I have reeled & staggered under the heavy weight. That burden is *my heart*. . . . How earnestly I have struggled to roll that burden upon the God of my childhood & youth. Oh—I have often looked into that deep concave above me & with tears of agony, sought to give my heart to that God who, I was taught [,] claimed it. . . . There was no rest, no holy & sublime rest, no swallowing up of my being. I could not give my heart to that being who was presented to me as a God. He always seemed a cold, stern, hard man. My soul turned away. There was nothing in him that filled myself.

After this review of the loneliness in the wide universe and the religious uncertainties that had plagued him since childhood, Wright turned directly to his marriage:

> I have been appropriated to one woman, as a wife, whom, in my ignorance, I promised to love, while we lived; but my heart never for one moment blessed & sanctified the deed. Within 24 hours after the ceremony—my eyes were open to see the gulf into which I had blindly leaped. I saw that my heart never had been & never could be, given to that woman. She could not receive it—nor understand it. From that hour I commenced a course of *concealment.* The shame of defeat kept me silent. I had no fault to find with her. She was not to blame nor was I.
>
> To this hour my heart has been in solitude, so far as Marriage is concerned. It never was merged with a woman. I die. I am oft in agony to give it all away. It is useless to try to give it to God, unless God be embodied in the soul of a woman. I never expect to find a wife, to experience the power, the saving, elevating influence, of a *love-wife,* a heart-wife, a wife of my heart's own choosing, & of my heart's own marrying. A conventional wife has utterly failed to elevate me to God. I cannot give her my heart—nature's heart. She can receive & understand only a conventional heart. I never had such an one to give.
>
> Oh that God would come to me, in the form of a pure, daring, fire-souled, great-souled woman, & take entire & eternal possession of my heart. With what devotion would I exhaust upon such a being all the divine energies of my soul. I would surround that loved one with the holy incense of love & worship.
>
> My heart aches—it is in a vice—it is crushed by loneliness & solitude. If my heart were in the possession of some loved woman & I had the sweet consciousness of feeling it to be at rest in her bosom—I never could be in solitude more.[64]

To this melancholia he gave the title "Unappropriated Heart." In other journals he professed shock at unorthodox views of marriage. Here he sounded like a prisoner of Victorian attitudes toward divorce, struggling to persuade himself of the legitimacy of flight and liberation.

Besides its frank discussion of marital failure, probably exaggerated over the years, and its references to father-God's coldness, leading to Henry's own blocked affections, this passage stresses another important theme. What exactly was it that his heart had never experienced? As the grand organ of romantic love, the heart performed many acts, including the swoons, faints, and aches that Wright detailed so poetically. But is it possible to substitute penis for heart in order to see what his father frightened him from using, what he feared might be swallowed up, what no man could absorb, what no woman had ever elevated, and what he had never merged in woman? Doubtless the reasons for his marital frustration were complex, but it seems likely that the discovery made within twenty-four hours—en route to Niagara—was sexual. The significance of the passage does not simply look backward. While it linked a yearning for potency with fantasies of exhausted energy and desires to worship a woman, it also pointed toward his eventual advocacy of retentive and infrequent coition.

To this private journal he confided years of sexual abstinence from his wife: "we have no desire for each other's society as male & female—she wishes not to be carressed by me, nor do I by her—we are simple friends—without one emotion of Marriage love between us." But the desires to be loved as a spouse and to join in the creation of children were essential to man's "harmonious development." Writing in Darlington in May 1843, Wright envisioned a clandestine marriage: "My heart finds its mate—twines around hers—my being is absorbed in hers & hers in mine." In secret they call each other husband and wife. "We sleep together. We long for a child." But why, he asked, need it be in secret? Since he had not had "conjugal-marriage intercourse" with his legal wife since the day when he discovered they had nothing more than friendship, he believed that natural and divine law allowed him and his love "to recognize each other as husband & wife—to live together as such—& to propagate." In 1843 such legal rationalizations were premature; his problem was still loneliness and self-absorption, if not impotency. "Oh that I might find before I pass into another state a woman,—who would thus become to me an essential element of existence—a Regenerator—a Redeemer—to lead me out of myself—into a kingdom of love & goodness."[65] But whatever Elizabeth Pease, Mary Martin, Maria Waring, and other miscellaneous women who were intimate with *cher papa* Wright may have thought was occurring in their relationships, this journal proves that he recognized, at least partially, that his purposes were sexual. Well might he worry whether the eyes of the world beheld him in moments of spontaneity. Men like Theodore Weld and Richard Webb who resented his manners with women—though they made their own projections, no doubt—were not wide of the mark. This nonresistant had "resistless" energies to disseminate among women; their innocent faces were "deguerreotyped" on his heart.

He tried hard to be fair to Elizabeth LeBreton Stickney Wright in these confessions, just as he honored her with mildly affectionate public letters. Yet he had begun to consider unhappiness a disease to be purged. To the ceremonial cleansing of aggression through the drama of nonresistance was being added a daily routine of bathing in clear cold water and restriction of diet to pure, plain foods. His loves were nurses. The paternal God of theology was giving way to the maternal nature-God of anthropology who viewed all social wrongs as pollution. It was not possible, in this frame of mind, to remain magnanimous toward Mrs. Wright. In July 1844, returning from the baths at Graefenberg, he compared her to a toxin: "I took her, & she me in good faith—thinking we could administer to each others social health & development. But I find, as she finds, that the woman is a poison to my social nature. She cannot develope the marriage nor the parental element of my nature, nor I hers. This noblest & purest part of my being must be crushed, crucified. Must I ask the consent of society before I cast out this poison?"[66]

Wright subsumed his private torments under the cause of physiological perfectionism. Not only did he need to eject a poison for the sake of his own growth, but the same condition existed globally. In what was supposedly his most private document, he was still representative of human life. Mankind's perfection depended on universalizing love matches, producing love babies. Writing in Austria in 1844, he depicted conventional loveless marriages as no better than prostitution because they let sexual relations follow the dictates of convenience and sensuality, unregulated by love. When man and woman propagated in a conventional marriage, the fetus's development suffered from the lack of a loving environment and the child was born "physically and socially diseased." As a corollary, there was no wrong in bearing children outside conventional marriage where love was the law. Children were so natural an expression of love that it was wrong to stay married without the possibility of bearing them. The state had no rightful control over affairs of the heart, except perhaps to record marriages and births.[67]

In May 1845 he returned to the same problem. Under the heading "Subjects for Reflection," he pondered whether the enactments of church or state could make a wrong right. Of course the Garrisonians had long since declared that nothing could legitimize slavery or murder, and now Wright added that only love could sanctify marriage, which was a necessity of nature just like eating and sleeping. When a man and a woman wished to "propagate," nature gave the only relevant license. Yet church and state proclaimed "procreative intercourse" a great sin until they authorized it; then they pretended "intercourse every day or hour is pure & right."[68] There was a logic in Garrisonian reform, in short, that allowed Wright to see society's rules as wanton and his personal rebellion as restraint.

In June 1845, under the heading "The design of this generative passion," Wright phrased the tacit question of Victorian reform: did the procreative act have two purposes—the creation of children and "simple gratification"? Plainly coitus was justified, inside or outside marriage, when a couple desired children. Plainly church and state could not sanctify unloving coitus. But was loving sexual intercourse for the purpose of gratification unhealthful, or was it natural? Certainly the "universal opinion" was that propagation was the sole end of coitus. Wright did not settle the question, which might have complicated his pose of restraint, but turned instead to a more shocking one, "Is it a crime in a man to solicit & have intercourse with a woman who does not love him but whom he loves?" To this question he knew the answer: "She is a prostitute for yielding & he is guilty of prostituting her."[69]

In July 1847, under the heading "Mystery," he hinted that even his intimacy with Maria Waring had not risen to the pitch of a love-marriage, although he experienced "daily" the sweetness of friendship. In spite of passionate relationships with young women, his sexual desires went unfulfilled. One part of his nature, he wrote, remained mysterious to him, "an ocean never fathomed." Only a love marriage could solve the mystery; meanwhile, his conventional marriage was "a living death," and he knew the wonders of love only as a starving man knows the taste of food. "Till my whole being is absorbed into that of some pure, generous, noble, high-minded woman—I can never understand myself." Most remarkably, this intimate of hundreds of families suffered whenever he saw others embrace, bear children, or nurse babies. As he admitted unhappiness with the itinerant life that he had spent years in shaping, he revised his watchword: "Why must I be alone in the universe? Be without God? For he that is without a wife—a *love-wife*, & she who is without a *love-husband*—is without God—in the highest sense. Science, Philosophy, Religion cannot teach him to know God—nothing but a love-wife—love-marriage—can reveal this mystery."[70] Even while probing his wish to be settled in a home, however, he was slipping from the first to the third person, from sufferer to expert on the problem, from patient to doctor.

It was not simply loneliness in this world that frightened him. In the private journal he confessed another fear, quite inconsistent with his visions of disembodied reunion with Maria. "A man who has no *love-wife* & no *love-children,*" he wrote, "(no matter how many conventional wives & children he may have had) cannot be fitted to enter upon that higher life." He faced immortality as a dwarf, an "abortion," because of his confinement in a conventional marriage with only stepchildren. His "imperative duty," therefore, was to violate society's laws so as to be "fitted to be born into another state."[71] Consider the analogy between two problems the private journal explored: absorption by a woman and birth-passage into the spiritual state. Although Wright blamed his cold father for his sense of inadequacy, complex feelings about his mother also haunted his search for sexual power over women whom he addressed as children. Consider, also, his repeated efforts to believe there was nothing wrong in gratifying his body: "there can be no more wrong, no more impurity, no more indecency, in the desire, nor in the act of propagation than in the desire for food & in the act of eating."[72] Behind this fear of not fitting into heaven lay anxiety that his need for sustenance had injured his mother. It was nearly impossible for him to straighten out his thoughts on purity, gratification, and the law of nature.

The secret journal includes only one woman's voice, one that could not offer him the appropriation he desired. On a loose leaf stuck in this volume appear extracts, in Wright's handwriting, from a letter or conversation. Since none of the women previously discussed had been married—legally, anyway—to a man named Joseph, this dialogue may reveal one more European liaison. Perhaps it was sheer fantasy. In any case, it showed how Victorian delicacy clashed with traditional habits of remarriage; and it brought together, in a new form, two of Wright's preoccupations—exalted intercourse with women and death. The quotation marks are Wright's:

> "I do not *pretend* to feel the emotions for you I did for Joseph; it would be a *sacralege* [*sic*] to make such a profession; but I love you tenderly, *truly,* & would love you *devotedly.*"
>
> "In that—(in intercourse with women) was Joseph superior to any man I ever knew. His love was a *delicate, sacred* thing, *an object of worship.*"
>
> "When my husband died I fully believed there could be but one righteous marriage & that was for Eternity."

"What the future life will bring I can hardly say I know, but let it bring what it will, let us meet it together. . . ."[73]

Wright's private journal, finally, was a place for quotations and page references on physiology and anatomy. Some pages resembled a commonplace book of the pudenda, a repository for scientific accounts of penis, testes and the "organs of generation" in general. These excerpts carried no commentary in Wright's words, no effort to tie them to the sorrows of his unappropriated heart; but they obviously belonged among his clandestine musings on pain and desire. He also used this journal, probably as he recrossed the Atlantic, to draft four chapters of a future book on marriage. Despite its secrecy, in other words, the journal experimented with a new public role. An expert on sexual relations was bound to face "*crucifixion*," he predicted, but the cause cried out for a champion. The lonely itinerant life beckoned. Wright returned to America not as lover, but as love reformer.[74]

Alone without God

When Henry Wright came home, Edmund Quincy noted in the *Liberator* that the news would please many Americans, "for no man in the country has more true friends, or has deserved to have them. . . ." Actually, his failure to return had puzzled abolitionists for some time. Garrison had expected to bring him back in 1846, but Wright's dread of seasickness stood in the way. When he finally separated from Britain in August 1847, he called the voyage "11 days of *Nausea, Vomit & Starvation*." In Halifax he was able to eat again, "in no limited measure," enjoying fresh fruit and berries. He stopped in Boston for another kind of enjoyment—to visit Garrison's wife and children, for their home was, "also, a sweet home to me." Then he made his way to Philadelphia, where Mrs. Wright and the girls (who were now grown up) received him with "merry-making" and "happy greetings." He told his rejoicing friends: "I speak for myself and all the members of my family, when I say that my long absence has only rendered us the dearer to one another, and disposed our hearts to still greater and more affectionate sympathy and confidence, till our final separation on earth." He took pleasure in sitting in his study once again, thinking of his loved ones everywhere. His tears flowed: "it is *glorious* to live."[75]

Probably his reception was just as warm as reported. It was good to be alive, to eat again, to be home. While he was away he had expressed homesickness for "my home in Philadelphia & its dear inmates": his family had written amiably to him and his friends abroad, including Maria Waring.[76] Even in his secret journal his wife was a good friend. After five years of agony and experimentation in Europe, however, it is doubtful that the warmth he found in her household lasted very long. He continued to write Maria. Gaps in his diaries seem to conceal new relationships with women. In 1857 (when Wright was sixty), Richard Webb inquired of Samuel Joseph May whether the rumor was true that Wright was living with a lady "out of marriage bonds." To his relief, May dismissed the story as a revival of earlier charges that had never been proved. May must have retained some doubts, but the episode illustrated the Garrisonians' collusion in Wright's separation of public from private life.[77]

First came a woman called Hetty with whom he perfected the amorous language in which each partner regarded the other as God. She dominated his journals of the late 1840s, and he had her in mind in 1850 when he surveyed vast changes in his character over the preceding decade: he was gentler, less reckless now—tamed by "a sweet child of love." Absence from her revived familiar strains of *Weltschmerz:* "I often dream about you & see you in much sorrow & suffering. I feel no heart for company & for forming new acquaintances. I just wish to be alone; & think over all my relations. Some of my memories of the past are very precious—more so infinitely than any thing present." He praised her aid in his discovery of new topics for the lecture platform—medicine, death, illegitimate children, the improvement of the race. As they exchanged journals (that was the "right way" to correspond, he taught her), she became the model for the perfect wife, named Nina, whom he introduced in *Marriage and Parentage.* He drafted letters that were addressed, almost interchangeably, to Hetty or Nina. On one page headed *Nina* he wrote, for example, "Hetty I love the memory of those sweet domestic hours when our spirit, [*sic*] mingled in sympathy over the great questions of Humanity." She was an important bridge from private analyses of his unappropriated heart to public professions of expertise on physical and spiritual relationships. She was also, quite likely, one of the women involved in rumors that reached Richard Webb.[78]

Wright's partner in this *affaire de coeur* was Esther Ann Lukens of New Garden, Ohio. She came from the Galbreath clan of stalwart abolitionists; although they were of Quaker descent, they took the lead in building "free churches" where humanitarian groups could look for inspiration without sectarian encumbrance. Though never accorded the historical attention given urban abolitionists, they were the sort of family on whom Garrisonism, and indeed all of antislavery, depended. Esther Lukens herself gained some national reputation as an early suffragist. Both she and Maria Waring sent letters to the 1850 Worcester convention on "The Sphere of Women," and her name appeared in newspapers periodically as a representative of the scattered feminist movement in Ohio. In an address published in 1851 (alongside one by Wright), she invoked Goethe's name to prophesy an approaching golden age of equal rights; then she indignantly attacked the view that suffragism made "war upon domestic life; that we would destroy its natural order and attraction by allowing women to mingle in the coarse and noisy scenes of political life." Among other faults, this view sabotaged men's useful participation in the home. Families like hers sustained Boston and New York reformers when they went forth to lecture (hers named children after Charles Burleigh, Parker Pillsbury, and Abby Kelley). When Henry Wright felt oppressed in Philadelphia, he longed for the lecture circuit and her peaceful domicile. "I must get a lease of" a room in her house, he wrote her, "for one year—of thee & David—to be my home—where I can retire when I want to write—as I must spend some time in doing during the coming year."[79]

There is no record of Hetty's family's attitude toward the relationship. But Henry clearly delighted in the blend of covertness and spontaneity that had previously typified his British experiments, and he returned to his old trick of half-exposing secrets to the light of day. In *Anthropology*, the book that marked his breakthrough into science and sexuality, his deception was more intricate than when he substituted wee Catherine for big Maria in his autobiography. This book consisted entirely of letters from Penmaen (Penname?), Ohio, to a lady named "L." in London who has questioned his opinions about the Bible. He assiduously manufactured connections among significant persons in his past, while telling his public to be more present-minded:

> I am in the house of a friend, on the banks of the beautiful Ohio—the most beautiful of all rivers. . . . The ground is covered with snow. I could not resist the temptation to join the children of the family and have a game of snow-ball and sliding down hill. I have just been on the sofa with the joyous group, telling them about my rambles in the Highlands, with "my wee darling," and in London with thee. It is sweet to live in the heart of

> childhood. Why need we become old in spirit? We need not: we should not, if we lived less in the future and more in the present—less in an abstract Divinity and more in an ever-present humanity.

Next his journal reminded him of conversing with L., "under the dome of St. Paul's Cathedral," where they concluded "it will take an eternity" to solve the mystery of human nature. Mostly, their conversation concerned the evils of slavery and war that had been Wright's forte, but he now altered the memory of it so that it alluded to the sexual mystery his private journal had probed: "A recuperative power—a Redeemer—is at work in man, to rescue him from violence and death, and make him what he is designed to be—the bright, beautiful and loved incarnation of Him who is Love and Justice, and whose 'dominion ruleth over all.'" "L." was in fact *El*izabeth Pease, with whom he had toured London and who had just written to condemn his view of the Old Testament. His efforts to couple her with Hetty, not to mention Wee and the sofa, are emblematic of the verbose, inconsistent theory of redemption by which he achieved a little control over his loneliness. Not only was he stuck with furtive gestures to escape from secrecy, but he was unable to justify personal gratification derived from the love of individual women unless he concocted an oceanic "Humanity" sweeping them all along.[80]

It was while writing Hetty that Wright contrasted the lively affection of four-year-old Sarah Gunn to the glacial formality of Mrs. Wright and her daughters. He and Sarah had to hug and kiss secretly, for "she has just had an *orthodox* training, to impress on her the idea that she is too old and too big to sit in my lap." "What would they say," he asked Hetty, "if they were to see some *children* that sit in my lap!" On the one hand, he wished to stress Sarah's innocence: she shared his feeling that it was "perfectly *Godlike* . . . to jump into my arms & nestle & squeeze herself into my heart." On the other, he enjoyed naughty deceptions and joked with Hetty about Sarah's belief that his Ohio friends were "little children—like herself."[81]

Wright went into a tirade about his stepdaughter Elizabeth's plan to take this little girl around Cape Horn to California. He was prepared to miss her terribly, and he was certain that her mother would not survive the voyage. Lewis Gunn he accused of forsaking reform and pursuing money. It embittered Wright that the family appeared "anxious to get them gone" rather than joining his opposition. Maybe it was better for the child to be "swallowed up" by the ocean than to continue in a Calvinistic household that blighted "sweet, noble young hearts."[82]

What an array of meanings children—especially little girls—held! He had given them sabbath schools and antislavery societies; capered with them during his travels; used them to make inquiries about motherhood; substituted them for illicit loves; taken them as pretexts for trysting; adopted their language in turning older women into sweethearts—and soon he would espouse their need of a loving birthright. As the products of sexual unions, they triggered anxieties concerning weakness and power. Instead of surrendering Sarah to the ocean, he wished to adopt her and place her under Hetty's training: "gladly would I maintain her—educate her—under thy care—for I know not the woman into whose hands, to whose heart, I would rather *such* a child should fall, if she were mine." This wish's impossibility reminded him of other shortcomings of his marriage; soon, however, he began to boast how much more assertive and successful he would be "in another state."

> . . . my Nature shall receive its fulfillment there—if Omnipotence comes not across my path—& sure I am no just & loving Omnipotence will; & other Omnipotences I'll just command to stand out of my way—to "go along"—they must obey me or there will be a rumpus. I'll not be crushed there, & *victimized* to a Bible, a Church, a Priesthood, a Government, a custom, a Heaven, a Hell, a Devil, an Angel, or an Abstract God as I have been here. . . . Tell me—Hetty—if thou knowest any thing about the matter—if I am to enter on that state under the Dispensation of a genteel *bow?* Must I formally, politely, genteelly, & properly make a *bow* as I enter that land? If so—I'd as leave not go.[83]

In railing freely against his Philadelphia family, Wright spilled out thoughts that had formerly been confined to his private journal. As he imagined himself in a new realm, spontaneous and powerful, he inspected his old theological slogan once more. "*Alone with God in the Universe!!* It is terrible; yet it was for years my stern, sepulchral, *world-defying* Motto—till I found that to be *alone with* God, was to be *alone without God in the universe;* for in trying to be *alone* without a *human being,* I was, in fact, alone without God." No longer resigned to the virtues of loneliness, he was not in the mood to humiliate himself in the mud. "I want a *home* for my spirit in the bosom of humanity, & must have it, or become severely stern, cold, distant, savage." The impending loss of Sarah dashed his optimism, however; as she approached her doom at sea, he returned to self-pity.

"Forgive all this about that child—Hetty—& all the rest who shall read it. *Alone with God*—without a human being to fill the soul! I repeat—it is terrible! It is to wander in perfect solitude, thro' an *empty* void of existence."[84]

Hetty nestled in his lap as a child. She sent letters that he treasured as "an account of thyself"; sometimes she gave him reminiscences of childhood. "How I love & reverence that divine child!" he responded to one tale. "Hetty—thinkest thou all thy divinity has left thee? I do not believe it has—I have read that history many times, but never so understandingly as this time."[85] In addition to giving him love, she aided his work by helping him see into the recesses of childhood. Wright had always been adept at winning women's confidence and thereby collecting case material for his books and lectures; Hetty carried this process to new psychic heights. The "history" that he reread so "understandingly" was, almost certainly, a curious manuscript that survives in his handwriting: "Antenatal History—or History & Education before my Birth." Although the original source is not identified, it seems likely that he copied her self-analysis, conducted perhaps under some kind of hypnotic trance, and took it with him as a keepsake and aid to reflection.[86]

Her memories of antenatal life—"that brief period between my conception and birth"—were not very detailed; they amount to little more than an assertion that the period *must* shape character and determine happiness. But they were combined with other colorful fragments that help us to comprehend Wright's emotional life. Together, they illustrate that spiritualism was the religion of the uterus just as certainly as Calvinism reflected the father's law. They show the juvenile preoccupations of the woman whose love sustained him at a critical transition point in his career. They also exemplify the romantic imaginations, however subdued, of the mid-nineteenth-century women to whom Wright wrote and spoke successfully. Through Hetty's snatches of memory may be detected the misgivings of a generation who had enjoyed youthful, secret reading in Madame de Staël, George Sand, and other bold writers, who had turned to benevolent reform to submerge selfish passions, and who were now headed, with mixed feelings, into polite, asensual gentility. Esther Lukens was, as we have seen, an advocate of women's rights who resented men's abdication of useful roles in the home. Even when Wright played Dimmesdale to her Hetty, however, he saw himself leaving an adopted child for her to bring up.[87]

There was a smouldering sexuality in her highly spiritual reminiscences. Her strategy resembled Wright's: denial of the body opened the way to explore loosely sexual thoughts. She had a keen sense of what she gave up by growing up. Her fascination with the bizarre, distant, and unconventional identified her as an American romantic. Her self-analysis must have thrilled Wright by fusing adolescent longings and religious visions with a practical commitment to Garrisonian reform.

One charming reminiscence summoned back yearnings for the most ethereal kind of love:

> When a child I was greatly dissatisfied with my *name*. I used to think I could never have a *lover* unless I changed my *name*. I did not suppose any true & noble *Man* could love me with such a name. I imagined how awkward, vulgar and unromantic it would seem to have a man tenderly & lovingly addressing me & calling me *Esther*. I had read several Novels, & thought how beautiful it must seem to a man to have the woman he loved, have some poetic & romantic name [like Corinne, no doubt, or Consuelo]. So I said to Mother one day—"Mother—are you willing I should change my name?" "Why child—said she—Why do you want to change it?" "Why Esther—I said—is so vulgar & common sounding—I don't believe I shall ever have a lover unless I change my name." Mother laughed in great merriment & asked—"What name would you take?" "Why—Mother I'd like to be called *Astrea*." She laughed in great glee—& I did not soon hear the last of it. She made it a source of fun at my expense till I was heartily disgusted with myself.

A scant dozen pages included three recollections of captivating men. The first derided fashionably dressed men, with neat beards and hair. While she began envisioning all good men as Christlike martyrs in loose flowing robes, her interest was not exclusively religious: "I could not imagine how a *woman* could fall in love with a little man in a *Bobtail* coat—or a Peaktail coat—strutting & capering & bobbing about. I thought the man, whom I *loved* when I came to be a woman, must have on a large, flowing gown, or *Toga*—& if he had any thing on his head, it must be a graceful, grand *Turban* & he must have an *August appearance*." The second focused on an oak tree near the steps of her childhood home. Watching it, she sometimes saw a vine-covered castle. "Sometimes the Oak would turn into a tall, noble manly looking man," in sandals and prophetic robe, walking toward her; "then I thought he'd spread out his arms, & pour out a flood of Eloquence—in such a grand musical voice that would shake the earth. [A]ll the people fall before him—the guilty be converted & the righteous rejoice." The third recollection described her search for an "*Ideal* Christ or Saviour," ending with the vision of a poet who was "far different from all the little *dapper* songsters the present day called poets." With divine inspiration, he would lead mankind to nobler ways of living. He would play the harp and walk in time with a flowing river.

Abolitionism sedated girlhood fantasies. Her mother—a central figure throughout these memories—worked hard to get her to stop confusing Bible stories with pagan mythology. Her mother was also a reformer who once rebuked a man for calling Garrison an incendiary. Intrigued by the conversation, little Esther asked whether there were "other men like Mr. Garrison? Why Mother, he seems to me just like Christ—for he pitied poor & outcast people & tried to relieve them & people then put him into prison just as the people in Baltimore treat Mr. Garrison." An abolitionist uncle encouraged this version of the martyr-poet-prophet, though not without wondering why a young girl had strong feelings about slavery. For twenty years her mother loyally subscribed to the *Liberator;* as a result, the paper had "a powerful influence on my mind"—an influence that presumably included Henry Wright's frequent communications. Apparently she did not cease the imaginary voyaging that her family disapproved: she thus had an ironic influence in releasing Wright's prose from the confines of abolitionism.

She recalled her childish resistance to the notion "of leaving the body—throwing off the body & being a spirit disembodied." She was reluctant to lose touch with familiar objects. But there came a time when she was looking at a stack of books and wishing to know all they could tell about the world without the time and labor required to read them. "A singular feeling came over me, such as I have often since experienced of being suddenly swung off into space; separated from all my material surroundings—at least, in the sense of identity with them." She went on:

> No one can know how wonderful & complete that separation may be without experience. How the objects of daily life that surround us are part of ourselves. The floor & the ceiling of the Chamber where I stood seemed to pass from under my feet & from over my head [.] I saw in the distance a vast dark object. I was conscious it was the Earth. It was round & rolling & I knew it was the earth. It revolved slowly & cities & forests, mountains & val[l]ies, rivers & lakes, oceans & Dry land uprose & passed on before & away from my sight: dreamlike, yet terribly distinct.

Although Wright prized introspection more than book learning, his meditations never lifted him so far above ordinary reality. But he had split off a portion of himself for a kind of extraterrestrial communication, and so he could appreciate Astrea's feats. Once she was pondering her appearance in the mirror, wishing she could alter it, when the "spirit eye seemed to become detached from what I saw in the glass": the "*Me*" that others addressed became a stranger. It became an object separate from herself, her possession to dispose of at her pleasure. That made her feel "rich & proud," and her body looked much better, much "as we respect those whom we just meet more than we do those with whom we are more familiar." Wright's experience differed significantly: it was his spiritualized self, an old intimate, whom he respected most. She was nonetheless a kindred soul who guided him toward the spiritualism and pseudoscience that he joined to marital reform in the 1850s.

Wright's romantic life in the middle of that decade is unknown, and the rumor Webb heard in 1857 cannot be verified. Wright's affectionate life was always seamless. One cannot discover a falling-out with his wife, nor trace the borders between relationships with British lovers and with Hetty; it is equally hard to determine what happened to his Ohio home. By the 1860s, however, he had moved on from the amateur seer Esther Ann Lukens to the professional medium whom he regarded as the culmination of a lifetime's search—Julia Wass Friend. She was the principal medium advising against his return to Britain in 1862: in a sense, then, she stepped between him and some old soul mates. A few years later, he began to address her so lovingly as his daughter that he sometimes appeared to believe literally that his anxiety about going childless to eternity was behind him. She was the only beneficiary named in Wright's will, giving her two lots of land and canceling her notes totalling $1,100.[88]

She was born at Cape Split on the "down east" coast of Maine. When Wright met her she lived with her first husband, Elbridge Harrison Friend, in Gloucester; at this time she was a medium. As we have seen, she conveyed messages back and forth between Henry and his brother Chester "within the veil." She was obviously a remarkable person. Professor Albert E. Carpenter, her second husband and a hypnotist, described a day in Maine when there was much alarm over a missing boat. When he placed her in "the subjective state" and summoned her "psychic powers," she received a vision of the harbor where it lay. In spite of this story (and Wright's infantilization of her), she had independent gifts. She had at least a quasi-therapeutic practice in the 1860s; in 1880 she gained a medical degree from Vermont Medical College, thus standing as one of America's earliest woman doctors.[89]

Wright lived with the Friends, who took some pains and expense to fit out his room. In 1865, if not before, Julia won acceptance as his child. Throughout his remaining years, he longed for Oak Hill in Gloucester, whenever he went off lecturing, as "My only Home!"[90]

Possibly her medical practice first lured him there, an old man, afraid of the closeness of death. If his cryptic notes are valid indications, her practice was a source of great strain. "Am anxious about My Home! Fear she is in trouble about her patients," reads a typical notation. The doctor was not herself the epitome of health: once she entered his room, lay down on his bed, then rolled off in convulsions. After several fits, she lay unconscious for over an hour. "Great terror" struck Wright that someone had come, presumably from the spirit world, "to take her off." In a few hours he felt happier about the intense experience: "*Heaven* has been mine this day. *Hell* has been mine *also*. This day will not soon be forgotten."[91] Her fits were not, of course, irrelevant to her psychic powers.

The basis of her intimacy with Henry was almost daily conversation about marriage. She may very well have shown more direct interest in his life than any previous acquaintance. When she asked whether he would go back to age twenty-five and begin all over, he replied that he would—on one condition, which she must guess. If she succeeded, he joked, he would believe in clairvoyance. On another occasion he noted "many pleasant talks with Julia about getting a *Wife* & making for myself a Home aside from her & E. H." There was a good house nearby (perhaps on one of the adjacent lots he willed her), but his mind was not made up whether to leave his child's home.[92] A few days later, on March 5, 1867, he couldn't sleep because of the excitement of a "never to be forgotten" talk with Julia. Then a week later: "Long talks with Julia on *Exclusive, permanent, Conjugal Love*." The breath of promiscuity in her beliefs threatened him in a way that echoed old conversations with Maria Waring. Julia declared "there is no such thing as a true, exclusive, concentrated, Conjugal Love that is *enduring*." "I know there is," Wright reflected: "I have & do experience it. It is & has been the life of my Manhood. It makes me very *sad*, & desolate & isolated to know that she above all others on earth holds such a view of life." It is pointless to guess whom Wright imagined, at that moment, to be his eternal wife; it was conversation with his "child" that filled the emptiness in his life, even when her conversation violated all-important proprieties.

Certainly he did not pretend to her that he was happily married. He told her instead of his "need of some one to care for & live for & *die* for. Want one worth dying for. I do—I do." And when one couple came to Julia for treatment of afflicted throats and lungs, he diverted the consultation to the great subject—"their having a *Home* & a *Child*."[93]

Wright liked Julia's frankness in exposing his faults and her refusal to let him dominate their talks. But there were limits to his pliancy. On March 18, 1867, several days after her opinion of marriage shocked him, she launched a long discussion "about my relations to women. She made a statement in writing of what she knows about it. Asked her if she felt she had a right to know & inquire about them?" It was unnerving to be the quarry rather than the expert; there were secrets to protect from all eyes. "It is some 18 months," the journal turned abruptly, "since I began to feel that my *Home* was going away from me & that I must soon be Homeless or *seek* & *make* another separate from this. O that I could be placed in my relations to this Home just where I was two years ago." There followed an illegible, anguished plea to "Julia My Child!" He fought off the impulse to flee, however, and soon reported that all was going well "as of old."[94]

Leave-taking was always difficult, whether from Hartwick, West Newbury, or Ireland, even though Wright had organized an Ishmaelite life of travel. His inevitable departure from Julia, later in March, raised pathetic echoes of earlier experiences. He predicted Julia's death. He used his diary as a self-accusatory device, addressing himself as though he were gone among the spirits. "I would commune with H. C. W. He tells me I am needed at Home, that I did not do wisely in leaving as I did. When shall I be at peace with H. C. W.? Never—I fear—in all things."[95]

As soon as he returned he was happy once more. Julia kept him busy caring for her headaches, fits, and what Wright called "piraxisms" of insanity. Sometimes she resisted help, but during late April and early May he served steadily as "Nurse." The reversal of roles moved him deeply. "At 3 P.M.," he noted on May 6, "experienced myself transfigured. Heaven came to me not through *Christ* but through my *child*." When he had to go off again, he sent an impassioned appeal from Ohio for her to trust him, to lean on him. Otherwise, he felt lonely, "*Homeless, Houseless—Childless*—so tempest-tost & driven." While in Ohio (where Hetty's name no longer came up), he loved the company of his sixteen-year-old niece named Nellie. "But [she is] not My own Child—God bless my own child."[96]

Remembering the desperate meditations on paternity that Wright inscribed in the secret journal of the 1840s, we may misread his assertions that Julia was *his own* child, closer to him than his niece. Had this salesman of ideas, somewhere on one of his journeys, sired a daughter outside of conventional wedlock? The thought was not remote from his fantasies, of course, but he had not been to Cape Split in the years before he went to Britain, and he had hardly won his emancipation early enough to have a grown-up daughter in 1865. Furthermore, his emancipation never reached far enough to permit casual conjugation. Julia was a daughter by transference, the surrogate for a string of previous affections. Her communion with the spirit realm enhanced both her powers as a healer and her fragility as a patient—she was in touch with the lost. But even the liveliest associations could not make her a real daughter, nor could they satisfy his need for a love wife.

By the theory of the "unappropriated heart," a surrogate daughter did no good at all. There was no such thing as step-salvation, adopted bliss. Julia did not end his sad quest: "Thought much of God today," he wrote in April 1867, "as incarnate in a Wife. Oh the folly of worshipping an abstract God or a *God in the Dead.*" But who was there for him to worship among the living except this married woman, whom he regarded as a child, whose death he expected soon, whom his vocation caused him regularly to desert? As he traveled, he reinvoked his motto, "Alone with My God."[97]

Julia could not be the culminating love Wright sometimes tried to see in her. She was simply one more evidence of the human capacity to repeat emotional patterns with remarkably little variation, each time with the conviction that a victory has been scored, a breakthrough accomplished. She might easily have spoken the words that Wright actually received in a letter from one of his British intimates as he boarded ship in 1847: "You have been a good kind father to me, Henry, you *know* you have, & I have been a very fond child to you. I only wish I could have had a thousand times more of you all my life & done ever so much more for you. I never said much to you about all you have been to me but you know I *feel it all.*"[98] Though sharing intensely in the emotional lives of others, Wright remained an outsider. Throughout the twenty-five years of covert relationships that Julia summed up, he probably never experienced the sexual gratification that he attributed to husbands and wives.

One fruit of the union between Julia and Henry was an 1869 novel entitled *The Chester Family*. He encouraged her to compose it, and used his reform contacts to defray publishing costs. He made several appearances in the novel, as we shall see, and in 1873 it was reprinted, alongside several of his books, in a library of spiritualism and reform.[99] Like Esther Lukens's fragmentary recollections, *The Chester Family* gives us a look at the mind of a woman whom Wright loved; it is also evidence of the mentality of American women in Wright's mid-century audiences. What is most striking in this instance is not lingering youthful fantasies regarding men. In spite of Julia Friend's liberated view of conjugal love, her novel shows hostility toward male appetites. She worked in a genre—the temperance novel—that forged some of the strongest connections between reform and the middle-class reading public, a genre which consistently presented the goal of an improved society in conjunction with new abstemious ideals of marriage.

The Chester Family purports not to be fiction, but Julia's memories of some Maine neighbors. The story unfolds through letters to Henry Wright (and the family in the title may be named after one of his brothers). He secured an introduction by the "well known" lecturer on geology Professor William Denton, whom he had met on the temperance platform in London twenty-five years before. Denton lent Julia's "report" some scientific authority; he also highlighted the theme of progress, as measured by the widening hegemony of temperance. Wright added his own prefatory letter, asking Julia to share with the public a story that he had found edifying in private conversation. Despite these signs of authenticity, however, most elements in the novel were familiar from *Ten Nights in a Bar Room* or any other temperance novel or play. It is the story of a good woman who made the mistake of marrying, for love, a man with a weakness for drink. The family goes from riches to poverty, from bliss to distress, from health to debility. On child is misshapen, another dies with tear-jerking appeals for father's reform. The father does experience a change of heart, but he continues in life as a helpless invalid.

Temperance literature explored vexing questions. Where do habits and urges come from, how can they be controlled? How can a family break free of a pattern of violence and mistrust? When may a wife leave an inadequate husband (and by implication, when may a man walk away from a wrong choice)? Who is guilty or innocent in a society where evil and degradation seem to be systematic? In this literature, political issues were explored within the limits of sexual and family relationships, and pure sentiment was commonly ranged against impure physical drives. In this literature children could vanquish fathers. Wright's prefatory letter showed how temperance sagas could retrieve fairly primitive anger against incontinent fathers. The man's addiction to drink, which drags down the mother, is a polite way of thinking about a ruinous lack of sexual control. It authorizes Wright's dream that by his purity, even his impotency, he can conquer—that his heart will be appropriated.

> Having committed the fatal mistake of accepting, as a husband, a victim of the drunkard's appetite, the great, tender, pitying Human Heart can not but pay homage to the patience, forbearance, the heroic and sublime self-abnegation, of the wife and mother. That noble son, too, who dedicated his young life to the welfare of his mother, brother and sisters! Before the devotion of that wife and mother, and of that son, how contemptible seems the glory of the warrior which is born of hot wrath and dripping with blood![100]

Through the nonsequiturs in the last sentence, Wright not only proclaimed a victory over the father but also denied the violence of birth. The poignance of these themes in Wright's emotional life, from his mother's death to his own conjugal failures, was clear enough. Temperance sagas caught up private male feelings and joined them with goals and anxieties that women were beginning to express; these sagas helped delineate an emerging public ethic founded on respect for sentimental, passionless women.

Temperance raised some of the problems of discipline that had concerned nonresistants. Instead of abstract discussions of divine sovereignty and corporal punishment, however, it presented homely images of masculine self-restraint and good environments for children. Politically, *The Chester Family* reflected the temperance movement's disillusion with voluntary measures: it criticized voters for permitting the murderous occupation of rum selling to continue. Law was necessary because many men could not control their urges on their own. Nonresistance might even be dismissed as feminine weakness. Mrs. Chester plainly was wrong to ignore appeals to be sterner with her husband—or even to leave him. She erred by persisting "in the use of the only true means to save my husband from drunkenness—GOOD FOR EVIL."[101] But if her gentle measures came to naught, they were signs of her noble womanly heart. In the long run sentiments like hers might open doors to a perfectly harmonious world where force would be unnecessary. Somewhat ambiguously, temperance advanced the vision of kisses triumphing over blows, feminine refinement over coarse masculinity.

Mothers counted most toward the progress of civilization. Their mother's kindness rescued some of the Chester children, for example, while their father's influence crippled others. But what of John Chester himself? What was the original sin that bent the senior Chester wrong? His mother confessed her failing to Julia Friend: a doctor advised her during pregnancy to calm herself with liquor. She had never been a drinker before or since, but in the fateful nine months she had imbibed several times a day, "whenever I felt any nervous depression or irritability." Even when the need was becoming "uncontrollable," the doctor still urged her on. Although she managed to give up the habit, her son carried an "educated" taste for liquor from the womb. Even as a child he loved its smell and could not keep his hands off it when it lay within reach.[102] The mother did not tell why she was originally depressed—an important omission in view of Wright's advocacy of children's rights to be loved and wanted by their mothers. But the physician's urging her to drink at least hints at the inconsiderate sexuality of males in general, as opposed to the more temperate advice of experts like Wright. Julia Friend (who had her own practice) discussed another physician who advised a woman to get rid of scrofula by bearing children and thus giving it to them. Fortunately, this woman got a new doctor and refrained from childbearing. Abstention from drink was not the only form of self-denial requisite to the perfection of the human family.

The temperance movement gained much of its popularity from the ambiguous way in which it blended scenes of inevitable sin with bland prophesies of improvement. As *The Chester Family* traced these ambiguities to the influences of the uterus, it resembled an advertisement for the advice that Henry Wright had been dispensing for two decades. The point of her novel, said Mrs. Friend, was "that our appetites, tastes, and, finally, our whole character, depend essentially on the influences brought to bear on us previous to our birth." In the last of a long series of public exposures of Wright's domestic conversations, she called her readers' attention to his remark that ". . . it is easier to start right and keep right, than to start wrong and then get right. I have heard you say often that it is much better and safer for the future character and destiny of a child, to place it on the *up-grade*, than on the *down-grade*, of humanity. You assert most truly, that those parents do a great wrong to their children, who place them on the *down-grade* before birth, and trust to domestic, social and religious influences to switch them off on to the up-grade afterwards." There were strong notes of biological determinism in his view that children born with disease-ridden bodies and degraded souls had no chance of a good life. "By a fixed law of reproduction, LIKE BEGETS LIKE."[103] He had moved far from the educational reforms that he once promoted. Only as men submitted voluntarily to the regulations women imposed on sexuality could society really be reformed.

The Chester Family, in summary, belonged to a genre of fiction in which male exploitativeness and female vulnerability were clichés; Julia Friend used alcoholism as a symbol for problems of wedlock on which Wright had been lecturing for two decades or more. As a public revelation of his closeness to the woman he called "my own child," the novel also recapitulated his long private quest for acceptance. Perhaps his public stand for sexual restraint will appear ironic in view of his own excruciating frustration. Despite his agonized complaints, however, we cannot overlook his success in maintaining intensely affectionate relations with a series of interesting partners, a success due in part to his respect for their feelings, his attention to their worries, and his merger, it appears, of high emotionality and sexual forbearance. His program for modern marriage had its basis in considerable practice as a lover.

His failures as husband and potential father had not blocked him from expertise in family life. To some extent, he had always kept a professional perspective on his romantic affairs. His inquiries respecting the emotions of women, furthermore, anteceded his quest for a "love-wife" and extended beyond its boundaries. His acquaintance with unpublicized sides of women's experience was exceptional in his day; modern scholarship in women's history tends to bear out the profundity of his insights. As we turn to his books on marriage and sexuality, we are not likely to forget that he was compensating in idealized fashion for gaps in his own life. But we must remember, also, that his work reflected unusual knowledge of what nineteenth-century women wanted.

Bonds

In the late 1840s Wright's public career refocused on marriage and sexuality. As Chapter 1 has explained, this was an act of professional self-discovery after many false starts. Other chapters have examined issues of childhood that gave continuity to his life and the religious restlessness that provided the vehicle for adjustments in his thought. This chapter has detected a sexual emancipation (of sorts) in his private life coinciding with his new professional standing. There is one additional level at which to examine Wright's career in marital reform: as an instance of the reexamination of marriage that permeated the antislavery movement and every other dimension of American intellectual life.

A look back at Wright's pre-Garrisonian career discovers so much emphasis on the institution of marriage—and especially on mothers—that the period of antislavery work after 1835 almost looks like a digression. No minister could ignore the family's impact on the moral sphere, segregated from politics, which the clergy claimed as their province. Throughout the nineteenth century, in fact, ministers saw their fortunes rise to the extent that softening feminine impulses overcame the rough edges of business and politics. This background did not, of course, make the Reverent Henry Wright the expert on the needs of husbands and wives that he later became; nor did he romp ostentatiously with wee children. Instead he called marriage "the nursery of heaven," and exhorted parents not to regard their child as "a mere animated play-thing" decked out in "gay attire." He was shocked when parents let their children out to play ball on Sunday, and advised Christian mothers to keep children safely home, protected from corrupt influences on the city streets, even if confinement injured their health.[104]

Wright's respect for mothers grew after he became minister to Boston's children. The family, he discovered, was even more important than sabbath schools, and in the family it was maternal discipline that counted. It distressed him to think about excessive maternal indulgence, which could be a curse leading to drunkenness and other varieties of intemperance. The character of its citizens, in sum, determined a nation's destiny, and that character resulted from "maternal relations." Meetings with sewing circles and maternal associations reinforced his opinion that "there is not a more interesting object in this world than an infant just come from the hands of its Creator." From one group he gathered evidence that the first five years were the crucial period of education. To another, he explained the effects of "Maternal influence . . . on . . . our destiny in Eternity." He reprimanded a third club for their inability to subordinate earthly affections to the love of God.[105]

Questions of order preoccupied an urban minister acutely aware, as all members of profession had to be, of the fluidity of American society. If children did not grow up in a clearly defined hierarchical structure, then character was all that could keep them out of trouble. As men ranged far from home in search of more money and more goods, the importance of God's moral law was magnified: it established an "outer rim" of permissible behavior and encouraged individuals to hold themselves accountable.[106] Similar questions of order concerned American wives, particularly in a city like Boston where the chasm between men's and women's daily occupations was wider than in the Essex County and New Hampshire towns where Wright had promoted Sunday schools. As new economic institutions took "work" away from farm and household, man's realm was defined as economic, woman's as domestic. In his advice to Boston's mothers, Wright simply echoed numerous books and sermons charging mothers with the tasks of training the next generation to a standard of moral conduct that would make an open, shifting society endurable. These socially momentous responsibilities, imposed just when women had reason to feel lonely and useless, caused many worries about personal inadequacy.[107]

Wright's work in Boston acquainted him with the strains inherent in the family's newly altered structure. In the family he admired most, the husband excelled in the subsidiary role of "backing up & sustaining the influence & authority of his wife, by his precept & example." He criticized another father for being absent too frequently to give the mother much support; there was danger that the children, wishing to imitate their father, might fly away too soon. While pondering this increasingly prevalent family pattern (of which his own was a clear instance), he urged mothers not to reason with their children—it was better for young people to regard maternal command as law. The mother constituted the only fixed point in the growing child's world.[108]

After joining the antislavery fellowship Wright continued to advise mothers and guide children, but to these solemn concerns he added a passionate interest in sexuality. Once again he was in close touch with popular anxieties: the imperiled octoroon and lustful slaveowner eventually became as familiar stock characters as the drunken, inadequate husband. These images took such deep hold in American thought that historians connot always determine the significance of sexual overtones in antislavery propaganda. In Wright's case, however, it is clear that the misfortunes of slaves had strong familial connotations. In his first pseudonymous appearance in the *Liberator*, the Genius of Africa lambasted William Ellery Channing's genteel indifference to the annihilation of marriage down south. "Incontinence, fornication, adultery and bigamy are unmeaning words among one sixth of this nation!" He needled the Unitarian to imagine his loved ones torn away into bondage, to envision how masters "outrage every feeling of modesty and delicacy in the female heart—they sport with the agonized husband's groans—they mock the delirium of maternal anguish and jest at the orphan's tears."[109] Writing from that rage at pretense and display that typifies many newly converted radicals, Wright set out to restore meaning to puritanical words like continence.

His predilection for sexual and familial imagery was unusual even among Garrisonians who regularly denounced Southern panders in the brothels of slavery. Contacts between Bostonians and Southern churchmen were, in his eyes, "Slavery and Liberty Kissing Each Other in Tremont Temple." The issue was "Fidelity to Principle"; there must be either "an eternal DIVORCE; or an indissouluble MARRIAGE between Liberty and Slavery." Not only was disunion analogous to a broken marriage, but nonresistance—the movement in which Garrisonians escaped all compromises—was "my own child."[110] There is no point in conflating more of these images. But it is important to notice that they run far beyond fascination with lust in the South; they identify ideals of pure marriage and parenthood. They are not simply projections of prurient interests or signs of dissatisfaction with the repressions of Northern life. Antislavery was, above all, a source of support to aspirations for control and cleanliness that were extremely important elements in Wright's conception of worthy manhood.

The border between prurience and the protection of chastity was hard to draw, as Rev. John R. McDowall had sadly learned. The escalating numbers of prostitutes in Northern cities well symbolized the vicious consequences of social dislocation; speculation over how these fallen women might be redeemed was a good method of tinkering with the adjustments in psychology and theology that a new era demanded. For a time, therefore, McDowall's Magdalen or Moral Reform Society, as it was euphemistically called, occupied a proud place in the empire of benevolent reform and missionary work. But after publishing detailed information concerning New York's bordellos, McDowall was charged with aggravating evils instead of rectifying them; his charges that well-born men frequented New York's ten thousand prostitutes set off angry outcries. When he refused to curtail his plain dealing, a nasty division took place in the empire. Expulsion from the ministry and, soon after that, death made this foe of prostitution, in the eyes of radicals, a martyr crushed by the same powerful forces that shielded slavery. In a moving account of McDowall's funeral, Wright's mind raced back to Garrison, whom churches and state equally scorned. In addition, he commented on the blacks in attendance. They recognized the deposed minister as a friend of the downtrodden, and they appreciated the threat that antiprostitution posed to slavery: "is not every slaveholder an adulterer and a fornicator?"[111]

The Liberator had a keen interest in marriage from the outset, and its purpose was to protect the institution, not to radicalize it. If we look over its steady stream of domestic advice in the 1830s, we are reminded that Garrison's boyhood was overshadowed by his father's desertion. Although he kept silence about Wright's fractured marriage and opened up his blissful home to less fortunate reformers, Garrison opposed the liberty of fugitive husbands. Some of the advice—it is seldom clear when the editor wrote it, when he gleaned it from other papers—tells how to choose a spouse or keep one at home. A piece on "The Fatherless Household" bemoaned the plight of those abandoned by an insensitive brute, but also noted the problems caused by a nagging wife who failed to "chain him to his home by the sweet enchantment of a cheerful room and a cheerful heart."[112]

As a nonresistance lecturer, Wright often portrayed his cause as submissive and feminine, and thus as an alternative to aggressive forces transforming the land. Sometimes this terminology disclosed important limitations to his belief in women's rights. Women were not equal to men, but fundamentally different. They were a protected, dependent class. Because they represented civilizing influences one could speak of them as superior to men, but they needed to operate in a restricted sphere of activity where their influence was unimpeded. Consider, for example, Wright's account of "a social party" in Duxbury, Massachusetts, to which some persons walked three miles in order to hear Wright speak. In advance of his talk, conservative abolitionists branded him an anarchistic spokesman for licentiousness and prostitution. But he and his friends concluded: ". . . women must rise or fall in society, as brute force or moral power prevailed. Women sink beneath the throne of violence. She [*sic*] rises into her appropriate sphere in society, in proportion as society comes under the dominion of truth and love."[113] The liberation of women imagined here is a rescue from seduction, the liberty to preside chastely over domestic scenes. The other side of his stress on self-discipline was a belief in woman's inablility to compete in the physical male world. There were political and economic corollaries to the mid-nineteenth-century theorem that woman's natural bent was moral, not carnal—that sex satisfied male lust but violated female spirituality.

In the preceding century popular attitudes toward the sexual drives of men and women had been dramatically reversed. Once viewed as passionate, sensual, ruled by insatiable appetites arising from the womb, preying on the Adamic modesty of men, women were by 1830 more often regarded as chaste, sexually reluctant, spiritual. It was still "unnatural" for a woman to take precedence over men in public, no longer because chaotic forces were rumbling out of control but because of feminine preferences to rule quietly in the moral realm. And some overtones of the older scheme persisted. The immensely popular novelist George Lippard pointed out repeatedly that if wicked men prodded a woman's normally passive "animal nature" too far, sensuality would rise "like a vapor" and destroy her capacity for holy devotion in the home. Let wise men learn "that no angel around God's throne is purer than Woman when her intellectual nature alone is stirred into development, that no devil crouching in the flames of hell is fouler than Woman, when her animal nature alone is roused into action!"[114] Wright's version of nonresistance, with woman's fate resting on the outcome of the battle between morality and brutality, similarly viewed female nature as historically undecided, oscillating between polar images of sensuality and refinement, and dependent on male restraint for its resolution.

It is tempting, but wrong, to see this rhetoric as irrelevant to the lives of real women. Of the many indications that changes in sexual behavior coincided with the newer asensual images of women, the clearest is the declining fertility rate in the more developed sections of the Northeast. Along with the separation of male and female spheres, the magnified importance of motherhood, and the shifting mythology of sexual desire went measurable decreases in family size—decreases that historians can best explain as the consequences of sexual abstinence. It is possible that women, left alone in the changing household, showed less sexual initiative, although the diminished value of children in nonfarm families must have impressed men too. These historical trends emerged most clearly among the leisurely, benevolent women whom Wright knew best; they were brought home to his consciousness by his wife's failure to give him a child and his lifelong feelings of incompleteness despite intimacy. Some of his feminine friends regarded the sexual purification of women as indispensable to their rights and dignity. Women in the antislavery movement, including famous visitors to his own home, began, tentatively, to express such views.[115]

"I feel as if it is not the cause of the slave only we plead but the cause of Woman as a responsible & moral being," wrote Angelina Grimkė at the time when she first entered Garrisonian circles. Her exertions, more than any other factor, shifted the antislavery controversy to the rights of women. In this letter to her most trusted confidante she made it clear that her new cause had strongly antisexual implications. She and Sarah had told the women in a moral reform society—that is, an antiprostitution organization like McDowall's, calling on the time and energy of religious ladies—"this reform must begin in *ourselves,* we were polluted by it, our moral being was sear[e]d and scathed by it."

> Look at our feelings in the Society of *men,* why the restraint & embarrassment, if we regarded each other as moral & intellectual beings merely, how pure & elevated & dignified would be our feelings towards & intercourse with them. How is the solemn & sacred subject of marriage regarded & talked about; my heart is pained—my womanhood is insulted, my moral being is outraged continually, & I told them so. After we had finished, many women came up & expressed their pleasure & satisfaction at this part particularly of our remarks—they were their own feelings, but had never heard them expressed before.[116]

What makes this letter unusual is its explicit comment on a process that historians usually see only by inference: the acceptance of asexual ladyhood as a precondition for women's rights. Even this outspoken abolitionist regretted an undertow of carnality that prolonged her subjugation. In her own life, as is well known, she did not marry until she and her man had agreed that sexual desire played no legitimate part in wedlock. Her practice, in this instance, anticipated the advice that Wright and other reformers dispensed across the North. Her comments well illustrated, furthermore, the general assumption that self-reform makes social reform possible. Sexual impulses were, after all, lively symbols of animal and emotional tendencies that might have to be checked before one could participate contentedly in a complex society. To Wright's movement to restore meaning to words like incontinence the Grimkės and other modern women attached a movement in favor of respectful friendships between men and women at a level secure from any secret carnality.

Many scholars have noted connections between antislavery and feminism. The Grimkés' antislavery speeches called attention to outmoded proprieties restricting talented women, and the restless Garrisonian wing of the American Anti-Slavery Society gave much impetus to feminism. Just as bondage was an ambiguous concept, suggesting emotional attachment as well as imprisonment, relations between antislavery and feminism were sometimes puzzling (the collaboration eventually broke down in the 1860s when the ex-slaves' suffrage set back the rights of women).[117] Perhaps some feminists imagined a male-female warfare analogous to that of slaves and their owners; certainly some compared marriage to slavery. Typically, however, abolitionists struggled toward a mutual ethic, not an exclusively female one. Henry Wright is an instance of their experimentation with uncoercive forms of intergender friendship. Antislavery raised the positive hope of men and women joined together, not by lust or economic coercion, but as comrades seeking humanity's greater good. Other men besides Wright felt imprisoned by moral codes that allowed great intimacy within genders, little between them; others realized that sexual restraint might ease the way to intimacy with women.[118]

This cause was impermissible in American culture in the 1830s. As an aftermath of the animosities and schisms of that decade, the *Liberator* became silent on the question of marriage. Even the little paeans to considerateness, thrift, and industriousness in the household vanished. Marriage did not reemerge as the abolitionists' public concern until it was subtly redefined. What Angelina Grimké had called the morality and responsibility of women took second place to the maternal defense of civilization: the liberation of mature women disappeared behind the progress of children. A radical movement has a way of pounding at the perimeters of acceptable belief and action at any given moment in a culture. In the process it discovers what is too delicate to be challenged, but it also carries out adjustments in customs that are ready for change. Abolitionists bumped up against stubborn resistance to women's liberation, but they discovered how much could be gained—for husbands and wives—by expanding the significance of motherhood.[119]

The slavery controversy tested the definitions of freedom and authority in a period of rapid social change. Abolitionists might have preferred to keep discussion on the safe ground of denouncing plantation slavery: most Northerners could see that slavery was an unjustifiable sort of unfreedom even if they could not agree on the abstract principles and procedures that made one form of coercion or deprivation tolerable and another less so. The abolitionists' opponents refused, understandably, to restrict debate to this ground and, in lieu of slavery, offered marriage as the clearest illustration of the need for bonds to keep society from flying apart. It was no accident that abolitionists reexamined the degree of subordination required to make marriage an orderly, yet satisfying institution. The tentativeness of social conditions, within which they and their opponents pretended to have a fixed grasp on righteousness, made the subject unavoidable.

Southern intellectuals frequently framed a comparison between marriage and slavery, not to criticize the former but to defend the latter. This tactic even allowed them to champion the higher law (within sensible social limits). In J. W. Page's *Uncle Robin in His Cabin in Virginia and Tom without One in Boston*—one of the better known replies to Mrs. Stowe's novel, which dealt repeatedly with disruptions of marriage—the wife of a slaveowner allays the doubts of a soon-to-be-married slave girl. How can she pledge to obey her husband when the law enjoins her to obey her master?

> You will have to obey three masters, Cecelia, instead of one or two, and I must try and explain this matter to you. In the first place, you must obey God (who is your Heavenly Master) above all others. . . . He tells you that you must pray to him, and if your earthly master was to tell you not to pray to God, you are bound to obey God rather than man, and you could pray in secret. . . . There are a great many things for you to do, about which your master in heaven is silent, and gives no instruction. In every one of those things you must obey your master upon earth. . . . When your husband tells you, however, to do something which is not forbidden by your earthly master and is not contrary to his interest, you are bound to obey your husband.[120]

George Fitzhugh's *Cannibals All* and *Sociology for the South* cleverly taunted the North to distinguish its declining respect for obligation from the cultural weaknesses that commonly preceded anarchy and decay. Fitzhugh took "Free Love" (which included all the agitation for women's rights) as a talisman of worse things ahead for the business society that found slavery discomforting.[121] In pitting a traditional view of hierarchical authority against the novelty of free labor,

Page, Fitzhugh, and other Southerners appealed to values that had once been articulated superbly in the North. John Winthrop, in particular, had envisioned a good society, bonded by love, united by interlocking vows of obligation, a society in which lines of subservience and command were unmistakably clear. In such a society there existed no meaningful liberty beyond that of doing right within the duties of one's station. By insisting that Northerners now discuss one institution that they preferred not to regard as economic—marriage—the South asked what limits contained the free labor system that supposedly indicted slavery. How willingly would abolitionists accord to wives the sympathies they flung to subjugated bondsmen in far-off plantations? How freely would the Northern consensus on problems of order permit abolitionists to redefine the marital yoke?

Only the uncertain perimeters of freedom in the North allowed Southerners to take radicals like Wright as delegates of a society that often watched their movements with suspicion. Many representatives of denominational religion in the North had deep misgivings about the disintegration of hierarchy. Men like Wright's associates in Andover, Essex County, and Boston usually shared the ideological distaste for black slavery that won much of the nation after the Revolution. Colonization provided one outlet for that feeling, and there was an impressive amount of prayerful opposition to bondage in the 1830s before Garrisonian immoderation blackened the cause. Before long, however, many evangelicals drew a line separating themselves not only from the Garrisonians but from abolitionism in general. The complex issues over which they made this often painful choice included their strong residual respect for institutional order and the prerogatives of rank. In explaining themselves they fell back on marriage as an instance of the intricate dovetailing of freedom and authority. Since their purpose was not to defend slavery but to brake impetuous social change, they were at liberty to admit the hard realities of marriage while still approving the institution.

One example will suffice. Joseph Tracy, the leading spokesman for orthodox Boston, maintained that, in England, a man could sell his wife as property, although recent cases were rare. This did not make marriage woman-stealing. United States law gave husbands considerable leeway for punishing and correcting their wives. The fact of legalized coercion did not make marriage sinful. There were differences in practice, Tracy conceded, between marriage and slavery; masters were more likely to make vile use of their legal power. But the comparison indicated that slavery should not be attacked as a *malum in se;* its sinfulness resulted from the masters' acts in individual cases, not from legal powers defining its existence. There were ironies in the argument that Tracy could not suspect. The historian E. P. Thompson has discovered in "the sale of wives" a practice that was not lawful, a folk ritual by which communities governed crises of divorce and remarriage. "The law" was itself the modern alteration of customary ways of resolving conflict, not the effective tradition to be modified only with caution. But it was, in any event, the disposition of official powers, as reflected in the law, that men like Tracy wished to perpetuate. While there would inevitably be abusive individuals, they said, the task of correcting them must not endanger the system as a whole.[122]

To compare this view, or Fitzhugh's, with the Garrisonians' is to catch hints of divergent perspectives on social mobility. What Wright and his comrades sought was not the preservation of power, but the consolidation of newly gained respectability. What they opposed to the law was not plebeian custom but a new class's universalized sense of how things ought to be. It is easy to misconceive the radicalism of their position. The tokens of respectability included blameless behavior in mixed company—for example, the exchanges of solemn words at reform meetings that Tracy and the Andoverites found so shockingly "promiscuous." The universal emancipation of women that Garrisonians advocated was the reverse of sexual release; it bore a resemblance to John Winthrop's distinction between liberty and unregulated carnality. Theirs was the Christian reformer's freedom to please God rather than man. Accused of encouraging free love, Garrison indignantly asserted the divine status of marriage regardless of whatever "initiatory rites" churches and states devised. When his accuser conceded that Garrison never "held it to be morally right to desert one's wife and family, or to neglect the duties arising from such a relation," he touched on "all that is essential to moral purity and connubial integrity."[123]

Lasting married love was, in fact, one of the most promising territories to search for some degree of permanency amidst all the customs and offices whose "arbitrary" law-made character was only too apparent in a period of rapid social change. "Slavery, and governments of human will and brute force," Wright reported in 1841, "all assume that marriage is a *civil* institution, to be put up and put down at human will and pleasure—to be annulled at the discretion of individuals and legislatures. Non-resistants assume it is a divine institution, and that God alone has a right to annul it." He took umbrage at charges from men who voted for proslavery politicians, and who therefore "voted for *concubinage* and *adultery*," that he was anti-marriage.[124]

The permanent affections of happily married couples were easily connected with another expression of divine law—the unfettered conscience. In the "Domestic Scenes" Wright explained how wise parents turned their children into autonomous moral agents by surrounding them with good influences instead of relying on corporal punishment.[125] In the years ahead, as we shall see, he attributed the same effect—the development of conscience—to the mother's blissful acceptance of the child's growth in the womb. In addition to his newly confessed longing for an "appropriated heart," this formulation brought together numerous themes of self-ownership and propriety that his prior emergence as an abolitionist had refined: young minister Wright's ruminations on America's destiny; the Genius of Africa's fascination with "continence"; the Grimkés' and other intelligent women's aversion to carnality; the philosophical exchanges on law versus natural institutions that antislavery prompted; and the nonresistants' quest for a universal code of discipline.

Although Wright's approach to marriage resulted in many ways from his antislavery experience, we should neither overstress the radicalism of his position nor overlook the larger cultural dimensions of his work. Images of happy mother and innocent child, as well as counter-images of dark continuities of inheritance, circulated widely during Wright's lifetime. The family was the subject through which a society bursting across the continent, fighting over servitude, and locking deviants in penitentiaries and asylums, imagined its own confinement. It was the subject where the interests of uncompromising radicals intersected those of a host of other public men and women. Wright stepped forward, as abolitionist, to join a field already discovered by ministers issuing advice to young men and women, doctors specializing in the complaints of women, lecturers demonstrating new theories of mind and body, songwriters, playwrights and novelists wringing tears from domestic setbacks and victories. All of them—hacks and artists, conformists and reformers—agreed on the immeasurable importance of motherhood. Perhaps this importance was first brought home in revivalistic counterattack against secular republican forces. In 1834, for example, an Andover graduate told Wright of a class meeting in which each student related the religious experiences leading to the ministry; one after another gave the same testimony "till all but four attributed their hopes to the influence of mothers on their infant minds."[126] It was a politician, however, who gave motherhood its most famous celebration. Down to the mid-twentieth century schoolboys memorized the sentiment of that child of a nomadic family who rose to become the sixteenth president: "All that I am or hope to be, I owe to my angel mother."

The Importance of Being Ernest

I have sometimes been asked what would have happened to Henry Wright if he had lived today. It is a silly question, but one that arises inevitably, in our day of frequent divorce, when we survey the four decades of loneliness following his unfortunate marriage. The obvious speculation is that he would have left his wife after a half dozen years or so, had affairs with various women who attracted him, remarried, remained productive in his chosen career. It is not obvious that he would have been less lonely. My point, in any case, is to underscore the importance of seeing him as the nineteenth-century man he was. Disloyalty in marriage appalled him; his apparent impotency brought him close to the women he wanted; and worshipping motherhood permitted him, much of the time, a self-image of continence and purity.

His writings on marriage reflected the leading values of his culture more often than opposing them. He was expert in making his ideas sound novel—who, after all, would read an authority on sex who promised to reveal what everyone already knew and was unafraid to ask? And certainly they were not the ideas of his parents' generation. In his culture there was hardly a received body of truth to be handed down; his professionalism and itinerancy were signs of disintegrated community. Men and women, aware of the changes around them, wondered what alterations in personal habits and outlooks might improve their families' futures. Wright's task was, in a sense, to tell them what they already believed, or what they were on the verge of believing, to codify the emerging judgments of a population in flux. Each year's books and lectures were a slight "advance" over last year's dicta, but they also reiterated what had stimulated previous audiences.

Besides this give-and-take with men and women who came to hear him, Wright passed on the views of other writers too. Never a thorough or philosophical reader, he absorbed just enough to put current fads into the "progressive" jargon his audiences favored. He could not quite be called a "carrier" in the sense in which today's sociologists use the term: he did not convey news from a fully modernized world to backward peoples.[127] On his circuits he tested and consolidated the value system of a society that was already in motion.

His case is an exception to familiar shibboleths about social control and the motives of reformers. He was not a utopian modernizer ignorant of, or warring against, persistent folklife. There were undoubtedly large segments of the American populace with whom he had no rapport and in whom he took little interest. But there was a striking degree of flexibility in his ideological work, and a reciprocal relation existed between his self-discovery as a lecturer and the anxieties of the uprooted, forward-looking Protestants who comprised his audience. Traveling among them, observing them, asking them questions—these things pointed him toward his teachings; he spoke to them, for his part, about his own autobiography, the ephemeral customs of the "dead past," and the promising science of "human life." Through such exchanges between reformer and audience, unarticulated plans were given voice, and cultural goals were redefined. He captured a trade-off between pleasure and progress that described what some men and women had already passed through, while it set goals for others. He delineated the existence of an audience of couples who were learning to regard male sexual drives as a problem to be curbed, to treat motherhood as a sacramental profession, and to strive for deepening intimacy between husbands and wives in lieu of the compulsions of bygone communities.

Each year he went forth with a new topic. "The One Supreme Object of Devotion" (1855), for example, drew attention to the child who issued from a glad antenatal experience. "The Hat for the Head, Not the Head for the Hat" (1857) showed the adaptibility of human institutions, ending with "Home and its influence"; it overlooked his own false start as a hatmaker. Normally lectures came in sets of three, but there might be as many as twelve (with a return to the same town in a year or two for more). Reports of Wright's talks tended to emphasize avant-garde qualities, especially the bravery of discussing matters that "false delicacy (the legitimate offspring of lechery and prudery . . .)" branded lubricious. But they also emphasized the audience's "propriety and seriousness of deportment," the speaker's "serious earnestness of manner." Despite his tilting against respected institutions, despite the fluidity of their busy lives, audiences understood that Wright championed domestic stability. "And who like Mr. Wright can portray a happy, peaceful and loving home?" An exciting, exploratory aura surrounded these occasions, but they remained soberly, irrevocably middle-class.[128]

Wright's diaries seldom gave more than the titles of his lectures: to be earnest, talks had to be off-the-cuff. Less perishable evidence remains in the books he sold, books that were not always consistent in the views they promoted, but that seldom strayed from the central conviction that a changing society required new outlooks on marriage and sexuality. As he discussed the family, in fact, Wright turned his back on abstract theological issues and focused increasingly on the Northern economy.

Before turning to free-lance lecturing Wright wrote remarkably little about the family. One searches in vain through *Man-Killing, by Individuals and Nations* (1841) or *Defensive War* (1846) for discussions of peacekeeping between husbands and wives. And *The Dissolution of the American Union* (1846) made no mention of Wright's emotional preference for seamless relationships. His one long discourse on the family, *A Kiss for a Blow* (1842), envisioned a male-governed home, analogous to God's kingdom, and strikingly at variance with his later celebrations of maternity. But he preferred to write about children and ignore the relationships of parents. Even *Six Months at Graefenberg* (1845), composed in the shade of Mount Maria and Mount Elizabeth, kept silence on the theme of a "love-wife," although its recommended program of exercise, hiking, chopping wood, and cold water referred obliquely to restraining sexual impulses.

The manuscript survives of an unfinished essay on "The Blood of Woman & the Blood of Christ," written in Rosneath, August 1845, and arguing that women had more impact on human destiny than Christ. While working with Boston's mothers a decade before, he restricted his attention to their moral influence, particularly in disciplining children. Now he adapted the beliefs, honored in both folklore and medical literature, that mother's milk flowed out of the bloodstream and determined the infant's character. Within the womb and without, all the materials of body and soul descended from the mother. Christ's blood was powerless to help purity or health, while woman's would redeem mankind from disease. His own emancipation being mixed with convalescence, Wright prepared to tell audiences that heaven was a healthy body, hell an unhealthy one—nothing more. And yet woman would destroy man, instead of redeeming him, if her blood remained as cancerous and corrupting as evil practices often rendered it. While praising women, he displayed suspicions of sexuality that went back to the supplies he took from the mother he had lost. He had begun to polish his as yet unspoken message that woman should be "to *man,* a Messiah, a *Saviour.*"[129]

In *Anthropology, or the Science of Man* (1850), lecturer Wright came out in the open to combat paternal theology. Life was not, as he had so often said, the nursery of heaven; man was already in eternity, and would so continue in the next state. Rather than obeying regulations that repressed current needs and justified present dissatisfactions, it was time to study the laws evident in human nature. There was a clear strain of perfectionism in this work: all evils were inexcusable, and hell was merely the suffering that inevitably followed them. Ill health was the common metaphor for imperfection: just as a cut causes pain, a sin like slavery leads to vengeful destruction. Ostensibly a challenge to theology, *Anthropology* also reflected Wright's search, and his readers', for an adequate account of sex and affection. Not surprisingly, marriage was the key to emotional health. Instead of the prevailing government-regulated kind of marriage, however, with its contractual inequalities and penalties, Wright sketched a looser state of affairs that would in reality be governed by firm bonds of sentiment.

> MARRIAGE is a law of our social nature. . . . I mean, a mutual love between one man and one woman, which unites the soul of each to that of the other, leaving neither an independent existence in any of the interests of life: and fidelity to that love. This is marriage; and, as I view it, nothing else is. No man can be what he was designed to be, till by marriage, the spirit of a woman has entered into him, to refine, beautify and strengthen his peculiar nature, and assimilate it to the divine. No woman can be what she was designed to be, till the spirit of a man has entered into her, to purify, elevate and adorn her peculiar nature.

Written in the form of letters to "L." in London, *Anthropology* depicted love matches obeying laws of the human constitution similar to those that indicted war or slaveholding. In a world peopled by the offspring of such matches, social evils would disappear. The natural operation of the law of marriage cured all antagonisms. These extravagant expectations were barely elaborated in *Anthropology,* but they gave marriage a dominance in its pages that was not apparent from its title or table of contents.[130]

Wright began his most influential book, *Marriage and Parentage* (1854), by declaring: "To create a conscience in men and women, as to the use of their sexual nature and relations, is the great end at which the ensuing work aims. This is THE want in every class of society." This book took "the reproductive element in man" as its subject; to this new interest it joined the older one in internalized moral values. It formulated the ideology for a classless or, more accurately, a fluid society that repaid planning and restraint with economic advancement. Popular slang already connected the "spending" and "getting" of copulation to the market place; Wright went further and compared a man prodigal with his semen to "him who was ever toiling for wealth, but who could derive no enjoyment from it, except by throwing it, fast as he earned it, into the fire or sea." Wright's purpose was, then, not to disparage the acquisition of wealth, but to propose a ratio of enjoyment and accumulation by which couples would find their lives improving as they went along. His model husband promised his wife to be her "possession," guided by conditions she placed on the "reproductive element." Their motto was: "Progress, not pleasure, is our aim." Out of his own frustrations, Wright saw the redirection of sexuality as the basis of social behavior. The links between sexuality and the economy, moreover, were not simply theoretical. Declining fertility rates suggested how many couples were learning, during Wright's lifetime, that fewer children meant better material conditions, how many families accorded wives greater authority in the home. In a sense Wright was creating a science and mythology to justify their decisions.[131]

Whereas old-style religion told man to look "to a power outside himself" for personal salvation and social perfection—and we might add, for discipline—Wright now divulged the Promethean secrets of the power within. For all its vaunted freedom from autocratic religion, *Marriage and Parentage* presented a science of reimposed controls. Like sexologists ever since, Wright alleged that he was disclosing secrets about the health and happiness of the human body that previous generations had mistakenly suppressed. The distinction between men and women, far from being lewd, was central to the "general economy of human existence." While God was self-sufficient male and female, mother and father, He and/or She had provided for human moral behavior by requiring the union of distinct parts to propagate the species. Isolation coarsened and degraded human beings, but properly self-regulated marriages would improve civilization.[132] (Despite his efforts to rest morals on biology, Wright usually avoided intervening stages between isolation and marriage; he had nothing to say about the moral implications of "the chase."

Wright gave considerable space to describing the reproductive system, male and female, and the stages of fetal growth. He quoted frequently from scientific works, especially the *Physiology* of William Benjamin Carpenter (previously copied in his secret diary). In leaning on this authority, he chose respectable, even distinguished opinion. That Carpenter came from good British antislavery stock was additional, tacit proof of the power of heredity.[133] From science Wright found out that sexual relations were injurious. One perceptive review of *Marriage and Parentage* regretted Carpenter's influence and questioned whether the Creator would ever make a necessary function harmful. But the view that the expenditure of semen depleted masculine well-being was scientifically plausible, and Wright, for all his longing to be a father, quoted this principle: "*the development of the individual, and the reproduction of the species, stand in inverse ratio to each other.*" Thus in urging frankness regarding the reproductive system Wright also publicized fear of it. The sexual emancipation that promised health, happiness, and social harmony began with control over emission.[134]

The first token of progress was cessation of masturbation. Having won his own victories over masturbation with the help of Jesus, Wright was outraged that doctors advised nervous men to marry in order to cure the malady (much as their advice on drink ruined the Chester family). Imagine the immoderate man who married for that reason:

> He gets a wife, not to restrain him from pollution, but that he may indulge his sensuality under legalized and social sanction. In solitary indulgence, he ruined only himself: now, he victimizes wife and children to his passion. Death to a pure-minded woman were preferable to such a doom. Yet multitudes are sought, in legal marriage, by men whose aim is to save themselves from what they have come to consider an indulgence which they must and will have alone, if they cannot get legal control over the person of a woman. Such men had better be left to die as solitary sensualists, than to enter into relations by which others must be destroyed with them.

Horrors like these might have sprung out of one of George Lippard's gothic novels. Yet Wright printed letters tracing how the unremedied sin of masturbation brought the hell of anguish and disease into his readers' actual lives. Masturbation was, in any case, only one dimension of the larger problem of restraint. Other letters documented the ruined characters of infants whose sensualist fathers molested wives during pregnancy. The spermatic improvidence of one generation exacted heavy physiological tariffs on the next. When a man laid his mate's "womanhood" on "the altar of his sensuality," his children proved deficient in "reproductive power."[135]

Wright's message, ostensibly hopeful, was hemmed in by frightening case histories and predictions. Social reform would succeed when husbands and wives ceased to resign themselves to all the children "God sends." Men must beware the effects of sensual gratification; spouses should plan together how many children they could nourish and protect. Couples, before marrying, should inspect each other's mental and physical states. If everything was in order, they should still limit male ejaculation in intercourse to moments when they planned to conceive a baby. These infrequent moments demanded perfect health, happiness, and refinement. There should be no coarseness, no tobacco, no alcohol. During gestation, too, the child required parental love and happiness: a "love-origin" meant more than princely descent. Disease, anger, drugs, carnality—all passed through the mother's constitution into her progeny's body and soul. How misleadingly religion preached a postponed second birth: love-children were society's only hope of eluding physical degeneration, conflict, meanness of spirit. The pursuit of the millennium called for romantic marriage and a scientific approach to sex: "The kingdom of heaven is within those, and only those, who understand and comply with the conditions of present life and health to body and soul."[136]

About 180 pages of *Marriage and Parentage* featured affectionate, philosophical letters between an ideal husband and wife whom Wright named Ernest and Nina. Theirs was marital pleasure at its most purified and elevating. Each paid sonorous tribute to the other's influence on their mutual contentment. Their efforts to extinguish selfishness allowed Wright to make public a trace of his personal meditations on divorce. While making their match perpetual, Ernest and Nina criticized sham, state-sanctioned marriages that amounted to loveless entrapments. The absence of love, in fact, constituted divorce. But they did not publicize his complaints of a sexless marriage. Selfish gratification, instead, was connubial harmony's direst foe; and sexual problems stemming from inconsiderate behavior wrecked more marriages than any other cause. The goal of Ernest's letters, therefore, was the development of a restrained character. He made himself Nina's "possession," as we have seen, and crowned her "the regulator" of sexual intercourse. It was his belief that "all that is noble in manhood points to the subjection of the *passion* to the *sentiment* of love." The premise of their marriage was that strong emotions could only result in resented conquest; refined sentiments, on the other hand, created bonds of intimacy. Their marriage exemplified, in short, the theme of blows versus kisses, violence versus internalization, that defined Wright's intellectual life.[137]

When Ernest asked Nina, "Is reproduction the only object for which the sexual element may be rightfully expended?" she answered *yes;* she knew other ways to express her adoration of him. Ernest breathed his wish not to victimize her to his lust, especially since the loss of semen, however essential to procreation, injured men. Ernest also ventured some extraordinary fantasies about human history—fantasies that jumbled traditional issues of religious faith together with new concerns over commercial prospects, physical well-being, and luck with children:

> Failures in business, without any apparent cause; imbecility and folly in plans and purposes, and indecision in execution, where strength, wisdom and promptitude were expected; dyspepsia, rheumatism, gout, apoplexy, paralysis, consumption and disease . . . and a premature and agonizing death, where a healthy, vigorous youth gave promise of a long life . . .; a morose and selfish temper, where, in youth, a loving and manly spirit reigned; domestic circles converted into scenes of discontent, strife, cruelty and blood . . .; women, whose girlhoods were seasons of health, beauty and joyous life and activity, become prematurely nervous, fretful, sickly, helpless and deformed; . . . children . . . dead under five years of age . . .; the many premature births; the sufferings and deaths in child-birth; the inconceivable amount and variety of disease and suffering peculiar to the female organism; idiots, born of intellectual parents; insane, born of the sane; diseased and deformed, born of the healthy and beautiful; hating, revengeful and bloody spirits, born of the loving, the forgiving, and the gentle;—these and many other facts connected with human life, are ever before us, and ever marvellous.

All these vicissitudes, which "Religion and Public Opinion" blamed on Providence, actually were owing to "THE UNNATURAL AND MONSTROUS EXPENDITURE OF THE SEXUAL ELEMENT, FOR MERE SENSUAL GRATIFICATION."[138] It was very important to be earnest.

This fantasy oscillated between cruel and sentimental images. What impeded male renunciation of brutality was fear of appearing unmanly and of leaving one's mate unsatisfied. Stress on women's peculiar diseases might replace traditional beliefs in their strong sexual appetites. But how would Nina feel about her husband if he failed to expend his "sexual element"? Ernest draws an anxious picture, familiar throughout the literature of sexual advice, of cooling affections. We see the wife "pining for expressions of love she cannot get," and the husband, who once disliked even brief absences, now able to stay away for weeks "and yet return to her with measured steps and greet her with formality." He cannot respond to her outpouring affection; "she sinks in loneliness and anxiety." He becomes lifeless with his children, dull at business. Why? "Ask that husband how he has treated her, in reference to passional intercourse, and all is explained." The explanation is not inadequate or infrequent sexual performance; it is excess. "The very life of his manhood . . . has been expended in mere sensual indulgence, till, as a husband, he is an imbecile,—as a lover, well-nigh an idiot." Reconstruction of masculine character required a complicated denial of female sexuality and confinement of erotic pleasure to male bodies. There are undertones conveying Ernest's—and Wright's—fears that women might indeed have strong sexual needs and their own species of cruelty; but their explicit program is the conservation of semen and respect for feminine coolness. This program placed them at the fore in developing a new ideological view of women, regardless of contradictory evidence.[139]

Was there no pleasure, then, for married lovers? By announcing his subservience to Nina's sexless will Ernest made "his home an Eden of Love to his wife." She in turn praised the "manliness" of his restraint. *"Marriage, to me, is no romance,"* she told him, *"but an ennobling fact."* Bonds of domination gave way to bonds of intimacy. For Ernest there was an additional pleasure: "retention." The same sexual element that pleased the wife when released at an instant of high moral seriousness, and that gave a child its first vital impulse, was, when not secreted, the source of "magnetic power" between man and woman. It inspired them to the fullest development of love and intellect. Lest Nina worry that he resented the shortage of chances to ejaculate, he assured her that their intimacy was consistent with his self-improvement. "In all ages, men who have sought to improve themselves in physical beauty, strength and activity, have been abstemious in this regard. Witness the athletæ of Rome, the wrestlers, boxers and runners of all ages. They knew full well, that the life-energies required to supply the means of indulgence should be restrained, for the perfect development of the body in beauty, activity and power." He told Nina that the retention of the sexual element, "except for offspring," was "deep, vitalizing, ennobling, and intensely joyous and elevating." At times it sounds very much as though they practiced a form of genital intercourse without ejaculation.[140]

Beneath the surface, however, Ernest's letters—like Wright's intimate journal—entertained the opposite case: there would be a fit occasion for guiltless sexual release. Ernest and Nina desire a child, as their author so desperately did: "a child is the want of our nature, and an essential element in the happiness of our home. This, Nature allows," even though it costs some depletion of the father. "We stake, it may be, a trifle of individual growth, but we gain a crown of parental glory." And so Ernest enjoyed the pleasure of expenditure, then abstained scrupulously while Nina was pregnant and lactating. His reward was that his partner treasured, rather than resented, his moment of passion. "The memory of the act in which this new life originated is sacredly cherished," Nina wrote. "It was rendered delicate, and most acceptable, by the assurance that it was but the expression of your soul's deepest love. *In our passional relations, there is not a single memory or association which is not refined and noble.* I cannot conceive of the aversion some wives express in speaking of the animal passion of their husbands; it can never be associated in my mind with thee. I owe thee a deep debt of gratitude for this experience."[141] How skillfully this passage, like so much of Wright's later work, blended fantasies arising from his personal conflicts with telling responses to the complaints of wives and mothers!

The sexual ideology of *Marriage and Parentage* may be clarified by contrast with that of John Humphrey Noyes. Wright and Noyes had been religious radicals in the heady days of nonresistance; both were important influences on Garrison; both gained reputations for radical opinions on sex. But Wright's nomadic popularizing differed from Noyes's insulation in the Oneida Community, a vantage-point from which he passed caustic judgment on fads and compromises in the world outside.

Noyes is the best-known advocate of male continence, or coitus reservatus, in which ejaculation was inhibited during genital intercourse. At the simplest level Noyes offered a means of contraception, an alternative to coitus interruptus, withdrawal prior to ejaculation, a traditional means currently advocated by the notorious Robert Dale Owen. Interruptus, in Noyes's view, and the "various French methods" were unnatural; because they encouraged emissions without fear of pregnancy they were "wasteful of life." Abortions, of course, were worse. But some contraceptive scheme was desirable, Noyes thought, to render sexual intimacy something more than "a bait to propagation." Proffering love was a social function separate from breeding; "the grand problem," then, was to find a healthy, natural, effective method of contraception that did not retard "amativeness." By experimentation with his wife Noyes settled on male continence and recommended it to religious comrades who, after practice, were equally impressed by its virtues. The method later proved essential to extended family relations within the Oneida Community. Having eliminated fear of pregnancy, Noyes placed "amative sexual intercourse on the same footing with other ordinary forms of intercourse, such as conversation, kissing, shaking hands, embracing, &c." If a man paid a social call and left a baby, that would be immoral; but there was no need to be watchful over forms of intercourse that imposed no subsequent burdens. Noyes's community was freed from incest taboos; nor did it confine love and sex to conjugal couples. Expanding circles of sexual reform were part of the work of redemption: as men and women approached perfection they cast off Adam's legacy of shame.[142]

Like Wright, Noyes favored economic metaphors for his new system. He took a keen interest in profit and expense, cost and waste.[143] Despite his religious beginnings, he was a true modernizer who wrote about sex much as the farm journals criticized old-fashioned instruments and practices. His theory, in his own words, "opens the way for *scientific* propagation." Like Wright he deplored the costs to civilization of the multitudes of unwanted babies, but he cast no aspersion on sexual desire. His hope lay not in Wright's sentimental love babies, but in children bred according to principles of scientific agriculture. If no one had to give up amative intercourse, no complaints were justified concerning selective rules for propagation. Noyes also quarreled with American economists who thought the continent could absorb unlimited population. Sooner or later, the reserves of good land would run out and the limits of technological improvement would be reached; then the alternatives would be Malthusian or Noyesian, starvation or control.[144]

While other means of contraception weakened sexual pleasure in Noyes's view, his system "*vastly increases*" it. Ordinary intercourse was "a momentary affair, terminating in exhaustion and disgust." Male continence lasted as long as desired, produced a sensation of enhanced power, and left no feelings of shame. Many marriages sank into a "process of cooling off" because of self-reproach and resented temptation. Noyes's version of continence, in other words, remedied the same connubial maladies that Ernest had depicted for Nina. Instead of widely scattered moments of passion, however, Noyes promised that "lovers who use their sexual organs simply as servants of their spiritual natures . . . may enjoy the highest bliss of sexual fellowship for any length of time, and from day to day, without satiety or exhaustion; and thus marriage life may become permanently sweeter than courtship, or even the honey-moon."[145]

Wright and Noyes were both Victorian ideologists who prescribed versions of male restraint to intensify the pleasures of marriage. Wright was perhaps less insightful a psychologist, more sentimental a rhetorician, more embarrassed in admitting either partner's enjoyment of coition. His work is utterly ambiguous on the question of coitus reservatus. Is that what Ernest and Nina found so elevating, or were they simply thrilled by daily reassurances of respect? There is no answer.[146] But if Wright's books were muddier than Noyes's, his audience was wider. Noyes commented on honeymoons from an extended-family community where marital permanence was not a leading concern. He was distant from his countrymen's typical experience, while Wright covered East and West as an expert on marriage. Some came to him for practical counsel, some for clarification and reassurance. The "science" they sought from him was not a drastic overhaul of their behavior, not scientific propagation, but simply a new mythology giving legitimacy to changes in feeling that were already under way.

This "science" was most easily presented as an antitheology. In *The Errors of the Bible* (1857) Wright justified change by enunciating a *"fixed Revelation"* that various theologies had ignored. His argument turned swiftly to the body and marriage. The Bible tolerated polygamy and encouraged a double standard of sexual conduct, while hinting that there would be no distinctions of sex "in the resurrection state." It contradicted Wright's faith, dictated by "Nature," that he would be joined in reciprocal fidelity to one woman in the spirit world. Scriptural wives were conquered and purchased, rather than submitting to the subtler bonds of sentiment that Wright preferred.[147]

The Bible also erred on the fascinating subject of parentage outside of wedlock. In a characteristic twist of meaning, Wright called the birth of an illegitimate child "one of the greatest crimes against Nature which human beings can commit; and, of course, one of the greatest sins against God." What he meant, however, was that becoming a parent without love was illegitimacy, regardless of the technical legality of marriage. Loveless matches led to polluted children, the "offspring of shame," who were given "the wrath nature" instead of gentle dispositions. "A son or daughter asks, 'Am I the child of prostitution?' I answer, you are the offspring of prostitution and shame, if your parents did not love each other with marriage love. No use in blinking that fact, and human beings, as they now exist, are very frequently the offspring of prostitution and shame, their parents not being married." The Bible frustrated the cause of sexual realism by glorifying a woman who lied about an immaculate conception and a man who failed to assume his gender's highest responsibilities. To preach celibacy was as absurd as to teach abstinence from air or water! A permanent wife was prerequisite to salvation, and Jesus mistook the nature of true purity.[148] While defending adaptibility and change, in other words, Wright pretended that true reform was impossible until all commitments were lasting ones, until all children were wanted.

Old-fashioned religion ignored questions that really gripped men and women. *The Unwelcome Child* (1860) starred Wright in the role of advisor to unhappy husbands and bitter wives. The book consisted of letters to one worried man, and within these letters appeared many others, generally from women. Some testified to great help derived from reading Ernest and Nina and striving to resemble them; others sang the benefits of Wright's lectures or personal consultations. Nowhere else did Wright make himself sound so much like a twentieth-century marriage counselor. Many of the women he counseled plainly abhorred sex. Certain case histories, furthermore, were borrowed by other writers and played a significant part in shaping Victorian conceptions of women.[149] And his stereotype of a marriage in trouble indicated an increasingly disturbing pattern of experience, in which the husband was frequently away from home, and the wife aspired to reach his intellectual level. She dreaded sex and maternity; he viewed "passional intercourse" as a right. Having children widened the distance between them; the wife resented motherly duties. *The Unwelcome Child* made clear how Wright's favorite topics—heredity and children's rights—enabled fairly candid discussion of women's roles in society.

From behind all the quaint circumlocutions there also emerged the view of marriage as a pleasurable institution. If sex was unwelcome because it was associated with coercion and maternity, then men had an interest in learning about contraception. Wright avoided specific advice on that score—in print at least—but he clearly indicated that men needed more from wives than intellectual and spiritual respect. A man needed his "*physical* nature to be tenderly cherished and reverenced . . . in all the sacred intimacies of the home." Perhaps the husband's "uncalled-for passional manifestations" had rendered his "physical manhood disagreeable"; if so, he could hardly, "in her presence, preserve a sense of manly pride and dignity." In a successful marriage the husband had no fear of rejection:

> His physical manhood, as well as his soul, is dear to the heart of his wife, because through this he can give the fullest expression to his manly power. But if such manifestations are made when the wife is not prepared to receive them, and when she repels them and dreads the consequences, his physical nature becomes associated, not with the pure joy of a longed for maternity, but with a deep sense of shame and degradation, with an outrage on her nature. . . . How can she cherish, and proudly care for, the purity, health and comfort of his physical nature? He has made it disgusting to her. She regards it as the deadliest enemy of her purity and peace as a wife, and as the bane of her home.[150]

Once we observe that "a longed for maternity" stands for other longings and that man's "physical nature" is essentially phallic, we see that Wright's advice pointed toward a surprisingly modern view of marital sexuality, one that envisioned men giving up primitive notions of right in order to enjoy greater intimacy with their women. When the "manly passion" is "controlled by a love for her," the wife will love it. The "very power" that causes shame and wretchedness when unregulated "does but ennoble her, add grace and glory to her being, and concentrate and vitalize the love that encircles her as a wife, when it is controlled by wisdom, and consecrated to her highest growth and happiness, and that of her children. "It lends enchantment to her person, and gives a fascination to her smiles, her words and her caresses, which ever breathe of purity and of heaven." Wright continued: "Manly passion is to the conjugal love of the wife like the sun to the rosebud, that opens its petals, and causes them to give out their sweetest fragrance, and to display their most delicate tints; or like the frost, which chills and kills ere it blossoms in its richness and beauty." A true husband, in Wright's view, will not take any caress, let alone "the passional surrender of a woman to his passion," solely as a matter of right or even when "it is made solely to please him." Wright's advice, at least partly intended to enhance the joy of sex, was a somewhat manipulative form of role playing. "Whatever manifestations of yourself you would make to your wife, before offering them, create in her the necessity of demanding and receiving them. If your nature prompts you to reveal yourself to her in the relation that leads to maternity, control yourself . . . until, by all other loving and endearing manifestations, you have created in her nature an earnest call for maternity. Then would she joyfully accept of you the germ of a new life." The language strikes modern ears as cloyingly pious. But the objectives of reciprocal pleasure, the suggestion that anxiety can be overcome by self-control, and the scenarios of dissimulation and sincerity that it lays out—these aspects of *The Unwelcome Child* place it near the enduring paradoxical heart of sexual advice.[151]

Wright keenly understood the importance of unspoken sexual codes in a rapidly changing culture. He made skillful use of formulas found in American popular literature in order to interpret puzzling experiences and new goals. One hears echoes of George Lippard in the perils caused by the monster husband who does not respect the slow sexual rhythm of women. The result may be death, virtual imprisonment, or a long chain of abortions. One hears the drama of the revival or temperance novel in the case of the husband who, at his wife's begging, reads *Marriage and Parentage* and overcomes his maddening urge to excrete semen. I will be an Ernest, he proclaims. Wright's books accord scientific status to the popular wisdom that the world will be a better place when all children benefit from motherly affection. They also employ the reformer's slogans of the higher law: no couple, no wife, should disobey the promptings of their highest nature regardless of what church and state presume to sanction. These themes converge in the advice that couples should experiment with their sexual patterns and avoid the stony silences of bad marriages. Raising the ideal of a wife as a companion, equal in intelligence, Wright's books urged couples to discuss their sexual expectations before and during marriage. Conventional reticence on this subject left too many men unloved, too many timorous wives living as though caged with an untamed animal.[152]

The Unwelcome Child included many signs of Wright's fascination with motherhood. He gave considerable attention to mother's milk, which he located in the reproductive system. Resentment, he had learned, affects the flow of milk. What he stressed, however, was the utopian alternative that loving mothers will pour forth the material elements of a sweet nature.[153] In his next book, *The Empire of the Mother over the Character and Destiny of the Race* (1863), he revised this view: mother's milk and all other postnatal influences meant little compared to the "organization" of body and soul imparted in the uterus.

The determinism of this message, if taken literally, was as implacable as Calvin's. Many things that Wright had once celebrated—home influences and childhood education, for example, or sexual counseling for adults—he now called ineffectual; a person's bent was fixed in the womb. Even variations in sexual customs around the world derived from "differences in organic conditions and constitutional tendencies of the soul, created before birth." Wright's anthropology did not favor cultural explanations: the egg had come before the chicken. Like many other prophets of determinism, he ignored the inconsistency in exhorting men and women to break loose from forces that shackled them. But his exhortations were cold and muted. A key example of the social evils that might be escaped with greater wisdom was the death of children. This evil held deep personal meaning. It was also important to his audiences: one third of New England's children, he said, died before the age of five; another third before fifteen; more survived in pain. If by some chemistry of abstinence a cleaner generation of mothers came into being—if, in other words, embryos and fetuses could construct their consciences and physiques out of unpolluted materials, devoid of illness, anger, and intemperance—then history's cycles of inhumanity and suffering would be broken. There was a disturbed underside to Wright's public celebrations of womanhood and maternity. *The Empire of the Mother* gave few glimpses of happy marriages and blissful sex. Whatever cheer came from knowing that the genius of a Mozart or John Brown—his improbable pair—surfaced in early youth was dispelled by a mother's chilling first-person account of raising a murderer by bathing him in the womb with foul sentiments of resentment. Mother's empire was a troubled realm, auguring grimly for the future.[154]

This bleak vision represented something beyond echoes of Calvinism or comments on the author's disappointments: it conveyed an outlook on social inequality. If Americans chose not to breed persons like pigs or ears of corn, they might prefer Wright's science emphasizing the material supplies and liquid sentiments of the uterus. If so, theirs was a limited and chastened perfectionism whose purpose was ideological accommodation to the present rather than utopian planning for the future. The grandeur of his theme and some of his rhetoric may blur this accommodation, but it was there. When this grim book restated Wright's old call to look for God in living human beings rather than in far-off abstractions, femininity and poverty served as interchangeable examples. Men should accustom themselves to seeing God "in the poor, the oppressed and suffering, and in those who seem most lovable to us, who live in most endearing and intimate relations with us, and whose interests and happiness would be most essentially promoted by such love and worship of a manifest God." Let husbands see God in their wives, and let all see Him in "the oppressed, the despised, the outcast and the suffering."[155] Reciprocal pleasure did not mean equal power. If we read Wright's sexual teachings outward to their social implications, important limits were being set around how much improvement—even in the name of perfectionism—ought to be anticipated.

The Self-Abnegationist; or, The True King and Queen (1863) clarified Wright's ideological purposes. His message plainly was not self-fulfillment, but denial. This book canceled even the cryptic allusions to self-gratification that he had toyed with in previous sexual advice and tried to justify in his secret life. He fell back heavily on notes of selflessness and restraint held over from the trials of childhood. God speaks through human cravings, such as the laws of supply and demand that tell us to eat or drink. Commencing in this way, Wright nearly syllogized himself into hedonism, but he swiftly turned back: since self-abnegation was the most enduring basis for social life, it was divine law.[156]

The language of this book was economic, and the problem it addressed was one that Adam Smith, among others, found central to moral philosophy. The echoes of ironclad economic laws were not accidental. Wright's goal was to show that necessary adjustments in society would occur automatically, that men would regulate their behavior according to natural inclinations toward goodness. Wright approached this goal with the rhetorical emphasis on private property and individual autonomy that C. B. Macpherson has described as "possessive individualism." In Wright's formulation: "If a man is sole and absolute owner of anything he must be of his own body and soul with all their functions. We instinctively recoil from the thought that our bodies and souls are at the disposal of others. . . . We cannot help but feel outraged when others, whether acting individually or collectively, assume or exercise the right to dispose of our physical life and powers without our consent, and for their benefit." In the beginning all persons stand encapsulated in the lonely equality of "self-ownership." But their isolation is theoretical and temporary; they are constantly sensitive to the needs and wishes of others. Social order depends not on the maintenance of a fixed hierarchy, but on the natural tendency of human nature to approve self-abnegating acts. All applaud spectacular feats of self-sacrifice to help others. Indeed, the altruism of reformers like Garrison and John Brown, by this analysis, serves the same purpose: the dramatization of a universal moral consciousness.[157]

At its heart *The Self-Abnegationist* was a book about business, an early contribution to cultural controversies that scholars sometimes associate with Darwinism. The theory of possessive individualism outlined criteria for distinguishing the good businessman from the bad, the sharp exploiter from the fair trader. It was hard, Wright admitted, to extend the rule of self-abnegation to the commercial sphere, where deceit and ruthlessness slipped by prevailing ethics. He denounced the pervasiveness of "slavery" in the North:

> Who are the slave-breeders, slave-traders, slave-drivers, slave-hunters and slave-holders of America . . .? Without exception, they are men who hold that self-preservation, by arms and blood, and at the expense of others is the first law of nature. . . . They insist that Nature prompts them to seek to become rich by making others poor, if need be; to feed themselves by starving others; to house and warm themselves by making others houseless and cold. . . . [W]hosoever and whatsoever, intentionally or unintentionally, justly or unjustly, innocently or guiltily, endangers the existence, safety, comfort or gratification of Self, they may kill, slay and destroy, as the anaconda crushes in its snaky folds whatever crosses its path.

If this description of "slavery" was really thought to define Northern business practice, Wright's argument might have been radical. A more likely effect of such exaggerated denunciation was to confer legitimacy on most familiar practices. Wright paid no attention to discrepancies between "self-ownership" and the lot of numerous Americans; his views anticipated the ideology of the impartial citizen and harmony of interest between workman and boss. Under ordinary circumstances there was an ebb and flow of reciprocal sympathy alleviating whatever personal tragedies were incidental to a free labor society.[158]

This book about business consisted of letters to "Julia, my child." What did they say about marriage and the family? Domestic life furnished exempla of the sacrificial behavior, crucial to a free, mobile, prospering society, that made governmental regulations irrelevant. Conflicts were less obvious if one ignored the economic relations of free males; perhaps for that reason Wright noted that "in contemplating the relations of human beings, in the family, or in the general society, I instinctively and of necessity, think of the relation of man to woman, and of woman to man, and never of man to man, nor of woman to woman." Wright did not think of heterosexual love as enslaving or hierarchical: his type of pregnancy was an image of free labor. His appreciation of links between domestic behavior and the economy was also revealed by commonsense boundaries he placed on "self-abnegation." He kept in mind what kinds of husbands and children would go forth into the world. There were false forms of sacrifice, as when parents through reluctance to discipline their children spoiled them or when wives by pampering their husbands made them vain and delicate. No one should lead a loved one to excessive habits of self-gratification. Although women were assigned imperial significance for the destiny of the race, furthermore, Wright did not call for any change in the division of labor.[159] Wright's vision of self-abnegation could be summarized as follows: glorification of the mother's domestic role; redefinition of the attitude of the mobile, economic male with regard to wife and mother; celebration of sacrificial conduct in private and social life; and the focusing of the family's ultimate concern, rather fearfully, on the growth and welfare of children—the true beneficiaries of their predecessors' self-restraint.

It was in his last book, *The Living Present and the Dead Past* (1865), that Wright disclosed bizarre assignations with his split-off self and, figuratively, with his mother.[160] His drift toward solipsism added urgency to his recurrent contention that God must be revealed in the person of a true mate, a loving "other." The links between this contention and the mainline of evangelical Protestantism emerge in references to Henry Ward Beecher, who also criticized abstract images of God in favor of the "pictorial" reality of Jesus. Wright's style demanded some antagonism: "Tell me, Henry Ward Beecher, tell me, each and every man, can you not see your 'Personal God', the object of your heart's deepest love and worship more clearly presented to you in your wife, the angel of your home, and the mother of your child that nestles in your bosom, than in a picture?" But by acknowledging some consensus with Beecher, Wright called attention to the reorientation of Protestantism that was an important context of his own work on the hustings. The famous Brooklyn preacher spoke constantly—and just as ambiguously as Wright—in praise of "Love." It was the hope of many of his generation's Protestant leaders that sentiment would stave off intellectually confusing and socially disintegrating aspects of their times. Although it is hard to imagine the two men holding much of a conversation, Beecher hardly needed Wright to lecture him on the unbounded significance of the home.[161]

Beecher later endured a storm of controversy over his intimacies with a parishioner's wife—an episode probably resembling Wright's amours with Esther Lukens or Julia Friend. In *The Living Present,* Wright published hints that he had found an earthly love. It was always his custom to *almost* unveil his secrets; here he mentioned fear that his opinions might hurt his lover, thus making it advisable to converse instead with his better self! It is a familiar enough irony of the century that men who extolled marriage had affectionate partners who were extramarital. The important point, however, is that they were searching for a deeply intimate match, a condition visualized less as liberation than as control and worthiness. Among the most poignant themes of *The Living Present* is a need for belonging and protection, recognized in his own life and then generalized to all of humankind. A remote God, projected outside the sphere of human needs, could not be satisfactory; neither could fantasies of mother sustain him forever. What was required, as the world revolved from an age of fiction to one of fact, was for each person to translate qualities once associated with God to his or her spouse. In his wife's face let each man identify his savior. This tactic threw up defenses against unwelcome instincts, also against threatening circumstances of a fluid market society that constantly pressed men like Wright to define who they actually were and what they actually did. After comparing mating to ingesting food and water "to protect me from hunger and thirst," Wright insisted: ". . . God can do nothing to shield me from harming myself and others, and others from wronging themselves and me; nor can he control my passions and appetites, words and acts, except as he is personified in me, and in those with whom I am associated in intimate relations; and *the more intimate the relation,* the more complete is my salvation."[162]

The Living Present defended private indiscretions with publicly worthy purposes. It was also a passionate effort to unite love with continence, one more instance of a long-standing campaign to subdue aggression. "In the forbearance, the self-forgetting, consecrating love felt by the husband and wife, the parents and children, and brothers and sisters for one another, God is as really manifest as he was in Christ." It is "madness," Wright continued, for a man to pretend to worship God and "see *only* the animal in his wife." Sexual relations was a subject clarifying the meaning of submissiveness in a world that was often brutal and unfair. Consider, for example, Wright's repeated insistence that it is not in homosexually defined relationships—father-son or brother-brother—that God is realized. Clearly there was a personal homosexual aversion at work, but more interesting is the meaning of this aversion in terms of the world's discipline. Male relationships conjure up images of force; heterosexual ones evoke the rule of love. "Human nature recoils from man and woman, when either attempts to rule over the other by brute force". Perhaps human nature could learn that unlimited authority did not require violence. "God, incarnate in woman as love, forbearance, patience, self-abnegation and good for evil, in true relations, exercises 'supreme, uncontrolled, absolute and irresistible power' over the interior and exterior life of man." The internal quotation, unattributed, might well have referred to the powers of God, or of a Mississippi tyrant; the analogy between these powers and woman's influence shows how earnestly Wright turned to guilt and family obligation as sources of social discipline.[163]

The Living Present reiterated Wright's belief that the economic world of men was inevitably competitive and, therefore, always possibly coercive. But there were forms of self-abnegation in the family to temper dread of that possibility. The influence of women, standing by definition outside the battles, promised that the adversaries might meet in the future with well-regulated consciences. And yet, deeply as Wright's teachings drew on his knowledge of women, the most that he expected of them was to soften the conflicting masculine world.

Wright was nevertheless a radical, a hero to those who were fed up with marital slavery. Perhaps the best testimonial came from Lucy Stone, the sturdy abolitionist and suffragist who caused a great stir by refusing to alter her name at marriage. She wrote Wright that she had read parts of *Marriage and Parentage* "over and over, and every time, see more clearly its absolute truth, and exceeding beauty." It was wonderful that correspondence like Ernest's and Nina's could be imagined, more wonderful still that a few such lives were already being lived. (She was probably unaware of Wright's experiments.) When she praised "that *conscious purity,* strong in its truth, which dares to reveal its most intimate life," she found exactly the phrases to describe the merger of sexual control with elevated communication that Wright identified with progressive marriage. Although one of Stone's friends called the book unfit to read and refused to show it to a daughter on the verge of marriage, Stone was giving copies to other young people. "Very truly yours for all that is pure, and true between man and woman," she signed herself.[164]

"The marriage question will and must some day be discussed," Lucy Stone reportedly said; but feminists must first secure political rights.[165] Her admiration of *Marriage and Parentage* might be interpreted as part of a strategic evasion of conflicts and complaints that rendered marriage oppressive to women. Although Wright sometimes asserted that divorce was nothing more than the cessation of love, requiring no churchly or governmental sanctions, these were experimental remarks, offered in passing. Divorce was one thing he did not dare in his personal life; disclosure of his extramarital loves was another; and he laid emphasis, resoundingly, on the permanence of conjugal love. His books might be assigned, then, to that side of feminism determined not to offend public taste, but to take what advantage it could from sentimental visions of domestic life, so long as men and women were politically unequal.

The fact that women's movements usually kept disagreements out of sight does not mean that there was consensus on these priorities. A conflicting viewpoint came to light at the 1858 Rutland "Free Convention," at which radicals were invited to speak without restraint and let their deepest convictions emerge. At this gathering Julia Branch criticized Lucy Stone's timidity on the marriage question; only widespread knowledge of their wedlock shielded Stone's cohabitation with her husband from attack. When one of the radicals, possibly Wright, presented a resolution defying polygamy and celebrating domesticity, Branch caused a furor by opposing it. Until legal marriage was a repudiated version of slavery, she said, men would continue to pick wives like items of exchange, and not much would be gained by seeking women's suffrage. It was the reformers' ignorance of working-class life, she suggested, that explained this oversight. Criticizing Wright and others who praised mothers' influence, Branch said that she preferred to "go a step further back"; instead of worshipping child-bearing women she would turn attention to the binding legal ceremony of marriage that kept them "degraded in mental and moral slavery." Wright himself revealed considerable sympathy with Branch's remarks. Her criticisms of him were not altogether fair, for in glorifying motherhood Wright always distinguished his portrait of true wedlock from customary practices and legal codes. Nor did she admit that he at least hinted at making marriage more easily terminable. Her criticisms nevertheless point to boundaries that Wright, Stone, and many others carefully did not overstep. Wright's audience was middle-class, and a celebration of pregnancy, delineating woman's place in history, overshadowed his attack on that species of legalized prostitution and slavery that, in his view, passed for marriage.[166]

The issue of divorce tested the preoccupation of antebellum reform with order and authority. If one granted that sexually unhappy marriages amounted to slavery—and granted, moreover, the social costs of unwanted children—troublesome questions still surrounded the obligations of marriage partners. Probably most reformers preferred to criticize existing arrangements, to envision undying unions, and to leave other questions buried. But Wright's antislavery friend Charles K. Whipple questioned his assumption that "reproduction is the one object of marriage." Wasn't it more accurate to call marriage a complex contract serving many purposes? And wasn't Wright's view of divorce too simple? Regardless of the problems in enforced continuance of a cold marriage, was it clear that greater wrongs would not befall women without the existing protective laws?[167] Other critics revealed the lack of a reform consensus on the issue of divorce.

Andrew Jackson Davis, the famed clairvoyant whom Wright hailed as "a Jesus of this day," was a competitor in the growing market for reform/spiritualist/marital authorities. Perhaps because he was reeling from a scandalous divorce and allegations of extramarital sex, he treated *Marriage and Parentage* a bit gingerly, even calling it a "New Testament" from the "Heaven of the Soul," and "the code of the New Jerusalem." The Ernest-Nina correspondence, in particular, was "the truest, fullest, highest exposition of the hypothesis of an indissoluble, eternal marriage," a display "of the *head* declaring positively that the desires of the cultured *heart* shall meet with boundless, everlasting gratification." (This sounds suspiciously like wishful thinking.) According to Davis, the children of love matches would easily reach the "harmonial" state of spiritualism. Welcoming Wright to the quest for uncoercive paths to orderly community life, Davis thought he heard echoes of the French utopian Charles Fourier's analysis of human affections. Actually Wright had not read so widely, and his consuming interest in indissoluble marriage outweighed the appeal of community. But he surely must have appreciated such progressive credentials.[168]

After praising Wright, Davis turned to the thorny topic of marital fidelity. Had Wright foreseen all the difficulties inherent in saying that couples are divorced when they find they do not love? How could couples know their love was perpetual? How did easy divorce differ from the polygamy both he and Wright detested? In order to raise issues that were normally unthinkable in Victorian America, Davis summarized a review of *Marriage and Parentage* by two notorious radicals, Thomas Low Nichols and Mary Gove Nichols. Wright's admirable book would obviously play a role in dispelling the conspiracy of silence cloaking marriage, they said; but its emphasis on monogamy was unfortunate. Assumptions that love is eternal and exclusive were contradicted whenever persons ceased to love or loved more than one. The Nicholses disagreed, furthermore, that sex's only object was offspring (though sexual relations *should* be infrequent). As for Davis, he admittedly quoted the radicals so as to hedge his own opinion. He hoped spiritualism could designate temperamentally harmonious mates, but also predicted that the marriage question would merge with women's rights, thus forcing a "desperate struggle between heart and head—between Law and Love."[169]

Ordinarily Wright skirted threats of struggle: he was simultaneously a radical "progressionist" and a defender of restraint and fidelity. The Nicholses and other dissenters from the gospel of conjugal bliss were, in his language, polygamists; they handily demonstrated that his views were not too outlandish.[170] But this game could be reversed—the dissenters could turn Wright the iconoclast into a guardian of tradition. The most revealing instance occurred in 1856, after Wright dispatched to the *Liberator* an excited report of the Sheboygan Falls convention on spiritualism and its enemies. In Berlin Heights, Ohio, a reader named Francis Barry took offense at resolutions equating "free love" with the polygamy and concubinage of the Old Testament. All advocates of free love, in his opinion, disavowed enslavement; when it came to shackling women, modern monogamy was more obnoxious. It was specious for Wright and other sentimentalists to advocate a form of marriage based on love: everyone knew the term *marriage*, like slavery, referred to a system in which love was at best fortuitous.[171]

Barry understood the midwestern audiences on whom Wright depended, and he cleverly challenged Wright to justify bad marriages (and thus antagonize some of them) or to propose easy divorce (thus irritating others). On the defensive, Wright stuck to the marriage-as-procreation formula: he merely tried to point out at Sheboygan Falls that the Bible sanctioned polygamy while spiritualism advocated "*exclusive* conjugal love . . . as the only basis of a happy home, and a spiritual and healthy offspring." Some champions of free love wanted "Free Lust"; others—perhaps including Barry—sought exclusive love, and would find no slander in the Sheboygan Falls resolutions. Attacks on the Bible and slavery were helpful in sidestepping tricky questions about marriage: "Every eulogy on the Bible, *as a whole,* is a eulogy on polygamy and prostitution; every apology for slavery is an apology for the abolition of marriage and universal concubinage. May Spiritualism, with her purer and more ennobling views of marriage and parentage, and of the relations of the sexes, go forth to the conflict with Sexualism, under every name and form, until men and women shall more perfectly understand and accomplish the true and exalted mission of each to the other!"[172]

Barry, unbeguiled, had no use for Wright's categories. Free love had nothing in common with polygamy. Some "free lovers" preferred exclusive unions, but he did not. "Free lovers demand perfect and unconditional freedom . . . and they are perfectly willing that the heart shall decide for itself whether it will have one or more objects; at the same time they believe . . . that variety in love is not only natural, but in the highest degree promotive of purity, happiness and development." The cause of "affectional freedom" could not be accused of enslaving women. Poor Wright, who needed to count his meager intimacies as liberating, received this condescension: "you will know us to be your equals in purity, and your superiors in philosophy. In the meantime, we will love and honor you for your great heart, and the good you are doing, and pity you as the victim of a false and merciless system."[173]

Seldom was Wright hit so cleverly by the taunting style that was his own specialty. If there had been more "free lovers" willing to cast aside prudence and monogamy, he might have been pushed to examine divorce and nonprocreative sex more openly. Already Barry indicated how sexual radicals cleared the way for more conventional theorists and kept the liberation of women near the forefront of changing patterns of marital life. Their uninhibited views made Wright's seem more legitimate. Barry and other critics revealed that Wright took a complex middle way between marital freedom and marital happiness, between individual needs and social order. By directly addressing sexuality and divorce at all, he was overstepping boundaries and dissipating silence. There were contemporary manuals for newlyweds, supposedly giving frank, practical advice, that made no reference to sexual intercourse or parental responsibilities. They talked about in-laws, servants, and the perils of trying to change a spouse's habits, but they came nowhere near Wright's treatment, cautious as it was, of sexual pleasure and women's rights.[174] Bold as he was from this perspective, however, Wright stopped short of publicly justifying the need for "affectional freedom" to which his secret diaries testified.

Wright spoke instead for the couples in his audience who aimed to control themselves and get ahead, who at the same time looked forward to a bright new era of intimacy and freedom. What kinds of behavior—they asked—were too free, or unfree, for a new economic order? Wright answered by sketching out a formula of sexual restraint and political progress; at the same time, as we shall see, he contrasted a dark European past to America's glorious future.

Five

Change—Revolution

Alfred de Musset, *Confession of a Child of the Century* (1835)

Three elements entered into the life which offered itself to these children: behind them lay a past forever destroyed, moving uneasily on its ruins with all the fossils of centuries of absolutism; before them the aurora of an immense horizon, the first gleams of the future; and between these two worlds—something like the Ocean which separates the old world from Young America, something vague and floating, a troubled sea filled with wreckage, traversed from time to time by some distant sail or some ship breathing out of a heavy vapor; the present, in a word, which separates the past from the future, which is neither the one nor the other, which resembles both, and where one can not know whether, at each step, one is treading on a seed or a piece of refuse.

Child of the Century

"My father was a Federalist, and sided with England in the wars of Napoleon": this memory indicates one source of Henry Wright's lifelong hostility toward party politics.[1] He echoed the fear, voiced by eminent men of the Revolution, that factionalism would stir up the rabble, impede the rule of the meritorious, and destroy the republic. With the overthrow of

Federalism—"the Revolution of 1800"—dire fears came true; and complaints about the vulgarity of politics became almost ritualistic among devotees of New England's lost cause. Fervent antipartyism was part of the family baggage transported to New York by disenchanted veterans of the Revolution. In decades to come their children might well attempt to ignore the squalid rivalries of office seekers while maintaining a keen interest in the nation's morality and progress. When Henry went back east and rose within the Federalist world of Newburyport, his ambitions matched Seth Wright's priorities. Under the pseudonym "Sincerity" he criticized politicians, especially Democrats, for their lack of independent judgment; servile Americans, to his regret, chose their rulers by factional maneuver instead of reason.[2] In later explorations of the nonpolitical realms of education and genetics, Henry showed the creative side of a post-Federalist temper that too often was provincial and reactionary.

The political milieu of his boyhood did not lead automatically to Federalism or antipartyism. Erastus Wright, beloved brother toward whom Henry never showed the slightest ambivalence, born during the Revolution, supervisor of the farm during Seth's absences, "was a Democrat, and sided with Napoleon." Arguing over "Napoleon's progress," father and brother dramatized, within a single family, one of American history's deepest ideological cleavages. Loyalty to England's cause, or Napoleon's, signaled how one felt about violence, aristocracy, and economic mobility. Those who favored France placed their hopes in international insurgency; the other side backed its repression. Verbal battles between Erastus, a grown man still residing in his father's house and a partisan of the Man of Destiny, and his aloof father must have been fascinating.[3]

Young Henry took part in the cult of Napoleon that seized many young Europeans: ". . . with what absorbing interest I used to hear and read of that man's movements; for though a child, my heart always triumphed in his victories, his rapid movements, his sudden encounters with the combined armies of all Europe. It was the fearful daring and energy of the man that kindled up my young heart. Many a stirring speech have I made, in the dreams of my childhood, to an army, to animate them to battle and to victory."[4] During his *Wanderjahre* on the Continent friends remarked how closely Wright's head resembled Napoleon's.[5] And there was always in his breast a glimmer of the young romantic Julien Sorel's "sacred fire with which one makes oneself a name."[6] The dangerous virtue that Napoleon symbolized—"daring and energy"—was a version of that "itching to be *known*" that Theodore Weld, among others, detected in Wright. Marriage into respectable Federalist society could not quench dreams of self-advancement and dangerous liaisons. Around a statue of Wellington he cavorted with his Wee Darling, careless of the world's opinion. Nonresistance and sexual continence were means he developed to keep these Napoleonic impulses from overpowering him. Sometimes the example of Napoleon reminded him that it was sinful to win praise through violence and selfishness.[7] But the sacred fire still smoldered.

His first manly venture was wrecked by England. After serving his apprenticeship he set out as a hatter, but "trade was very dull, in consequence of the immense importations from Britain since the close of the war in 1815." Since no laws protected American hatmakers, he did not make his living. When he returned to his father's house, gave up dreams of writing, and bowed to suggestions that he study for the clergy, he severed his fate from Napoleon's.[8] If he wished to rise, it would be in black cloth, not military splendor.

On a trip to Rhode Island in 1828 Reverend Wright observed the rising factory system and predicted that economic changes would destroy farm families and weaken American morals. Sharing a coach with two Southerners led to political debate in which Wright, as a good representative of his section, favored Adams over Jackson. Then conversation turned to the French Revolution and the influence of "circumstances" in raising obscure men to fame. How many would never have been known, the travelers wondered, had it not been for Revolution? In some ways faithful to American Federalism and the traditional order, in others Wright was a child of France and circumstances, looking for vocation.[9]

Wright's life belongs to the history of romanticism. Of course hundreds of ill-defined and incompatible things have been termed "romantic"; the term can serve historians clearly, however, when it refers to "ways in which man's self-awareness was affected by the Revolutionary-Napoleonic disruption,"[10] more particularly to efforts to discover one's bearings or assert one's freedom in a world where old institutions and sources of value could no longer be taken for granted. Wright's generation searched for new definitions of political and economic obligation, new methods of harnessing individual drives to the public good. We can place Wright in the context of international romanticism by examining, first, his youthful statements of taste and aspiration. Then we shall attend closely to his mature reports of historical grandeur in Europe and the sublimity of nature in America. We shall encounter, throughout his life, images of mobility and insurrection that harked back to his initial searches for a place in the economy and to controversies over foreign policy in his boyhood home.

Fiction

One recurrent sign of Henry Wright's romanticism was his feeling of unutterable loneliness. Usually he cast this mood theologically—"alone with God"—but there were aesthetic precedents for his nighttime wanderings beside rivers in Norwich and Newbury. By the time he left home he had read Goethe's *Sorrows of Young Werther* and was acquainted with popular modes of acting out and savoring sadness. Sometimes he actually posed as a sensitive, weary young man in a world that had lost its meaning. On the cover of his student commonplace book, preceding pages of ecclesiastical history, he copied twelve lines from Byron on the universality of *Weltschmerz:* "Who hath not shared that calm so still and deep / The voiceless thought which would not speak but weep?" Who had not experienced the ecstasy of a "sweet dejection," of unmotivated tears?[11]

He had also read Scott's *Scottish Chiefs.* His father had marched in uniform and pioneered the Cooper country, while little Henry imagined himself in front of armies. In his crises we may hear overtones of the *mal de siècle* defined by Alfred de Musset: what agonies were endured by sensitive youths, born too late for glorious endeavor.[12] Taught at Andover to be critical, relativistic, dryasdust, Wright thirsted for historical purpose, for ennobled *action.* Donning the cloth was a temporary retreat; he still dreamed of a mission among simple tropical peoples. How long would he leave his genuine self, the source of those powerful feelings associated with Byron, Werther, and Bonaparte, imprisoned in a world of dusty books and lifeless conventions? How long would his genius remain frozen?

Itinerant reform could be pursued as a Byronic pilgrimage.[13] It relieved the hero's sorrows to be among plain people—wives and children, especially—living authentic lives. Like Werther, the reformer could pause for meditations in graveyard or forest, while brooding thoughts of death heightened his awareness of the historical conflict between great principles vying for authority to reconstruct society. Would men be free or slaves, would they be ruled by superstition or science, would they run society or be crushed? To discontented women the reformer confided both thoughts of death and his commitment to right principle. In his journals Wright addressed himself as a Cain or Manfred, bearing a guilty secret, doomed to wander without solace.

Like romantics who dismissed social conventions as meaningless versions of playacting, Wright detested ministerial histrionics. In regretting that children were taught to show off, he expressed a mixed ideal of spontaneity and self-effacement: "Once a child gets the idea that she is acting a part—that she has a right to be looked at & admired—she is ruined so far as beauty & interest of character are concerned. She becomes stiff, formal, awkward, selfish—a torment to herself & associates. I hate to see human life performed—acted—Rather see it felt & lived." His uncertainty about self-exposure diminished when walking in the Highlands with Wee, feeling "confident, easy, *graceful* . . . because I am a child of nature, and can speak, laugh, walk and act with perfect ease and naturalness." Yet returning to society made him "an *artificial* man." "There I, like others, *perform* humanity." A muted protest against modern society was common to romantics for whom authentic lives were undermined by the economy, and professional life defeated the self.[14]

Despite his professed aversion to playacting, Wright allied himself with the romantics' revaluation of Shakespeare and demolition of classical unities that falsified the theater. During an interlude from the theological grind at Andover he read Macbeth. His scholarly relativism allowed him to tolerate "ludicrous" scenes of witchcraft; he appreciated the inevitable connections between monarchy and murder that he took to be the play's message. Most important, the play was serious—"not a fiction" but a fact of human history. Although some critics complained that the bard had violated dramaturgical rules by compressing too much historical time into an evening's entertainment, this cavil "will have weight with those only who censure all that chooses to be guided by their genius rather than by given rules."[15] In obvious ways *Macbeth* echoed the meanings of Napoleon: self-expression, advancement, and "genius."

There were inconsistencies in approaching a work in terms of its own age and yet with an eye for universal moral teachings. There were ambiguities, furthermore, in praising *Macbeth* simultaneously for not being a fiction and for its intimations of creative genius. These obscure student notes set down perplexities of motive that typified Wright's life. How could one distinguish falsified from authentic theater, heartfelt from deceiving performance? Similar questions plagued Wright's romantic contemporaries. Doreen Hunter and other scholars have detected the painful efforts of early American artists, the children of Federalism, to explore the creative side of personality without letting go of universal moral law. They experienced strains between artistic production and the marketing of commodities, between literary creativity and public demands for works that were morally unchallenging.[16]

Literature was a subject of delicate importance in the testing of modern attitudes toward personal feelings and social obligation. To authors it evoked ambition (or "genius"); to readers it afforded vicarious experiences that conventional moralities intended to suppress. The paradigmatic case was Rousseau, whose widely read *Confessions* recounted uninhibited nights spent with his father over his dead mother's supply of novels, nights that gave him, too early, troubling acquaintance with the passions and foreshadowed the fantasy-haunted qualities of his adult life. While Rousseau sometimes attributed the artificiality of modern civilization to literature, he also reported that only by imagining fictional worlds could he turn his back on intrigues and conflicts that in reality surrounded him. Despite his complaints about literature, moreover, Rousseau was himself the author of fictions that experimented rather freely with the psychology of sexual attraction, and he suggested that novels might usefully support public morals in a republic. As in many other instances, Rousseau had touched on an issue of intersecting private and public experience, the significance of which became clearer for later generations. Was the rehearsal of inner fantasies, especially when prompted by commercial literature, more conducive to disorder or to restraint?[17]

It is clear that numerous middle-class Americans in the nineteenth century used novel reading as a testing ground for the ability to control erotic drives. Trying to resist the lure of fiction safely reenacted men's efforts to cease masturbating: it was a step toward emancipation and maturity. It was also a step from frivolity to earnest purpose, as Wright's employers in the sabbath school work recognized when they eschewed fiction as an injurious influence on children. The proper task—performed so successfully by Wright in *A Kiss for a Blow*—was to use fact creatively. Just as novels could retard young men's growth, they could carry old men backward: Wright's teacher, Moses Stuart, avoided them until retirement, then succumbed to a compulsion that used up his time and conversation.[18]

Wright's journals regularly bemoaned his inability to put aside his thirst for fiction. For example, in 1833 he wrote: "I will subdue my love for such pernicious books. O how much has my soul suffered & how much happiness & spiritual joy I have lost by reading Shakespear[e] & Scott. I believe those two writers have ruined many souls. Would [to] God they had never seen the light of day & that I had more strength to resist temptation." So much for youthful aspirations to romantic genius! The next day he evoked some of the sexual struggle associated with novel reading: "Suffered much during the night from the novel I had read yesterday. Though designed to be religious it had any other effect on my mind than religious. My dreams were horrible—my sleep disturbed. I had no sweet communion with God in the night-watches & this morning." He preached listlessly that day. "Felt cold & heartless—the effect of the novel. My mind always sinks into a state of insensibility to all the realities of this world after reading a novel."[19]

Nevertheless he felt no compunction about enjoying Rebecca Read's tremendously popular *Six Months in a Convent.* To modern readers the entire genre of revelations from nunneries reeks of demipornographic fiction; to Wright, however, it bore "the impress of Truth." He also approved of *The Armadeers, or the Mysteries of Upper-ten-dom Revealed in New York,* an exposé of the unscrupulous aristocracy that foiled the dreams of bright young men. He loved Richard Hildreth's early antislavery novel, *The Memoirs of Archy Moore,* which followed the economic and marital tribulations of an upwardly mobile, pale-skinned slave. "No man can read this book & not feel that a *desire* to hold power over a fellow being, is in itself most wicked & [that] possession of power [is] most corrupting to the heart." Such fiction braked desire and thus did not violate resolutions or trouble sleep. It helped set guidelines for a young man growing up in the post-Napoleonic world and wishing to earn a reputation free from all taints of sin.[20]

It is almost humorous to observe Wright feeling guilty after reading a novel, vowing to break the habit, distracting his mind with sober thoughts, giving in again and renewing the cycle. We are unlikely to see excessive eros in Scott's novels or the cheap sentimental books from which sprang remorse, but Wright's generation was unschooled in the harmlessness of emotional escapes. The choicest example of his use of reform to paper over illicit feelings evoked by even the most moralistic fiction is a scrapbook of clippings about his antislavery work in England and Scotland: the clippings hide the pages of a novel called *The West Indian, or the Brothers.*[21]

Because intellectual guides equated the sublimation of erotic wishes with the outreach of human sentiment, Wright attacked his inveterate novel reading as an impediment to his ability to do good in the world. He admired "Abercrombie on intellectual powers," because of its emphasis on duty and character building. It outlined the components of "a well-regulated mind": steady concentration, control over the succession of one's thoughts, inquiring habits, care in selecting objects of study, restrained imagination, unprejudiced judgment, sound moral feelings. Nothing was more important than "maintaining harmony between the moral emotions & the conduct. Every good emotion should be followed with corresponding actions. Hence the injurious effects of *Novels*—which excite emotions by fictions." There should be no undischarged fantasy, no purposeless exploration of consciousness. Room should be allowed for the play of the emotions, but always within the bounds of prescribed Christian action.[22]

Yet Wright became the author of untrue sketches of family life—think of Ernest and Nina. He must have suspected that many of his own works appealed to curiosities and anxieties similar to those that made fiction popular. There is a nimble *volte-face* in his *Human Life* where he praises novels for their nonresistant subject matter, and then condemns them for misguiding energies:

> I love to trace a man or woman into the scenes, the joys and sorrows, the ups and downs of social and domestic life. My soul gets weary of the history of corporations in church or state. . . . I am weary of tracing the history of weathercocks and bombshells. I love to enter into the feelings, plans, sympathies, joys and trials of human beings. Novels give the history of individuals. . . . My individual human sympathies are called out, and answer to those of the fictitious individuals with whom I commune for the time being. My desire to read a novel is gone, whenever I come into exciting sympathy with living human beings around me. But I am well assured that sympathy with fictitious weal or wo does not qualify me to sympathize with the human beings with whom I daily live. Novel reading has produced in me a kind of sickly, morbid sensibility, that unfits me to feel a deep interest in human suffering. . . . It cannot be right for any one to expend the energies of his feelings and sympathies on fictitious joys and sufferings, when there are so many living men, women and children who might be blessed if the same were given to them. This passion for novels I'll set myself resolutely to subject to righteousness.[23]

Political consciousness emerged from Wright's struggles to overcome literary appetites. In his politics the past reeked of blood shed by corporate power, the future belonged to free individuals. But would anyone care for the unfortunate if corporations ceased their watch? The self-involved novel reader might well find his powers so totally "expended" that charity would be beyond him. A more factual literature would encourage the moral feelings needed to curb the prospective heartlessness of the new era. But at the same time it would have to accept the breakdown of traditional bonds that set men and women loose to go up and down in social life.

These vexations of individual consciousness, in which moral law competed with genius, charity with fantasy, history with fiction, subsided into comparisons between the Old World and the New. In 1849 Wright visited Fort Ancient with several other reformers. After a quiet picnic he reflected that the great mysteries of the place surpassed all the monuments of Europe. He called it, with approval, "a world of fiction." When all questions about the mound builders were answered, the scene would "one day be worked into the world's wildest and most thrilling creation of human imagination."[24] So much for Shakespeare and Scott! They were to be surpassed by glimpses of ancient life, brought to life through scientific inquiry and enhancing appreciation of the dynamic growth of the Ohio civilization. Other romantic writers lamented America's lack of ruins. But to Wright the West arose as a theater of history more awesome, and more conducive to meditation, than all European competitors. By the time he was prepared to convey that vision to others, he had made his own tour of the old continent whose battlefields and graveyards had once quickened his imagination.

The European Scene: Free Trade

In Britain in the mid-1840s, Henry Wright ruminated on the "cash nexus."[25] All the controversies in which he enlisted questioned the morality of monetary exchanges. He scolded his co-worker Frederick Douglass for letting friends compensate his former owner: why dignify a robbery with a bill of sale?[26] When Irish Quakers took funds from the American South for famine relief but disdained proceeds from a theatrical benefit, he asked why brutal enslavement was less sinful than voluntary playacting.[27] His attacks on the Free Kirk conflated their acceptance of Southern money with the acts of those "who breed and rear men for the market." The Scots had prostituted themselves, bartering away their souls like Judas and paying "the

DREADFUL PRICE."[28] Longstanding antagonism toward the hireling ministry gave rise to a lurid concentration on the cash exchange itself as the index of sin.

Money questions dominated the Scottish fray. According to Wright the Free Kirk had withdrawn from the establishment only because "they would not allow the state to look after the expenditure of the people's money." Money questions shaded into considerations of class. One abolitionist broadsheet charged that the Free Kirk conspired to "rob servant girls of the hard-won money that ought to have gone for ribbons and gum-flowers, weavers of their snuff and tobaccos, and washerwomen of their savings-bank accumulations—and all to reward them for their disinterested contempt of lucre." There were tales of Dundee apprentices running through the streets with the cry, "Send Back the Money." But there were pitfalls for abolitionism in enlisting non-middle-class elements in popular agitation. Such steps appeared sinister to defenders of the top-heavy hierarchy of the Scottish church and to those who trembled at political turmoil. The shouting apprentices stood, as Duncan Rice reports, as "an apparent Scottish approximation to the urban mob of the continental revolutions." Henry Wright, in particular, drew angry fire for fomenting disorder among the working classes and turning "the people" against the clergy.[29]

The concern may have been genuine, but the threat was illusory. In actuality Wright had scarcely a shred of support among Britain's exploited poor. Ranting against the cash nexus presented no danger to the social order so long as it remained focused on philanthropic donations from the far-off South. Sending back the money was a cause that drew support from some tories. It excited only the "more respectable elements" of the working class, and it offended militants who sought coalitions on issues more directly affecting the distribution of wealth and power. Scottish antislavery leaders reportedly scoffed at "poor inhabitants of Glasgow" who sought their support: ". . .abolition as it respected the colored man was popular, but it was not popular to speak of equal suffering at home." American abolitionists contributed rather tactless letters informing the "Christian peasantry of Scotland, grievously as they suffer," that their lot was superior to the slave's.[30] In general there was a cautious purpose running through the issues that Wright and his friends selected for emphasis. If he appealed to the working class at all, his goal was not to foment disorder but to promote reforms that transcended class interests and united mankind.

The Garrisonians have sometimes been faulted for obliviousness to the miseries of the poor in Victorian cities or—more kindly—for their principled inability to see the working class as an aggregate rather than as individuals.[31] The criticism usually centers on Garrison, whose trips to Britain were too brief to clarify all the implications of what he saw. Wright is a more valid case because he spent five years overseas, much of the time in Engels's Manchester, Dickens's London, or in famine-stricken Ireland. During his travels, which gave him the standing of a transatlantic expert on social upheavals, he saw little of the poor. The selectivity of his European acquaintance was striking. His closest Scottish friends were the family of a Glasgow merchant who speculated in the cotton trade.[32] His Irish companions still had nightmares about the 1798 uprisings. In 1844—the year of *The Condition of the Working Class in England*—he visited Manchester and stayed with his dear friend John Thompson, a mill owner, and his wife Deborah. In 1847 he described Deborah as a "noble woman" and John as "a pleasant man; but sorely tried in business as [are] all cotton manufacturers."[33]

His failure to observe the poor is remarkable when we recall that in his conversion to antislavery he cast his lot with working folk and that he now traveled constantly, often on his own, recording thousands of pages of observations. For one thing, his vision was restricted to what he came to see: after landing in Liverpool he noted the prevalence of police, and since he came to preach nonresistance, he continued to regard Britain as the stronghold of militarism. For similar reasons, he saw drunkenness more easily than poverty.[34] Further restrictions went along with the company he kept. During one visit to Rosneath with his "wee darling" and her merchant father, he noted that all the land for miles was entailed to the Marquis of Lorne and that evictions were causing distress throughout the Highlands. One day about thirty persons found temporary quarters in a barn next to the cottage where he had his adored little room—destitute folk in search of seasonal woodcutting jobs or heading to Glasgow to make vinegar. There is no sign that Wright made any contact with them. He was, after all, the Patons' guest, and on that day read them the manuscript of his forthcoming tract on the sabbath.[35]

Wright's mission among British abolitionists put him in touch with evangelicals who deplored the customary habits of the working classes and were in turn despised. It also introduced him to zealous champions of free trade. He wrote glowing reports of speeches by Col. Perronet Thompson and Daniel O'Connell at Free Trade Hall.[36]

He was on cordial terms with John Bright, and added the anti-Corn Law message to his repertory alongside temperance, nonresistance, and antislavery. He won the friendship of the well-known authors William and Mary Howitt and various other "moral-suasion" (as distinct from "physical-force") Chartists, preeminently William Lovett and Henry Vincent. His explanations of the Garrisonian position on the union saddened Vincent, who loved America's republican institutions. Despite these friendships, Wright made only a partial commitment to moral-suasion Chartism. On the one hand, he approved its renunciation of violent means; on the other, his New England-style nonresistance left him suspicious of the Charter, which would merely widen the base of political participation in a coercive system. "It matters little whether human life be at the disposal of one man, or of millions of men," he wrote. "Should it be at the disposal of *man* at all? That is the question."[37] It was difficult for an American reformer, displeased by the impact of public opinion on politics, to appreciate the urgency that his British friends attached to extending the franchise. But it was not difficult to understand their dread of lower-class rebellion, and he admired the respectability and orderliness of those disfranchised elements for whom Lovett, Vincent, and the Howitts presumed to speak. Almost imperceptibly, Wright acquired a vision of reform intended to mollify class conflicts and impose a logic of Christian morality on surfacing discontents.

Lovely tableaux survive from Wright's time among British reformers. Lovett recalled a "delightful evening" in London when Frederick Douglass, "who had a fine voice, sang a number of negro melodies," Garrison performed "several anti-slavery pieces, and our grave friend H. C. Wright, sang an old Indian war song." Others did what they could to enhance "the amusement of the evening," including Vincent's rendition of "The Marseillaise."[38] On another occasion Wright enjoyed pleasant conversation with a London circle that included James Webb from Dublin, the wit and melodramatist Douglas Jerrold, and the exile Giuseppe Mazzini, whom he found "altogether an interesting man" despite being a political leader. Also present was the wealthy philanthropist and socialist Robert Owen: Wright thought him kind-hearted and benevolent, but detested his doctrine that environment—or circumstances—excused human failings. The next day Wright hurried off to visit the Howitts and their children in Epping Forest.[39]

If Owen's doctrine accounted for what the evangelicals viewed as lower-class depravity, it still blurred, in Wright's mind, the

Napoleonic possibility of a man seizing his destiny and rising in society. Wright did not think this required a man to dissemble or to take advantage of others, but simply to work at improving his character and getting ahead. Acceptance in British society may have heightened Wright's personal awareness of having done well on his own. Certainly his "circumstances" were often impressive. In between stints of hard work and illness, he rested in "delightful" spots. His hostile missives to American slavers and the Free Kirk bore such charming addresses as "Mamore Cottage, Rosneath" or "Druid Cottage, Killiney Bay." He romped with children in green forests and weighed grand measures of reform on country lawns.

When he did take notice of the poor, it was from the standpoint that Harold Perkin has termed "the entrepreneurial ideal," lauding both active capital and labor for wages while condemning the idleness and luxury of an older way of life.[40] The entrepreneurial ideal, while firmly antislavery, enabled Wright to compare America and England to the latter's detriment: the broad base of poverty in the Old World was owing to an archaic, extravagant social system. The contrasts he drew could lead to moments of almost comic rage, as when Richard Webb showed him the Tower of London and the crown jewels:

> H. C. Wright was, of course, in a great taking—he was fit to be tied. It was worth any money, beside the shilling [admission] to be there with this apostle of non-resistance, amidst so many implements of murder and refined Christian cruelty . . . his heart heaving, his eye flashing, his brows (and he has brows) lowering with righteous indignation. Indeed, I am beginning to look as he does on all the stupendous churches, the stately abbeys, the royal hospitals as costly as palaces, the triumphal arches, and all the other indications of imperial wealth with which London abounds, as built up with the hard earnings of the poor, wrung from them by the hands of royal and aristocratic power, and cemented by their blood and sweat.[41]

In fact Wright, whose vague economic opinions previously leaned toward protectionism, became a free trader. Competition was the best method to free the respectable poor from exploitation. Looking out over Scottish lochs, he was pleased to see "hundreds of steamers & ships from every clime & country." Looking far into the future, he imagined years of remarkable revolution in which bloodless natural forces would triumph. In this revolution Britain's anti-Corn Law movement stood side by side with American antislavery, and free trade became a kind of nonresistance applied to economics. Turn the other cheek translated into hands-off.[42]

Wright's schooling in the entrepreneurial ideal could sometimes sound quite revolutionary. High above Glen Fruin in August 1845, he and Wee watched moorfowl darting about and sheep grazing among the rocks. Knowing that the land could be used in that wild way only because families had been driven off, he reflected "with pain how few of the laborers of this kingdom own a foot of land or the hut they live in!" After denouncing landlords "who riot and fatten on the heart's blood of the people," he dared imagine a day—"nearer at hand than most think"—when the people would cease to be "law-abiding" and take back the land.[43]

Since Jefferson's time Americans had believed that the laws of primogeniture and entail explained the miseries of the Old World. This traditional belief helped Wright understand the sight of hundreds of Irishmen on the docks awaiting passage to America. To the *Liberator* he expressed the wish that money collected for Irish relief should go instead to combat the ancient laws that propped up aristocracy and caused famine. Even the free trader John Bright thought this was "casuistry," but there appeared to be no limit to Wright's hardening faith in the economic view of man. In an extraordinary letter on the Irish, published in 1847, he spoke out against "feeding and clothing a population without labor," regardless of their desperation. Such misdirected aid created mendicants for life; it was especially ruinous in Ireland where native character preferred one begged meal to three gained by honest work. "It may seem a hard doctrine; *but I know it is a wicked and impolitic system, which, in seeking to relieve human suffering, only tends to increase and perpetuate the very evils which it seeks to remedy*. Every piece of bread given to a door beggar, and every bauble given to a street beggar, no matter how importunate his calls for help, only tends to multiply beggars, and to pauperize their souls."[44] To put the matter mildly, Wright more readily empathized with distant bondsmen than with needy whites whom he passed on his travels.

While his antiaristocratic statements showed contempt for the poor, transposition into an alien social system also revealed ambiguities in his antislavery commitment. Passing through Wales in 1843 he reflected: "The servility of the great masses in England to the contemptible distinctions that pride and ambition have set up, is not less complete than is the servility of the Southern slave." The abolitionists' disappointment in black acquiescence in slavery was usually repressed, but it emerged clearly when Wright was figuring out the logic of a competitive society. Scorn for the English "masses" and Southern slaves was a step toward favorable discussion of the political economy of New England where men owned their own land, moved freely to new jobs, and escaped the burdens of a huge public debt—where men, in short, were not "governed to death."[45] Nonresistance audiences of earlier years might have been amused by this hearty praise of New England's institutions. In Britain Wright was ceasing to speak for an anarchistic remnant and approaching the middle-class ideology of later works on marriage and the family.

His comments on women's work in Europe were equivocal. He frequently took notes on women laboring in the fields (he perceived them more often than men). These premodern work habits were, in his mind, exploitative, degrading violations of women's domestic nature. But this indignation did not apply to the new industrial order. He observed in Wigan that women in bad times sought work down in the mines until a well-intentioned but misguided law shut them out. Unemployed women received the same "protection" as orthodox clergymen had given the Grimkés and other female lecturers in Massachusetts—they were kept in their sphere.[46] It was not yet clear how far reformers might choose to go in placing women under the rules of the entrepreneurial world; it was uncertain whether liberation always voided the need for protection. But Wright would shortly join in assigning women to the realm of domesticity. From that time on, the free trade argument that he rehearsed in England sounded less harsh because it featured the silent operation of "self-abnegation."

Some of his remarks in Britain simply show how impressionable he was. He applied to the British poor, whose acquaintance he did not make, catch phrases learned from liberals he got to know in Glasgow and Manchester. But these phrases conformed to his own ambition, his long-standing interest in the mobility of individuals. What he learned in Britain, in sum, was to appreciate the openness of American society where circumstances favored rising destinies as they did not in post-Napoleonic Europe: ". . . there is more hope for a man in America than in Europe. There are no old institutions to crush by their authority and antiquity. The spirit of change . . . is the real regenerating, conservative spirit. . . . Society cannot grow in Europe, as it can in America. Man must be cut and carved to fit institutions in Europe—*vice versa,* to some extent, in America."[47] In order to emphasize this revaluation of America he grumbled and shouted at the tourist sites of London. Alleging his contentment with the flux and growth that characterized his homeland, he was prepared to pay the ultimate debt: "I would rather my body should be buried . . . beneath some beech, sugar-maple, or hemlock tree in the wild woods of America, than to sleep with *reverend* and *anointed* robbers and murderers" in Westminster Abbey.[48]

The European Scene: Revolution and Cold Water

Rail as he might against Tower and Abbey, the fact remains that in Europe Wright combined reform with tourism. In Rosneath Castle's crumbling ruins he devised his attack on the first-day sabbath. On Loch Long's shingly shores, away from "the haunts of men" and "the din of perpetual conflict," he composed a tract for the Scottish fray. And he visited Dunsinane to renounce the unquenchable interest in the past that his journals and publications betrayed. With all the scenes of *Macbeth* around him, he reflected how vile leaders dominated church and state because of public concern with history instead of character. It was an occasion to shudder at "the hell of an unjust, hating, revengeful heart, and a polluted life."[49]

Walter Scott was a symbol of ambition outweighing character, a cold stylist performing for "money and honor." But his novels immortalized many of the battlegrounds where Wright skirmished with the Free Kirk, and the opportunity to visit Abbotsford, the castle Scott had built for himself, was irresistible. Over the course of ten days he perused every item of Scott's memorabilia. At Scott's grave he was scornful of others who flocked to the same place as though to a shrine. He passed on stories about the novelist's deathbed peevishness and Mrs. Scott's alcoholism. After all this compulsive tourism he concluded: ". . . never did I feel so deeply the insignificance of such a reputation as Scott has left behind." At the same time he gladly recorded the dissemination of thousands of his own writings in Scotland. This was not ambition, simply the creation of "a healthful commotion." His goal was "to stamp on the world, CHANGE—REVOLUTION"; his adversaries sought, "on the contrary, to perpetuate SAMENESS."[50]

His journey to Graefenberg and back, carefully chronicled in the *Liberator*, played up the ironies of viewing the European past through an American's eyes—and a nonresistant's at that. These skillfully written public letters had a large audience; they were followed closely by many American readers. Garrison was delighted that "thousands at home and abroad" enjoyed them. "Never was there such a blending of graphic description and reformatory matter in the journal of any individual and tourist before," but there had never been another traveler like Wright, "so anti-national, so world-embracing, so brotherly, so deeply imbued with the spirit of universal philanthropy, so ready to communicate his 'ultra' thoughts and feelings to all with whom he came in contact."[51]

To Richard Webb these travels afforded a wonderful test of Wright's naiveté, forcing him "to use his eyes, and to cease for a while his endless discussion." The Continent confronted him with a variety of peoples whom he had never before observed, with genuinely despotic societies in comparison with the free institutions he so tediously denounced in America and Britain. "I look on him as just now going to school," Webb gloated. Thus the public account of his travels began with the tables turned, the educator on the verge of being educated, the peaceable American plunging into unfamiliar tyranny. Wright himself justified the trek away from his British assignment as an opportunity to study the differences in human beings as they were shaped by national institutions.[52] It was this educational quest, indeed, that kept his experience under control and gave his reports their unity. By using his eyes he sharpened his understandings of "circumstances" and mobility, poverty and progress, obedience and revolution.

He went by steamer from Hull to Hamburg, where he compromised with the state and got a passport. It described him thus: "Age, 46 years—stature, five feet ten inches—forehead, high—eyes, light blue—nose, common—mouth, small—chin, round—hair, dark—complexion, fresh—face, oval." by his own account he was struggling to think of himself as a man, not the subject of a particular state; most of all, he was appalled by other travelers' incessant smoking.[53]

This carping about smoking announced a persistent theme: studying mankind often amounted to rather shrill complaints about the ways in which people ate, drank, smoked, or picked their teeth. His next letter discovered more serious subject matter: a visit to the fortifications and cathedral in Magdeburg prompted his wrath against Europe's monuments to war and superstition. This theme, too, persisted. The same letter contained the first of many ambivalent passages that kept his education from becoming predictable. In Berlin he exclaimed: "*Unter den Linden* is by far the finest street I ever saw in a city." But it was the result of planning, and lacked a "legitimate birth" in the workings of commerce. From the viewpoint of the gospel of free trade he therefore prophesied: "A tyrant's word might create it, but no tyrant's word can perpetuate it. Berlin must become desolate—grass will grow in her beautiful streets—foxes will look out the windows, and owls will scream and hoot in her palaces. Nothing can save a city, thus located amid a sandy waste of hundreds of miles in extent, from such a doom, in this age of commercial tendencies." No Manchester there! Since he was in a hurry to Graefenberg, he bypassed Potsdam, the favorite city of the tyrant Frederick the Great (as his guidebook pointed out). "I hardly can make up my mind to go on and not visit it; but I must; time will not allow." He also skipped Luther's Wittenberg.[54]

At Leipzig he experienced a twinge of horror. There in 1813: "Three hundred and sixty-six thousands of human beings, children of one common Father, members of a common family—*brothers*, spent three days, under the eye of their common Father, cutting one another's throats, and cutting and tearing one another's bodies to pieces." These atrocities were somehow "the legitimate fruit of the religion preached by Luther in this very town, and by Calvin in Geneva." Wright was melding memories from boyhod—Protestant orthodoxy and Napoleonic insurgency. But in Dresden he also observed vulgar people at a fair, cleaning their teeth, smoking, fearing to criticize the ubiquitous soldiers except in whispers. Like the British plebs and American slaves, they were "governed to death"; they were a "slow" people with "little energy or activity of mind."[55]

Next he proceeded by stagecoach through Breslau and Niesse, with sour remarks on the people's habits and the government's surveillance. Soldiers watched him closely as he took notes in his diaries. In every city, it seemed, "the church and the barracks, the priests and the soldiers, the soul-savers and the body-killers, are side by side." Unharmed and unsaved, he finally arrived in Graefenberg, with the temperature at zero, and secured room and board. "At once I threw off my flannel, put on linen shirts, began to be wrapped up twice a day in a sheet dipped in cold water, and then to plunge into cold water bath; and then to go out and get warm by exercise." Rumor had it that the government employed a spy among the convalescents.[56]

In contrast to the oppression and secrecy of Europe stood Vincent Priessnitz, the man of genius who had ascended from the peasantry to the status of "Water King." Wright also contrasted his therapist's straightforwardness to the hocus-pocus of doctors and other professionals. Priessnitz was uneducated, though his "reserve" and "calm" revealed a meditative temperament. He read no books, and had "no *theory* at all"—he simply looked at the skin. Even the moment of triumph, when he declared Wright cured of lung disease, required nothing more than the patient's stripping for an external examination. The man who judged by appearances was himself open and candid. In his face there was "no secrecy, no mystery, nor oracular pretension."[57]

The external means of the water cure, such as baths, massage, and strenuous exercise, had their internal counterparts. Wright told his public that "all the morbid matter, secreted in my system, has been put in motion . . .; and . . . by the time I have gone through the ordeal enough, these morbid secretions will be entirely expelled from the body."[58] It seems clear that Priessnitz intuited the nonsomatic sources of some patients' ailments. All they needed was to relax, put away "anxiety, despondence, and gloomy forebodings," and let liquid nature take effect. A person would be cured at Graefenberg if he could forget the past, shut out the world, avoid the expenditure of strong feelings. Wright found that "to keep my mind tranquil and amused was . . . the most difficult part of the cure."[59] Life on the magic mountain cured him, nevertheless, and we may pause to speculate on the reasons: the immobility and prolonged contact with a community that he could not easily manipulate; the moratorium in which to examine tangled feelings about women in England, Ireland, and America; the rituals of immersion and purification; the liberating emphasis on the open air instead of oppressive parlors and sitting rooms. In this situation Wright gained more insight into the belligerent origins of nonresistance than at any other time of his life; here, too, he tried to face up to the reality of his unhappy marriage.[60] By imposing a temporary respite from analysis of the great issues of the age, convalescence permitted Wright to explore the meanings of force and fraternity in his own psyche.

The baths were a diffuse sexual environment in which he could explore, at least peripherally, a problem that even the secret diary ignored: homosexual love. In contacts with men he was usually combative and restricted, or else sanctimonious, but at Graefenberg he belonged to an intimate trio with the Byronic Joe Poole and another comrade named Willie. He kissed Willie affectionately when they separated—a kind of detail lacking in previous diaries. And Joe, before leaving, bent over Henry and kissed his lips. Then Henry went off to a frigid plunge bath and reflected on his unappropriated heart.[61] At Graefenberg he placed himself under the authority of another male—Priessnitz—and stripped for examination without a dissenting murmur. But it was particularly Lawrence, the *badediener* assigned to care for him, who focused the issue of homosexuality. It was while Lawrence wrapped him in a wet sheet that he bade his sorrowful adieu to Joe Poole. It was Lawrence who waited at the end of the path to the douche, where he walked with fear and anticipation. After each plunge it was Lawrence who rubbed him dry with the "friction" that Priessnitz recommended. Instead of brushes or harsh cloth, "the hand only should be used"; and "delicious sensations" came afterward when the skin felt "clear, smooth, [and] soft." Lawrence's playfulness surpassed his instructions: "My badediener, when in a frolicsome mood, greatly enjoyed administering" the *Abreibung,* or standing bath, covering the patient with a cold, wet sheet and rubbing vigorously. "He delighted to throw the sheet around me when my eyes were turned away, so that it might take me unawares."[62] Never before or after was Wright quite so ready to place himself under the loving care of another man, and the experience may help explain why he gained at Graefenberg something approximating psychotherapy.

Homosexuality threatened nineteenth-century men with images of submission in the realm of sexuality that they were supposed to dominate. The issue of submission versus dominance connects Wright's cure at Graefenberg to the social investigations that he would shortly resume. Lawrence was a menial servant, unmistakably a member of a class lower than Wright's. What made him important was his fusion of puzzling considerations of love and class. When they parted Lawrence kissed Wright's hand (not his lips), and cried. "Dear fellow!" exclaimed Wright to the *Liberator;* "he felt it hard to lose sight, forever, of the form that he had nursed and cared for so long and kindly." The scene resembled his mother's death. Only wishful thinking, however, allowed Wright to claim: "At that moment, Humanity asserted her prerogative in us both, and overleaped all the miserable and wicked distinctions of rank or station." Wright was "disgusted" with himself for holding back his own tears, a suppression showing that he was all too conscious of behavior appropriate to his sex and station. The tenderness of the water cure was over. At the first stop after this parting Wright got into a "warm argument" over agrarian reform; tenantry, he argued, bred servility.[63]

Protest as he might his transcendence of class feelings and his belief in competition, his Graefenberg experiences pressed Wright to think clearly about the options of lower-class men. He reworked the theme of nonresistance, with the increasingly clear implication that those who were not upwardly mobile must be disciplined to accept the rule of the strong and privileged. Nonresistance had always counseled against slave revolts in the South; at Graefenberg the doctrine was applied to the convalescents' fears of impending democratic upheaval. Wright embraced the others' hopes, on the eve of 1848, that there would be peaceful political change, not class warfare.

Curiously, class barriers were more relaxed on the Continent than in England, where aristocrats jealously guarded their privileges and commoners seemed awed by their superiors. On the Continent, Wright observed, "the titled and untitled familiarly meet and mingle; and it is often difficult to distinguish the one class from the other." Actually, as he was informed, the comparison was deceptive. Regardless of the visible informality, there was "more deference" to rank in Austria: "because the line that separates the two classes is so distinctly drawn . . . the aristocracy do not fear that the people will encroach upon their privileges, and the people have no fears that their superiors in rank will encroach upon theirs." Familiarity between classes indicated "abject servitude" on the bottom. The tensions between England's strata resulted, on top, from the aristocracy's fears of losing prerogatives and, on the bottom, from the assertiveness of a "people [who] are of great importance in affairs of state, and . . . are vigorously pursuing measures to obtain still greater power." English social structure, with its unmistakable class lines and continuing political tumult, was more stable; the Continent's, more dangerous. Many had fearful expectations that "a bloody struggle for mastery,—not as in the French revolutionary days, between nation and nation,—but between the people and the aristocracy, will, at no distant day, desolate Europe."[64]

I do not question the sincerity of Wright's pacifism or the ardor of his romanticism. What is striking, however, is his acceptance of the notion that a peaceful, democratic society may be consistent with—and even dependent on—rigid divisions between classes. Nonresistance simply required that classes should not bully one another, not that they should cease to exist. Wright and other Garrisonians, like the radical socialists of Europe, boasted that they would dig out the roots of social injustice, but in pre-1848 Europe this radicalism sounded ambiguous:

> It is hardly to be wondered at, that men should dread civil revolution, for in their minds a change of government is inseparably associated with bloodshed. But a change is coming over the world; and men are beginning to see that a revolution effected by violence, instead of infusing into society a more kindly spirit, and purer and more unselfish principles of action, only takes the power to oppress out of the hands of one set of men, to put it into the hands of another. There is no real gain to humanity when despotism merely changes hands. Despotism itself must be destroyed. Lay the axe unto the root of the tree.[65]

No doubt the twentieth century has substantiated the fear of new despotisms replacing old. But it has also shown that "infusing" society with "a kindly spirit" could be a tactic to leave serious inequalities undisturbed. Wright was learning, in any case, to substitute consensual politics for the military clashes of his childhood dreams.

He returned at a leisurely pace to Britain after Preissnitz declared him cured. As he journeyed by Danube and Rhine and through the Swiss Alps into France he was more than ever a self-conscious literary traveler, dispatching reports to an American public. He dwelt once more on the annoying personal habits of Europeans; he also recognized how freakish he appeared to them, particularly because of the open collar he affected after the cure. His dispatches, often duplicitously addressed to his wife, paused with fascination over "classic ground," where the reporter's head swelled with "historical recollections." But Europe's past abounded in hypocrisy and carnage, thus reminding him of the present-day horrors of American slavery.[66] Literary tourism collapsed personal and public, old and new, and allowed some dramatic reflections on social change. His conservative moods alternated with some of the most uncompromisingly anarchistic statements he ever uttered. The world traveler reflected in Geneva that "all the arrangements and institutions of this world . . . tend to a practical dethronement of God over human hearts and actions." Other men might have fixed interests, but from his footloose viewpoint: *"Treason against any human institution is no crime."*[67]

Among the Alps Wright was inevitably drawn to Manfred-like poses and experiments with the demonic. In Basel, for example, he conjured up an equivocal world reminiscent of *Macbeth*—and plainly enjoyed it. The night was too hot for comfort, he couldn't sleep, and awoke in a panic. He got up, found a cathedral, and watched the mass. His conventional hatred of priests welled up, as he must surely have expected; and when he heard loud thunder outside, the forces of nature seemed triumphant over human artifice. But he denied thinking of vengeance: "How great is God! yet how kind and Fatherly!" The rumbling was benign: "Men talk of the glories of eternity. *I am in eternity now*—as truly as I expect to be—except that I am in the body; but no less are the glories of eternity around me. The outer edge of the storm passes over the city. I am between fair and foul—storm and sunshine—on the confines of light and darkness—of chaos and order. But the rain begins to drop on my book, and I must find a shelter."[68] It is interesting to wonder what this flirtation with chaos meant to the polite reformers who read the *Liberator*. For Wright himself it symbolically revoked the abject apology to his Father years earlier in the White Mountains of New Hampshire. It also captured the paradox of his sense of freedom, roaming across Europe at a perilous moment for the old order.

Vienna beguiled him. The visit began inauspiciously, when armed police grabbed his passport and customs officials poked through his trunk and scanned his diaries for evidence of sedition. The experience deepened his commitment to the new philosophy: "FREE TRADE, the world over, and unrestricted intercourse between man and man, is my motto." Once in the city, he hurried to a bath "as a starving man goes to food," then indulged in a ten-course *table d'hôte* that was too heavy after Graefenberg's healthy fare. He paid a traveler's price of several days' illness. To make matters worse, getting his passport back from the police was time consuming and irritating, though one could do nothing but "submit good naturedly" to such indignities.[69]

But a concert by Johann Strauss and his band was a thrilling display of virtuosity. "Strouss [*sic*] throws his whole body and soul into his violin, and plays with his head, shoulders, arms, fingers, legs, feet, and whole body. He makes his instrument speak." Although Wright normally sated his longing for spontaneity far away from cities, in the People's Garden unrestraint coexisted with urban life. The music enthralled him, even though it depended on Habsburg munificence. He wondered at Vienna's gaity, its absence of poverty: "there are not the stiffness, coldness, coarseness, and surliness that appear on the surface of society in the cities of England and America." People were polite and gentle, and showed no trace of class hostilities. Only as an afterthought did he claim that these merry folk were cowed by fear.[70]

A visit to the great educator Philipp Emanuel von Fellenberg reminded the traveler of the links between nonviolence and education; everywhere else, Europe gave evidence of recent slaughter. Wright's sustained commentary on the battlefields and ruins reached a crescendo in Belgium, where he found himself "running, like one mad, here and there, to see this and that—to ask questions, Yankee fashion." His guide, a veteran of Waterloo, admitted, under questioning, that he had felt like a tiger, not a man, during the conflict. Not only would God require an account of the blood he spilled, as Wright told him; every person who defended defensive wars—that is, everyone outside the handful of nonresistants—shared the guilt of forty thousand crushed lives. It was a day of "deep and mingled emotions."[71]

He took more satisfaction at St. Joux, scene of the captivity of Toussaint, "greater than Bonaparte," a hero who joined military glory with the worthy cause of racial liberation. Wright's traveling companions all declared that America's slaves ought to rise up—their safe way of contemplating lower-class revolt—and Wright was "obliged to admit" that if there were any such thing as a "holy war" a slave uprising would be an instance. But he held fast to moral suasion. Slavery could not be ended by war, for then ex-slaves would rule ex-masters. "Slavery is not abolished. *Tyranny has changed hands*—that is all."[72] This was not the first time that the example of St. Domingue served to warn against precipitate experiments with liberty. Although Wright, by his own account, advocated "CHANGE—REVOLUTION," he did so only if change were carried out at a natural pace and accompanied by widening adherence to moral principle, not by abrupt reversals of labor discipline.

Another name for peaceful change was free trade. Each time he passed through customs, Wright denounced artificial obstacles to human commerce.[73] On a steamer on the Rhine, however, he met a formidable adversary who believed in protecting culture as a national economic asset—Friedrich List, once an exile in Philadelphia, now an enormously important economist. Like the youthful Henry Wright, List had witnessed advantages to home industry when the Napoleonic wars had cut off English goods. Rejecting the economic system of Adam Smith, he had served the protectionist cause in America and devoted most of his life to the economic unification of Germany, the erection of tariff barriers, and the development of railroads and industry. No one could have stood in sharper contrast to the international-minded reformer carrying free trade doctrines on his Continental travels; their discourse was unpleasant. But List's scorn only intensified Wright's faith in the entrepreneurial ideal. By arguing that Britain should never have freed its slaves and that widespread land ownership conflicted with national interests, List reinforced Wright's conviction that Manchester political economy was a philosophy of universal reform.[74]

The traveler's most remarkable encounter occurred one night on the Danube after sparring with a Southerner on the sinfulness of slavery. A passenger named John Paul Rath, a former professor who now earned his living as a tutor, introduced himself and two charges, who had listened to the contest and wished to meet the abolitionist. They were Metternich's children! When they went to bed, next to the childless American lay the prince's son. "Rank, and station, and title are levelled by sleep, as well as death; and I only wish the levelling were as permanent in the one case as in the other."[75] "Levelling" for Wright encompassed equality of opportunity and termination of aristocratic prerogatives—not the classless sharing of wealth and esteem, but freedom to strive, to make oneself known. What a magical voyage it was, however, that united the son of a New York revolutionary with the son of the foremost custodian of a crumbling order.

The American Scene: Free Labor

"Eastward I go only by force; but Westward I go free": thus spake Thoreau. For a long time Henry Wright's ambition carried him eastward, to Andover, to Newbury, to Boston and Philadelphia, finally to Britain and Silesia. After returning from Europe in 1847, however, he spent most of his life traveling in the trans-Appalachian West. He took long treks from New York's "western country," where his family had migrated at the opening of the century, westward through Pennsylvania's hills into Ohio, then on to Michigan, Indiana, Illinois, Wisconsin, Minnesota, Iowa, and Missouri. He always had business to perform—addressing a convention of spiritualists, perhaps, or rallying support for Lincoln—though there were pleasant sojourns with kinfolk and lovers as well. He was always a tourist with a writing assignment, for while surveying the Old World's institutions he had discovered how to see the West.

While logging thousands of miles in the West, Wright grappled with disrupted meanings of time. His own career exemplified the compression of sweeping changes in a few years: trained as an apprentice, residing under his master's watch and care, he recalled an old protective system that the century had cast aside; educated for the ministry in one of the earliest postgraduate institutions, he joined many classmates in devising modern careers outside the cloth. After an abrupt conversion to antislavery, his work had spun in so many radical directions as virtually to epitomize the fluidity of a new order. In the year of his conversion, moreover, he had frequently reflected on *"Rapidity of motion,"* first out of amazement at how swiftly a reform agent could get from one city to the next, then with the breathless hope that Christianity might be rushing ahead with open throttle. Would the shrinking of time, in other words, lead to meaningless bustle or to the advancement of worthy purposes? Sometimes he feared that farm families would dissolve, and the nation would suffer from having a "distinct class" of common laborers, "out of reach of all moral & religious influences," in which case the characteristic monument of American civilization would be the grog shop alongside the canal or railroad line. There was hidden allure in the prospect of throngs visiting Niagara Falls and other shrines, but improved transportation might also subvert respect for work: "To ride about the country & play the idle gentleman & lady raises man in his own estimation."[76]

In succeeding years travel for pleasure did attract classes for whom it would once have been unthinkable: whether or not the middle class assumed gentle airs, their appetite for vicarious travel benefited Wright's literary career. It is unlikely, however, that westward migration destroyed the traditional family. It may actually have been easier to preserve familiar patterns after relocating on new land,[77] and Wright certainly discovered a western audience that viewed family loyalties with extreme seriousness. He had been correct on one point—the making of a "distinct class" of unskilled transients excluded from the respectable life promoted by the churches. But in Britain he became practiced at ignoring those who failed to taste the advantages of progress: neither published nor intimate accounts of his American travels give any hint of the existence of poverty.[78]

After his repatriation Wright dashed to Cleveland (where Garrison was convalescing from serious illness), and let *Liberator* readers follow the trip by means of public letters to Elizabeth Pease. He left Boston on October 8, 1847, and covered eight hundred miles by October 14 in spite of Lake Erie's gales. On the way back he disclosed some discomforts of railroad travel, especially on the line from Buffalo to Rochester. Then crossing over the Genesee, a larger river than the Clyde, he looked down at two giant falls and imagined "instant death" if the railway bridge collapsed. How terrible to be tossed and battered—a fate he did not wish even for enemies. He controlled this terror with jokes about Graefenberg's icy plunges, and hastened to point out that not all railway lines were uncomfortable. And if the falls were frightening, he could relate the exciting story of the growth of Rochester, all within his lifetime, to a city that produced flour for Europe. There was also the astonishing sight of Syracuse, his next destination, where intense fires and steam from salt works produced "a wild and romantic effect."[79]

The West, like Gaul, was divided into several parts. Our attention today drifts so inexorably with pioneers across the Rockies that we overlook the excitement—and fears—awakened by the development of the trans-Appalachian region. This hither West gave Wright recognition and money. It was the scene of his son-in-law's vacillations between otherworldly schemes and slick promotions (before Gunn stole away to California); it was the stage where his English friend Joseph Barker mixed economic gambles and religious heresies.[80] To Wright's readers it was a rapidly expanding market, holding out new opportunities and risks for merchants, new dependencies for consumers, new competition for skilled workers. It also held out new anxieties that summoned a selfless ideal like antislavery to temper guilt and screen ambition.[81] It was a hard task to reconcile modern economic ventures with the warnings of religion and folk tradition against greed and pride.

And yet the hither West meant something beyond personal acquisitiveness. The strivings of mobile individuals occurred within new systems of interconnectedness. For those who migrated or speculated across the mountains, the collaboration of others was usually desirable; for those remaining behind, it was still necessary to conceive of larger entities of time and space. Not only were men and women covering more ground in their lifetimes; they also found themselves in an expanding, and increasingly more integrated, political and economic system. A certain degree of amusement over regional customs and character types accompanied this process, together with acceptance of the inevitability of unceasing social change. The belief spread, moreover, that God approved the development of the West. "This is civilization," exulted a Cincinnati literary man, "the bridal of nature and art; the beautiful consummation of that promise, 'Thou shalt have dominion over all the earth.'" No obstacle could long deter the course of progress, "the bloodless triumph of mind over matter."[82]

Wright's lectures, as we have seen, instructed couples to regulate their behavior so that the spirit of progress would be incarnate in their offspring. Quite apart from the specific shifts in outlook they upheld, these lectures prompted a compliant attitude toward change. After all, new authorities might come by with altered formulas for changed conditions, but the very act of attending a lecture on pregnancy, marriage, or death was a recognition of the transitory nature of community. It reinforced habits of turning to experts, rather than neighbors or kin, as life revolved from one phase to another. Furthermore, Wright's travel reports supplied a wide-scale national vision to replace local perspectives. Although he boasted of cosmopolitan antinationalism, the kind of nation he opposed was premodern and aristocratic, not the efficient, integrated state that was in the making.

There were two important themes in his exploration of the West. First, it was young green land. From awesome spectacles like Niagara to dark forests and vast prairies America exhibited no end of opportunities to venerate nature. Second, it was a land of economic improvement. Wright regularly described the uninhibited growth of cities and the incredible fertility of newly cultivated earth. As memories of the depression of 1837 receded, Wright bore the good news that in beautiful America civilization had attained a distinctive triumph characterized by movement and speed. Buildings sprang up, harvests boomed, populations hurtled westward. Unlike the Old World with its aristocracies and unnatural stability, this was a world of change.

Wright had visited Niagara as a bridegroom and returned for many subsequent experiments with fear and self-composure. In 1853 he marveled at the torrents below—"the combination of all that is powerful, grand, majestic, *free,* wild, daring"—and confessed his insignificance as a man. On second thought, high atop a sightseeing tower, he viewed himself as "King over this wild, rushing, roving, *anarchical* Kingdom of brute matter." As the nonresistant enjoyed his throne, he meditated on mind's domination over matter, on the ascendancy of principle over social chaos. The importance of Niagara, as he described the experience, was not simply its awe-inspiring natural beauty, but also its reminders of man's necessary discipline over riotous powers. It provided symbolic expression of the individual's rise from bondage to impulse and of the spread of orderly civilization westward.[83]

Niagara also led to reflections on the boundaries of race and social class. Wright identified the falls with earnest truth, distinguished from the idle pretension of the watering spots of the rich. Niagara blessedly lacked Saratoga's balls, and no one came to show off. The churches at Niagara were superfluous because the experience of the falls, particularly if one sailed on the *Maid of the Mist,* conveyed its own intimations of immortality. Religious observances pointed backward "to the dispensation of Art, not of Nature; to the era of Romance, and not of Reality." But if the churches were discordant, it was fitting that the simple Indians of the forest, so frightening in the old days when his family first entered New York, sold their wares nearby. His mind turned to the slaves, and he wished they could all get across this chasm, like the spectacular leaping performers in popular "horse dramas," perhaps, or the Lizas in later "Tom shows."[84]

Wright also recorded lovely descriptions of what life was like for whites in the forest. Some of his hosts, though farmers and abolitionists, lived in an eerie quiet that eastern readers would find strange; reports like Wright's, therefore, contributed to forging a national consciousness in the midst of great diversity of experience.[85] The quietude inspired reflections on favorite themes of Ralph Waldo Emerson and other successful lecturers—the divinity of man in the woods, the permanence of all truth. But Wright did not neglect the economic importance of clearing the forest: in Ohio's lull he was awed by America's dizzying prospects. In autumn 1848 he observed the leaves changing color, falling to earth, and merging, like human bodies, into dust. "Think of this process, going on annually for ages, and then calculate the power of the land of Ohio to produce human food."[86] The tensions in this report (which took the form of a letter to Wee's father) go to the heart of Wright's ideology.

The *Liberator* was a forum not only for abolitionism and radical ideas but also for economic information and praise of the interdependent free-labor economy. On another trip through Ohio, for example, Wright stopped to describe splendorous fields of grain and fruit—and to advise that bread prices would be cheap that winter and everyone should wait to buy flour. To the itinerant reformer "it was amusing to pass from the power of the bear in Boston to that of the bull in Ohio," one seeking low prices, the other high. "'Down! down!' is the cry of the consumer; 'Up! up!' that of the producer. Are these two classes antagonisms? They should not be; they will not always be. Perfect love and harmony should exist between the consumer and producer. The interests of both are the same. What is good for either is good for the other."[87]

The ultimate sign of progress was not wheat fields but cities. It took historians many years to discover urban civilization in the early West, but contemporaries saw it at once through ebullient reports like Wright's "Chicago, as a Monument of Human Power."[88] One day, after complaining of the monotony of waiting in railway stations, Wright wrote that there were few places where the "Infinite speaks to me" as clearly as in Pittsburgh. Man's accomplishments were impressive enough, but in addition "geology, that vast, ponderous science, here speaks . . . with authority." The city, "like Jerusalem of old," lay among mountains and rushing rivers; coal, iron, and salt—"so essential in the economy of life" were abundant nearby. It overwhelmed one's sense of time to think of the aeons of compression and decay that created coal ("man can no more compute the age of this globe than the age of God"). On the same trip he had inspected wells of natural gas and other wonders, all promising incalculable economic benefits. Long before the Darwinian controversies, he used these sights to fortify his attacks on institutional churches and biblical orthodoxy. "How certainly must an abstract theology bow to facts!" he wrote. "How futile the efforts to maintain the authority of a book, or books, against the stern realities of Geology! In the coal, salt and iron mines of Pittsburg and vicinity, may be found the true word of God, that speaks as never man spake." The assault on religion was keyed to a national ideology of economic growth. The mines advanced the comfort and health of nearly "every domestic circle" in the United States. But it was utility, not acquisitiveness, that gave them the sanction of "God's Word" and made them unlike the gold mines of the thither West that blighted mankind with contention and avarice. Lust to get rich was out of keeping with Wright's quasi-religious vision of a unified economy based on the profitable commerce of widely scattered peoples.[89]

Wright often pointed out that western settlers knew him from reading his divagations among castles, cathedrals, and battlegrounds: they were well prepared for comparisons between America's changing institutions and the fixities of Europe. His reform-minded audiences were probably also inclined to join him in espousing obedience to natural law as well as rapid economic change, in prophesying slavery's doom while imagining economic bounty. Especially in public letters to Irish reformers, he condemned political compromises, and then praised northern cities when compared with European dwellings. Through dual comparisons with Europe and the South he underscored a revision of the "philosophy of slavery," which formerly placed man in lonely solitude at God's feet, while simultaneously according him dominion over nonhuman aspects of creation. With man's visible conquest of nature, "philosophy" now gave way to ideology, and attacks on slavery openly celebrated the free labor system and the West's booming growth. The dual comparisons made it possible to appreciate salt works, fertile fields, coal mines, and bear markets, without sacrificing a note of moral earnestness. While political events confirmed his antislavery denunciation of American politics, as he let his friends overseas know, other marvelous news led to the exclamation: "The world has no monument of human greatness and glory like the state of Ohio." The works of free men in the new world made the landmarks of the old look "contemptible."[90]

The linkage between free labor and reform was further defined in letters to James Haughton, published in the *Liberator* in that year of destiny 1848. It was like a dream, Wright felt, that a "social earthquake" had overthrown the terrible despotisms he had so recently toured. Though welcoming the liberation of repressed peoples, he reiterated the belief that freedom would prove illusory if new governments relied on military force. America, in one sense, exemplified the illusions of democracy: slaveholders in Washington, in their slaves' presence, cheered Europeans for ending tyranny; later in the same week they sent armed men to keep a band of those slaves from escaping to Canada. Haughton had often "chid" his immoderate criticism of America's "misnamed" democracy, but in 1848 Wright still prayed for its downfall.[91]

That side of Wright's argument is familiar to students of disunionism and anti-institutionalism in America; the other side, less well known, became apparent when he turned from political revolution to images of a free economy. He then gave Haughton an idyllic view of American liberty. Under the title "Old England and New England Laborers on Land Contrasted," he depicted his host, J. T. Everett of Princeton, Massachusetts, owner of the soil he farmed, employer of a young man who doubtless in a few years would also acquire land, marry, and start a family. Everett had been a legislator. His library included Orson Fowler, Andrew Jackson Davis, and other authorities on slavery, peace, capital punishment, diet, mental science, and water cure; among his six subscriptions were the *Liberator* and *Non-Resistant*. He enjoyed time to read, in other words, and his womenfolk did not toil in the fields—a state of affairs that had "horrified" Wright in Europe. Like nine out of ten New England families (by

Wright's estimate) the Everetts imbibed no alcohol, not even cider. They produced all their own grain, and ate a diversity of meat, vegetables, and cheese unknown among British commoners. Their floor was made of handsome boards rather than dirt or stone, their taxes were low, and at their piano someone played a song by the Hutchinson Family. This enviable tally subsided with the inevitable strophe, "This is a glorious country; but I cannot bear to speak of its advantages, for it is cursed with slavery."[92] No one could argue, of course, that the Everetts of North America were responsible for the wicked institution. They represented, instead, ideal readers of the *Liberator*, ideal audiences for Wright and other experts of reform, ideal beneficiaries of the free labor system. Prophetic denunciations of slavery served to justify the economic system in which they reaped advantages untold in the history of the Old World.

Certain strains had vanished from the romanticism of Wright's youth as he put his energies to spreading a new vision of economic life. He was less intrigued by heroes, less devoted to literary genius. There was an occasional Faustian moment in his hymns to wild nature and demonic factories in the West. But he had encapsulated restless preoccupations with opportunity and mission within new images of the self-improving proprietor, Mr. Everett, and his refined family. Wright's personal itinerancy may have typified the liberated expectations that reached a climax among his generation of easterners, but in imagination he and his friends were settled people, enjoying an easy balance of work and leisure. Admitting no fear of popular uprisings, they paid no heed to the questions of submission and dominance that defined European classes. One reason why their way of life kept extending its boundaries—Wright told them—was its success in pacifying unrest by opening up circumstances for individual competition. A kiss for a blow!

Let us not forget the South. Traveling through regions where no one feared revolution, Wright silently dropped the class-conscious habit of identifying himself with the honest poor against gown-men and aristocrats. Down south, however, masters boasted of familiarity with slaves much as the casualness of Continental ruling classes masked explosive inequalities and resentments. How would the black lower orders respond to whispers of rebellion? When Wright ruminated, at St. Joux, whether slave revolts were justifiable, he dreaded tyrannical aftermaths of violence. But he recognized that *L'Ouverture* excelled Bonaparte in the depths from which he climbed and the moral cause he led: dread might be joined to admiration of the black revolutionary's striving against adverse circumstances. After the dashing of Europe's romantic hopes, Wright turned willingly to that emblematic possibility. If American slaves took up arms, they would certify the obsolescence of social systems that stifled initiative; and whites would have to join the rebels in order to show fidelity to the logic of modernity. The more clearly Wright understood free labor, the more stridently he welcomed manly combat.

Some contemporaries balked at the gymnastics whereby Wright (and other pacifists) tried to adhere to principle and defend violence. As early as 1847 the *Liberator* carried criticism of speeches on natural law in which Wright urged listeners both to live out their convictions and to renounce violence. Did he mean they should follow their consciences to war or simulate an unfelt nonresistance?[93] Eventually Wright discovered in John Brown the genius to override all inconsistencies, the martyr of a new religion of self-abnegation. In the meantime he endured—or reveled in—interminable controversies over means and ends. At the 1857 meetings of the Massachusetts Anti-Slavery Society, for example, he announced that his opinions were irrelevant; he held the nation to "its own acknowledged rule of action," violence. His old friend James Buffum wondered whether it would then be obligatory for Brigham Young to stick to the polygamy in which he believed. Wright had no good answer.[94] And yet to focus exclusively on tactical disputes is to miss ideological meanings of slave revolts and white violence, issues that revised family excitement over the sweep of Napoleon's armies, that tested the vision of society developed on his mission abroad. A philosopher could make short work of Wright's preachings on natural law, and an expert strategist might challenge his credentials to hold office in the antislavery army. But logic and strategy were not essential to the work of constructing and transmitting a sense of reality consistent with a new America.

Wright was preoccupied by the universality of the revolution out of which the modern world was born. Would the slaves, he asked, be allowed to shout the battle cries of their eighteenth-century forerunners? Some Jacksonian intellectuals looked back wistfully to a patriotic past that they imagined to have been peaceful, but Wright's specialty was change, the future, the children, and he came to terms with a legacy of violence. He turned his back on the God of his Andover teachers who declared "that if the slave dare to draw the sabre of revolution, and imitate your Kossuths and Lamartines, if he dares to strike for liberty," the law of the land should strike him down. Instead of this deity Wright honored "the God of humanity" who commanded free men to support the cause of liberation everywhere.[95] Wright's apparent defection from the pacifism he had championed for decades, on two continents, signified his continuing extension to all men of the right of self-determination. Against his selective inattention to the poor we must place his widening embrace of revolution.

Wright's contempt for acquiescent slaves has already been noted: servility and aristocracy alike were out of place in the bustling, entrepreneurial world. He did not, however, imitate the bigotry that sometimes accompanied the West's hatred of the slave power. "I am a *Negro,*" he declared in 1861. "The scorn & hate cast on him are cast on me." Even though the union represented the "hope of oppressed Millions in other lands," it could not endure so long as the white American refused to accept the black "as a *Man.*"[96] This declaration recalls how his evangelical colleagues' racism had once driven him toward Garrisonism, how he then attempted to adopt the voice of Africa. But Wright never laid eyes on slavery, and an unmistakable irony clung to habits of empathy developed while he was discovering his own role in a fluid society. Some of the motives that made him an abolitionist also explained an ultimate inability to comprehend the existence of slaves. Back at the 1836 training sessions he had attacked servitude as a way of eschewing passivity in himself; if a slave voluntarily remained servile, it seemed, then no one was accountable.[97] Out of rigorous Northern concern for self-improvement arose the call for Southern blacks to strike off their chains.

Wright's views clashed with the events of his day: the "Marseillaise" was not sung in Dixie, circumstances unleashed no American Toussaint. His views clash also with the themes of recent historiography. According to the controversial study called *Time on the Cross,* black Horatio Algers found sufficient incentives in bondage to surpass farmers and workers of New England and the West in efficient production. If this contention were accurate, then the free-labor abolitionists may have been racist promoters of a false psychology of human motivation. The contention has fared poorly, however, under scrutiny by historians and economists,[98] though even its critics appreciate complexities of slave life that Wright, to whom slaves were a simple category contrasted with free laborers, could hardly have fathomed. While the problems facing a white youth in an age of romanticism were to learn the best ways to express his feelings and to find himself through work, the problem of the slave was to endure in peace. The slave's work was assigned without vocational crises, and self-expression came through religion. What Wright overlooked in Europe he could scarcely have imagined in the black South: even when men, women, and children accept their lots as fixed, their lives may still be rich, their visions of redemption inspiring.[99]

"Institutions for men, not men for institutions,": this 1848 motto became the public counterpoint to private meditations where Wright remained "Alone with God."[100] He lived with a keen sense that his world was shifting, that new arrangements were still being created. We may regard him as the citizen of a transitional world, no longer traditional, but not yet modern, a world characterized by unsettling change, one in which nostrums and slogans conveyed the hope that society was headed in the direction of liberation and progress. In this world Wright traveled with a classless, raceless dream of rewarding individual freedom and tidy social order. It may not have fit the South very well, but it was not so wild a dream when we keep in mind the vast distances covered in the life of a boy who eyed his father in revolutionary regalia, who slept as a man beside Metternich's offspring, who led enthusiastic crowds in singing the John Brown doxology and invoked American leadership in "planetary redemption."

The promise of the future was shining in well-planned, virtuous communities of reformers where he lectured and resided right up to his death. "Progression" was, for example, the leading idea exhibited in the beautifully laid out town of Vineland, New Jersey. "Here, as in all places there are but two classes: i.e. the progressive party and the stationary party." One was "holding back, and trying to back the wheels and put on the brakes to the car of progress, and pointing the world to the dead past," while the other called, "put on the steam, ease the brakes, and rush on to the final station; with the sublime watchword, 'Nearer to man, nearer to God!'"[101]

Epilogue

Last Work

These old P.M.s are gruesome, but I often find them . . . a help before embarking on a new . . . (hesitates) . . . retrospect.

Samuel Beckett, *Krapp's Last Tape* (1958)[1]

In view of Henry Wright's celebration of forward-rushing political and economic change, his introspective and backward-looking habits are ironic. This advocate of "Revolution" retired for hours of diary-keeping; this champion of "Progression" referred compulsively to experiences on his boyhood farm. To Wright these preoccupations counted among the rewards of modernity: man was freely exploring his consciousness as never before. And modern readers may agree that Wright attained impressive, if limited, knowledge of the psychological sources of that lonely defiance which characterized many stands he took.

But self-knowledge came at a price. Looking back over Wright's career, we sense that personal insight was a way of reversing public setbacks; it compensated for lost definitions of power and fame. He retreated from the ministry at a time when its traditional civic leadership was challenged; he turned his back on the benevolence societies when their millennial program faced competition from local ministers. He soon forgot the nonresistants' ardent belief that through peaceful words and deeds they could change history. By the mid-1840s every route to civic influence had proved disappointing. Making a virtue of political impotence, Wright became an expert on the offstage worlds of bridal bed, nursery, and sewing circle. In the process, no doubt, he learned much about himself and helped others to voice hitherto repressed feelings. The fact remains that failure in various collective public endeavors prepared him for the success he eventually attained.

His authority as lecturer and author was predicated on his understanding of marriage and acquaintance with women. In this respect, too, his expertise reversed personal frustrations, particularly in his married life. More important, Wright exemplified a common pattern among ministers (and renegades from the profession) who asserted that feminine "influence" outweighed more visible, masculine expressions of power. His books and lectures experimented with a new sense of history in which politics seemed immaterial, in which the slightest incidents of domestic life were totally absorbing.[2] There were momentary fears that society might be beyond control, but they subsided when he remembered the new age's invitation to penetrate the mysteries of human nature.

But human nature might also run out of control, in spite of the skillful efforts of a nineteenth-century man of progress to prevent a breakdown. There are undertones of desperation throughout Wright's last work, an unpublished *magnum opus* entitled "Mine and Thine, in the Realm of Thought."[3]

This work survives in four manuscript volumes, running well over one thousand pages in length. In these volumes he arranged extracts from scores of letters to and from his wife—not Elizabeth LeBreton Stickney Wright in Philadelphia, but a younger woman named Helen. The letters are numbered and dated, and his alternate with hers; but the extracts do not appear chronologically. They are grouped instead under topics in religion, motherhood, and sexuality. Wright left blank space for letters that he did not have at hand, and Helen regretted that distance prevented her from helping him copy "Mine and Thine" for publication. She showed no alarm at his use of her letters on the lecture platform or in evening conversations.

He concealed her name (which was probably not Helen), but despite the clandestine necessities of their relationship, both obviously felt they were living out the model marriage of their century. She marveled: "What a man is my own husband! Reaching out everywhere & clasping the whole world of human beings to his heart. Feeling the heart throbs of the mighty multitude—knowing their weaknesses & shortcomings; & while pitying them with a loving tender heart, seeking all available means to ameliorate & perfect their condition."[4] In his eyes, she was nothing less than a "Mother-God," the epitome of womanhood.

I cannot establish her identity. Some of her words, especially on religion, sound like Wright's. Her fulfillment of his marital fantasies is so complete that at times I have felt she must be an imaginary creation, perhaps the outcome of a bizarre spiritualist episode. But if "Mine and Thine" is partly fiction, it includes many passages that seem authentic. As a seventy-year-old man, Wright was making a last overture to the conjugal happiness that life had always denied him. He found his mate, I suspect, among some Rhode Island Quaker families whom he visited frequently in his declining years.[5] Whoever she was, she embraced his fantasies because she was his equal in loneliness.

"I have been lonesome all my life," she confessed in her first letter, dated August 22, 1868. They had spoken only a few words during an interval at a camp meeting, probably of spiritualists, at which Wright performed. He invited her to communicate "all I had to say," but she decided to wait until she was home in her own room. "But then, that word *Home* does sadly mock us poor mortals sometimes. I feel often like some weary wanderer, in a foreign land, with kindly faces around me, but strangers as if they did not know me. *I look away, away, & reach out my hand imploringly* for those of my own household to take me & hold me tenderly, as one who has been sick & absent a long while." She had "accidentally poisoned" her face and hands ("I can almost hear thee say now—*'Dear little Darling!'* "), but as soon as she recovered she planned to go sit on an ancient Indian throne and *"think great loving thoughts of thee."* At this stage she signed as "thy affectionate friend."[6]

We do not have Henry's reply. Her second letter, dated September 11,[7] indicates that he struck just the right chord by saying, "we would have a good time being *lonesome* together." It makes her very happy that "thou dost bid me come into thy heart; & lo! behold me, right in *my own place.*" She denied any jealousy that others abided there too. (In a subsequent letter she thought it natural for other women to feel attracted to the handsome lecturer, but he denied the problem's existence.)[8] She showed a tendency to deprecate herself, wishing to "sit at thy feet," to crown him and wait upon him, and she is afraid to burden him with her troubles. But his complaint moves her deeply: "Forty years—not so much as a Wigwam! A Wanderer! No shelter in the wilderness that thou couldst call thy own." Already she says a prayer to him in the morning, and wishes she had a home to offer him. Then she analyzes her lonesomeness: "How can I help it when my mother was lonesome before I was born? She would rather the baby that died before I was born had been her last." How greatly she needed him to accept her "just as thou wouldst if thou hadst me really to be all thine own—with all the years of a woman, but I fear many childish ways."

By the fourth exchange he had asked whether she desired to be owned by a man, and she had replied that she thirsted for such possession.[9] Although it is impossible to trace all the steps toward "Mine and Thine," it is clear that they contracted an ethereal marriage which both hoped would endure, and take on greater reality, beyond the grave. She continued to feel inferior, calling herself "*thy Gypsey-Wife . . . thy Girl-Wife* . . . I am so *small!* . . . my husband . . . has taken this *Waif* to his heart as a Wife."[10] She allowed him to dream that in "the inner temple" he would finally taste the pleasures of paternity. Already in the realm of thought they could assert that their irrevocable union included a baby; the manuscript, improved by Wright, made the wish tangible.

While telling all too little about Helen, the letters in "Mine and Thine" reveal permanent, troubled strata of Wright's mind that the social changes of his lifetime barely touched. There are scattered remarks on evolutionary science (confusing in view of his lifelong insistence on sharp distinctions between man and the animals), but few other references to contemporary culture. There is only sparse mention of Garrison, Lincoln, Toussaint, or John Brown; the Negro question gives way to "the baby question" as the foremost human concern.[11] As the great causes recede from consciousness, Wright's life of service to humanity appears principally as Byronic journeying, "Houseless, Homeless, Wifeless, Childless!"[12] No longer proud to be alone with God, he sought to nestle in a comfortable embrace, even if that meant death. "Mine and Thine" is the literary expression of the withdrawal from politics that was an implicit feature of Wright's life.

The terms "Mine" and "Thine," as exchanged by Henry and Helen, posed a contradiction to the risky modern economy. Henry repeatedly calls himself "a billionaire in love," and criticizes the incursions of the marketplace into the domain of affection. When couples convert weddings into bargains, they conceal and deceive; the results are their own degradation and their progeny's disease. Henry's life maxim is "*Earn it & Own It,*" which means, in the first instance, that the virtuous, candid man will take more complete possession of a spouse than will a conniving sensualist. Far away from the world of barter, playacting, and divorce, it is possible to imagine an unselfish world of fixed identities and undying affections.[13]

One public matter is not ignored—religion. Hundreds of pages rail against the wrathful, hateful God whose vengeance he had been educated to fear. There is a tender adolescent memory of holding a baby while a revivalist expatiated on the blackness of human nature and the need for a second birth. He harks back as well to the discovery at Andover of his inability to entertain the idea of a meaningless universe, devoid of God.[14] After dreaming of God throughout childhood, what a shock to discover that He was not physically there. And Wright correctly saw it as his consistent life purpose to bring God down to earth and associate Him with man. For many years this purpose had inspired his faith in social progress; but at the verge of death such faith disintegrated, and it became apparent just how tortured human consciousness may become when God is not projected far enough away. Wright spoke effusively of "family-worship" as a surrogate for Christianity, with domestic sentiments replacing piety, with each kiss a prayer. We are most struck, however, by layer upon layer of reversals and denials of long-standing disappointments.

On some pages Henry and Helen have a daughter, named Helen in his letters, Henrietta in hers. On other pages they only think of having a daughter, at least for the time being. Sometimes the child is herself called "Mine and Thine," the conjunction of two individual wishes. She represents the theme of the book, the superiority of idealization over temporary material reality. And yet when Henry calls the baby God, and swears fealty to her, he has in mind some of the practical duties of modern fathers. He imagines himself getting up in the middle of the night to attend to her majesty's cries—and finding his character softened by such obedience.[15] In the idealized realm, along with its other advantages, he was released from self-centeredness.

Henry scarcely described Helen, whom he loved as God rather

than as a flawed individual. She was no one in particular. She personified categorical needs emerging from his own psyche—somewhat painful needs even when mixed with words of exaltation:

> I look to the earth! I *see, hear* & *feel* then, nothing but Wife! On every blade of grass is written—Wife. The fragrance & beauty of every flower are but the fragrance & beauty of my wife—Helen! Every shrub, bush & tree, ever speaks to me that one potential, *killing, piercing, stiletto* word—"*Wife.*" On every Rock, Pebble, & Grain of Sand, is written *Wife.* Every breeze whispers softly & sighs so sweetly & gently—*Wife.* Every storm, hurricane & tornado shrieks & roars—*Wife.* The leaves & limbs of every tree as they gracefully wave & toss themselves proudly ring out—*Wife.* Every lightning, as it flashes out over the gloom of midnight, emblazons *Wife* on the night.[16]

Marriage fulfilled visions of self-control. The condition of "wife on the brain," as Henry half-jokingly called it, kept "the animal in me" under subjection and gave him self-confidence. Helen had broken his will, and when passion surged within him she was the "Nurse & Physician" who sedated him. "The most striking result of thy power over me as a wife," he reported, "is the absolute control it gives me over myself." "*I trust myself. Canst thou trust me?*"[17] Inevitably the problem that focused this drama of self-government was sexuality. That was the point of Helen's recurrent protests that she, unlike most other women of her acquaintance, saw nothing vile in sexual relations: their object, after all, was to conceive godlike Henrietta. When Henry drew on conversations with women who loathed intercourse with their husbands, that was Helen's cue to say that she could never feel such aversion to her controlled, loving, masculine God. By summarizing divorce statistics and guessing at the incidence of contraception and abortion, Henry demonstrated how many other matches were merely provisional, but in the realm of thought his worthiness was verified by Helen's eternally undisgusted embrace.

Where were the origins of the destructiveness and unworthiness that Henry denied so artfully? They referred back to what he feared had been the effects of his needs on his mother, and these were anxieties that not even Helen could suppress. He tried to believe, as another life maxim put it: "*Man's Natural Demands are God's only Commands.*"[18] They could not be harmful. But supplying his needs remained a version of cannibalism, as was clearest perhaps in his negation of the eucharist: "*Man can be saved only through Woman as a*

Wife. Only by Eating a Woman can Man be saved. . . . *To eat Christ* cannot meet the demands of the Masculine Element of Human Nature. Man's Nature demands, as a necessary condition of a full salvation, of a perfect growth & development of his Manhood, that 'he should eat the flesh & drink the blood of Woman. . . . [']"[19]

Henry professed to regard Helen as God, and "God as the mother of my child," he said, "is even nearer & dearer to me, if possible, than is God as my own Mother." But the comparison could not result, finally, in Helen's favor. Near the beginning of his *magnum opus* he planted the wish that life as a reformer could never eradicate, the wish that burst from some substratum of consciousness as he arranged his papers for oblivion: "My own mother left the body when I was four years old [*sic*], but how sweet is her name to me. As a fond loving mother Mother-God ever holds me, & nurses me in her bosom. I think more of God as a Mother, than as a Father." This, he concluded, was his "deepest experience."[20] Even in the four volumes that trumpeted his sweet love match, he was unmistakably alone.

Death claimed Henry Clarke Wright suddenly, in August 1870, during a visit with his Rhode Island friends. In good health at breakfast, he was "taken with a fit" at seven o'clock while riding into town. He died at midday.[21] *Mine and Thine* remained unfinished.

Henry Clarke Wright with Catherine Paton. Inscribed, "My Wee Darling," this picture appeared in *Marriage and Parentage* (1855). Copies were also sold on Wright's midwestern tours.

Abbreviations

AEG Angelina E. Grimké.

Anthropology Henry Clarke Wright, *Anthropology; or, The Science of Man: In Its Bearings on War and Slavery, and on Arguments from the Bible, Marriage, God, Death, Retribution, Atonement and Government in Support of These and Other Social Wrongs* (Cincinnati: E. Shepard; Boston: Bela Marsh, 1850).

ASSU American Sunday School Union.

Birney Letters *Letters of James Gillespie Birney, 1831–1857*, ed. Dwight L. Dumond, 2 vols. (1938; reprint ed., Gloucester, Mass.: Peter Smith, 1966).

BPL Boston Public Library, Boston, Mass.

Brit. and Am. Abolitionists Clare Taylor, ed., *British and American Abolitionists: An Episode in Transatlantic Understanding* (Edinburgh: Edinburgh University Press, 1974).

Def. War Henry Clarke Wright, *Defensive War Proved to Be a Denial of Christianity and of the Government of God* (London: Charles Gilpin, 1846).

DFHL Society of Friends Historical Library, Dublin.

EI Essex Institute, Salem, Mass.

"1818 Address" Henry Clarke Wright, "1818 Address" (delivered before the Ladies Missionary Society, Hartwick, N.Y.), Boston Public Library, Boston, Mass.

Empire Henry Clarke Wright, *The Empire of the Mother over the Character and Destiny of the Race* (Boston: Bela Marsh, 1863).

Eng. Let. Henry Clarke Wright, English, Irish, and Scotch Letters, Harvard College Library, Cambridge, Mass.

EP Elizabeth Pease.

Errors Henry Clarke Wright, *The Errors of the Bible, Demonstrated by the Truths of Nature; or, Man's Only Infallible Rule of Faith and Practice* (Boston: Bela Marsh, 1857).

Fragments Henry Clarke Wright, Fragments of Diaries Written in 1832, 1835, 1845, 1847, 1848 and Miscellaneous Papers, Harvard College Library, Cambridge, Mass.

GAL-S George Arents Research Library, Syracuse University.

Garrison Wendell Phillips Garrison and Francis Jackson Garrison, *William Lloyd Garrison, 1805–1879: The Story of His Life Told by His Children,* 4 vols. (New York: Century Co., 1885–89).

HCL Harvard College Library, Cambridge, Mass.

HCW Henry Clarke Wright.

HSP Historical Society of Pennsylvania, Philadelphia, Pa.

Kiss Henry Clarke Wright, *A Kiss for a Blow; or, A Collection of Stories for Children Showing Them How to Prevent Quarrelling* (Boston: Bela Marsh, 1858).

Lib. *The Liberator.*

Life Henry Clarke Wright, *Human Life: Illustrated in My Individual Experience as a Child, A Youth, and a Man* (Boston: Bela Marsh, 1849).

Living Present Henry Clarke Wright, *The Living Present and the Dead Past; or, God Made Manifest and Useful in Living Men and Women as He Was in Jesus* (Boston: Bela Marsh, 1865).

Man-Killing Henry Clarke Wright, *Man-Killing, by Individuals and Nations, Wrong—*

Dangerous in All Cases (Boston: Moses A. Dow, 1841).

Marriage Henry Clarke Wright, *Marriage and Parentage; or, The Reproductive Element in Man, as a Means to His Elevation and Happiness* (Boston: Bela Marsh, 1855).

Merits of Christ and Paine Henry Clarke Wright, *The Merits of Jesus Christ and the Merits of Thomas Paine: As a Substitute for Merit in Others—What Is the Difference between Them?* (The Author, 1869).

Misc. Writings Henry Clarke Wright, Miscellaneous Writings on Theology and Education, Harvard College Library, Cambridge, Mass.

Natick Resolution Henry Clarke Wright, *The Natick Resolution; or, Resistance to Slaveholders the Right and Duty of Southern Slaves and Northern Freemen* (Boston: The Author, 1859).

Notes on Eccl. Hist. Henry Clarke Wright, Notes on Ecclesiastical History, Andover, Mass., 1820–21, Boston Public Library, Boston, Mass.

Notes on Script. Henry Clarke Wright, Notes on Scriptural and Theological Studies, Andover, Mass., 1819–20, Boston Public Library, Boston, Mass.

NYSHA New York State Historical Association, Cooperstown, N.Y.

PHS Presbyterian Historical Society, Philadelphia, Pa.

Rad. Ab. Lewis Perry, *Radical Abolitionism: Anarchy and the Government of God in Antislavery Thought* (Ithaca, N.Y.: Cornell University Press, 1973).

Self-Abnegationist Henry Clarke Wright, *The Self-Abnegationist; or, The True King and Queen* (Boston: Bela Marsh, 1863).

Six Months Henry Clarke Wright, *Six Months at Graefenberg; with Conversations in the Saloon, on Nonresistance and Other Subjects* (London: Charles Gilpin, 1845).

Unwelcome Henry Clarke Wright, *The Unwelcome Child; or, The Crime of an Undesigned and Undesired Maternity* (Boston: Bela Marsh, 1860).

Weld-Grimké Letters Gilbert H. Barnes and Dwight L. Dumond, eds., *Letters of Theodore Dwight Weld, Angelina Grimké Weld, and Sarah Grimké, 1822–1844*, 2 vols. (1934; reprint ed., Gloucester, Mass.: Peter Smith, 1965).

Whittier Letters John B. Pickard, ed., *The Letters of John Greenleaf Whittier*, 3 vols. (Cambridge, Mass: Harvard University Press, 1975).

WJ Journals and diaries of Henry Clarke Wright. Volume numbers change back and forth between roman and arabic numerals, sometimes with letters added, and in overlapping series.

WLCL William L. Clements Library, University of Michigan, Ann Arbor.

WLG William Lloyd Garrison.

WRHS Western Reserve Historical Society, Cleveland, Ohio.

Notes

Chapter One

1. See, e.g., the inaccurate sketch in *National Cyclopaedia of American Biography* (New York: James T. White, 1899), 3:332.

2. "A Christian Reformer," *Union Herald* (Cazenovia, N.Y.), as reprinted in *Lib.*, Mar. 27, 1840, p. 4.

3. The classic discussion is Whitney R. Cross, *The Burned-Over District: The Social and Intellectual History of Enthusiastic Religion in Western New York, 1800–1850* (New York: Harper & Row Torchbooks, 1965). Extremely valuable is Paul E. Johnson, *A Shopkeeper's Millennium: Society and Revivals in Rochester, New York, 1815–1837* (New York: Hill and Wang, 1978).

4. The best discussion is Perry Miller, *The Life of the Mind in America: From the Revolution to the Civil War* (New York: Harcourt, Brace & World, 1965), pp. 3–95.

5. "1818 Address."

6. *Life*, pp. 167–68.

7. Hannah F. Gould's "Epitaphs," in John J. Currier, *History of Newburyport, Mass., 1764–1909* (Newburyport, Mass.: The Author, 1906, 1909), p. 556.

8. The license itself is tucked into WJ (BPL), II (May–June 1828). His later report of this "farce" is in *Life*, pp. 228–29.

9. On his ministry see *Life,* pp. 236–324. His silk gloves and other personal habits are mentioned in Hannah Lee to Susanna ——, Feb. 12, 1844, a postscript on Mrs. E. L. B. Wright to Hannah Webb, Feb. 8, 1844, Garrison Papers, BPL.

10. WJ (BPL), I, 126–27 (Sept. 19, 1829). Emphasis added.

11. *Essex Gazette* (Haverhill, Mass.), Oct. 10, 1829, p. 1; drafted in WJ (BPL), I, 109–15 (Sept. 19, 1829).

12. *Contributions to the Ecclesiastical History of Essex County, Mass.* (Boston: Congregational Board of Publications, 1865), pp. 147–48, 254–55, 375–81. This source was antagonistic toward HCW. For more on revivals, see WJ (HCL), LIII, 5 (Nov. 11, 1832).

13. *Contributions to the Ecclesiastical History;* manuscript records of the Essex County North Association of ministers, EI.

14. WJ (BPL), I, 89 (July 18, 1828); *Life,* p. 275.

15. *Salem Gazette,* Jan. 1, 1830, pp. 2–3; *Essex Gazette* (Haverhill, Mass.), June 11, 1831, p. 3; *Salem Gazette,* Jan. 4, 1831, p. 1; Charles W. Upham, "Memoir of Francis Peabody," *Essex Institute Historical Collections* 9 (1868–69): 51.

16. "On Crime" (1829–30), "Schools and Industry" (1827), and "On Industry" (1830), three manuscript essays (BPL). On the effects of alcohol, see Fragments, pp. 1242–1307, and a speech on "Teetotalism," Aug. 16, 1829, folded inside WJ (BPL), LIII.

17. "Schools and Industry"; "Common Schools" (1829), manuscript essay in Misc. Writings. The significance of district schools and academies is clarified in Michael B. Katz, *The Irony of Early School Reform: Educational Innovation in Mid-Nineteenth Century Massachusetts* (Cambridge, Mass.: Harvard University Press, 1968), pp. 50–80.

18. See James M. Banner, Jr., *To the Hartford Convention: The Federalists and the Origins of Party Politics in Massachusetts, 1789–1815* (New York: Alfred A. Knopf, 1969), p. 55.

19. "Common Schools," pp. 1–8.

20. William Seymour Tyler, *History of Amherst College during Its First Half-Century, 1821–1871* (Springfield, Mass.: C. W. Bryan, 1873), pp. 181–85. The man quoted was a Universalist. For another comment on the crowded state of the professions, also related to antislavery commitment, see *Whittier Letters,* 1:16.

21. WJ (HCL), I, 8–9 (Dec. 1, 1832).

22. HCW to Frederick W. Porter, ASSU Correspondence, PHS. The six societies were the American Sunday School Union, the American Education Society (which supported the education of ministers), the American Home Mission Society, the American Board of Commissioners for Foreign Missions, the American Tract Society, and the American Bible Society.

23. Quoted in David Tyack, "The Kingdom of God and the Common School: Protestant Ministers and the Educational Awakening in the West," *Harvard Educational Review* 36 (1966): 456. Important studies of the empire of

benevolence include: Charles I. Foster, *An Errand of Mercy: The Evangelical United Front, 1790–1837* (Chapel Hill: University of North Carolina Press, 1960); Bertram Wyatt-Brown, *Lewis Tappan and the Evangelical War against Slavery* (Cleveland: Press of Case-Western Reserve University, 1969); Clifford S. Griffin, *Their Brothers' Keepers: Moral Stewardship in the United States, 1800–1865* (New Brunswick, N.J.: Rutgers University Press, 1960); Lois Banner, "Religious Benevolence as Social Control: A Critique of an Interpretation," *Journal of American History* 60 (1973): 23–41; and Lois W. Banner, "Religion and Reform in the Early Republic: The Role of Youth," *American Quarterly* 23 (1971): 677–95. The latter article discusses the origins of many reformers at Andover.

24. WJ (HCL), III, 19, 230 (July 22, Dec. 31, 1833).

25. WJ (HCL), VI, 4–12 (June 1, 1834).

26. Raymond B. Culver, *Horace Mann and Religion in the Massachusetts Public Schools.* (New Haven, Conn.: Yale University Press, 1929), p. 22, 42.

27. "Christian Education," manuscript essay, BPL. HCW, "Christian Education," *Boston Recorder,* May 1, 1833, p. 72; May 8, 1833, p. 76; May 15, 1833, p. 80; May 22, 1833, p. 84; June 5, 1833, p. 89. In September 1834 he read over old diaries and retracted old views of the possibly harmful competition of Sunday schools with the common schools (WJ [BPL], IX, 148–49).

28. HCW, "Christian Education," *Boston Recorder,* May 1, 1833, p. 72; HCW, "The Family Circle, the Nursery of Heaven," *Boston Recorder,* Feb. 20, 1835, pp. 29–30; HCW, "The Family Institution," *Boston Recorder,* Jan. 23, 1835, p. 13.

29. HCW, "Infidelity Upheld by Christians," *Boston Recorder,* Mar. 27, 1833, p. 49; "How Ministers May Get Access to Neighborhoods and Districts, from Which They Have Been Excluded," *Boston Recorder,* Aug. 22, 1834, p. 133.

30. ASSU, Missions Committee, Minutes, July 31, 1833, PHS. HCW to Frederick W. Porter, Dec. 27, 1833, Jan. 10, 1834, Jan. 23, 1834, ASSU Correspondence, PHS. On the Southern campaign see *The Southern Enterprize . . .* (Philadelphia: American Sunday School Union, 1833); and on the English experience see Thomas Walter Laqueur, *Religion and Respectability: Sunday School and Working Class Culture, 1780–1850* (New Haven, Conn.: Yale University Press, 1976).

31. WJ (HCL), XII (1834), passim; XIII, 80 (Jan. 13, 1835), and passim. WJ (BPL), X, XI, XII, XVI, XXVI, numerous entries on maternity in 1834 and 1835. Mary Howitt, "Memoir of Henry Clarke Wright," *Howitt's Journal* 2 (1847): 133.

32. WJ (BPL), X, 9 (Sept. 22, 1834); WJ (HCL), V, 202 (May 6, 1834); Peter Berger, Brigitte Berger, and Hansfried Kellner, *The Homeless Mind: Modernization and Consciousness* (New York: Random House, 1973), pp. 176–77.

33. WJ (HCL), VII, 63 (July 29, 1834); XII, 400 (Dec. 10, 1834); XXIII, 39–40 (Aug. 20, 1835); XII, 394–95 (Dec. 9, 1834). WJ (BPL), VIII, 50–57 (Aug. 23, 1834); XIV, 32 (Feb. 10, 1835); XIV, 99 (Feb. 24, 1835); X, 7–19 (Sept. 23, 1834).

34. WJ (BPL), XVI, 52 (Apr. 13, 1835); XXVII, 156 (Mar. 21, 1836); XIII, 29–32 (Jan. 5, 1835); XIV, 100, 113 (Feb. 24, Feb. 26, 1835).

35. WJ (HCL), XII, 120, 464 (Nov. 10, Dec. 20, 1834). WJ (BPL), VIII, 114–15 (Aug. 27, 1834); XIII, 19 (Jan. 3, 1835); XIV, 31 (Feb. 10, 1835); XVI, 97 (Apr. 23, 1835).

36. WJ (BPL), XIV, 4–9, 57 (Feb. 5, Feb. 13, 1835). WJ (HCL), XII, 173, 181, 200, 218–19, 260, 324–25, 381, 442–43 (Nov.–Dec. 1834); XIX, 26–29 (June 11, 1835).

37. WJ (BPL), XVI, 87–88 (Apr. 21, 1835); XXVI, 119 (Dec. 12, 1835).

38. WJ (HCL), XII, 287 (Nov. 25, 1834); XXVIII, 4, 138 (Apr. 2, May 28, 1836); XXI, 27 (Aug. 29, 1836).

39. *Memoirs of American Missionaries, Formerly Connected with the Society of Inquiry Respecting Missons. . .* (Boston, 1833), pp. 296–317; *Life*, p. 211.

40. *Life*, p. 212.

41. *Sabbath School Visiter* 1 (Apr. 1833): 7.

42. WJ (HCL), III, 56 (Oct. 8, 1833).

43. WJ (HCL), IV, 63–64 (Jan. 28, 1833).

44. WJ (HCL), III, 47–48 (Oct. 7, 1833).

45. WJ (HCL), I, 89 Dec. 20, 1832); LIII, 29–30 (June 18, 1833); V, 308–9 (May 24, 1834).

46. WJ (HCL), V, 41 (Mar. 26, 1834).

47. WJ (HCL), VI, 30, 36–38, 179–80, 301–2 (June 5, June 6, June 25, July 14, 1834); II, 53 (Oct. 11, 1834).

48. WJ (HCL), VI, 217 (July 2, 1834). The man was Rev. John Frost.

49. WJ (HCL), VI, 30 (June 5, 1834). When Essex County ministers debated the merits of the colonization society in 1833, five frankly opposed it and three others doubted "it ever could do away slavery"; only four were its "warm friends." Opposed to colonization, Wright still felt: "Best way to abolish slavery is to help carry into effect the designs" of the Sunday School and Home Mission Societies (WJ [HCL], II, 8–9 [July 15, 1833]).

50. WJ (HCL), II, 92–93 (Sept. 11, 1834).

51. WJ (BPL), XIII, 86–90, 93–94 (Jan. 14, Jan. 15, 1835). See also his prior meeting with Tracy: WJ (BPL), XIII, 49–50 (Jan. 8, 1835).

52. WJ (BPL), XVIII, 5–6, 30–34, 105–7 (May 25, May 27, June 5, 1835); WJ (HCL), XVII, 133, 139, 142–52 (May 23–25, 1835); *Lib.*, May 30, 1835, p. 2.

53. WJ (HCL), XXI, 84 (July 10, 1835). *Lib.*, Sept. 4, 1840, pp. 1–2; Mar. 5, 1841, p. 4.

54. WJ (BPL), XVIII, 17 (May 26, 1835).

55. WJ (BPL), XIII, 39–43 (Jan. 6, 1835); Fragments, pp. 17–21 (Jan. 6, 1835); HCW to WLG, Nov. 26, 1835, Garrison Papers, BPL; Sarah H. Southwick, *Reminiscences of Early Antislavery Days* (Cambridge, Mass.: Privately printed, 1893), p. 13; *Brit. and Am. Abolitionists*, p. 26.

56. WJ (HCL), XXV, 168 (Nov. 6, 1835); XXIII, 16–21 (Aug. 18, 1835). *Garrison*, 2:115.

57. WJ (HCL), XIX, 78–80 (June 14, 1835); WJ (BPL), IX, 45, 48 (Sept. 3, 1834).

58. WJ (HCL), XIX, 7–15 (June 10, 1835). For another meeting with Blagden, see WJ (BPL), XVI, 68–69 (Apr. 16, 1835).

59. *Garrison*, 2:136–37.

60. WJ (BPL), XVIII, 71–75 (June 2, 1835).

61. WJ (HCL), XXII, 73–74 (July 28, 1835); Howitt, "Memoir," p. 133.

62. WJ (HCL), XXVIII, 144 (May 30, 1836).

63. See WJ (BPL), XVI, 134 (Apr. 29, 1835), for an account of a man named Twining who was traveling from city to city in the hope of uniting the organizations. HCW wished him Godspeed. See WJ (BPL), XIII, 170–72 (Feb. 4, 1835), for a lecture by the Garrisonian Amasa Walker on the American Union and the antislavery views of the rich and haughty.

64. WJ (HCL), XVII, 85–86, 96–97 (May 16, May 18, 1835); XXI, 144 (July 17, 1835).

65. WJ (HCL), XXV, 79–82, 84, 168 (Oct. 23, Oct. 24, Nov. 6, 1835). In his conversion, violence conformed to the pattern described in Silvan S. Tomkins, "The Psychology of Commitment: The Constructive Role of Violence and Suffering for the Individual and for His Society," in *The Antislavery Vanguard: New Essays on the Abolitionists*, ed. Martin Duberman (Princeton, N.J.: Princeton University Press, 1965), pp. 270–98.

66. WJ (HCL), XII, 530–31 (Dec. 31, 1834); XXV, 171–72, 176 (Nov. 7–8, 1835). WJ (BPL), XXVI, 23 (Nov. 9, 1835).

67. WJ (HCL), XXV, 119–22 (Nov. 2, 1835).

68. *Boston Recorder*, July 24, 1835, p. 118; July 31, 1835, p. 123. *Lib.*, Aug. 1, 1835, p. 3.

69. WJ (HCL), XXII, 7 (July 22, 1835); *Lib.*, Oct.–Nov. 1835. The HCL set of *Lib.* has HCW's annotation of pseudonyms.

70. *Lib.*, Dec. 19, 1835, p. 2; Dec. 26, 1835, p. 2; Jan. 2, 1836, pp. 2–3. WJ (BPL), XXVI, 93 (Dec. 5, 1835). These references also apply to quotations from the Genius of Africa in the following paragraphs. On the theme of empathy, see Aileen S. Kraditor, *Means and Ends in American Abolitionism: Garrison and His Critics on Strategy and Tactics, 1834–1850* (New York: Alfred A. Knopf, 1968), pp. 237 ff.

71. WJ (HCL), XXII, 55–56 (July 27, 1835); XXXIII, 251 (Mar. 30, 1837). HCW, *Dick Crowninshield, the Assassin, and Zachary Taylor, the Soldier: The Difference between Them* (n.p., n.d. [1848]). *Lib.*, Sept. 27, 1850, p. 4.

72. Ronald G. Walters, "The Erotic South: Civilization and Sexuality in American Abolitionism," *American Quarterly* 25 (1973): 177–210.

73. WJ (HCL), XXIII, 26–27 (Aug. 18, 1835); XXV, 89–90 (Oct. 26, 1835); XXVIII, 38 (Apr. 21, 1836); WJ (BPL), XVIII, 40 (May 28, 1835).

74. *Def. War*, pp. 47–48; *Six Months*, p. 248.

75. WJ (BPL), XII (Apr.–May 1830).

76. WJ (HCL), I, 106–8 (May 7, 1833).

77. WJ (BPL), XIII, 146–50, 167 (Jan. 29, Feb. 3, 1835); Fragments, p. 33 (Jan. 29, 1835).

78. WJ (BPL), XVI, 33–34 (Apr. 11, 1835). WJ (HCL), XVII, 88 (May 16, 1834); XVII, 29 (May 7, 1835). *Lib.*, Apr. 11, 1835, p. 3.

79. *Lib.*, Oct. 10, 1835, p. 2.

80. WJ (HCL), XXIX, 81 (June 25, 1836); XXXI, 88–89, 115 (Sept. 12, Sept. 20, 1836).

81. Ladd to HCW, July 23, 1836, Garrison Papers, BPL; WJ (HCL), XXX, 66–68 (Aug. 2, 1836). On the background of the American Peace Society and its conflicts, see Peter Brock, *Pacifism in the United States from the Colonial Era to the First World War* (Princeton, N.J.: Princeton University Press, 1968), chap. 11.

82. The account in this and the following paragraphs depends on Wright's diary account of the training sessions in WJ (HCL), XXXII, 142–397 (Nov. 15–30, 1836). See also John L. Myers, "Organization of 'The Seventy': To Arouse the North against Slavery," *Mid-America* 48 (1966): 29–46.

83. WJ (HCL), XLIII, 42 (Apr. 20, 1840). Weld's mother told Wright of the relation.

84. AEG to Jane Smith, November —, 1836, Weld Papers, WLCL.

85. WJ (HCL), XXXII, 210 (Nov. 19, 1836).

86. WJ (HCL), XXXII, 239 (Nov. 21, 1836).

87. WJ (HCL), XXXII, 428 (Dec. 9, 1836); *The Slave's Friend* (New York, 1836), vol. 1; *Lib.*, Feb. 25, 1837, p. 3.

88. AEG to Jane Smith, July 25, Oct. 26, 1837, Weld Papers, WLCL. There is no definitive list of the Seventy, but Wright's notes indicate that the Grimkés were in New York as participants and trainees.

89. AEG to Jane Smith, June 26, July 25, Aug. 26, 1837, Weld Papers, WLCL; AEG to HCW, Aug. 12, 1837, Garrison Papers, BPL; WJ (HCL), XXXIII, 277 (Apr. 6, 1837).

90. AEG to Jane Smith, July 25, 1837, Weld Papers, WLCL.

91. *Lib.*, July 21, 1837, p. 2.

92. Ibid., Wright's italics. He clarified these views in "Family Government," *Lib.*, Dec. 1, 1837, p. 2.

93. Quoted in *Garrison*, 2:143.

94. WJ (BPL), XIII, 38 (Apr. 1832).

95. *Lib.*, July 28, 1837, p. 2; July 27, 1838, p. 4; Aug. 4, 1838, p. 4; emphasis mine.

96. WJ (BPL), XXXIV, 18–24 (Apr. 29, 1837).

97. *Lib.*, June 23, 1837, p. 3; July 21, 1837, pp. 2–3.

98. WJ (BPL), XXXV, 99–100, 132–33, 219–20 (Aug. 14, Sept. 28–29, 1837).

99. Gilbert H. Barnes and Dwight L. Dumond in *Weld-Grimké Letters*, 1:419 n.

100. *Garrison*, 2:148–149; *Weld-Grimké Letters*, passim. The best study of the marriage is Katherine Du Pre Lumpkin, *The Emancipation of Angelina*

Grimké (Chapel Hill: University of North Carolina Press, 1974).

101. Benjamin P. Thomas, *Theodore Weld: Crusader for Freedom* (New Brunswick, N.J.: Rutgers University Press, 1950), p. 142; Gerda Lerner, *The Grimké Sisters from South Carolina: Rebels against Slavery* (Boston: Houghton Mifflin Co., 1967), pp. 176–81; AEG to Jane Smith, July 25, 1837, Weld Papers, WLCL.

102. WJ (BPL), XXXVI, 50 (Nov. 8, 1837).

103. *Birney Letters*, 1:418, 421–22; *Whittier Letters*, 1:250–54.

104. WJ (BPL), XXXV, 178, 217 (Aug. 30, Sept. 26, 1837); XXXVI, 48–49 (Nov. 8, 1837).

105. My view of nonresistance is developed at greater length in *Rad. Ab.*, chap. 3.

106. WJ (BPL), XLVI, 86 (Sept. 23, 1841). Cf. the "heresy of the Free Spirit" as discussed in Norman Cohn, *The Pursuit of the Millennium*, 2d ed. (New York: Harper & Row, Torchbooks, 1961).

107. *Man-Killing*, p. 44.

108. Sarah Grimké and AEG to HCW, Aug. 27, 1837, Garrison Papers, BPL.

109. *Non-Resistant*, Feb. 2, 1839, p. 3.

110. *Lib.*, Nov. 7, 1840, p. 4.

111. *Lib.*, Sept. 9, 1842, p. 3.

112. Editions of *Kiss* continue down to Boston 1890 and a 1908 Welsh translation. *Advocate of Peace* is quoted in *Lib.*, June 23, 1843, p. 4; Phillips is quoted in *Catalogue of Spiritual, Reform, and Miscellaneous Publications* (Boston: Colby & Rich, 1873).

113. *Lib.*, Sept. 4, 1850, pp. 1–2.

114. *Lib.*, July 3, 1840, p. 4; Mar. 27, 1840, p. 4.

115. WJ (BPL), XLV, 224–25 (May 26, 1841); XLVI, 1, 83 (June 18, Sept. 21, 1841). *Non-Resistant*, June 1, 1839, p. 2; Nov. 24, 1841, p. 1. *Lib.*, July 16, 1841, p. 2; Aug. 27, 1841, p. 2.

116. *Lib.*, Mar. 23, 1842, p. 3.

117. *Whittier Letters*, 1:556; Charles Spear, Journal, May 22, 1842, BPL; *Lib.*, Apr. 8, 1842, p. 2.

118. William Benson, secretary, "The Manchester Peace Society to the London Peace Society. Report for 1843 Spring Quarter," BPL; *Lib.*, Apr. 24, 1836, p. 3; *Six Months*, pp. 26–27.

119. *Lib.*, Sept. 29, 1843, p. 3.

120. WJ (BPL), XXXVI, 4 (Dec. 30, 1846); Richard D. Webb to HCW, Feb. 22, 1846, Eng. Let. Less tactful is this correspondence about a poem he found, written in cipher, and making fun of an abolitionist blackbird: WJ (BPL), XXXVI, no pp. (Jan. 23, 1847). Zip Coon was a blackface dandy in the minstrel shows.

121. Wright's battles can be traced through his diaries and the "Scrapbooks of anti-slavery newspaper clippings, 1844–45, made by H. C. Wright," HCL. In this and the following paragraphs I am much indebted to C. Duncan

Rice, "The Scottish Factor in the Fight against American Slavery, 1830–1870" (Ph.D. diss., University of Edinburgh, 1969).

122. Louis Billington, "Some Connections between British and American Reform Movements, 1830–1860" (M.A. thesis, University of Bristol, 1966), p. 181. See also *Brit. and Am. Abolitionists,* p. 13 and passim.

123. Billington, "Some Connections," chaps. 2, 3.

124. I continue to follow Rice, whose view of Wright is a caustic one. See also George Shepperson, "The Free Church and American Slavery," *Scottish Historical Review* 30 (1951): 126–43; idem, "Thomas Chalmers, the Free Church of Scotland, and the South," *Journal of Southern History* 17 (1951): 517–37; idem, "Frederick Douglass and Scotland," *Journal of Negro History* 38 (1953): 307–21.

125. Rice, "Scottish Factor," pp. 316–17; Shepperson, "Free Church"; HCW, "Is Mamon or Is Not Mamon the Divinity of the 'Free' Church Folks," clipping from *Abroath Guide,* pasted in "Scrapbooks . . . 1844–45"; *Lib.,* June 19, 1846, p. 1.

126. *Farewell Letter from Henry C. Wright to the Committee of the Glasgow Emancipation Society* (Glasgow: D. Russell, 1847).

127. Sydney V. James, *A People among Peoples: Quaker Benevolence in Eighteenth-Century America* (Cambridge, Mass.: Harvard University Press, 1963).

128. WJ (HCL), XXXII–XXXIII, passim (1836–37); XXX, 103 (Aug. 9, 1836); XXXIII, 4 (Jan. 14, 1837).

129. *Lib.,* Jan. 26, 1844, p. 3; Feb. 9, 1844, pp. 1–2; Apr. 5, 1844, p. 2. The latter is "Letter from Henry C. Wright. No. 1," the first of dozens of such letters. See also the letter from Elizabeth Pease, *Lib.,* Feb. 2, 1843, p. 4.

130. "Letter from Richard [should read: James] Haughton," *Lib.,* Sept. 6, 1844, p. 3; Webb's letter in *Lib.,* Feb. 9, 1844, pp. 1–2; *Six Months,* pp. 9, 47, 86–88, 120–21, 269.

131. Steven Marcus, *Engels, Manchester, and the Working Class* (New York: Random House, Vintage Books, 1975) pp. 83–86.

132. *Practical Christian,* Jan. 8, 1848, p. 3; *Non-Resistant and Practical Christian,* Apr. 29, 1848, p. 1; WJ (BPL), no. 38b, unpaginated (Jan.–Apr. 1849); Adin Ballou, *History of the Hopedale Community, from Its Inception. . .* (Lowell, Mass.: Thompson & Hill, 1897), p. 181.

133. A striking contrast to Wright may be found in the Journal of Charles Spear (BPL), which frequently comments on the sales of Spear's book on *The Names and Titles of Jesus.* Spear thought that in doing good he was also doing well, and hoped that he would have taken the same radical course even if it were not profitable. For a study of an abolitionist who preceded Wright (and probably influenced him) in turning to health reform and pseudoscience, see J. R. Jacob, "La Roy Sunderland: The Alienation of an Abolitionist," *Journal of American Studies.* 6 (1972): 1–17. The best-known study of a reformer who began as a peddler and continued to search for wider audiences is Odell Shepard, *Pedlar's Progress: The Life of Bronson Alcott* (Boston: Little, Brown &

Co., 1937). Whittier had fantasies about himself as "a tin peddler," as I have noted in "The Panorama and the Mills: An Essay on *The Letters of John Greenleaf Whittier,*" *Civil War History* 22 (1976): 240. Weld was a traveling promoter of the "science of Mnemonics" prior to his evangelical career (Gilbert Hobbs Barnes, *The Anti-Slavery Impulse, 1830–1844* [New York: Harcourt, Brace & World, 1964], p. 12). Elizur Wright also had experience as a peddler, going from door to door with carpetbag in hand (Jane H. Pease and William H. Pease, *Bound with Them in Chains: A Biographical History of the Antislavery Movement* [Westport, Conn.: Greenwood Press, 1972], pp. 238–39). But no one has as yet written a general essay on this theme. There are suggestive comments, however, on reformers and new popular markets in Leonard Richards, *"Gentlemen of Property and Standing": Anti-Abolition Mobs in Jacksonian America* (New York: Oxford University Press, 1970), 68–73, 165–70; and David Brion Davis, *The Slave Power Conspiracy and the Paranoid Style* (Baton Rouge: Louisiana State University Press, 1970), pp. 24–31. I should also note that no one has surveyed the popular market for health, spiritualism, pseudoscience, and "progress" in the antebellum years, though a number of works comment on it indirectly. See, for example, Walters, "Erotic South" (n. 72 above); Constance Rourke, *Trumpets of Jubilee* (New York: Harcourt, Brace & Co., 1927); Kathryn Kish Sklar, *Catherine Beecher: A Study in American Domesticity* (New Haven, Conn.: Yale University Press 1973), pp. 205–6 and passim; Gail Thain Parker, *Mind Cure in New England: From the Civil War to World War I* (Hanover, N.H.: University Press of New England, 1973); Harry B. Weiss and Howard R. Kemble, *The Great American Water-Cure Craze: A History of Hydropathy in the United States* (Trenton, N.J.: Past Times Press, 1967); and most recently, R. Laurence Moore, *In Search of White Crows: Spiritualism, Parapsychology, and American Culture* (New York: Oxford University Press, 1977), pp. xiii, 13–14, 41, 61.

134. See WJ (BPL), nos. 38b, 39, unpaginated (June 1849).

135. Emma Hardinge, *Modern American Spiritualism: A Twenty Years Record. . .* (New York: The Author, 1870); *Lib.*, Jan. 21, 1853, p. 4; and the many attacks on the Old Testament in spring and summer 1849.

136. One Hopedalian remembered, probably falsely, that Wright had been "frozen out" of the community for this reason. See *Hopedale Reminiscences: Papers Read before the Hopedale Ladies' Sewing Society and Branch Alliance* (Hopedale, Mass.: 1910), p. 20.

137. WLG to Elizabeth Pease, July 2, 1842, Garrison Papers, BPL; *Kiss*, p. ix.

138. "Fate," in *Selections from Ralph Waldo Emerson*, ed. Stephen E. Whicher (Boston: Houghton Mifflin Co., 1957), pp. 330–31. On religious and physiological perfectionism, see Ronald G. Walters, *The Antislavery Appeal: American Abolitionism after 1830* (Baltimore: Johns Hopkins University Press, 1976), pp. 84–87; and Walters, *American Reformers, 1815–1860* (New York: Hill and Wang, 1978), pp. 145–172.

139. *Empire*, pp. 65–66.

140. *Rad. Ab.*, pp. 234–39, 257–58, 278–82. *Lib.*, Oct. 3, 1862, p. 2; Oct. 17, 1862, p. 2. HCW to Charles Sumner, Nov. 26, 1861, Sumner Papers, HCL.

141. *Lib.*, July 21, 1861, p. 3; *Garrison*, 4:110. For evidence of his search for information on war and politics with which to bolster his speeches and of the way in which politicians benefited from his soundings of public opinion, see HCW to Charles Sumner, Dec. 20, 1863, May 22, 1866, Sumner Papers, HCL.

142. HCW, *The War a Rebellion of Capital against Labor, to Enslave the Laborer* (n.p., n.d. [1864]). HCW, *The War: A Rebellion of the Minority against the Majority, to Sustain Slavery* (n.p., n.d. [1864]). *Lib.*, May 31, 1861, p. 3; Aug. 16, 1862, p. 3; Feb. 13, 1863, p. 3; Oct. 23, 1863, p. 3. HCW to Gerrit Smith, Smith Papers, GAL-S.

143. *Lib.*, Feb. 24, 1863, p. 4; Feb. 17, 1863, p. 2.

144. WJ (BPL), XLII, unpaginated (Jan. 14, Jan. 15, 1867).

145. *Lib.*, Dec. 15, 1865, pp. 3, 4; May 19, 1876, p. 4. HCW, *The Ballot: What Does It Mean? Who Shall Use It?* (n.p., n.d. [1865]).

146. WJ (BPL), no. 42, unpaginated (Jan. 18, Jan. 24, 1867).

147. *Garrison*, 4:279; WLG to Oliver Johnson, Nov. 7, 1870, WLG to Wendell Phillips, Nov. 27, 1870, Garrison Papers, BPL.

148. *Garrison*, 4:252–53; WLG to Oliver Johnson, Nov. 7, 1870, Garrison Papers, BPL; Lyman F. Hodge, *Photius Fisk: A Biography* (Boston, 1891), p. 138.

149. When *Garrison* appeared in the 1880s, it created an unpleasant stir among polite Bostonians by revealing the radical, schismatic, and contentious side of the now worshipped antislavery figure. Some persons argued that this aspect of the past ought to have been left buried (see *Whittier Letters*, 3:518–19). Wright's importance may first have been recognized in Louis Filler, *The Crusade against Slavery, 1830–1860* (New York: Harper & Row, 1960); further study of Wright is called for at p. 288.

150. *Living Present*, p. 11.

Chapter Two

1. *Life*, quotation from "History" on title page.

2. Perry Miller, ed., *The Transcendentalists: An Anthology* (Cambridge, Mass.: Harvard University Press, 1966), p. 496.

3. Max Stirner, *The Ego and His Own*, trans. Steven T. Byington (New York: Libertarian Book Club, 1963).

4. Philip Rieff, *Freud: The Mind of the Moralist* (Garden City, N.Y.: Doubleday & Co., Anchor Books, 1961), p. 57.

5. WJ (HCL), IV, 93 (Feb. 3, 1834).

6. *Living Present*, p. 10.

7. *Merits of Christ and Paine*, pp. 37–39.

8. WJ (HCL), IV, 159 (Feb. 12, 1834).

9. WJ (HCL), II, 47 (Oct. 11, 1833).

10. Quoted in Rieff, *Freud,* p. 45.

11. *Natick Resolution,* pp. 8–10.

12. Given the assumptions about human nature and self-examination underlying his autobiographical writings, we may take Wright as an exception to historians' complaint that their sources limit the validity of their essays in psychology. His scores of confessional diaries make the exception stronger. Because he lived in an era of different psychological assumptions from our own, however, this chapter ultimately depends on a kind of loose analogy with twentieth-century case histories, an analogy that may help us to comprehend, in the terms we know, the liberation and control Henry Wright secured from the professional life he made for himself. There are pitfalls in this kind of interpretation. The question of distinguishing unhealthy from adaptive defenses has vexed historians writing about controversial movements whose purposes they approve or deplore. Much of the scholarship on the psychology of antebellum reform has advanced or rebutted the charge that abolitionists were generally unhealthy. The relevant distinction in the literature of psychotherapy is whether a particular defense leads to symptom formation or healthy social adaptation, but this distinction may tempt the historian into useless polemics. On the one hand, much of the evidence on Wright's career could be characterized as symptom formation, as this chapter may indicate. On the other hand, if we view agitation against war, slavery, and familial oppression as beneficial service to society, then we are likely to stress social adaptation. It may be significant that other reformers, even when strenuously disagreeing with Wright, did not usually characterize him as unhealthy or mad. In addition, his contemporaries were either ignorant of, or extraordinarily discreet concerning, his terrible loneliness and sad attempts to assuage it—two salient themes of his personal papers. For further discussion of the problem of psychohistory and antebellum reform, see Lewis Perry, "Psychology and the Abolitionists: Reflections on Martin Duberman and the Neoabolitionism of the 1960s," *Reviews in American History* 2 (1973): 309–22.

13. *Life,* p. 24. For excerpts from *Life* placed in the context of pioneer experience in the "Cooper country," see Louis C. Jones, ed., *Growing Up in the Cooper Country: Boyhood Recollections of the New York Frontier* (Syracuse: Syracuse University Press, 1965).

14. *Life,* pp. 28, 140. For genealogy see p. 414 and nine back pages of WJ (BPL), no number, unpaginated (1848).

15. *Life,* pp. 27–28. Sometimes in later years, Wright confused the year of his mother's death with that of Miles's birth.

16. WJ (HCL), VII, 32–36 (July 26, 1834).

17. *Life,* p. 28.

18. Since World War II the loss of parents, temporarily or forever, has become a perennial subject of psychoanalytic studies. The classic work has been done by John Bowlby, whose writings have spurred comment by many

others. (See, for example, his "Grief and Mourning in Infancy and Early Childhood," *Psychoanalytic Study of the Child* 15 (1960: 9–52; and his latest statement, *Separation: Anxiety and Anger* [New York, 1973]). There is considerable controversy over Bowlby's formulations, which take their terminology from ethology. Is he wrong, for example, in assuming that behavioral responses to separation are the same for children as for adults? Does he neglect the stage of ego development of the mourner and propose, instead, an essentially physiological theory? Does he underemphasize the baby's physical and psychological needs for maternal *care* rather than "attachment"? (Some of these questions may be found in Anna Freud, "Discussion of John Bowlby's Work on Separation, Grief, and Mourning," *Writings of Anna Freud* [New York, 1969], pp. 167–86; or in Robert A. Furman, "Death and the Young Child: Some Preliminary Considerations," *Psychoanalytic Study of the Child* 19 [1964]: 321–33. Helpful summaries of the controversies may be found in Leopold Bellak, Marvin Hurvich, and Helen K. Gediman, *Ego Functions in Schizophrenics, Neurotics, and Normals* [New York: John Wiley & Sons, 1973], pp. 151–52; and Elsa Furst's review article in the *New York Times Book Review*, Nov. 25, 1973, pp. 31–37.) I do not think that the refinements of these controversies must influence our consideration of Wright's loss of his mother. What he recalled was confusion over whether she would return, profound feelings of desolation, and solace from conversations with an older sister about the lost mother. Such reactions are found throughout modern studies. What he did not recall was any experience of anger at her departure, probably because to have done so would have raised the question of his responsibility for her death. It would be hard to interpret Wright's grief work as successful because it did not meet Bowlby's criteria of protecting his ego and enabling him to withdraw from the love object.

19. *Six Months*, pp. 59, 142–43, 301, 305.

20. WLG to Elizabeth Pease, Feb. 28, 1843, Garrison Papers, BPL.

21. Misc. Writings, notebooks 4, 5. See WJ (BPL), IX, 148–49 (Sept. 19, 1834), where he said he would have cut out some remarks except for his desire to preserve the record.

22. WJ (BPL), XXIX, 62–65 (Jan. 1, 1846). When advised to hold back damaging information, Wright noted that he hated a cool, suspicious character. "There are those whom I wish to know all that is in me—to whom I would be perfectly transparent if I could. . . . I'll trust so fully that none will feel inclined to betray me" (WJ [BPL], no vol., p. 27 [July 27, 1843]). For other examples of the goal of transparency and the early loss of mother, see Jean Starobinski, *Jean-Jacques Rousseau, la transparence et l'obstacle* (Paris: Plon, 1957); Lewis S. Feuer, "The Dreams of Descartes," *American Imago* 20 (1963): 3–26.

23. *Living Present*, pp. 7, 13.

24. *Lib.*, July 28, 1843, p. 4.

25. WJ (BPL), IV, 16–17 (Feb. 10, 1844).

26. *Living Present*, pp. 95–99.

27. "Henry C. Wright's Manuscript," WRHS. On the identity of this woman, see chapter 4, pp. 204–11.

28. *Empire*, pp. 113–14.

29. *Empire*, p. 96. See also p. 130, where he traces a case of scrofula to a family background resembling his own.

30. *Empire*, pp. 69–70. His journals for 1834 and 1835 contain frequent accounts of his work with maternal associations, but I find no mention of intimate diaries kept by mothers.

31. Sarah H. Southwick, *Reminiscences of Early Anti-Slavery Days* (Cambridge, Mass.: Privately printed, 1893), p. 13.

32. *Helen Eliza Garrison: A Memorial* (Cambridge, Mass.: Riverside Press, 1876), p. 40; *Garrison*, 4:328.

33. *Lib.*, Aug. 22, 1862, p. 3.

34. HCW to Gerrit Smith, Jan. 19, Apr. 17, 1839, Smith Papers, GAL-S.

35. HCW to Gerrit Smith, Mar. 23, 1839, Smith Papers, GAL-S; *Union Herald*, quoted in *Lib.*, Mar. 27, 1840, p. 4.

36. *Life*, p. 23.

37. *Life*, p. 26; WJ (HCL), V, 199 (May 5, 1834); Henry Glassie, "The Variation of Concepts within Tradition: Barn Building in Otsego County, New York" (reprint ed., Cooperstown: New York State Historical Association, n.d.). Conversations with Henry Glassie have been very helpful to me in formulating this paragraph.

38. *Life*, p. 22.

39. From the Schreber case, as quoted in Morton Schatzman, *Soul Murder: Persecution in the Family* (New York: Random House, 1973), p. 160. On ruling by eye movements, see pp. 30, 36.

40. *Life*, p. 23.

41. *Life*, pp. 22, 91–92.

42. *Life*, pp. 81–84; *Six Months*, pp. 133–34.

43. John Demos, *A Little Commonwealth: Family Life in Plymouth Colony* (London: Oxford University Press, 1970), pp. 69, 149–50.

44. *Life*, pp. 35–36, 78–80; *The Journal of John Woolman* (New York: Corinth Books, 1961), pp. 2–3.

45. *Lib.*, Sept. 25, 1857, p. 4.

46. *Life*, pp. 29–31. In view of his own needs, discussed above, the "perplexities" arose from the lack of opportunity, at first, to dramatize and express his feelings.

47. *Life*, pp. 55–57. For an extremely important letter to his brother Moses, Dec. 6, 1848, written at the scene where Miles was almost suffocated, and professing his eternal love for all his brothers, see *Life*, pp. 409–10.

48. *Life*, p. 29.

49. *Life*, pp. 32, 40–41, 52–54.

50. *Life*, pp. 50–52, 62–63, 65; WJ (BPL), no number, pp. 85–87 (Apr. 16, 1843).

51. *Life*, pp. 63–65.

52. On the stage of "youth" and the emergence of adolescence, see Joseph F. Kett, "Adolescence and Youth in Nineteenth-Century America," *Journal of Interdisciplinary History* 2 (1971): 283–98.

53. *Life*, pp. 124–27. His sorrow at his treatment of his brother is underscored by repetition.

54. *Life*, p. 127.

55. *Life*, p. 132. Previously (p. 130) he links his vow not to show anger to sorrow over his treatment of Miles. Wright drafted an account of another whipping episode, but finally omitted it from *Human Life*. It was the story of a fellow apprentice, Chelson Cleavland, who had formerly been a schoolmate of Wright's. He was catlike, always in trouble, and much whipped. While watching him being severely whipped for breaking into the Brights' house, Wright reported: "I said nothing, but rather felt then that the whipping might have some effect to cure him of a habit of which I alone knew he had been guilty from a mere child." But Cleavland gave no tears and no confession. It was puzzling to Wright that he never stole for use or gain; he just plain was a thief. Phrenologists might discover that he had large organs of theft, theologians that he had too slight a conscience; and Wright reports asking why, if it was his natural propensity, chastisement was justified. But it was an unthinkable question: Wright did not yet have a theory of natural deformity from birth. He simply concludes that the episode strengthened his own aversion to stealing and cheating in business—a further step in his internalization of the whip. It is not hard to see why the anecdote did not fit in the final version of *Human Life*. See Fragments, pp. 611–26.

56. *Exercises at the Annual Examination of the Theological Society*, Andover, Mass., Sept. 26, 1821.

57. Misc. Writings, no. 2, inside cover; no. 4, covers; no. 5, covers and inside pages. Notes on Script., p. 1.

58. *Life*, pp. 204, 210; Misc. Writings, 1821, no. 5, unpaginated.

59. WJ (HCL), LII, 1–2 (Aug. 29, 1832); II, 9–10 (July 18, 1833); II, 39–40 (Aug. 8, 1833); II, 47 (Aug. 11, 1833); IV, 34 (Jan. 21, 1834). In this and the following paragraph I am obviously indebted to Sacvan Bercovitch, *The Puritan Origins of the American Self* (New Haven, Conn.: Yale University Press, 1975), esp. pp. 15–25, 165. The links between abolitionism and self-forgetfulness are discussed in my "The Panorama and the Mills: A Review of *The Letters of John Greenleaf Whittier*," *Civil War History* 22 (1976): 238–40.

60. *Kiss*, p. x; WJ (HCL), XLVIII, 65 (Apr. 12, 1842).

61. *Kiss*, p. 43 and passim.

62. *Kiss*, pp. 23, 24, 27, 34, 36, 45.

63. *Rad. Ab.*, pp. 32–54. For a contrasting side of reform, see David J. Rothman, *The Discovery of the Asylum: Social Order and Disorder in the New Republic* (Boston: Little, Brown & Co., 1971).

64. *Six Months*, pp. 285, 312, 338.

65. *Kiss*, pp. 51–58.

66. *Glasgow Argus*, reprinted in *Lib.*, Oct. 20, 1843, p. 4; *Six Months*, p. 102.
67. *Lib.*, Sept. 28, 1838, p. 2.
68. *Lib.*, May 28, 1841, p. 4.
69. *Def. War*, pp. 47–48; *Lib.*, Mar. 27, 1840, p. 4.
70. *Life*, p. 78. See also n. 55 above.
71. *Six Months*, pp. 89–91.
72. *Lib.*, Oct. 9, 1840, p. 3.
73. *Lib.*, Nov. 10, 1848, p. 3; Sept. 9, 1842, p. 3; WLG to Elizabeth Pease, Feb. 28, 1843, Garrison Papers, BPL.
74. *Salem Gazette*, quoted in *Lib.*, Sept. 23, 1842, p. 3; *Birney Letters*, 1:418; Susan Dow to Maria Weston Chapman, July 13, 1839, Weston Papers, BPL.
75. Bradford Torrey and Francis H. Allen, eds., *The Journals of Henry D. Thoreau* (New York: Dover Books, 1962), 5:264–65.
76. *Lib.*, May 24, 1839, p. 4.
77. *Lib.*, June 12, 1840, p. 4.
78. *Lib.*, July 24, 1840, p. 4.
79. *Lib.*, Nov. 22, 1839, p. 4; July 3, 1840, p. 4. HCW, *Duties of Abolitionists to Pro-Slavery Ministers and Churches* (Concord, Mass.: John R. French, 1841); Essex North Association Papers, EI.
80. *Lib.*, Apr. 13, 1838, p. 2. For discussion of the ability of abolitionism to identify itself with the cause of free speech, see Russel B. Nye, *Fettered Freedom: Civil Liberties and the Slavery Controversy, 1830–1860* (East Lansing: Michigan State University Press, 1963).
81. *Six Months*, pp. 238–45. Wright's 1838 reports make it seem doubtful that he faced the mob (*Lib.*, May 25, 1838, p. 3). The incident, as reported in *Six Months*, might be compared with Garrison's teasing of the mob that threatened him in 1835. "Are any of you *ladies*-in-disguise," he asked, in his account (conveniently available in George Fredrickson, ed., *William Lloyd Garrison* [Englewood Cliffs, N.J.: Prentice-Hall, Inc., 1968]). In Garrison's case there is an element of cowardice—of not facing up to a challenge—that is dealt with awkwardly. This taunting style of nonresistance might be contrasted with other styles stressing the bravery, dignity, or stoicism of the victim.
82. *Six Months*, pp. 125–26, 133–34, 275.
83. *Six Months*, pp. 195–97.
84. Karen Horney, *Neurosis and Human Growth: The Struggle toward Self-Realization* (New York: W. W. Norton, 1950), pp. 221–23. In a sensible essay on "Psychoanalysis and History," Fritz Schmidl argued that what the historian might gain from the psychoanalyst is not so much theoretical models as a "feel" for various *Gestalten* familiar in therapeutic practice, a recognition of ways in which symptoms and traits often fall together (*Psychoanalytic Quarterly* 31 [1962]: 532–48).
85. See Leon Salzman, *The Obsessive Personality: Origins, Dynamics, and Therapy* (New York: Science House, 1968).

86. Lewis Perry, "'We Have Had Conversation in the World': The Abolitionists and Spontaneity," *Canadian Review of American Studies* 6 (1975): 3–26.

Chapter Three

1. WJ (HCL), III, 83–87 (Oct. 16, 1833).
2. *Catalogue of Spiritual, Reform, and Miscellaneous Publications* (Boston: Colby & Rich, 1873), p. 8.
3. See Joseph F. Kett, "Growing Up in Rural New England, 1800–1840," in *Anonymous Americans: Explorations in Nineteenth-Century Social History,* ed. Tamara K. Hareven (Englewood Cliffs, N.J.: Prentice-Hall, Inc., 1971), pp. 1–16; Donald Scott, "Abolition as a Sacred Vocation," in *Antislavery Reconsidered: New Perspectives on the Abolitionists,* ed. Lewis Perry and Michael Fellman (Baton Rouge: Louisiana State University Press, 1979); and especially on revivalism in the cities, Paul E. Johnson, *A Shopkeeper's Millennium: Society and Revivals in Rochester, New York, 1815–1837* (New York: Hill & Wang, 1978). To counterbalance these discussions of male experience with a view of the meanings of submissiveness and role consciousness on the part of women, see Nancy F. Cott, *The Bonds of Womanhood: "Woman's Sphere" in New England, 1780–1835* (New Haven, Conn.: Yale University Press, 1977), pp. 126–59, 180.
4. *Life,* p. 147. See Kett, "Growing Up," p. 10, for the shift from the eighteenth-century pattern of conversion in one's late twenties to the nineteenth-century pattern of teen-age conversions.
5. *Life,* pp. 138–39.
6. Ibid., pp. 132–33.
7. Ibid., pp. 141–42; C. R. Johnson, *History of the First One Hundred Years of the First Congregational Church, Norwich, New York, 1814–1914* (Norwich, N.Y.: Chenango Union, 1914), pp. 32–35. On interdenominational cooperation, specifically in Norwich but also as typical of the New York revivals, see Whitney R. Cross, *The Burned-Over District: The Social and Intellectual History of Enthusiastic Religion in Western New York, 1800–1850* (New York: Harper & Row, Torchbooks, 1965), p. 42. Truair was a man of greater achievement than Wright's account of frontier revivalism may suggest. An engraved portrait (biographical file, PHS) shows a handsome, Napoleonic figure. His publications included *The Alarm Trumpet* (Montpelier, Vt., 1813); *A Discourse, Delivered at Shelburne, Nov. 24, 1814, Being the Day of Public Thanksgiving . . .* (Utica, N.Y.: Merrell & Camp. 1815); *A Short Treatise on Baptism* (Sangerfield, N.Y.: Tenny & Miller, 1816); and *A Call from the Ocean; or, An Appeal to the Patriot and Christian in Behalf of Seamen* (New York: American Seamen's Friend Society, 1826). Like Wright, he moved up from the western country via the empire of benevolence: he became minister of the Mariners' Church in New York and corresponding secretary of the American Seamen's Friend Society.

8. *Life*, pp. 142–43; Johnson, *History of the First One Hundred Years*, pp. 34–36. On the implications of revivalism for communities, see Perry Miller, *The Life of the Mind in America: From the Revolution to the Civil War* (New York: Harcourt, Brace & Co., 1965), bk. 1.

9. *Life*, pp. 146–49.

10. Ibid., p. 146.

11. *Lib.*, Nov. 6, 1857, p. 4.

12. *Life*, pp. 150–51.

13. Ibid., pp. 153–65.

14. Ibid., pp. 165–67.

15. "1818 Address." See also John A. Andrews, *Rebuilding the Christian Commonwealth: New England Congregationalists and Foreign Missions, 1800–1830* (Lexington: University of Kentucky Press, 1977).

16. HCW to Laura West Hartwick, July 20, 1818, BPL.

17. HCW to Laura West Hartwick, Sept. 2, 1818, BPL.

18. HCW to Laura West Hartwick, Sept. 25, 1818, BPL.

19. See generally: Daniel Day Williams, *The Andover Liberals* (New York: King's Crown Press, 1941), pp. 1–30; Leonard Woods, *History of the Andover Theological Seminary* (Boston: James R. Osgood, 1885); and Oliver A. Taylor, "Sketches, Statistics, Etc., of the Theological Seminary of Andover," *American Quarterly Register* 11 (1839): 63–81. For an excellent brief account of Andover's origins, see Henry F. May, *The Enlightenment in America* (New York: Oxford University Press, 1976), p. 318. On missionaries and distinguished graduates, see: Henry K. Rowe, *History of Andover Theological Seminary* (Newton, Mass., 1933), pp. 93–95 and passim; Leonard Woods, intro., *Memoirs of American Missionaries, Formerly Connected with the Society of Inquiry Respecting Missions . . .* (Boston: Peirce & Parker, 1833); and *A Memorial of the Semi-Centennial Celebration of the Founding of the Theological Seminary at Andover* (Andover, Mass., 1859). On the college backgrounds of Wright's classmates, see *Catalogue of Those Who Have Been Educated at the Theological School in Andover . . .* (Andover, Mass., 1821). On the origins of reform societies, see Woods, *History*, p. 199. On the origins of graduate education, see Natalie Ann Naylor, "Raising a Learned Ministry: The American Education Society, 1815–1860" (Ph.D. diss., Teachers College, Columbia University, 1971). On Wright's regimen, see *Life*, pp. 184–5, 203–7; on his membership in the Society of Inquiry see the manuscript records of that organization (Andover Newton Theological School).

20. *Life*, pp. 168–69, 210; Jerry Wayne Brown, *The Rise of Biblical Criticism in America, 1800–1870: The New England Scholars* (Middletown, Conn: Wesleyan University Press, 1969), p. 117; Taylor, "Sketches, Statistics," p. 69; *Catalogue of the Professors and Students of the Theological School, Andover, Mass.*, Feb. 1820; *Lib.*, Mar. 23, 1849, p. 4.

21. Sarah Stuart Robbins, *Old Andover Days: Memories of a Puritan Childhood* (Boston: Pilgrim Press, 1908), pp. 11–12, 29–55.

22. *Life*, pp. 207–8; Frank Hugh Foster, *A Genetic History of the New England Theology*, (1907; reprint ed., New York: Russell & Russell, 1963), p. 379; Woods, *History*, pp. 180–81; J. Earl Thompson, Jr., "Church History Comes to Andover: The Persecution of James Murdock," *Andover Newton Quarterly* 15 (1975): 213–27.

23. Williams, *Andover Liberals*, esp. pp. 11–12; Foster, *Genetic History*, p. 379.

24. *Memorial of the Semi-Centennial*, pp. 181–82.

25. In this paragraph I am much indebted to Brown, *Rise of Biblical Criticism*, esp. pp. 169–78.

26. Ibid.; *Memorial of the Semi-Centennial*, pp. 169–78.

27. Woods, *History*, pp. 173–78.

28. See Perry Miller, *The Transcendentalists* (Cambridge, Mass.: Harvard University Press, 1966); and more generally, Henry A. Pochmann, *German Culture in America: Philosophical and Literary Influences* (Madison, Wis.: University of Wisconsin Press, 1957), pp. 114–255, 304–7.

29. Notes on Script., pp. 69 ff.; *Life*, pp. 187–93.

30. Notes on Eccl. Hist., cover. It is instructive to compare the student's disciplined notes on the Bible with the superficial attempts to figure out the gospel meanings of "baptism" in his old preacher's *Short Treatise* (see n. 7 above).

31. *Life*, pp. 193–97; Notes on Script., Jan. 1, 1820, p. 37.

32. Misc. Writings, 1821, no. 2, covers and unnumbered back pages; no. 5, covers.

33. Misc. Writings, 1821, no. 1, unnumbered back pages.

34. Misc. Writings, 1821, no. 1, cover; WJ (HCL), VI, 315–25 (July 15, 1834).

35. Notes on Script., cover. Misc. Writings, 1821, no. 2, covers; no. 3, inside cover.

36. Misc. Writings, nos. 2, 5, unpaginated; Notes on Script., p. 116.

37. Misc. Writings, no. 2, back pages.

38. May, *Enlightenment*, esp. pp. 337–57; Morton White, *Science and Sentiment in America: Philosophical Thought from Jonathan Edwards to John Dewey* (New York: Oxford University Press, 1972), esp. pp. 11–24; Misc. Writings, nos. 1, 4, unpaginated; Notes on Script., pp. 12–16.

39. WJ (HCL), IV, 16–17 (Jan. 29, 1834).

40. Notes on Eccl. Hist., pp. 3–35, 59.

41. Ibid., p. 37.

42. Ibid., pp. 51–52.

43. Ibid., p. 58.

44. Notes on Script., pp. 5–10.

45. Misc. Writings, no. 2, unpaginated.

46. Ibid., nos. 1–3, unpaginated.

47. Ibid., nos. 1, 6, unpaginated.

48. Ibid., no. 3, esp. concluding pages; no. 4, unpaginated. The standard discussion of this subject, which strikes me as one that would repay further

examination, is H. Shelton Smith, *Changing Conceptions of Original Sin: A Study in American Theology since 1750* (New York: Scribner, 1955).

49. Misc. Writings, no. 5, unpaginated.

50. Misc. Writings, no. 6, unpaginated.

51. Misc. Writings, passim (quotation in no. 4, unpaginated).

52. *Life,* pp. 228–29; the license is tucked inside WJ (BPL), II (May–June 1828).

53. *Life,* pp. 248, 298; WJ (BPL), III (June–Aug. 1828), on the Book of Job; Misc. Writings, no. 6 (Oct. 1828–July 1829), on "The Hebrew Prophets & Their Writings."

54. *Life,* pp. 209, 237–38; Rev. C. D. Herbert, "Historical Sketch of the First Church & Parish of West Newbury," p. 49 and insert, EI. The latter was much edited and abbreviated when it appeared as "First Church in West Newbury, formerly Second Church in West Newbury," in *Contributions to the Ecclesiastical History of Essex County, Mass.* (Boston: Congregational Board of Publications, 1865), pp. 375–81.

55. Herbert, "Historical Sketch," p. 50. Rev. S. J. Spalding also conceded that HCW was "highly esteemed and eminently successful among his people" ("Sketches of the Members of the Essex North Association," in *Contributions to the Ecclesiastical History,* p. 148). For HCW's reflections on the children of his parish, see *Life,* pp. 245–46; "How Ministers May Get Access to Neighborhoods and Districts, from Which They Have Ever Been Excluded," *Boston Recorder,* Aug. 22, 1834, p. 133. HCW is conspicuously omitted from an account of church life in Newbury in *Whittier Letters,* 3:500–2.

56. Herbert, "Historical Sketch," pp. 51–52.

57. Ibid., pp. 54–55.

58. Spalding, "Sketches," p. 148; Essex North Association Papers, numerous entries, EI; Minutes of Council of Ministers, West Newbury, July 5, 1833 (copy), Garrison Papers, BPL.

59. *Life,* pp. 267–82.

60. WJ (HCL), LII, 51–52 (July 8, 1833); LII, 5, 27–28 (Nov. 11, 1832; June 2, 1833). For further examples of his monitory attitude, see *Life,* pp. 248–49, and a speech on "Teetotalism," tucked inside WJ (HCL), LIII, on the text, "Am I my brother's keeper."

61. *Life,* pp. 294–95.

62. See above, chapter 1, pp. 5–6.

63. "Christian Education," WJ (BPL), XIV, (n.d. [ca. 1829]); *Boston Recorder,* June 5, 1833, p. 89.

64. WJ (HCL), XL, 1 (Feb. 3, 1839); WJ (BPL), loose (Dec. 21, 1847).

65. WJ (HCL), LII, 48–52 (July 7–8, 1833).

66. This paragraph and the next are much indebted to Donald Scott, *From Office to Profession: The New England Ministry, 1750–1850* (Philadelphia: University of Pennsylvania Press, 1978).

67. Essex North Association Papers, EI, Jan. 15, Feb. 26, Apr. 23, June 26, Oct. 30, 1839; Jan. 1, 1840. WJ (HCL), XL, 25–38 (Feb. 26–28, 1839). WJ (BPL),

XLV, 105 (Dec. 17, 1840). *Lib.*, Nov. 22, 1839, p. 4; Feb. 19, 1841, p. 4. HCW, *Duty of Abolitionists to Pro-Slavery Ministers and Churches* (Concord, N.H.: John R. French, 1841).

68. "The Anti-Ministry Convention," clipping from *New York Evangelist* in Amos Bronson Alcott Papers, XIV, HCL; HCW, *Christian Church: Anti-Slavery and Non-Resistance Applied to Church Organizations* (Boston: Anti-Slavery Office, 1841), p. 7; *Lib.*, Mar. 14, 1845, p. 3. For discussion of similar events, see *Rad. Ab.*, chap. 4.

69. Notes on Eccl. Hist., pp. 69–72; Misc. Writings, volume on "Common Schools," pp. 1–8.

70. Nathaniel Hawthorne, *The American Notebooks,* ed. Charles M. Simpson (Columbus: Ohio State University Press, 1972), p. 178. I have discussed these themes in the lives of Theodore Dwight Weld and John Greenleaf Whittier in "'We Have Had Conversation in the World': The Abolitionists and Spontaneity," *Canadian Review of American Studies* 6 (1975): 7–14, and "The Panorama and the Mills: A Review of *The Letters of John Greenleaf Whittier,*" *Civil War History* 22 (1976): 236–53.

71. WJ (HCL), III, 27–28 (Sept. 28, 1833); XXXI, 27 (Aug. 29, 1836); III, 12 (Sept. 23, 1833).

72. WJ (HCL), VI, 174, 178 (June 24–25, 1834); IX, 45, 48 (Sept. 3, 1834).

73. WJ (HCL), II, 16, 92–93 (July 20, Sept. 11, 1833); XXIII, 151 (Sept. 5, 1835).

74. WJ (HCL), II, 21–22 (July 23, 1833). I am also instructed by conversations with Richard E. Ellis on the national debate over nullification.

75. WJ (HCL), IV, 92 (Feb. 14, 1834). See also my account of this view of the millennium in "Adin Ballou's Hopedale Community and the Theology of Antislavery," *Church History* 39 (1970): 6–7, 14–18.

76. WJ (HCL), IV, 194 (Feb. 14, 1834); XXVI, 152–53 (Dec. 20, 1835).

77. Notes on Eccl. Hist., pp. 3–28; Moses Stuart, Sermon of March 1818 (probably repeated for subsequent classes) on "My kingdom is not of this world" (microfilm, Stuart Manuscripts, Andover Newton Theological School). But the ambiguity of Wright's religious heritage becomes clear when we examine a controversial sermon by John Truair on the duty of Christians to oppose blasphemous and tyrannical rulers *(Discourse* [see n. 7 above]). Though his text was Daniel in the lion's den, he also referred to Jesus' response to oppression—*"resist not evil"*—very much as Wright would in later years. Truair warned that the irreligious constitution of the republic made it oppressive and impeded the approaching millennium.

78. HCW, *Self-Convicted Violators of Principle* (n.p., n.d. [ca. 1840]), p. 7. In 1838 WLG and Edmund Quincy reportedly declined to publish a similar tract on the grounds that it was too incendiary and would worsen existing controversies *(Garrison,* 2:253–54).

79. WJ (BPL), XLV, 37 (Oct. 31, 1840).

80. *Lib.*, Feb. 2, 1844, p. 4.

81. WJ (BPL), XXXVI, 134 (Jan. 8, 1838).

82. Ibid.

83. See these classic works on the logic of nonseparating Congregationalism: Perry Miller, *Orthodoxy in Massachusetts, 1630–1650* (1933; reprint ed., Gloucester, Mass.: Peter Smith, 1965); Edmund S. Morgan, *Visible Saints: The History of a Puritan Idea* (1963; reprint ed., Ithaca, N.Y.: Cornell University Press, 1965).

84. *Weld-Grimké Letters,* 2:705–6; *Lib.,* Oct. 28, 1838, p. 4; Sarah Grimké to HCW, Nov. 19, 1838, Garrison Papers, BPL; *Def. War,* p. 214 and passim.

85. Brown, *Rise of Biblical Criticism,* pp. 45–59, 94–110.

86. *Lib.,* Dec. 22, 1848, p. 1; Nov. 17, 1848, p. 1; Aug. 11, 1848, p. 1; Jan. 12, 1849, p. 3; Mar. 9, 1849, p. 4; Aug. 2, 1850, p. 3. *Brit. and Am. Abolitionists,* pp. 345–47, 358, 362–63, 440.

87. *Lib.,* Jan. 19, 1840, p. 4.

88. WJ (HCL), XV, 163 (Apr. 1, 1835); XXII, 122–23 (Aug. 6, 1835). *Lib.,* June 30, 1837, p. 2. For the student episode from the Andover side, see J. Earl Thompson, Jr., "Abolitionism and Theological Education at Andover," *New England Quarterly,* 47 (1974): 238–61.

89. *Lib.,* Mar. 23, 1849, p. 4.

90. *Lib.,* June 30, 1837, p. 2; Williams, *Andover Liberals,* pp. 24–25.

91. *Errors,* pp. iii–iv, 12, 76, 80, 85–91, 117–18.

92. Parker's *A Discourse on the Transient and Permanent in Christianity* is conveniently available, and well interpreted, in Miller, *Trancendentalists,* pp. 259–83.

93. HCW, *The Holy Bible and Mother Goose, As an Infallible and Authoritative Rule of Faith and Practice. What is the Difference between them?* (St. Louis: M. A. McCord, 1868); *The Blood of Christ and the Blood of Cock Robin. As an Atonement for Sin and a Means to Cleanse the Human Soul from Its Taint and Guilt—What is the Difference between Them* (n.p., 1869), esp. pp. 11–12; *Merits of Christ and Paine,* esp. pp. 18–19. These references apply to the following paragraph as well.

94. David Brion Davis, "The Nature and Limits of Dissent," in Bernard Bailyn et al., *The Great Republic,* (Lexington, Mass.: D. C. Heath & Co., 1977), pp. 544–58; Bertram Wyatt-Brown, "Prelude to Abolitionism: Sabbatarian Politics and the Rise of the Second Party System," *Journal of American History* 58 (1971): 316–41; Scott, *From Office to Profession.*

95. Emerson, "The Chardon Street Convention," *Lectures and Biographical Sketches* (Boston, 1884), p. 352.

96. WJ (BPL), no. 36, loose (May 16, 1847).

97. Walter M. Merrill, *Against Wind and Tide: A Biography of Wm. Lloyd Garrison* (Cambridge, Mass.: Harvard University Press, 1963), pp. 177–80, 243–44. *Lib.,* Nov. 27, 1840, p. 3. WJ (BPL), XXVI, 120 (Aug. 25, 1845); no vol. pp. 12–13 (Dec. 14, 1845); no. 36, loose (Dec. 2, 1847).

98. *Proceedings of the Anti-Sabbath Convention, Held in the Melodeon, March 23d and 24th,* reported by Henry M. Parkhurst (1848; reprint ed., Port Washington, N.Y.: Kennikat Press, 1971), pp. 4–5, 15–24, 42–50, 56–76, 117.

99. Ibid., pp. 7, 15, 30, 33–38, 118.

100. Ibid., p. 112.

101. *Garrison,* 3:219.

102. Quoted in *Proceedings,* p. 152. Wright's running notes at the convention convey a sense of personal contentment as well as admiration of his heroic friends—"a powerful fraternity of choice & tried spirits—that are thoroughly trained to face scorn, & obloquy with good-natured, but dauntless firmness." While marveling at the words of Burleigh, Parker, Mott, Alcott, Garrison, and Brown, however, he admitted there were "some curious & strange characters in this assembly—come here to let out their vagaries. Their dress & their hair & beard, & countenances, indicate a curious & strange empire in their souls" (WJ [BPL], XXXVIIb, 8–18, 1–8 [Mar. 23–24, 1848]).

103. HCW, *First Day Sabbath Not of Divine Appointment...* (Glasgow: William Symington Brown, 1846), p. 45.

104. Peter Gay, *The Enlightenment, an Interpretation: The Rise of Modern Paganism* (New York: Alfred A. Knopf, 1967); May, *Enlightenment,* pp. 253–304.

105. *Lib.,* Oct. 17, 1845, p. 3.

106. *Lib.,* June 18, 1852, p. 4.

107. *Merits of Christ and Paine.* On Paine's place in American radicalism, see Staughton Lynd, *Intellectual Origins of American Radicalism* (New York: Random House, Vintage Books, 1969); Eric Foner, *Tom Paine and Revolutionary America* (London: Oxford University Press, 1976). More particularly on religious free thought, see William O. Reichert, *Partisans of Freedom: A Study in American Anarchism* (Bowling Green, Ohio: Popular Press, 1976); and Albert Post, *Popular Free Thought in America, 1825–1850* (New York: Columbia University Press, 1943).

108. *Lib.,* Aug. 14, 1840, p. 4; and on the "philosophy of slavery," see above, pp. 30–31.

109. See HCW's reflections in WJ (BPL), XLI, 44 (Jan. 21, 1852). Adin Ballou and John Greenleaf Whittier were among the many reformers reaching similar resolutions. On the place of imposture in mid-nineteenth-century cultural experiences, see Neil Harris, *Humbug: The Art of P. T. Barnum* (Boston: Little, Brown, 1973), pp. 61–89; and on links between spiritualism and reform, see *Rad. Ab.,* pp. 213–22, 276–78, 292–93.

110. Emma Hardinge, *Modern American Spiritualism: A Twenty Years Record of the Communion between the Earth and the World of Spirits* (New York: The Author, 1870); J. R. Jacob, "La Roy Sunderland: The Alienation of an Abolitionist," *Journal of American Studies* 6 (1972): 1–17. For two more examples of local spiritualist conventions, see *Lib.,* July 25, 1856, p. 4; Oct. 17, 1856, p. 3. The importance of such events is noted in R. Lawrence Moore, "The Spiritualist Medium: A Study of Female Professionalism in Victorian America," *American Quarterly* 27 (1975): 211–12.

111. *Lib.,* Apr. 10, 1857, p. 4.

112. HCW to Chauncey Wright (his nephew), Aug. 6, 1862, Wright Papers, NYSHA; WLG to Julia Friend, July 31, 1862, Garrison Papers, BPL.

113. *Lib.*, Jan. 20, 1854, p. 1; Mar. 29, 1861, p. 3.

114. *Lib.*, Aug. 26, 1864, p. 4; Nov. 4, 1864, p. 4.

115. *Lib.*, Jan. 7, 1853, p. 4.

116. *Lib.*, Jan. 21, 1853, p. 4; May 27, 1853, p. 3; July 29, 1853, p. 4.

117. HCW to Chester Wright "within the veil," Jan. 11, 1863; HCW to Patience Wright, Jan. 13, 1863; and Chester Wright to HCW via Julia Friend, Jan. 12, 1863, all in Wright Papers, NYSHA.

118. "The Spirit of Jesus Communicating through the Rappings," as excerpted in *Practical Christian*, Sept. 13, 1851, p. 4. I have been unable to find this pamphlet, which is also apparently Emma Hardinge's source (n. 110 above), nor can I find it in the New York *Tribune*, Apr. 18, 1851, the source indicated in the *Practical Christian*. The excerpted version is, therefore, my source in these four paragraphs. On Leah Fox, see Herbert G. Jackson, *The Spirit Rappers* (Garden City, N.Y.: Doubleday & Co., 1972), pp. 20–57, 196–212.

119. *Practical Christian*, Aug. 2, 1851, p. 4.

120. *Lib.*, July 20, 1849, p. 2; Aug. 24, 1849, p. 4; Sept. 27, 1861, p. 4.

121. *Marriage*, p. 9.

122. WJ (BPL), XXXIX, loose (June 22, June 24, 1849); XXXVIIIb, loose (June 17, June 30, 1849). *Lib.*, Oct. 15, 1852, p. 4; Oct. 29, 1852, p. 3; Oct. 19, 1860, p. 3.

123. WJ (BPL), XLII, unpaginated (Mar. 26, Mar. 30, 1867).

124. HCW to Smith, Jan. 15, 1861, Jan. 13, 1861, Oct. 26, 1869, all in Smith Papers, GAL-S.

125. *Errors*, pp. 12–13.

126. The source for this and the following paragraph is: HCW to Smith, Mar. 16, 1865, Smith Papers, GAL-S. On HCW's conversion to abstinence, see *Life*, pp. 241–42.

127. *Oxford English Dictionary*, s.v. "Anthropology."

128. *Anthropology*, pp. 10, 14, passim; *Life*, p. 385 (Dublin quotation); and for some of the abundant examples of similar themes, *Lib.*, Aug 24, 1849, p. 4; Sept. 13, 1850, p. 4.

129. WJ (BPL), XI, 89 (Oct. 22, 1834).

130. Donald H. Meyer, *The Instructed Conscience: The Shaping of the American National Ethic* (Philadelphia: University of Pennsylvania Press, 1972). Meyer's attention to a "crisis of faith" among late-nineteenth-century intellectuals may appear to contradict my assertion of the sturdiness of orthodoxy. But he stresses that this relatively small intellectual class was ahead of the times in its "crisis" as in other things, and in fact sees the crisis "dramatized" as late as the Scopes trial of 1925. In pointing to a more widely held intuitive faith, rooted in a sense of dependency on a supreme being, he actually supports my view ("American Intellectuals and the Victorian Crisis of Faith," *American Quarterly* 27 [1975]: 585–603). The same points hold true

of many other analyses of nineteenth-century tensions between science and religion.

131. Eugene O'Neill, quoted in *Nine Plays,* intro. Joseph Wood Krutch (New York: Modern Library, 1932), p. xvii.

132. May, *Enlightenment,* pt. 4.

133. David Grimsted, "Melodrama as Echo of the Historically Voiceless," in *Anonymous Americans,* ed. Hareven (n. 3 above), pp. 80–98; Helen Papashevily, *All The Happy Endings* (New York: Harper, 1956).

Chapter Four

1. Natalie Zemon Davis, *Society and Culture in Early Modern France* (Stanford, Calif.: Stanford University Press, 1975), p. 120.

2. *Life,* pp. 209, 228; *Vital Records of Newburyport, Massachusetts, to the End of the Year 1849* (Salem, Mass.: Essex Institute, 1911), 1:365–67; Anna Lee Marston, ed., *Records of a California Family: Journals and Letters of Lewis C. Gunn and Elizabeth Le Breton Stickney* (San Diego: [The Editor], 1928), pp. 257–58.

3. John J. Currier, *History of Newburyport, Mass., 1764–1909,* 2 vols. (Newburyport, Mass.: The Author, 1906, 1909), 2:214–15; Marston, ed., *Records,* p. 7; Matthew Adams Stickney, *The Stickney Family: A Genealogical Memoir* (Salem, Mass.: The Author, 1869), pp. 257–58; "Deeds-Wills 1834–1846," Le Breton Family Papers, EI.

4. Stickney, *Stickney Family,* pp. 156–57; 257–58; Marston, ed., *Records,* p. 7.

5. "Bills and Receipts 1820 to 1829," "Deeds-Wills 1834–1846," Le Breton Family Papers, EI; Currier, *Newburyport,* 2:215.

6. "Deeds-Wills 1834–1866," "Deeds-Wills 1834–1846," Le Breton Family Papers, EI; Currier, *Newburyport,* 2:63.

7. Marston, ed., *Records,* pp. 7, 150–51.

8. *Life,* pp. 243–44.

9. *Life,* p. 209; Marston, ed., *Records,* p. 8. For stories about Mrs. Wright (and HCW) offending some parishioners by her pushiness on the temperance issue, see WJ (HCL), VI, 4–5 (Nov. 11, 1832). On early-nineteenth-century women and benevolence, see Nancy F. Cott, *The Bonds of Womanhood: "Woman's Sphere" in New England, 1780–1835* (New Haven, Conn.: Yale University Press, 1977), pp. 132–46.

10. *Life,* p. 247; Marston, ed., *Records,* pp. 9, 11; Angelina Grimké to Jane Smith, July 25, 1837, Weld Papers, WLCL; *Lib.,* Jan. 20, 1844, p. 4.

11. *Life,* p. 245; Hannah Lee Stickney to Susanna [Fisher], Feb. 12, 1844, postscript to Elizabeth L. B. Wright to Hannah Webb, Feb. 8, 1844, Garrison Papers, BPL; WJ (HCL), V, 314–16 (May 25, 1834).

12. WJ (HCL), II, 49 (Aug. 14, 1833); III, 50–51 (Oct. 8, 1833); IV, 26 (Jan. 16, 1834); VI, 16–17 (June 2, 1834); VII, 187 (July 13 [probably Aug. 13], 1834).

13. WJ (HCL), XII, 282 (Nov. 24, 1834); XXII, 141, 168–69, 177 (Aug. 12–14, 1835).

14. WJ (HCL), XXXI, passim (Sept. 1836).

15. Stickney, *Stickney Family*, pp. 373, 484; Marston, ed., *Records*, p. 6 and passim; Hannah Lee Stickney to Susanna [Fisher], n. 11 above; Hannah L. Stickney to Sarah Grimké, March 30, 1838, Weld Papers, WLCL.

16. *Lib.*, Dec. 19, 1835, p. 3; Oct. 22, 1836, p. 3; Sept. 27, 1839, p. 4; Nov. 22, 1839, p. 2. *Minutes of the Proceedings of the Requited Labor Convention, Held in Philadelphia . . . 1838* (Philadelphia: Merrihew & Gunn, 1838). Lewis C. Gunn, "An Address on [the] Duty of Abstaining from Slave Produce," ca. 1838, HSP.

17. Lewis C. Gunn, *The Age to Come! The Present Organization of Matter, Called Earth, to Be Destroyed by Fire at the End of This Age or Dispensation . . .*, rev. ed., Second Advent Library, no. 41 (Boston: Joshua V. Himes, [ca. 1844]); Marston, ed., *Records*, pp. 11–12.

18. WJ (BPL), no vol., p. 94 (Apr. 19, 1843).

19. Marston, ed., *Records*, passim.

20. Ibid., p. 11 and passim.

21. Ibid., p. 9. The quotation in the last sentence comes from a letter of one member of the family to me, May 14, 1973.

22. WJ (BPL), XL, 45–52 (Apr. 26, 1834). This citation supports the next paragraph too.

23. WJ (BPL), XL, 45–52 (Apr. 26, 1834); XVI, 142 (Apr. 30, 1835). WJ (HCL), XII, 325–26 (Dec. 1, 1834).

24. WJ (BPL), no vol., p. 12 (May 1843). For useful classifications of the ways in which older women avoided children, see "Victorian Women and Domestic Life: Mary Todd Lincoln, Elizabeth Cady Stanton, and Harriet Beecher Stowe," in *The Public and the Private Lincoln*, ed. Cullom Davis et al. (Carbondale, Ill: Southern Illinois University Press, 1979), pp. 20–37.

25. *Weld-Grimké Letters*, 1:455.

26. Sarah Grimké to Jane Smith, Mar. 24, 1838, WLCL; *Weld-Grimké Letters*, 2:661, 673; WJ (BPL), XXXVI, 217 (Apr. 24, 1838); Katherine Du Pre Lumpkin, *The Emancipation of Angelina Grimké* (Chapel Hill: University of North Carolina Press, 1974) chaps. 4–5.

27. Walter M. Merrill and Louis Ruchames, eds., *The Letters of William Lloyd Garrison* (Cambridge, Mass.: Harvard University Press, 1971), 1:570. Merrill notes a lovely example of children's love for HCW in *Against Wind and Tide: A Biography of Wm. Lloyd Garrison* (Cambridge, Mass.: Harvard University Press, 1963), p. 356.

28. Deborah Webb, "Reminiscences of Childhood" (1905), DFHL. For numerous other letters by and about children, see Eng. Let. On Elizabeth Pease Thompson, Wright's "playmate and comforter" before her death, see *Lib.* Sept. 18, 1846, p. 3; Jan. 29, 1847, p. 2.

29. *Life*, p. 70; and on the picture, *Lib.*, Aug. 18, 1848, p. 3; Sept. 8, 1848, p. 4.

30. Catherine Paton to HCW, Nov. 22, 1846, Nov. ?, 1846, Dec. 25, 1846, Eng. Let.; WJ (BPL), Aug. 7, 1845.

31. *Kiss*, p. 53.

32. *Life*, pp. 116–18.

33. *Life*, pp. 303–4.

34. WJ (NYHS), cover; Sarah Poole to HCW, Dec. 19, 1846, Eng. Let. Ages have been established with the aid of the staff of DFHL.

35. WJ (NYHS), pp. 99, 164 (Dec. 11, 1842, Jan. 20, 1843).

36. WJ (NYHS), p. 101 (Dec. 12, 1842); *Brit. and Am. Abolitionists*, pp. 97–98. The latter is an excellent source on the Irish women.

37. "Recollections of Lizzie Poole Addey. written about 1875," in Deborah Webb, "Reminiscences of childhood," DFHL.

38. Sarah Poole, "Short Account of the life of Joseph Poole up to 7 mo: 1852," DFHL.

39. WJ (BPL), no vol., p. 98 (Aug. 17, 1843). The best account of Pease is in C. Duncan Rice's forthcoming study of "The Scots Abolitionists."

40. WJ (BPL), no vol. pp. 148–70 (May 6–10, 1843), 134 (June 23, 1843), 2 (July 18, 1843), 25–26 (July 27, 1843), 101 (Aug. 17, 1843), 118 (Aug. 26, 1843), 122 (Aug. 27, 1843), 130 (Aug. 29, 1843). During the summer he covered his traces with a public letter (*Lib.*, July 28, 1843, p. 3), saying the artificiality of London was bearable only because of "The Company of E. P.," who had given him the same tour she gave Nathaniel Rogers and Garrison. He told the latter, again publicly, "You do, indeed, *live* in her heart. . . . It is very pleasant to live in such a heart as hers."

41. *Lib.*, July 28, 1843, pp. 2–3.

42. See, for example, EP to Ann Weston, Sept. 27, 1843, Weston Papers, BPL; EP to Sarah Grimké, n.d., Weld Papers, box 18, WLCL; or even EP to HCW, several examples in Eng. Let. To Wendell and Ann Phillips she wrote: "His company is a brook by the way, an oasis in a desert, a bright, delightful, heart-cheering one in the midst of this ceremony-ridden, formality-loving, etiquette-worshipping, caste-enslaving world" (Anna M. Stoddart, *Elizabeth Pease Nichol* [London: J. M. Dent; New York: E. P. Dutton, 1899], p. 145).

43. WJ (BPL), no vol., pp. 107 (Aug. 19, 1843), 122 (Aug. 27, 1843).

44. WJ (BPL), no vol., pp. 107 (Aug. 18, 1843), 113 (Aug. 24, 1843), 122 (Aug. 27, 1843), 135–36 (Sept. 1, 1843).

45. WJ (BPL), no vol., p. 137 (Sept. 2, 1843).

46. WJ (BPL), no vol., pp. 154–55 (Sept. 9, 1843), 164 (Sept. 11, 1843), 171 (Sept. 13, 1843). WJ (BPL), XVIII, unpaginated (Dec. 30, 1843). *Lib.*, Mar. 1, 1844, p. 3.

47. See Graefenberg diaries (WJ [BPL]) for Feb. 1844, passim.

48. E. A. Baker to HCW, Oct. 29, 1845, June 1846, Eng. Let. WJ (BPL), XIX, 1–14 (Feb. 28, 1844), 16, 46 (Mar. 1–2, 1844).

49. *Lib.*, Apr. 4, 1845, p. 1; June 20, 1845, p. 1.

50. WJ (BPL), I, 1–16 (Dec. 16, 1843).

51. *Life*, pp. 72, 75–76; WJ (BPL), XXXVI, loose pages (May 29, 1847).

52. WJ (BPL), no vol., unbound (Nov. 10, 1846); XXXVI, unbound (Jan. 8, Jan. 16, 1847).

53. WJ (BPL), no vol., unbound (Oct. 27–28, Oct. 31, Nov. 1–3, Nov. 9, 1846).

54. WJ (BPL), no vol., unbound (Nov. 1–2, Nov. 17, Dec. 12, 1846); WJ (BPL), XXXVI, unbound (Jan. 4, 1847).

55. WJ (BPL), no vol., unbound (Nov. 18, 1846).

56. WJ (BPL), no vol., unbound (Nov. 10, 1846).

57. Ibid.

58. WJ (BPL), no vol., unbound (Nov. 9, 1846); Sarah Poole to HCW, Mar. 19, 1846, Eng. Let.; Sarah Poole to HCW, Nov. 20, 1846, Eng. Let.

59. R. D. Webb to Edmund Quincy, Oct. 2, 1846, Webb-Quincy Papers, BPL; Webb to Samuel May, Jan. 9, 1857, May Papers, BPL; Webb to Quincy, Nov. 3, 1870, Webb-Quincy Papers, BPL. I am indebted for these references to Douglas Riach, the authority on Irish antislavery, who argues on the basis of Webb's responses to other scandals that he would not have hesitated to say so, "whatever the consequences," if he had had "definite evidence that anything untoward was going on" between HCW and Maria Waring (personal communication, Aug. 6, Sept. 6, 1973).

60. R. D. Webb to Anne Weston, Nov. 6, 1849; Webb to Maria Weston Chapman, July 5, 1849; Webb to [?] Weston, July 25, 1851; Webb to Maria Weston Chapman, Sept. 25, 1857; Webb to [?] Weston, Nov. 28, 1858; all in Weston Papers, BPL.

61. WJ (BPL), no vol., unbound (Nov. 20, Dec. 14, 1846); HCW to "M. W.," extract in WJ (BPL), no vol., "Miscellaneous" (Dec. 26, 1849).

62. WJ (BPL), no vol., p. 127 (July 1844). The BPL has recently catalogued this volume under the title: "Notes on theology of marriage and propagation, Darlington, Eng., etc., 1843–1844." Hereafter cited: "Notes on Marriage."

63. Derek Hudson, *Munby, Man of Two Worlds: The Life and Diaries of Arthur J. Munby, 1828–1910* (Boston: Gambit, 1972), p. 18. Munby, poet and student of lower-class life, lived for years with a wife who appeared to friends and company only as his maid.

64. "Notes on Marriage," pp. 1–7 (May 1843). At this time his hostess wrote: "It has nourished my unruly heart and done it good to hold communion with a man who has such a heart for humanity under every aspect. And such a heart, too. I'm sure there's not one beating on this globe . . . that surpasses it in size, in purity and in love" (Stoddart, *Elizabeth Pease Nichol*, p. 145).

65. "Notes on Marriage," pp. 9–17 (May 1843).

66. Ibid., pp. 138–39 (July 1844).

67. Ibid., pp. 143, 145, 148–51 (July 1844). See the discussion of physiological perfectionism in chapter 1 above, pp. 53–54.

68. Notes on Marriage," pp. 21–25 (May 1845).
69. Ibid., p. 236 (July 1847).
70. Ibid., pp. 27–30 (July 1847).
71. Ibid., p. 131 (July 1847).
72. Ibid., p. 59 (June 1845).
73. Ibid., loose undated fragment.
74. Ibid., pp. 75–81 (Aug. 1847).
75. *Lib.*, Sept. 10, 1847, p. 2; Sept. 17, 1847, p. 3. WJ (BPL), XXXIV, 8 (Aug. 31, 1847).
76. WJ (BPL), no vol. p. 119 (Apr. 24, 1843); no vol., p. 26 (June 14, 1843); no vol., p. 1 (July 18, 1843); no vol., p. 231 (Oct. 4, 1843). Elizabeth L. B. Wright to Hannah Webb, Feb. 8, 1844, Garrison Papers, BPL.
77. See 1857 letter in n. 59 above.
78. WJ (BPL), no vol. p. 119 (Apr. 26, 1850); XL, 113–14 (May 11, 1850); XLI, 18 (Jan. 13, 1852).
79. Elizabeth Cady Stanton et al., *History of Woman Sufferage,* 3 vols. (Rochester, N.Y.: Susan B. Anthony, 1876–85), 1:310–11; Charles Burleigh Galbreath, "Anti-Slavery Movement in Columbiana County," *Ohio Archeological and Historical Quarterly* 30 (1921): 355–95; WJ (BPL), XL, 58 (Apr. 27, 1850). The family may well have tolerated quite a show of affection, and there are indications in Wright's diaries that they shared most, if not all, of his intimacies with Hetty. The situation faintly resembles other marriages, analyzed by Carroll Smith-Rosenberg, in which husbands got out of the way of wives' intimacies with female friends. It is an instance of Smith-Rosenberg's generalization that nineteenth-century American culture permitted great diversity of sexual and affectionate practice. See her "The Female World of Love and Ritual: Relations between Women in Nineteenth-Century America," *Signs* 1 (1975): 1–29.
80. *Anthropology,* pp. 17–18; WJ (BPL), XXXVIIIb, unpaginated (Mar. 30, 1849).
81. WJ (BPL), XL, 53, 58 (Apr. 27, 1850).
82. WJ (BPL), XL, 53–54 (Apr. 27, 1850), includes this tirade. Wright disliked the idea of men leaving their families to look for gold. They went beyond the boundaries of permissible itinerancy, presumably because the quest for gain was so overt. "Husbands and fathers indeed!" he sneered to Hetty (WJ [BPL], XLI, 54 [Jan. 26, 1852]).
83. WJ (BPL), XL, 52 (Apr. 26, 1850).
84. Ibid., pp. 56–57.
85. WJ (BPL), XL, 45 (Apr. 25, 1850).
86. "Henry C. Wright's Manuscript," WRHS. This is the source for the succeeding paragraphs. It has been erroneously identified as a collection of Wright's fiction (see Louis Filler, *The Crusade against Slavery* [New York: Harper & Row, 1960], p. 120) or as Wright's memories (in my earlier papers and drafts of this book). The facts tracing it to Esther Lukens include: its references to a Garrisonian family, to the state of Ohio, to the name Esther, to

the names of other members of her family—and, of course, her intimacy with HCW. I could not have made this identification without genealogical references furnished by Mrs. Virginia R. Hawley of WRHS.

87. Among many useful guides to the experience of nineteenth-century women, this paragraph relies most heavily on Cott, *Bonds of Womanhood;* Perry Miller, ed. and intro., *Margaret Fuller: American Romantic* (Ithaca, N.Y.: Cornell University Press 1970); Kathryn Kish Sklar, *Catherine Beecher: A Study in American Domesticity* (New Haven, Conn.: Yale University Press, 1973).

88. HCW, Last Will and Testament, Sept. 3, 1866, Probate Court, Suffolk County, Mass.; Wendell Phillips to Julia Friend Carpenter, July 2, 1873, J. Hendrix McLane Papers, Yale University Library, New Haven, Conn. Where did HCW get the money? Probably from lecturing and from the Hovey bequest (see *Garrison,* 3:477–78).

89. The pitifully few facts about this remarkable life are taken from Albert Emerson Carpenter, *Plain Instructions in Hypnotism and Mesmerism, with Psychic Experiences* (Boston: Lee & Shepard, 1900); and Herbert J. Seligmann, *A South Carolina Independent of the 1880s: J. Hendrix McLane* (New York: Privately published, 1965). Her daughter, Fanny Clifford Friend, married McLane in 1887.

90. See, e.g., WJ (BPL), XLII, unpaginated (Jan. 9, 1867).

91. WJ (BPL), XLII, unpaginated (Jan. 28, Jan. 31, Feb. 16, Mar. 17, 1867).

92. HCW to Julia Wass Friend, July 7, 1865, extract in WJ (BPL), no vol., "Miscellaneous"; WJ (BPL), XLII, unpaginated (Mar. 2, 1867).

93. WJ (BPL), XLII, unpaginated (Feb. 16, Mar. 2, Mar. 5, Mar. 14, Mar. 17, 1867).

94. WJ (BPL), XLII, unpaginated (Mar. 18, Mar. 21, Apr. 13, 1867).

95. WJ (BPL), XLII, unpaginated (Mar. 26, Mar. 30, 1867).

96. WJ (BPL), XLII, unpaginated (Apr. 10, May 6, Aug. 9, Sept. 22, Sept. 24, 1867).

97. WJ (BPL), XLII, unpaginated (Apr. 15, 1867, Dec. 13, 1867).

98. Unbound diary, Aug. 19, 1867, Fragments, p. 129.

99. *Catalogue of Spiritual, Reform and Miscellaneous Publications* (Boston: Colby & Rich, 1873), p. 19; HCW to Gerrit Smith, Oct. 26, 1869, and Nov. 2, 1869, Smith Papers, GAL-S.

100. Julia M. Friend, *The Chester Family; or, The Curse of the Drunkard's Appetite* (Boston: William White, 1869), pp. 14–15.

101. Ibid., pp. 28, 35–36, 97, and quotation at 131.

102. Ibid., pp. 19–20, 141–46.

103. Ibid., pp. 18, 133–35.

104. WJ (HCL), V, 149, 215 (Apr. 20, May 9, 1843); XII, 127 (Nov. 10, 1834). *Boston Recorder,* Feb. 20, 1834, pp. 29–30. On the alliance between ministers and ladies, see Cott, *Bonds of Womanhood,* chap. 4; Ann Douglas, *The Feminization of American Culture* (New York: Alfred A. Knopf, 1977), pt. 1.

105. WJ (HCL), XII, 164–65 (Nov. 13, 1834); WJ (BPL), X, 44 (Sept. 25,

1834); XI, 3–4, 91–92 (Oct. 15, Oct. 24, 1834); XVI, 135–36 (Apr. 29, 1835); XXVI, 140 (Dec. 16, 1835).

106. The best analysis appears in David Brion Davis, "The Family and Boundaries in Historical Perspective," in *The American Family: Dying or Developing*, ed. David Reiss (New York: Plenum, 1979).

107. The outstanding guide both to changes in women's lives and to accompanying ideological shifts is Cott, *Bonds of Womanhood.* Still useful is Anne L. Kuhn, *The Mother's Role in Childhood Education: New England Concepts, 1830–1860* (New Haven , Conn.: Yale University Press, 1947).

108. WJ (HCL), XII, 91, 96–97, 174–75 (Nov. 8, Nov. 14, 1834).

109. *Lib.*, Dec. 26, 1835, p. 2; Jan. 2, 1836, pp. 2–3.

110. *Lib.*, Nov. 7, 1885, p. 4; Dec. 7, 1855, p. 4. WJ (BPL), XLIV, 48 (Aug. 29, 1840).

111. *Lib.*, Dec. 24, 1836, p. 3. On McDowall's early career, see Carroll Smith-Rosenberg, *Religion and the Rise of the American City: The New York City Mission Movement, 1812–1870* (Ithaca, N.Y.: Cornell University Press, 1971), pp. 98–109.

112. *Lib.*, Sept. 6, 1834, p. 4. The same article appeared again (Nov. 15, 1834, p. 4)!

113. *Lib.*, Aug. 30, 1839, p. 3.

114. Lippard, *The Monks of Monk Hall* (New York: Odyssey Press, 1970), p. 85. On the problem of woman's traditional image, see Davis, "Woman on Top," in *Society and Culture in Early Modern France* (n. 1 above), pp. 124–51.

115. Daniel Scott Smith, "Family Limitation, Sexual Control, and Domestic Feminism in Victorian America," *Feminist Studies* 1 (1973): 40–57; Robert V. Wells, "Family History and Demographic Transition," *Journal of Social History* 9 (1975): 1–19.

116. AEG to Jane Smith, May 29, 1837, Weld Papers, WLCL. Cf. the premarital discussions of sex in *Weld-Grimkė Letters*, 2:581–83, 587–88. On the expansion of "moral reform" to audiences outside New York, see Smith-Rosenberg, *Religion*, pp. 107–8, 119.

117. On the links between antislavery and feminism, see essays by Ellen Dubois and Blanche G. Hersh in *Antislavery Reconsidered: New Perspectives on the Abolitionists*, ed. Lewis Perry and Michael Fellman (Baton Rouge: Louisiana State University Press, 1979); Donald Meyer, *The Positive Thinkers* (Garden City, N.Y.: Doubleday & Co., Anchor Books, 1966) pp. 34 ff.; David J. Pivar, *Purity Crusade: Sexual Morality and Social Control, 1868–1900* (Westport, Conn.: Greenwood Press, 1973), pp. 34–43.

118. A good example is Charles Burleigh, whose diary (HSP) reveals clandestine relationships much like Wright's. He responded to scandal by asserting that "men and women should meet as equal human souls . . . [and that] sex should be no barrier to the exercise of intimacy and friendship" (p. 191).

119. My view of reform is influenced by Aileen S. Kraditor, "American Radical Historians on Their Heritage," *Past and Present* 56 (1972): 136–53; and David Brion Davis, *The Problem of Slavery in the Age of Revolution, 1770–1823*

(Ithaca, N.Y.: Cornell University Press, 1975), pp. 348 ff.

120. J. W. Page, *Uncle Robin in His Cabin in Virginia and Tom without One in Boston* (Richmond, Va.: J. W. Randolph, 1853), pp. 152–53.

121. George Fitzhugh, *Cannibals All! or Slaves without Masters,* ed. C. Vann Woodward (Cambridge, Mass.: Harvard University Press, 1960), chap. 20; Eugene D. Genovese, "The Logical Outcome of the Slaveholders' Philosophy," *The World the Slaveholders Made* (New York: Pantheon Books, 1969), pp. 118–24; *Rad. Ab.*, pp. 26–32.

122. *Boston Recorder,* Oct. 30, 1835, p. 175; E. P. Thompson, "The Sale of Wives in Eighteenth and Nineteenth Century England," paper delivered at Yale University, March 22, 1976.

123. *Lib.*, Nov. 26, 1841, p. 3.

124. *Lib.*, Feb. 26, 1841, p. 4.

125. See chapter 1 above, pp. 33–35.

126. WJ (HCL), XII, 165 (Nov. 13, 1834).

127. For a subtle discussion of institutional "carriers," see Peter Berger, Brigitte Berger, and Hansfried Kellner, *The Homeless Mind: Modernization and Consciousness* (New York: Random House, Vintage Books, 1974). On the pervasiveness of the theme of the wife's control over sexuality in the nineteenth-century manuals for married couples, see Smith, "Family Limitation," p. 50. According to one lecturer whom Smith cites, "marital excess was the topic best received by his female audience . . . of the 1850's."

128. HCW, "The One Supreme Object of Devotion—How to Attain It," broadside (Boston, 1855), also in *Lib.*, Jan. 11, 1856, p. 4; *Lib.*, Mar. 27, 1857, p. 3; Jan. 4, 1856, p. 4.

129. "The Blood of Woman & The Blood of Christ" (August 1845) in WJ (BPL), XI, "Lectures and Anecdotes on Slavery."

130. *Anthropology*, pp. 28–29, 61–62, and passim. Charles Rosenberg makes it clear that Wright's views of heredity were widely shared by other writers of the period. See Rosenberg's "The Bitter Fruit: Heredity, Disease, and Social Thought in Nineteenth-Century America," *Perspectives in American History* 8 (1974): 189–235.

131. *Marriage*, pp. 4, 242–43, 278. On declining fertility rates, see n. 115 above.

132. *Marriage*, pp. 22–27.

133. Son of a well-known Brisol Unitarian family, Carpenter studied medicine with a prominent abolitionist, Dr. John Estlin, with whom he visited the West Indies. He has been described as "an almost universal naturalist," whose curiosities ranged from shells to the unconscious mind, from the ocean to physiology. His work on *The Principles of General and Comparative Physiology* (1839) was "the first English book which contained adequate conceptions of a science of biology" (DNB, s.v. "Carpenter").

134. *Marriage*, pp. 268–69; review by Charles Whipple in *Lib.*, Sept. 29, 1854, p. 4. See also Ben Barker-Benfield, "The Spermatic Economy: A Nineteenth Century View of Sexuality," *Feminist Studies* 1 (1972): 45–74.

135. *Marriage*, pp. 66–136 (quotation at 78), 245–46. For echoes of HCW's bouts with masturbatory inclinations, see WJ (HCL), III, 12 (Sept. 23, 1833); cf. the struggle of another reformer in Bertram Wyatt-Brown, *Lewis Tappan and the Evangelical War against Slavery* (Cleveland: Press of Case-Western Reserve University, 1969), p. 41. Two of the many recent studies of nineteenth-century "anti-onanism" are Steven Marcus, *The Other Victorians* (New York: Bantam Books, 1966), chap. 1; and John S. Haller, Jr., and Robin M. Haller, *The Physician and Sexuality in Victorian America* (Urbana: University of Illinois Press, 1974), passim.

136. *Marriage*, pp. 10, 90–100.

137. *Marriage*, pp. 137–319.

138. Ibid., pp. 264–65.

139. Ibid., pp. 261–63; Carl N. Degler, "What Ought to Be and What Was: Women's Sexuality in the Nineteenth Century," *American Historical Review* 79 (1974): 1467–90.

140. *Marriage*, pp. 260–61; *Rad. Ab.*, pp. 226–27.

141. *Marriage*, pp. 269; 284. On the theme that women actually enjoyed sex, once freed from coercion and fear of maternity, see Linda Gordon, "Voluntary Motherhood: The Beginnings of Feminist Birth Control Ideas in the United States," *Feminist Studies* 1 (1973): 7, 13–14. I believe Wright's adoption of this theme reflected his numerous interviews with wives and mothers.

142. John Humphrey Noyes, *Bible Communism; A Compilation of the Annual Reports and Other Publications of the Oneida Association . . .* (Brooklyn: Circular, 1853), p. 46. Two recent studies of Noyes are Raymond Lee Muncy, *Sex and Marriage in Utopian Communities: Nineteenth Century America* (Bloomington: Indiana University Press, 1973), pp. 160–96; and Robert David Thomas, *The Man Who Would be Perfect: John Humphrey Noyes and the Utopian Impulse* (Philadelphia: University of Pennsylvania Press, 1977).

143. "Amativeness being the profitable part, and propagation the expensive part of the sexual relation, it is evident that a true balance between them is essential to the interests of the vital economy. If expenses exceed income, bankruptcy ensues" (*Bible Communism*, p. 46).

144. Ibid., pp. 51–52. For Wright's use of the analogy to scientific agriculture, see *Marriage*, p. 90; *Empire*, p. 12.

145. *Bible Communism*, pp. 50–51. Noyes's program was to widen the control of mind over supposedly involuntary aspects of the body.

146. If Wright favored the Noyesian system, he would probably have practiced it (and left some record in his journals). As an author, he left the inference open as part of his effort to secure the largest possible audience. But both points are far from certain.

147. *Errors*, pp. 16–19, 52–57, 115–116.

148. *Errors*, pp. 61–62, 71–72, 85–89.

149. See, e.g., John Cowan and W. R. C. Latson, *What All Married People Should Know* (1903), as quoted in *The Female Experience in America: A*

Documentary History, ed. Gerda Lerner (Indianapolis: Bobbs-Merrill Co., 1977), pp. 424–28. Lerner elsewhere described Wright as a "happily married man" who developed "strikingly modern ideas of marriage and education, which he published and dispensed by direct consultation in an informal marriage counseling service" (*The Grimké Sisters from South Carolina: Rebels against Slavery* [Boston: Houghton Mifflin Co., 1967], p. 177).

150. *Unwelcome*, pp. 31–32.

151. Ibid., pp. 33, 104.

152. Ibid., pp. 14–15, 26, 73–84, 88–89, 103. For the analogy between drink and sex, see this comment (p. 180) from a remorseful sensualist to his wife: "the blur of selfish, craving passion, would come over my sight, and I would go on my old way, cheating myself always, and sometimes you, into the feeling that it was all right."

153. *Unwelcome*, pp. 18–21. His authority on lactation was Carpenter (n. 133 above).

154. *Empire*, pp. 47, 54–58, 116.

155. Ibid., p. 15.

156. *Self-Abnegationist*, pp. 15–16, 51–52.

157. Ibid., pp. 23–29, 36–37, 97–100. C. B. Macpherson, *The Political Theory of Possessive Individualism: Hobbes to Locke* (Oxford: Clarendon Press, 1962); Genovese, "Logical Outcome," pp. 154–58.

158. *Self-Abnegationist*, pp. 36–37, 97–100. See also Davis, *Problem of Slavery in the Age of Revolution*, chaps. 8–9.

159. *Self-Abnegationist*, pp. 72–75, 85–89. In *Marriage* (p. 160) he had counseled that it was unnatural for a woman to "take the attitude of independence towards man," that it was natural for her "to rest in strength and wisdom superior to her own" (p. 171).

160. See chapter 2 above, pp. 68–69.

161. *Living Present*, pp. 70–79, 91–93; William G. McLoughlin, *The Meaning of Henry Ward Beecher: An Essay on the Shifting Values of Mid-Victorian America, 1840–1870* (New York: Alfred A. Knopf, 1970), chap. 4.

162. *Living Present*, pp. 86, 88–89 (emphasis added).

163. Ibid., pp. 76–78, 85–86. On woman's "influence," see Douglas, *Feminization*, pp. 347–48 and passim.

164. Lucy Stone to HCW, Apr. 23, 1854 [?], J. Hendrix McLane Papers, Yale University Library, New Haven, Conn.

165. *Proceedings of the Free Convention Held in Rutland, Vt. June 25th, 26th, 27th, 1858* (New York: S. T. Munson; Boston: J. B. Yerrinton, 1858), p. 52. Cf. *Marriage*, pp. 246–47.

166. *Proceedings of the Free Convention*, pp. 52–55; *Rad. Ab.*, pp. 229–30. On feminist strategies, see Linda Gordon, *Woman's Body, Woman's Right: A Social History of Birth Control in America* (New York: Penguin Books, 1977); Ellen Carol DuBois, *Feminism and Suffrage: The Emergence of an Independent Women's Movement in America, 1848–1869* (Ithaca, N.Y.: Cornell University Press, 1978).

167. *Lib.*, Sept. 29, 1854, p. 4. Whipple noted similarities between *Marriage* and Margaret Fuller's *Woman in the Nineteenth Century.* He may have been well enough acquainted with both for us to suspect they are the targets of irony when he complains of too much "speculation about marriage by incompetent persons, too much prescribing 'without experience.'" In making love and marriage identical, Wright—in Whipple's opinion—was open to the curious objection that "the terms of his *definition* [of marriage] do not even require that they [marriage partners] shall be of different sexes." In addition, Whipple thought sexual relations could be described more accurately as "*the sweetest and most perfect manifestation of love,* rather than as a conscious attempt, either at reproduction or at selfish sensual enjoyment."

168. *Lib.*, Apr. 2, 1854, p. 4. Davis's work was *The Genesis and Ethics of Conjugal Love* (New York: A. J. Davis, 1874).

169. *Lib.*, Apr. 2, 1854, p. 4.

170. HCW congratulated Adin Ballou for attacking Austin Kent and other champions of "Free Love." He enclosed a letter from a woman who abhorred the Nicholses' teachings, thus proving that free love was contrary to the heart of women *(Practical Christian,* Dec. 30, 1854, p. 1). Austin Kent Criticized HCW, among others, in *Free Love; or, a Philosophical Demonstration of the Non-Exclusive Nature of Connubial Love* (Hopkinton, N.Y.: Austin Kent, 1857).

171. *Lib.*, July 25, 1856, p. 4; Aug. 22, 1856, p. 4. There is no reliable study of antebellum "free love," but plainly persons like Barry existed and thought of themselves as respectable. See Constance Rourke, *Trumpets of Jubilee* (New York: Harcourt, Brace & World, 1963), p. 158; William O. Reichert, *Partisans of Freedom: A Study in American Anarchism* (Bowling Green, Ohio: Popular Press, 1976), pp. 281 ff. Gordon, in "Voluntary Motherhood," regards sexual radicals as an avant-garde clearing the way for more cautious groups with whom they shared essential areas of agreement.

172. *Lib.*, Sept. 5, 1856, p. 4.

173. *Lib.*, Sept. 26, 1856, p. 4.

174. See, e.g., Rev. Daniel Wise, *Bridal Greetings: A Marriage Gift, in Which the Mutual Duties of Husband and Wife Are Familiarly Illustrated and Enforced* (1850; reprint ed., New York: Carlton & Porter, n.d.).

Chapter Five

1. *Life*, p. 113.

2. *Essex Gazette* (Haverhill, Mass.), Oct. 10, 1829, p. 1. In stressing HCW's Federalist background I follow these accounts of reformers' motivations: David H. Donald, *Lincoln Reconsidered: Essays on the Civil War Era* (New York: Random House, Vintage Books, 1956), pp. 19–36; John L. Thomas, *The Liberator: William Lloyd Garrison* (Boston: Little, Brown & Co., 1963), pp. 32–33; and especially Linda K. Kerber, *Federalists in Dissent: Imagery and Ideology in Jeffersonian America* (Ithaca, N.Y.: Cornell University Press, 1970),

pp. 64 ff. On antipartyism, cf. Ronald Formisano, "Political Character, Antipartyism, and the Second Party System," *American Quarterly* 21 (1969): 683–709; William G. McLoughlin, *Modern Revivalism* (New York: Ronald Press, 1959), pp. 100–21; and see the views of the revivalist who converted HCW: John Truair, *A Discourse, Delivered at Sherburne, Nov. 24, 1814...* (Utica, N.Y.: Merrell & Camp, 1815).

3. *Life*, p. 113. On these ideological cleavages, see R. R. Palmer, *The Age of the Democratic Revolution*, 2 vols. (Princeton, N.J.: Princeton University Press, 1959, 1964); Richard Buel, Jr., *Securing the Revolution: Ideology in American Politics* (Ithaca, N.Y.: Cornell University Press, 1972).

4. *Life*, pp. 113–4. For an account of similar reminiscences, see my "The Panorama and the Mills: A Review of *The Letters of John Greenleaf Whittier*," *Civil War History* 22 (1976): 241–42.

5. Mary Howitt, "Memoir of Henry Clarke Wright," *Howitt's Journal* 2 (1847): 102.

6. Stendhal, *The Red and the Black*, trans. C. K. Moncrieff (New York: Modern Library, n.d.), p. 98; Pieter Geyl, *Napoleon: For and Against*, trans. Olive Renier (Harmondsworth: Penguin Books, 1965), pp. 26–33.

7. WJ (HCL), III, 221 (Dec. 24, 1833).

8. *Life*, p. 157. For HCW's early dreams of literary success, see chapter 3 above, p. 105.

9. WJ (BPL), I, 68 (July 10, 1828).

10. J. L. Talmon, *Romanticism and Revolt: Europe 1815–1848* (New York: Harcourt, Brace & World, 1967), p. 136. A similar view of "historical romanticism" was taken by Jacques Barzun in *Classic, Romantic, and Modern*, rev. ed. (New York: Doubleday & Co., Anchor Books, 1961).

11. *Life*, p. 323; Notes on Eccl. Hist., cover & unnumbered page.

12. Alfred de Musset, *Confession of a Child of the Century* (New York: H. Fertig, 1977).

13. Weld also exemplified the Byronic dimension of reform. See his fiancée's comparison to "The Corsair" (AEG to Weld, Mar. 4, 1838, Weld Papers, WLCL) and Weld's MS essays on Byron (WLCL, box 23).

14. WJ (BPL), no vol., p. 32 (July 30, 1843); WJ (HCL), XLVIII, 103 (May 28, 1842); *Life*, p. 170. On related themes of alienation and playacting, see David Brion Davis, *The Slave Power Conspiracy and the Paranoid Style* (Baton Rouge: Louisiana State University Press, 1969), pp. 26–31; Michael Paul Rogin, *Fathers and Children: Andrew Jackson and the Subjugation of the American Indian* (New York: Alfred A. Knopf, 1975); p. 258; David Grimsted, ed., *Notions of the Americans, 1820–1860* (New York: George Braziller, 1970), secs. 1–2; or Emerson's famous "American Scholar" address.

15. Unbound notes in Misc. Writings, no. 1.

16. Doreen Hunter, "America's First Romantics: Richard Henry Dana, Sr., and Washington Allston," *New England Quarterly* 45 (1972): 3–29; Perry Miller, "Thoreau in the Context of International Romanticism," *Nature's Nation* (Cambridge, Mass.: Harvard University Press, 1967), pp. 175–83; Ann

Douglas, *The Feminization of American Culture* (New York: Alfred A. Knopf, 1977).

17. *The Confessions of Jean-Jacques Rousseau,* trans. J. M. Cohen (Harmondsworth: Penguin Books, 1953) pp. 20–21, 400–401, and passim; Lionel Trilling, *Sincerity and Authenticity* (Cambridge, Mass.: Harvard University Press, 1972), pp. 60–61, 68.

18. Joseph Kett, "Adolescence and Youth in Nineteenth-Century America," *Journal of Interdisciplinary History* 2 (1971): 295–96; Gordon Wood, ed., *The Rising Glory of America* (New York: George Braziller, 1971), pp. 166–67 (but contrast pp. 170–71); Massachusetts Sabbath School Society, *Third Annual Report,* May 28, 1835, p. 10; Sarah Stuart Robbins, *Old Andover Days* (Boston: Pilgrim Press, 1908), pp. 185–86. Since the idea that girls had erotic fantasies jarred with increasingly important images of asensual domesticity, there was frequent vigilance to keep novels out of their hands. Somewhat contradictorily, novels were both vain luxuries and signs of the benevolent dispositions of women—they helped define the feminine sphere. Therefore the ability to discard one's novels could have complex significance. When Angelina Grimké, for example, found the nerve to tear up stories by Scott, she was renouncing the finery—we would say the exploitation—to which she was accustomed. She was also turning from the circles where women ordinarily dissipated their energies. It was a moment of economic, religious, and feminist rebellion (Catherine H. Birney, *Sarah and Angelina Grimké: The First Women Advocates of Abolitionism and Women's Rights* (Boston: Lee & Shepard, 1885), p. 51.

19. WJ (HCL), III, 27–29 (Sept. 28, Sept. 29, 1833).

20. WJ (HCL), XV, 47–48 (Mar. 19, 1835); XXXIII, 124 (Feb. 21, 1837). WJ (BPL), XLI, 11–12 (Jan. 10, 1852).

21. "Scrapbooks of anti-slavery newspaper clippings, 1844–46, made by H. C. Wright," vol. 1, HCL.

22. WJ (HCL), LII, 79–80 (Nov. 2, 1832). Such congruence of action to emotion was called "Practical Christianity." John Abercrombie (1780–1844), a physician noted for his close observations of Edinburgh's poor, was author of *Inquiries concerning the Intellectual Powers and the Investigation of Truth* (1830), a work that was very popular on both sides of the Atlantic (see DNB, s.v. "Abercrombie, John, M.D.").

23. *Life,* p. 324.

24. *Lib.,* Dec. 21, 1849, p. 4.

25. The phrase is Carlyle's in *Past and Present,* bk. 3, chap. 9. It represents one underlying theme in the nineteenth century's reexaminations of bondage and order.

26. HCW, *Letter to Frederick Douglass, with His Reply* (n.p., 1846); draft of same in WJ (BPL), no vol., unbound (Dec. 10, 1846).

27. HCW, *Slaveholders or Playactors, Which Are the Greater Sinners?* (Dublin: R. D. Webb, 1847).

28. *The Free Church and Her Accusers: The Question at Issue. A Letter from George Thompson, Esq. to Henry C. Wright; and One from Henry C. Wright to Ministers and Members of the Free Church of Scotland* (Glasgow: George Gallie, 1846).

29. *Lib.*, May 23, 1845, p. 1; C. Duncan Rice, "The Scottish Factor in the Fight against American Slavery, 1830–1870" (Ph.D. diss, Edinburgh University, 1969), pp. 331–32.

30. George Shepperson, "The Free Church and American Slavery," *Scottish Historical Review* 30 (1951): 137–38.

31. Cf. John L. Thomas, *The Liberator: William Lloyd Garrison* (Boston: Little, Brown & Co., 1963), pp. 297–99; Aileen S. Kraditor, *Means and Ends in American Abolitionism: Garrison and His Critics on Strategy and Tactics, 1834–1850* (New York: Pantheon Books, 1968), pp. 243 ff. For an important new look at this problem, see Jonathan Glickstein, "'Poverty is Not Slavery': American Abolitionists and the Competitive Labor Market," in *Antislavery Reconsidered: New Perspectives on the Abolitionists*, ed. Lewis Perry and Michael Fellman (Baton Rouge: Louisiana State University Press, 1979).

32. Andrew Paton to HCW, Nov. 13, 1848, Fragments, HCL, divulges that he and another man have bought an ocean vessel in the cotton trade to Mobile and New Orleans.

33. Unbound diary (Aug. 10, 1847), Fragments. For abundant evidence of the British abolitionists' anxieties about social unrest, see *Brit. and Am. Abolitionists*, passim. I have commented on this in my review in *Journal of Ethnic Studies* 5 (1977): 452–53.

34. WJ (NYHS), pp. 1 ff. (Oct. 22, 1842). Also see Steven Marcus, *Engels, Manchester, and the Working Class* (New York: Random House, Vintage Books, 1975), p. 44, on the difficulties of seeing the poor.

35. WJ (BPL), XXVI (Aug. 1845).

36. HCW to Elizabeth Poole, Feb. 3, 1843, Eng. Let. O'Connell was so funny-looking, however, that Wright reported: "My gravity was all overturned." The first person to meet him in Liverpool was the Owenite John Finch, representing the Anti-Monopoly League (WJ [NYHS]).

37. *Lib.*, Mar. 3, 1843, p. 1; Jan. 2, 1846, p. 3; Jan. 30, 1846, p. 3; Sept. 11, 1846, p. 2. On his friendships, see generally Eng. Let. and *Brit. and Am. Abolitionists*. Like Wright, Engels also saw the Charter as "a contradiction in itself"—but for entirely different reasons (Marcus, *Engels*, p. 90).

38. William Lovett, *The Life and Struggles of William Lovett, in His Pursuit of Bread, Knowledge, and Freedom* (London: Trubner, 1876), p. 321.

39. *Lib.*, Aug. 27, 1847, p. 3. For his pains to dissociate himself from an Ohio community that implicated him in their "circumstantialism" and opposition to private property, see HCW to EP, Mar. 12, 1843, Garrison Papers, BPL. For his argument that private property is a "settled principle of nonresistance," see the debate in *Non-Resistant*, Nov. 16, 1839, pp. 3–4.

40. Harold Perkin, *The Origins of Modern English Society, 1780–1880* (Toronto: University of Toronto Press, 1972), pp. 221 ff.
41. *Lib.*, July 28, 1843, pp. 2–3.
42. Draft of letter to WLG, Fragments; WJ (BPL), XXXII, 6–31 (Mar. 2, 1846). Free trade was troublesome to British abolitionists when the question arose of admitting slave produce into Britain. Wright's Scottish friend John Murray, for example, held that political morality in this case overcame free trade ("Free Trade and Anti-Slavery," *Glasgow Argus*, Apr. 18, 1844, p. 1). Howard Temperley, *British Antislavery, 1833–1870* (London: Longman, 1972), is particularly good on this problem.
43. *Life*, p. 119.
44. *Lib.*, Apr. 23, 1847, p. 2; May 28, 1847, p. 2; Aug. 6, 1847, p. 2. John Bright to HCW, Apr. 11, 1847, Eng. Let. For Richard Webb's moving account of the hunger, see *Lib.*, July 2, 1847, p. 3.
45. *Lib.*, Nov. 3, 1843, p. 4.
46. *Lib.*, Apr. 28, 1843, p. 2.
47. *Lib.*, July 11, 1845, p. 3.
48. *Lib.*, July 28, 1843, p. 3; Nov. 8, 1844, p. 3.
49. *Lib.*, July 31, 1846, p. 3; Feb. 6, 1846, p. 3.
50. WJ (HCL), IV, 29 (Jan. 20, 1834); WJ (BPL), XXX, 40–41 (Apr. 7, 1846); *Lib.*, May 8, 1846, p. 3.
51. *Lib.*, Feb. 13, 1846, p. 2. Garrison spoke of demands to have these reports in book form, but they were never republished.
52. *Lib.*, Feb. 9, 1844, pp. 1–2; Apr. 5, 1844, p. 2.
53. WJ (BPL), I, 119–20 (Dec. 27, 1843); *Lib.*, Apr. 12, 1844, p. 1.
54. *Lib.*, Apr. 19, 1844, p. 1.
55. *Lib.*, Apr. 26, 1844, pp. 1–2.
56. *Lib.*, May 24, 1844, p. 1.
57. *Six Months*, pp. 17, 21–23, 58, 324–26.
58. *Lib.*, May 31, 1844, p. 4.
59. *Six Months*, pp. 268–71.
60. See chapter 2 above, pp. 87, 92–93; chapter 4, pp. 191–92.
61. WJ (BPL), IV, 48 (Feb. 14, 1844); XIX, 1–14 (Feb. 28, 1844). Kathryn Kish Sklar has pointed out that the water cure furnished a therapeutic occasion for "female communality" for nineteenth-century women in America (*Catherine Beecher: A Study in American Domesticity* [New Haven, Conn.: Yale University Press, 1973], pp. 205–9). Wright's diaries suggest that for males, somewhat analogously, the baths provided outlets at varying levels of explicitness for forbidden feelings.
62. *Six Months*, pp. 46–47, 73, 118–21, 192–94.
63. *Lib.*, Oct. 11, 1844, p. 3.
64. *Six Months*, pp. 78–80. He was describing "the birth of a new society based on the horizontal solidarities of class in place of the old vertical connections of dependency or patronage" (Perkin, *Origins*, p. x).
65. *Six Months*, p. 103.

66. *Lib.*, June 20, 1845, p. 1.

67. *Lib.*, Dec. 12, 1845, p. 2–3; Oct. 24, 1845, p. 3. Calvinism was associated with his father, as was evident in many of his outbursts on the Continent.

68. *Lib.*, Oct. 31, 1845, p. 3.

69. *Lib.*, Oct. 24, 1844, p. 1; Nov. 1, 1844, p. 2.

70. *Lib.*, Dec. 13, 1844, p. 3; Dec. 20, 1844, pp. 1, 3. He was once more comparing customs in vertically and horizontally organized societies (see above, n. 64); his observations on street manners are confirmed by Engels and Dickens (see Marcus, *Engels*, pp. 146–53). It was also typical of Wright's life that he mistook professional culture for spontaneous folk life. A standard history of music attributes Strauss's success to a period when "a glittering eclectic society" took the place of the "original citizenry with its famous laisser aller temperament . . .; the bouquet of Austrian wild flowers was replaced by Parisian perfume" (Paul Henry Lang, *Music in Western Civilization* [London: J. M. Dent, 1963], p. 1003). The prospect of spontaneity in an increasingly commercialized cultural life was a crucial problem for American reformers, though it has never been adequately discussed.

71. *Lib.*, Jan. 16, 1846, p. 1; Feb. 13, 1846, p. 1.

72. *Lib.*, Sept. 5, 1845, p. 3.

73. *Lib.*, Nov. 14, 1845, p. 1; Feb. 13, 1846, p. 1.

74. *Lib.*, Dec. 19, 1845, p. 1; Othmar Spann, *The History of Economics*, trans. Eden and Cedar Paul (New York: W. W. Norton, 1930), pp. 187–201. List's belief in a later stage of European confederation and free trade is stressed by Emmanuel N. Roussakis, *Friedrich List, the Zollverein, and the Uniting of Europe* (Bruges: College of Europe, 1968).

75. *Lib.*, Dec. 27, 1844, p. 3; Feb. 7, 1845, p. 1.

76. WJ (HCL), XX, 11–16, 96–102 (June 20, June 29, 1835). For useful discussion of changing attitudes toward time, cf. Fred Somkin, *Unquiet Eagle: Memory and Desire in the Idea of American Freedom* (Ithaca, N.Y.: Cornell University Press, 1967); Major Wilson, *Space, Time and Freedom* (Westport, Conn.: Greenwood Press, 1974); and E. P. Thompson's seminal essay, "Time, Work-Discipline, and Industrial Capitalism," *Past and Present* 38 (1967): 56–97.

77. James A. Henretta, "Families and Farms: *Mentalité* in Pre-Industrial America," *William and Mary Quarterly*, 3d ser., 35 (1978): 29–32.

78. The relations between religion and the two working classes, one capable of rising, the other only of moving, are clarified in Paul Johnson, *A Shopkeeper's Millennium: Society and Revivals in Rochester, New York, 1815–1837* (New York: Hill and Wang, 1978).

79. *Lib.*, Oct. 29, 1847, pp. 2–3; Nov. 12, 1847, p. 1. On the juxtaposition of factory and wilderness, see Leo Marx, *The Machine in the Garden: Technology and the Pastoral Ideal in America* (New York: Oxford University Press, 1967).

80. For Lewis Gunn's peregrinations, see chapter 4 above, pp. 179–80. *The Life of Joseph Barker*, ed. John Thomas Barker (London: Hodder & Stoughton, 1880), is wildly unreliable on his early career. Therefore, to follow

his settlements in Ohio and Nebraska one must consult *Lib.*, Oct. 19, 1849, p. 2; July 18, 1851, p. 3; Nov. 14, 1856, p. 4; Feb. 6, 1857, p. 3. Staying with Barker in Newcastle, HCW called him "the most radical, consistent and independent-minded christian reformer I have yet met in England" (*Lib.*, June 25, 1843, p. 3); and he stopped with the Barker family many times after they became Americans. I do not know HCW's response to Barker's reversion to England—and proslavery views (*Lib.*, Nov. 6, 1863, p. 4).

81. This point emerges through the sensitive portraits of abolitionists in Peter Walker, *Moral Choices: Memory, Desire, and Imagination in Nineteenth-Century American Abolition* (Baton Rouge: Louisiana State University Press, 1978).

82. James Hall, as quoted in R. C. Buley, *The Old Northwest: Pioneer Period, 1815–1840* (Bloomington: Indiana University Press, 1962), 2:626. Of the many recent explorations of themes in this paragraph, I recommend Eric Foner, "The Causes of the American Civil War: Recent Interpretations and New Directions," *Civil War History* 20 (1974): 197–214, and Thomas L. Haskell, *The Emergence of Professional Social Science: The American Social Science Association and the Nineteenth-Century Crisis of Authority* (Urbana: University of Illinois Press, 1977).

83. WJ (BPL), no vol., back page (Aug. 24, 1853). *Lib.*, Sept. 9, 1853, p. 4. The public report is less psychological, more theological. The less Faustian public version places more emphasis on the indwelling of God in consciousness: "I am conscious that 'God is here,' not because of the exhibition of power in these Falls, but because I am here, amid the wild uproar; and where I am, there a consciousness of God is present with me." Thus the event recapitulates his Andover resolution (see chapter 3 above, pp. 115–16). On the connections of nature, emotion, and ideology, cf. Miller, *Nature's Nation*, pp. 197–207; David C. Huntington, *Art and the Excited Spirit: America in the Romantic Period* (Ann Arbor: University of Michigan Museum of Art, 1972).

84. *Lib.*, Sept. 9, 1853, p. 4. David Grimsted, *Melodrama Unveiled: American Theater and Culture, 1800–1850* (Chicago: University of Chicago Press, 1968), pp. 80–81, 101–3.

85. See the description of a house in Allan County, Indiana, in *Lib.*, Oct. 10, 1851, p. 3.

86. *Lib.*, Nov. 10, 1848, p. 1.

87. *Lib.*, July 27, 1855, p. 2.

88. *Lib.*, May 23, 1856, p. 4. Richard Wade's *The Urban Frontier: Pioneer Life in Early Pittsburgh, Cincinnati, Lexington, Louisville, and St. Louis* (Cambridge, Mass.: Harvard University Press, 1959), was a breakthrough in the historiography of the "frontier."

89. *Lib.*, Nov. 11, 1853, p. 4. For a curious sidelight on Wright and Darwinism, see *Garrison*, 2:150.

90. See, for example, *Lib.*, May 19, 1848, p. 3 (to Richard Allen); May 23, 1851, p. 4 (to Richard Webb). On the "philosophy of slavery," see chapter 1 above, pp. 26–41.

91. *Lib.*, May 12, 1848, p. 3.

92. *Lib.*, May 26, 1848, p. 1. In one respect this is mythology: Wright was ignoring persistent tenantry as well as poverty.

93. *Lib.*, Nov. 19, 1847, p. 4. I have discussed "accommodation to violence" at length in *Rad. Ab.*, chap. 8.

94. *Lib.*, Feb. 13, 1857, pp. 2–3.

95. *Lib.*, June 7, 1850, p. 1.

96. HCW to Gerrit Smith, Jan. 15, 1861, Smith Papers, GAL-S. On antislavery racism, cf. Eugene H. Berwanger, *The Frontier against Slavery: Western Anti-Negro Prejudice and the Slavery Extension Controversy* (Urbana: University of Illinois Press, 1967); Richard H. Sewell, *Ballots for Freedom: Antislavery Politics in the United States, 1837–1860* (New York: Oxford University Press, 1976), pp. 171 ff.

97. WJ (HCL), XXXII, 210 ff. (Nov. 19, 1836).

98. Robert William Fogel and Stanley L. Engerman, *Time on the Cross: The Economics of American Negro Slavery* (Boston: Little, Brown & Co., 1974). Of numerous critiques, especially cogent on the Horatio Alger theme are Paul A. David and Peter Temin, "Capitalist Masters, Bourgeois Slaves," *Journal of Interdisciplinary History* 5 (1975): 445–57, and David and Temin, "Slavery: The Progressive Institution?" *Journal of Economic History* 34 (1974): 739–83.

99. The most important reexaminations of slavery are John W. Blassingame, *The Slave Community* (New York: Oxford University Press, 1974); Eugene D. Genovese, *Roll Jordan Roll: The World the Slaves Made* (New York: Pantheon Books, 1974); Herbert Gutman, *The Black Family in Slavery and Freedom, 1750–1925* (New York: Pantheon Books, 1976); and Lawrence W. Levine, *Black Culture and Black Consciousness: Afro-American Folk Thought from Slavery to Freedom* (New York: Oxford University Press, 1977).

100. *Lib.*, Jan. 14, 1848, p. 4.

101. *Lib.*, July 14, 1865, p. 3. On Vineland, see William Chazenof, *Welch's Grape Juice: From Corporation to Co-operative* (Syracuse: Syracuse University Press, 1977), pp. 4–7.

Epilogue

1. Quoted by permission of Grove Press, Inc.

2. See Ann Douglas's elaboration of this pattern in *The Feminization of American Culture* (New York: Alfred A. Knopf, 1977). On the themes of this epilogue I also recommend Richard Sennett, *The Fall of Public Man* (New York: Alfred A. Knopf, 1977), and Carl Schorske, "Politics and Patricide in Freud's *Interpretation of Dreams*," *American Historical Review* 78 (1973): 347.

3. These volumes are at the Boston Public Library. Hereafter I refer to them as "Mine" and give volume and page numbers, though the order which Wright intended for the volumes is uncertain.

4. "Mine," 3:4–5.

5. The evidence, admittedly sketchy, includes several references to Rhode Island in Helen's letters and his references to their mutual friend "S. K." The Kenyon family were close Rhode Island acquaintances, and a letter concerning them is tucked into the first volume of "Mine." The letter is addressed to Elbridge Friend, however, and it should be recalled that during these years he still lived with Julia. The latter—not Helen—benefited from his will.

6. "Mine," 4:257.

7. "Mine," 4:277–78.

8. "Mine," 2:60, 67.

9. "Mine," 3:55.

10. "Mine," 3:59.

11. "Mine," 4:13, 53.

12. "Mine," 2:16.

13. "Mine," 1:204; 2:69–71. The reliance on maxims is another throwback to distant versions of folk memory and face-to-face community. But Wright speaks of keeping a book of maxims (2:237).

14. "Mine," 3:28–42, 237, 248.

15. "Mine," 4:22. Henry and Helen's child may remind some of George and Martha's in Edward Albee's *Who's Afraid of Virginia Woolf?* (New York: Atheneum, 1967). The nineteenth-century case may disprove the rumor that only homosexuality could explain George and Martha's delusion.

16. "Mine," 3:108.

17. "Mine," 1:123–26; 4:109, 140.

18. "Mine," 4:150.

19. "Mine," 2:35–36.

20. "Mine," 1:4. He was actually almost six at the time.

21. See Eunice Ann Kenyon's report, "Death of Henry C. Wright," a printed letter to Richard D. Webb, Aug. 16, 1870 (clipping in Garrison papers, BPL).

Bibliographical Note

Although Henry Clarke Wright appears frequently in books on antislavery, pacifism, and women's rights, he is not the subject of any previously published book. Works on Wright include: Gary D. Saretzky, "Henry Clarke Wright: Non-Resistant Abolitionist" (Master's thesis, University of Wisconsin, 1969); Jayme A. Sokolow, "Henry Clarke Wright: Antebellum Crusader," *Essex Institute Historical Collections* 111 (1975): 122–37; and Peter F. Walker, "Henry Wright: Abolition, Sexuality, and 'The Great Day Coming,'" *Moral Choices: Memory, Desire, and Imagination in Nineteenth-Century American Abolition* (Baton Rouge and London: Louisiana State University Press, 1978), pp. 278–304. Important discussions of Wright may also be found in these works: Merle E. Curti, "Non-Resistance in New England," *New England Quarterly* 2 (1929): 34–57; Peter Brock, *Pacifism in the United States from the Colonial Era to the First World War* (Princeton: Princeton University Press, 1968); Carleton Mabee, *Black Freedom: The Nonviolent Abolitionists from 1830 through the Civil War* (New York: MacMillan, 1970); Ronald G. Walters, *The Antislavery Appeal: American Abolitionism After 1830* (Baltimore and London: Johns Hopkins

University Press, 1976); Louis Billington, "Some Connections between British and American Reform Movements, 1830–1860. With Special Reference to the Antislavery Movement" (M.A. thesis, University of Bristol, 1966); and C. Duncan Rice, "The Scottish Factor in the Fight against American Slavery, 1830–1870" (Ph.D. dissertation, Edinburgh University, 1969).

The principal source for a study of Wright is his diaries, which are located in four collections. Harvard College Library has many volumes for the years between 1832 and 1842, in addition to student notebooks for 1821, ministerial drafts and notes for 1828–29, and fragments of diaries and other papers for 1845, 1847, 1848, and other years. Harvard also holds letters that Wright received in Great Britain in the 1840s. The largest collection of Wright's papers is at the Boston Public Library. This collection includes a few youthful writings of 1818, student notebooks of 1819–20, ministerial writings from 1827 to 1830, and diaries and other writings from 1830 to 1870. These two collections overlap one another in many respects; certain periods are missing from both. One missing diary for 1842–43 is at the New York State Historical Association, Cooperstown, along with other Wright family papers. The fourth collection of Wright papers is a small but important set at the Western Reserve Historical Society, Cleveland, Ohio.

Wright did not keep much correspondence. Aside from the British letters at Harvard, the rest of his correspondence appears to have been absorbed into the papers of William Lloyd Garrison and other abolitionists at Boston Public Library. Scattered letters from Wright show up in the correspondence of other abolitionists, such as Gerrit Smith (George Arents Research Library, Syracuse University), Theodore Dwight Weld (William L. Clements Library, University of Michigan), or Thomas Clarkson (Huntington Library, San Marino, California). Evidence of Wright's early career is scattered in the holdings of the Essex Institute, Salem, Massachusetts; and some clues to his later years rest in the John A. H. McLane Papers, Yale University Library. Except for the Friends Historical Society Library in Dublin, there is little on Wright in English, Irish, or Scottish collections.

Wright's published works are extensive and scattered. They include regular communications to the *Liberator* from 1835 to 1865. Among the papers to which he corresponded prior to 1835 are the *Essex Gazette, Sabbath School Visiter, Boston Recorder, Boston Mercantile Journal,* and *New Hampshire Observer.* Those that he favored after 1835, in addition to the *Liberator,* include: the *Non-Resistant,* the *National Anti-Slavery Standard,* the *Practical Christian, Union Herald, New England Spectator, Friend of Man, Zion's Watchman, Pennsylvania Freeman, Boston Daily Advertiser,* and other local papers in Britain and America.

Wright wrote numerous tracts, pamphlets, and broadsides. A list of these ephemeral works would include:

American Man-Stealing and the Alliance. Rochdale: Jesse Hall [1846].

American Slavery Proved to Be Theft and Robbery; with a letter to Dr. Cunningham, Containing the Doctor's Apologies for Slavery, an Account of Eight

Human Beings Sold by a Theological Seminary, and of the Sale of a Young Woman; and Also the Opinions of Thomas Clarkson and Dr. Andrew Thomson. Edinburgh: Quinton Dalrymple; Glasgow: George Gallie, 1845.

American Slavery Proved to Be Theft and Robbery, Which No Circumstances Can Justify or Palliate, with Remarks on the Speeches of Rev. Doctors Cunningham and Candlish before the Free Presbytery of Edinburgh. Edinburgh: Quinton Dalrymple; Glasgow: George Gallie, 1845.

American Slavery. Two Letters from Henry C. Wright to the Liverpool Mercury, respecting the Rev. Drs. Cox and Olin, and American Man-Stealers. Dublin: Webb and Chapman [1846].

Ballot Box and Battle Field. Boston: Dow Jackson's Press, 1842.

The Ballot: What Does it Mean? Who Shall Use It? N.p. [ca. 1865].

The Blood of Christ and the Blood of Cock Robin. As an Atonement for Sin and a Means to Cleanse the Human Soul from Its Taint and Guilt–What is the Difference Between Them? N.p.: the author, 1869.

Christian Church; Anti-Slavery and Non-Resistance Applied to Church Organizations. Boston: Anti-Slavery Office, 1841.

Christian Communion with Slave-Holders: Will the Alliance Sanction It? Letters to Rev. John Angell James, D.D., and Rev. Ralph Wardlaw, D.D., Shewing Their Position in the Alliance. Rochdale: Jesse Hall, 1846.

Declaration of Radical Peace Principles. Boston [no publisher] 1866.

Dick Crowninshield, The Assassin, and Zachary Taylor, The Soldier: The Difference Between Them. N.p. [1848].

The Dissolution of the American Union, Demanded by Justice and Humanity, as the Incurable Enemy of Liberty. With a Letter to Rev. Drs. Chalmers, Cunningham, and Candlish, on Christian Fellowship with Slaveholders: And A Letter to the Members of the Free Church, Recommending Them to Send Back the Money Obtained from Slaveholders to Build Their Churches and Pay Their Ministers. Glasgow: David Russell, 1845; London: Chapman, Brothers, 1846.

Duty of Abolitionists to Pro-Slavery Ministers and Churches. Concord, N.H.: John R. French, 1841.

The Employers of Dick Crowninshield, the Assassin, and the Employers of Zachary Taylor, the Soldier: The Difference. Hopedale: Non-Resistant and Practical Christian Office, 1848.

Farewell Letter from Henry C. Wright to the Committee of the Glasgow Emancipation Society. Glasgow: D. Russell, 1847.

First Day Sabbath Not of Divine Appointment: With the Opinions of Calvin, Luther, Belsham, Melancthon, Barclay, Paley, and Others. Addressed to the Rev. Justin Edwards, D.D., and to the Members of the American and Foreign Sabbath Union. Boston: Andrews and Prentiss, 1848.

First Day Sabbath Not of Divine Appointment, With the Opinions of Calvin, Luther, Belsham, Melancthon, Barclay, Paley, and Others. A Letter to the Committee of the Edinburgh Emancipation Society. Glasgow: William Symington Brown, 1846.

Free Church Alliance with Man-Stealers. Send Back the Money. Great Anti-Slavery Meeting in the City Hall, Glasgow, Containing Speeches Delivered by Messrs. Wright, Douglas, and Buffum, from America, and by George Thompson, Esq. of London. Glasgow: George Gallie, 1846.

The Free Church and Her Accusers: The Question at Issue. A Letter from George Thompson, Esq. to Henry C. Wright; and One from Henry C. Wright to Ministers and Members of the Free Church of Scotland. Glasgow: George Gallie, 1846.

Henry C. Wright's Peace Tracts. No. 1, The Heroic Boy. No. 2, Forgiveness in a Bullet! No. 3, The Immediate Abolition of the Army and the Navy. Dublin: Webb and Chapman, 1843.

The Holy Bible and Mother Goose, as an Infallible and Authoritative Rule of Faith and Practice. What is the Difference between Them? St. Louis: M. A. McCord, 1868.

John W. Webster, The Murderer, and Joseph Eveleth, The Hangman: The Difference between Them. Boston: J. B. Yerrinton, 1855.

Letter to Frederick Douglass, with His Reply. N.p.: 1846.

Man-Killing by Individuals and Nations, Wrong—Dangerous in All Cases. Boston: Moses A. Dow, 1841.

Manstealers: Will the Free Church of Scotland Hold Christian Fellowship with Them? Glasgow: David Russell, 1845.

The Merits of Jesus Christ and the Merits of Thomas Paine. As a Substitute for Merit in Others—What is the Difference between Them? N.p.: the author, 1869.

The Natick Resolution; or, Resistance to Slaveholders the Right and Duty of Southern Slaves and Northern Freemen. Boston: The Author, 1859.

Non-Resistance. In Two Letters, the First from H. C. Wright, of America, and the Second from J. Barker, of England, with an Appendix Containing Answers to Questions on the Subject. London [?] [ca. 1843].

No Rights, No Duties: Or, Slaveholders, as Such, Have No Rights; Slaves, as Such, Owe No Duties. An Answer to a Letter from Hon. Henry Wilson, Touching Resistance to Slaveholders being the Right and Duties of the Slaves, and of the People and States of the North. Boston: the author, 1860.

The One Supreme Object of Devotion—How to Attain It. Boston [no publisher], 1855.

Rev. Doctors Cox & Leifchild and American Man-Stealers. Rochdale: Jesse Hall [ca. 1847].

Self-Convicted Violators of Principle. N.p.: [ca. 1840].

Slaveholders or Playactors, Which are the Greater Sinners? Dublin: R. D. Webb, 1847.

The War: A Rebellion of the Minority against the Majority, to Sustain Slavery. N.p. [1864].

The War a Rebellion of Capital against Labor, to Enslave the Laborer. N.p. [1864].

William Lloyd Garrison. Glasgow: David Russell [1845].

This list is incomplete. Contemporaries refer, for example, to a pamphlet entitled *The Spirit of Jesus Communicating through the Rappings* (ca. 1851), but it has not been found. Wright's habits almost guarantee the disappearance of other ephemeral writings.

Wright also published eleven book-length works, which are listed below. There is a strong possibility of missing editions—further evidence of the itinerant and transitory character of his work.

Anthropology; or, The Science of Man: In Its Bearings on War and Slavery, and on Arguments from the Bible, Marriage, God, Death, Retribution, Atonement and Government, in Support of These and Other Social Wrongs. Cincinnati: E. Shepard; Boston: Bela Marsh, 1850.

Defensive War Proved to be a Denial of Christianity and of the Government of God. London and Dublin: Charles Gilpin, 1846.

The Empire of the Mother over the Character and Destiny of the Race. Boston: Bela Marsh, 1863. Also listed in *Catalogue of Spiritual, Reform, and Miscellaneous Publications* (Boston: Colby and Rich, 1873).

The Errors of the Bible, Demonstrated by the Truths of Nature; or, Man's Only Infallible Rule of Faith and Practice. Boston: Bela Marsh, 1857. Also listed in *Catalogue of Spiritual, Reform, and Miscellaneous Publications* (Boston: Colby and Rich, 1873). In the 1880s Colby and Rich offered a "fifth edition."

Human Life: Illustrated in My Individual Experience as a Child, a Youth, and a Man. Boston: Bela Marsh, 1849.

A Kiss for a Blow; or, A Collection of Stories for Children Showing Them How to Prevent Quarrelling. Boston: Bela Marsh, 1842. Another edition was published by Marsh in 1858. Other editions include: Boston: Benjamin B. Mussey, 1848; London: Charles Gilpin, 1851; London: Thomas H. Keble, 1853; Halifax, Eng.: Milner and Sowerby, 1855; London: George Routledge, 1874, and 1877. It was reprinted as *Forty Stories about Forgiveness; or, a Kiss for a Blow* (London: Ward and Lock, 1862). It was also reprinted with the subtitle, *A Collection of Stories for Children Inculcating the Principles of Peace* (Boston: Lee and Shepard, 1890). For a Welsh translation, see *Cusan am Gernod: neu, Gasgliad a hanesion i blant* (Wrexham: Hughes a'i Fab, 1908).

The Living Present and the Dead Past; or, God Made Manifest and Useful in Living Men and Women as He Was in Jesus. Boston: Bela Marsh, 1865. Listed in *Catalogue of Spiritual, Reform and Miscellaneous Publications* (Boston: Colby and Rich, 1873). "Third edition," Boston: W. White, 1873.

Marriage and Parentage; or, The Reproductive Element in Man, as a Means to His Elevation and Happiness. Boston: Bela Marsh, 1854. Marsh issued a second, enlarged edition in 1855, an 1858 edition, and a "Fifth Thousand" in 1866. For a so-called "sixth-edition," see *Works on Phrenology, and Kindred Subjects,* ed. Orson S. Fowler (London: John Heywood [1877?]). Another edition was published in Manchester by John Heywood, 1888.

The Self-Abnegationist; or, The True King and Queen. Boston: Bela Marsh, 1863. Also listed in *Catalogue of Spiritual, Reform, and Miscellaneous Publications* (Boston: Colby and Rich, 1873).

Six Months at Graefenberg; with Conversations in the Saloon, on Nonresistance and Other Subjects. London: Charles Gilpin, 1845.
The Unwelcome Child; or, The Crime of an Undesigned and Undesired Maternity. Boston: Bela Marsh, 1858. New edition, 1860. Also listed in *Catalogue of Spiritual, Reform, and Miscellaneous Publications* (Boston: Colby and Rich, 1873).

Index